HISTORICAL DICTIONARY

The historical dictionaries present essential information on a broad range of subjects, including American and world history, art, business, cities, countries, cultures, customs, film, global conflicts, international relations, literature, music, philosophy, religion, sports, and theater. Written by experts, all contain highly informative introductory essays of the topic and detailed chronologies that, in some cases, cover vast historical time periods but still manage to heavily feature more recent events.

Brief A–Z entries describe the main people, events, politics, social issues, institutions, and policies that make the topic unique, and entries are cross-referenced for ease of browsing. Extensive bibliographies are divided into several general subject areas, providing excellent access points for students, researchers, and anyone wanting to know more. Additionally, maps, photographs, and appendixes of supplemental information aid high school and college students doing term papers or introductory research projects. In short, the historical dictionaries are the perfect starting point for anyone looking to research in these fields.

HISTORICAL DICTIONARIES OF U.S. POLITICS AND POLITICAL ERAS

Jon Woronoff, Series Editor

From the Great War to the Great Depression, by Neil A. Wynn, 2003.

Revolutionary America, by Terry M. Mays, 2005.

Early American Republic, by Richard Buel Jr., 2006.

Jacksonian Era and Manifest Destiny, by Terry Corps, 2006.

Reagan–Bush Era, by Richard S. Conley, 2007.

Kennedy–Johnson Era, by Richard Dean Burns and Joseph M. Siracusa, 2008.

Nixon–Ford Era, by Mitchell K. Hall, 2008.

Roosevelt–Truman Era, by Neil A. Wynn, 2008.

Eisenhower Era, by Burton I. Kaufman and Diane Kaufman, 2009.

Progressive Era, by Catherine Cocks, Peter C. Holloran, and Alan Lessoff, 2009.

Gilded Age, by T. Adams Upchurch, 2009.

Political Parties, by Harold F. Bass Jr., 2010.

George W. Bush Era, by Richard S. Conley, 2010.

United States Congress, by Scot Schraufnagel, 2011.

Colonial America, by William Pencak, 2011.

Civil War and Reconstruction, Second Edition, by William L. Richter, 2012.

Clinton Era, by Richard S. Conley, 2012.

Old South, Second Edition, by William L. Richter, 2013.

Carter Era, by Diane Kaufman and Scott Kaufman, 2013.

Historical Dictionary
of the Carter Era

Diane Kaufman
Scott Kaufman

The Scarecrow Press, Inc.
Lanham • Toronto • Plymouth, UK
2013

Published by Scarecrow Press, Inc.
A wholly owned subsidiary of The Rowman & Littlefield Publishing Group, Inc.
4501 Forbes Boulevard, Suite 200, Lanham, Maryland 20706
http://www.scarecrowpress.com

10 Thornbury Road, Plymouth PL6 7PP, United Kingdom

British Library Cataloguing in Publication Information Available

Library of Congress Cataloging-in-Publication Data

Kaufman, Diane.
Historical dictionary of the Carter era / Diane Kaufman, Scott Kaufman.
pages cm. — (Historical dictionaries of U.S. politics and political eras)
Includes bibliographical references.
ISBN 978-0-8108-7822-8 (cloth : alk. paper) — ISBN 978-0-8108-7968-3 (ebook)
1. United States—Politics and government—1977–1981—Dictionaries. 2. Carter, Jimmy, 1924– —
Dictionaries. I. Kaufman, Scott, 1969–. II. Title.
E872.K385 2013
973.926092—dc23
2012042456

♾™ The paper used in this publication meets the minimum requirements of American
National Standard for Information Sciences Permanence of Paper for Printed Library
Materials, ANSI/NISO Z39.48-1992.

Printed in the United States of America.

Contents

Editor's Foreword

Hindsight is always better than foresight but not always perfect. When James Earl Carter Jr.—better known far and wide as Jimmy Carter—was elected president in 1976, he aroused great expectations in many sectors of the American population and possibly even more so abroad. While in office, he did achieve much in fields such as civil rights, energy, and foreign policy. But the country was badly punished by the economy, and he certainly lost face in his dealings with Iran. Thus, when he left he was not greatly missed or lamented, and his weaknesses were more often recalled than his achievements. However, with greater perspective over the past 30 years or so, he does not appear to have been all that bad, or, more exactly, others who followed or preceded him to do not appear to have been that much better. If nothing else, as a person, he was certainly honorable and forthright, and at least he did not get his country into a war. Oddly enough, during the period since he left office, Carter entered into a second career, one of do-gooder in humanitarian dramas and troubleshooter in international crises. This has won him accolades as the best ex-president the United States ever had. So, to say the least, the views are mixed if gradually improving.

This rather unusual and in some ways intriguing president is certainly an interesting figure in any study of American history, and this series would be seriously incomplete without a *Historical Dictionary of the Carter Era*. Obviously, the focus is clearly upon the period when he was either running for or serving as president, and that is covered in some detail in the chronology. But the introduction takes a longer view and also puts the assorted events in a broader context. The dictionary section, as per usual, then looks into the doings of President Carter, his family, and his supporters and detractors, with most emphasis on those persons who were in higher office during his one term. And other entries address his policy in various fields, including the economy, energy, defense, foreign policy, human rights, and so on. But this all takes place within a context, that being American society and culture during that period, and thus there are also entries on cinema, television, sports, and the like. For those readers who want to know more, a good first step is to browse through the bibliography, which includes useful titles on the most important aspects of the period.

This volume was written by Scott Kaufman and Diane Kaufman. Scott Kaufman is professor of history and codirector of the Robert E. McNair Center for Government and History at Francis Marion University, where he teaches American diplomatic and military history. As it happens, his main focus thus far has been Jimmy Carter, writing numerous articles and three books on the Carter era: *Rosalynn Carter: Equal Partner in the White House*; *Plans Unraveled: The Foreign Policy of the Carter Administration*; and, alongside his father, Burton I. Kaufman, *The Presidency of James Earl Carter, Jr.*, 2nd ed., and editing *The Companion to Gerald Ford and Jimmy Carter*. Diane Kaufman has taught in elementary and secondary education for many years. She was a reference librarian at the public library in Manhattan, Kansas, and the Newman Library at Virginia Tech. She also served on the board of Scholastic Books. Of particular interest, she was the coauthor of the *Historical Dictionary of the Eisenhower Era*. Between them, they have given us a very insightful glimpse into the career of a president whose tenure to this day generates intense debate.

Jon Woronoff
Series Editor

Acknowledgments

I especially want to thank our son-in-law, Steve, for helping me use Word. I want to thank my husband, Burt, for his help and patience after I suffered a brain aneurism. I cannot appreciate enough my physical therapist, Cameron Garbner, for his help as I regained my strength. Finally, I would like to thank Marty and Don Marks—your memories of the 1970s were very helpful.

—Diane

I cannot thank enough my wife, Julie, and "four-legged daughter," Lexi, particularly on those days when I retreated to my office as I worked on this project. My love goes as well to my parents, Burton and Diane; my sister and brother-in-law, Heather and Steve; and my in-laws, Sylvia and George.

—Scott

Acronyms and Abbreviations

AAM	American Agriculture Movement
ABA	American Basketball Association
ABC	American Broadcasting Company
ABM	antiballistic missile
ACLU	American Civil Liberties Union
AEC	Atomic Energy Commission
AFL-CIO	American Federation of Labor and Congress of Industrial Organizations
AIDS	acquired immune deficiency syndrome
AIM	American Indian Movement
ALS	amyotrophic lateral sclerosis
AMC	American Motors Corporation
A&T	agricultural and technical
AT&T	American Telephone & Telegraph
BCCI	Bank of Credit and Commerce International
BOB	Bureau of the Budget
CAB	Civil Aeronautics Board
CAC	Consumer Affairs Council
CAE	Council of Economic Advisers
CB radio	citizens band radio
CBS	Columbia Broadcasting System
CCC	Commodity Credit Corporation
CCP	Chinese Communist Party
CERCLA	Comprehensive Environmental Response, Compensation, and Liability Act
CIA	Central Intelligence Agency
CNN	Cable News Network
COWPS	Council of Wage and Price Stability

C-SPAN	Cable-Satellite Public Affairs Network
CTBT	Comprehensive Nuclear Test Ban Treaty
EPA	Environmental Protection Agency
ERA	Equal Rights Amendment
ERDA	Energy Research and Development Administration
ERW	enriched radiation weapon
ESPN	Entertainment and Sports Programming Network
FBI	Federal Bureau of Investigation
FCC	Federal Communications Commission
FISA	Foreign Intelligence Surveillance Act
FLRA	Federal Labor Relations Authority
FRB	Federal Reserve Board
FTC	Federal Trade Commission
GM	General Motors
HA	Bureau of Human Rights and Humanitarian Affairs
HBO	Home Box Office
HEW	Department of Health, Education, and Welfare
HUAC	House Un-American Activities Committee
HUD	Housing and Urban Development
IBM	International Business Machines
IFA	International Franchise Association
IVF	in vitro fertilization
MCAT	Medical College Admission Test
MGM/UA	Metro-Goldwyn-Mayer/United Artists
MRI	magnetic resonance imaging
MTV	Music Television
NAACP	National Association for the Advancement of Colored People
NACW	National Advisory Committee on Women
NARAL	National Abortion and Reproductive Rights Action League
NASA	National Aeronautics and Space Administration
NATO	North Atlantic Treaty Organization

NBA	National Basketball Association
NBG	National Bank of Georgia
NEA	National Endowment for the Arts
NFL	National Football League
NFW	National Farm Workers Association
NHI	national health insurance
NOW	National Organization for Women
NPT	Nonproliferation Treaty
NRA	National Rifle Association
NRC	Nuclear Regulatory Commission
NSC	National Security Council
NYPD	New York Police Department
NYPSC	New York Public Service Commission
OAS	Organization of American States
ODAP	Office of Drug Abuse Policy
OMB	Office of Management and Budget
OPEC	Organization of Petroleum Exporting Countries
OPL	Office of Public Liaison
OSHA	Occupational Safety and Health Administration
PD	Presidential Directive
PLO	Palestine Liberation Organization
PRC	People's Republic of China
PUSH	People United to Save Humanity
SALT	Strategic Arms Limitation Treaty
SAVAK	National Information and Security Organization (Iran)
SDP	Socialist Democratic Party
SLA	Symbionese Liberation Army
SNL	*Saturday Night Live*
SSI	Supplemental Security Income
TAA	Trade Agreements Act
TCM	Turner Classic Movies
TNT	Turner Network Television

UAW	United Auto Workers
UFWO	United Farm Workers Organizing Committee
UMWA	United Mine Workers of America
UN	United Nations
UNCF	United Negro College Fund
USDA	United States Department of Agriculture
USSR	Union of Soviet Socialist Republics
VCR	videocassette recorder
WTA	Women's Tennis Association

Chronology

1974 12 December: Jimmy Carter announced his candidacy for president.

1975 27 January: Jobless rate 9.3 percent; highest since Great Depression. **11 February:** Margaret Thatcher became the first woman to head Britain's Conservative Party. **22 February:** First Vietnamese refugees arrived on the West Coast. **9 March:** Alaska pipeline begun. **17 April:** Cambodia fell to communists. **30 April:** Saigon fell to communist North Vietnam. **7 May:** President Gerald Ford proclaimed the Vietnam War officially ended. **5 June:** Suez Canal reopened after eight years. **8 July:** Ford to seek reelection. **17 July:** United States and Union of Soviet Socialist Republics astronauts rendezvous in space. **1 August:** U.S., USSR, and 33 other nations signed the human rights agreement in Helsinki, Finland. **3 August:** Federal Bureau of Investigation began search for Jimmy Hoffa. **11 August:** U.S. vetoed Vietnam's entrance into the United Nations. **21 August:** U.S. lifted the 12-year ban on exports to Cuba. **4 September:** Israel and Egypt signed an interim peace pact in Geneva. **5 September:** Lynette Alice "Squeaky" Fromme attempted to assassinate President Ford. **8 September:** Forced busing in Boston to integrate schools began. **15 September:** Microsoft founded. **16 September:** Civil war erupted in Lebanon. **18 September:** Patty Hearst arrested. **22 September:** Sara Jane Moore made a second attempt to assassinate Ford. **12 November:** Alabama's governor George Wallace entered the presidential race. Supreme Court Justice William O. Douglas resigned due to ill health. **20 November:** Ronald Reagan entered the presidential race. **17 December:** The two women who attempted to assassinate Ford were sentenced to life in prison.

1976 22 January: Peace reached in Lebanon. **30 January:** U.S. Supreme Court banned spending limits on campaigns. **7 February:** Metropolitan areas in South and Southwest showed greatest population growth. **16 March:** British prime minister Harold Wilson resigned. **5 April:** James Callaghan elected new British prime minister. **20 April:** Barbara Walters became first woman news anchor. **20 May:** Concorde began service between U.S. and France. **28 May:** U.S. and USSR signed a pact limiting atomic tests. **1 June:** Syria sent troops into Lebanon. **16 June:** Six died in race riots in South Africa. **18 June:** President Ford ordered evacuation of Americans from Lebanon. **2 July:** U.S. Supreme Court ruled the death penalty was not cruel or unusual punishment. **3 July:** Israeli freed hostages at Entebbe airport in Uganda. **4 July:** U.S. celebrated its 200th birthday. **8 July:** Richard Nixon disbarred by

New York Court. **15 July:** Jimmy Carter and Walter Mondale chosen at Democratic Convention. **20 July:** Last U.S. G.I.s left Thailand. **3 August:** Twenty dead from Legionnaires' disease. **19 August:** Republicans nominated President Ford and Senator Robert Dole. **24 August:** Jimmy Carter booed by American Legion after he promises to pardon draft resisters. **25 August:** Raymond Barre became the new French premier. **14 September:** 165,000 UAW members strike Ford. **16 September:** Anwar Sadat reelected in Egypt. **17 September:** Space Shuttle unveiled in California. **18 September:** Mao Zedong died. **24 September:** Ford and Carter held first debate. **4 October:** Secretary of Agriculture Earl Butz resigned after racist remark. U.S. Supreme Court lifted ban on the death penalty in murder cases. **7 October:** Second debate between Ford and Carter. **24 October:** Hua Guofeng declared new leader of China. **2 November:** Jimmy Carter elected president. New Jersey approved casinos in Atlantic City. **12 November:** Vietnam and U.S. began talks in Paris. **14 November:** Jimmy Carter's Georgia church lifted ban on blacks. **19 November:** Patty Hearst freed on $1.5 million bail. **6 December:** Tip O'Neill elected Speaker of the House. Billy Carter lost his bid for mayor of Plains, Georgia. **7 December:** Kurt Waldheim reelected secretary general of the United Nations. **28 December:** President-elect Carter pledged not to let New York City go bankrupt.

1977 20 January: Jimmy Carter sworn in as president. **21 January:** He pardoned all Vietnam War draft resisters and urged homeowners to keep their thermostats at 65 degrees during the current energy crisis. **2 February:** He signed the Emergency Natural Gas Act. **25 February:** Uganda's Idi Amin held 240 Americans hostage. **1 March:** Amin freed American hostages. **19 March:** Adults living alone doubled since 1970. **28 March:** Two 747 jets collided over the Canary Islands, killing 574. **30 March:** SALT II proposals rejected by Soviet Union. **4 April:** Carter and Egypt's President Sadat met in Washington, D.C. **6 April:** Carter signed Reorganization Act. **9 April:** Supermarkets reported in trouble due to more people eating in restaurants. **14 April:** Carter rescinded proposed $50 tax rebate. **18 April:** Carter addressed the nation for second time on energy. Alex Haley received special Pulitzer for *Roots*. **28 April:** Department of Health, Education, and Welfare banned discrimination against 35 million disabled Americans. **7 May:** Carter attended the London Economic Summit. **25 May:** George Lucas's movie *Star Wars* hit the theaters. **16 June:** Leonid Brezhnev named first Soviet president. **30 June:** B-1 bomber production halted by Carter. **14 July:** New York's power was restored after massive blackout. **19 July:** Israel's Menachem Begin and Carter met in Washington. **4 August:** Department of Energy established. **16 August:** Elvis Presley found dead. **30 August:** New York's Son of Sam killer was captured. **7 September:** Panama Canal Treaty signed. **21 September:** Bert Lance resigned. **27 September:** Soviet Union agreed on

SALT II. **5 October:** Carter signed International Covenant on Human Rights. **14 October:** Singer and golf enthusiast Bing Crosby died. **1 November:** Minimum wage increased from $2.30 to $3.35 an hour by 1981. **4 November:** *Reader's Digest* lost nation's largest sex discrimination lawsuit. **19 November:** Egypt's President Sadat visited Israel. **22 November:** Civil Aeronautics Board banned smoking of pipes and cigars on U.S. airlines. **6 December:** Some 165,000 United Mine Workers members walk off the job. **21 December:** Organization of Petroleum Exporting Countries froze price of barrel of oil at $12.70.

1978 6 March: Carter used the Taft-Hartley Act to get mine workers back to work. **16 March:** Panama Treaty ratified by Senate. *Hustler* magazine owner Larry Flynt shot. **24 March:** United Mine Workers ended 109-day strike. **3 April:** White House against neutron bomb development. **10 April:** First American-made Volkswagen rolled out of Pennsylvania assembly plant. **18 April:** Senate voted to turn over Panama Canal to Panama on 31 December 1999. **16 May:** Shah of Iran stated country's modernization to continue despite opposition. **28 June:** Supreme Court upheld affirmative action in *Regents of the University of California v. Bakke* but said Bakke must be admitted to California medical school. **14 July:** Lee Iacocca resigned as president of Ford Motors. **25 July:** First test-tube baby born in Great Britain. **4 August:** Families left Love Canal, site of former chemical dump. **17 September:** Camp David Accords signed. Mohammad Ali won unprecedented third heavyweight boxing title. **6 October:** France granted asylum to Iran's exiled Ayatollah Khomeini. U.S. Senate extended deadline for Equal Rights Amendment. **13 October:** Civil Service Reform Act signed. **15 October:** First energy package passed by Congress. **2 November:** Iacocca became Chrysler's president. **6 November:** Iran comes under military control. **8 November:** American painter Norman Rockwell died. **15 November:** Margaret Mead, noted anthropologist, died. **29 November:** 909 died in Jonestown mass suicide. **5 December:** Soviets and Afghanistan signed 20-year friendship pact. **8 December:** Golda Meir, Israel's first woman prime minister, died. **10 December:** Begin and Sadat jointly won Nobel Peace Prize. **15 December:** Normalization of relations with the People's Republic of China announced.

1979 16 January: The Shah fled from Iran. **19 January:** China's Deng Xiaoping met with President Carter. **26 January:** Nelson Rockefeller died. **29 January:** Carter commuted Patty Hearst's sentence. **31 January:** U.S. and China resumed relations. **1 February:** Ayatollah Khomeini returned to lead Iran. **5 February:** Three thousand farmers marched on Washington, demanding higher price supports. **8 February:** Washington, D.C., broke military ties with Nicaragua. **14 February:** Armed insurgents attacked U.S. embassy in Tehran. **8 March:** Carter traveled to Egypt and Israel. **14 March:**

The movie *Hair* was released in the U.S. **15 March:** AP poll gave Carter a 29 percent approval rating. **26 March:** Egypt and Israel signed a peace treaty. **28 March:** Three Mile Island nuclear accident occurred. **30 March:** Iranians voted overwhelmingly to establish an Islamic republic. **1 May:** George H. W. Bush announced bid for Republican presidential candidate. **3 May:** Great Britain's Margaret Thatcher became Europe's first woman prime minister. **12 May:** Carter proposed his National Health Plan to Congress. **23 May:** Bert Lance indicted in bank conspiracy. **7 June:** Carter approved MX missile program. **11 June:** Actor John Wayne died. **18 June:** Brezhnev signed the SALT II Treaty in Vienna. **28 June:** OPEC raised oil prices 16 percent, up 50 percent from 1978. **15 July:** The president's "crisis of confidence" speech was televised to the nation. **17 July:** Somoza resigned as Nicaragua's president and fled to the U.S. Carter accepted resignations of cabinet members Joseph Califano, Michael Blumenthal, Griffin Bell, James Schlesinger, and Brock Adams. **25 July:** Anastasio Somoza Debayle ousted in Nicaragua. **31 July:** Chrysler Corporation reported largest quarterly loss in history; asked government for $1 billion in cash to keep company afloat. **3 August:** Patricia Harris, first black woman to occupy a cabinet post, was sworn in as new HEW secretary. **15 August:** Andrew Young resigned as ambassador to the United Nations. **31 August:** Reports of Soviet troops in Cuba. **27 September:** Congress approved the Department of Education. **6 October:** Pope John Paul II became the first pope to visit the White House. **20 October:** Carter decided to admit the Shah of Iran to the U.S. for medical treatment. **4 November:** The U.S. embassy in Tehran invaded; Americans became hostages. **7 November:** Democrat Edward Kennedy formally announced bid for the president. **13 November:** Actor and former California governor Ronald Reagan announced his bid for Republican presidential candidate. **4 December:** Carter announced his campaign for reelection. **10 December:** Mother Teresa won the Nobel Peace Prize. **15 December:** Former shah leaves U.S. to live in Panama. **20 December:** Congress gave Chrysler Corporation $1.5 billion to avoid bankruptcy. **27 December:** Soviets invaded Afghanistan. **30 December:** Composer Richard Rodgers died.

1980 4 January: Sanctions announced against Soviet Union for invasion of Afghanistan. **10 January:** President of the American Federation of Labor and the Congress of Industrial Organizations George Meany died. **11 January:** Honda announced its first U.S. automobile plant, to be built in Ohio. **21 January:** "Carter Doctrine" outlined to nation. **29 January:** Comedian Jimmy Durante died. **2 February:** Abscam charges announced against congressional members. **17 February:** Israel opened first embassy in Arab world in Cairo, Egypt. **20 February:** Moscow 1980 Olympic Games boycott announced. **3 March:** Banks raised prime rate to 16.75 percent. **14 March:** Balanced budget sent to Congress; anti-inflation program outlined. **21**

March: Carter announced U.S. boycott of Olympics in Moscow. **31 March:** Deregulation of banks began. **2 April:** Carter announced U.S. windfall profit tax on oil industry. **7 April:** U.S. broke diplomatic ties with Iran. **11 April:** Carter decided to free embassy hostages. **17 April:** John Anderson announced bid for president as an independent candidate. **21 April:** Secretary of State Vance resigned. **24 April:** Military rescue mission of embassy hostages failed. **29 April:** Director Alfred Hitchcock died. **1 May:** U.S. jobless rate hit 7 percent. **18 May:** Mount St. Helens erupted; eight killed. First woman graduated from West Point. **3 June:** A. C. Nielsen, inventor of Nielsen ratings, died. **5 June:** Gulf and Western announced battery for electric car. **10 June:** OPEC raised oil price to $32 a barrel. **13 June:** AT&T fined $1.8 billion in antitrust conviction. **19 June:** Olympics began in Moscow without U.S. athletes. **20 June:** Trucking industry deregulated. **30 June:** Carter signed Energy Security Act. **2 July:** Carter signed bill for draft registration of American men at age 18. **14 July:** Billy Carter registered as agent of the Libyan government. **16–17 July:** Republicans nominated Ronald Reagan for president, with George H. W. Bush as vice president. **22 July:** Carter explained Billy Carter's Libyan relationship. **23 July:** Actor Peter Sellers died of a heart attack. **27 July:** Shah died in Egyptian exile. **31 July:** Chrysler Corporation reported largest loss ever by an American carmaker, $536.1 million. **13–14 August:** Democrats again nominated Carter for president and Walter Mondale for vice president. **17 September:** Somoza assassinated in Paraguay. **22 September:** Iraq invaded Iran. Fatal toxic shock syndrome linked to tampons. **26 September:** Iraq halted oil exports. **2 October:** Senate investigations acquitted Billy Carter in Libyan dealings. **14 October:** Communist Party of North Korea named Kim Jong Il to succeed his father as president. **28 October:** Carter-Reagan debate. Ford set U.S. record loss of $595 million. **2 November:** Iranian parliament approved conditions for release of embassy hostages. **4 November:** Reagan defeated Carter. **7 November:** Actor Steve McQueen died. **12 November:** Congress approved Alaska Lands Bill. **2 December:** Carter signed Alaska Lands Bill. **8 December:** John Lennon murdered. **11 December:** Carter signed Superfund Bill to clean up toxic waste dumps. **16 December:** President Reagan named Alexander Haig secretary of state.

1981 16 January: Terms for release of American embassy hostages finalized. **19 January:** U.S. and Iran signed accord on release of American hostages. **20 January:** 40th president Ronald Reagan inaugurated at noon. American embassy hostages were released. **21 January:** President Reagan sent Carter to Germany to greet the embassy hostages.

Introduction

Jimmy Carter became the 39th president of the United States on 20 January 1977 at a time of transition. The Vietnam War and the abuse of power by President Richard Nixon during the Watergate scandal had upset both members of Congress and the U.S. public, and led lawmakers to try to rein in the executive branch. Meanwhile, sentiment among many on and outside Capitol Hill was that the liberalism of the 1960s had taken the country in the wrong direction. Government programs aimed at helping the poor, minorities, and women were now seen as a waste of money. Furthermore, there was a feeling that the movements of the 1960s, including the women's rights, civil rights, and gay rights movements, and their demands for affirmative action, abortion, and equal rights for homosexuals had gone too far. A conservative political and religious backlash emerged, one that called for curtailing government spending and restoring America's moral compass. Reports that the U.S. government had supported repressive regimes abroad and tried to throw out of power or kill foreign leaders intensified the conclusion held by many in the country that America's leaders had lost all sense of morality.

Jimmy Carter, the Democratic presidential candidate in 1976, played upon this sentiment. The former governor of Georgia and a born-again Christian, he advertised his status as a Washington outsider and advocate of decency who would bring honesty and new ideas to the nation's capital, be fiscally responsible, and restore the reputation of the United States as a defender of all that was good. In a close election, he defeated the sitting president and Republican candidate, Gerald R. Ford. Four years later, however, the American people overwhelmingly voted to remove Carter from office.

A ONE-TERM PRESIDENT

One of the reasons for Carter's failure to win a second term was his inability to prioritize. Trained as an engineer, the president saw his job as one of solving problems. He identified numerous matters he felt had to be addressed. Domestically, he wanted to stimulate the economy, cut water projects he regarded as a waste of money, protect the environment, establish a comprehensive energy program, formulate a program of national health insurance (NHI), and reform the nation's tax, welfare, and Social Security programs. His foreign policy included promoting human rights worldwide, sign-

1

ing a Strategic Arms Limitation Treaty (SALT II) with the Union of Soviet Socialist Republics (USSR), halting the proliferation of nuclear and conventional weapons technology, stimulating the world economy, returning the Panama Canal to Panama, achieving a comprehensive Middle East peace settlement, and normalizing relations with Cuba and the People's Republic of China (PRC).

Trying to do so much was tied to a second explanation as to why Carter was a one-term president, which was his relationship with lawmakers. On the surface, it would appear Carter and Congress would get along well. Not only had a Democrat won the White House, but the Democratic Party had overwhelming control in Congress, holding 61 of 100 seats in the Senate and 292 of 435 in the House of Representatives. But seeing himself as an outsider, Carter believed he owed only himself and his campaign staff for his victory in 1976, not the party. Moreover, the president viewed himself as a trustee of the American people, one who knew what was best for the United States; as such, he expected others, including lawmakers, to see the righteousness of his proposals and adopt them. Finally, Democrats in Congress were at odds, with those who favored liberal, New Deal–style policies facing a challenge from those who were of a more conservative fiscal, social, political, and diplomatic mind.

A third issue was the president's poor managerial skills. Because he failed to prioritize, Carter expected his subordinates to act on nearly all of his programs at the same time. Those subordinates became overwhelmed and unable to devote as much attention as they might have had they been allowed to focus on only one or two issues. Congress, which only had so much time on its calendar, had no way to tackle numerous requests at once. Complicating matters was that one policy could and did interfere with another, making it even more difficult for Carter to achieve what he wanted.

Finally, the president never put all of these initiatives into a coherent vision that could explain to the American people where he wanted to take the country. Theodore Roosevelt, for instance, had talked of a "Square Deal," while Woodrow Wilson had emphasized the creation of a world based upon free market economics and democratic values. Franklin D. Roosevelt had had the "New Deal," Truman the "Fair Deal," and Lyndon B. Johnson the "Great Society." Carter never provided Americans with a vision, in either a domestic or a foreign political context. Consequently, it was unclear what the overarching goal of the president's initiatives was.

1977: YEAR OF TROUBLE

These shortcomings became clear almost immediately. With inflation standing at about 6 percent and unemployment about two points higher, Carter considered it essential to stimulate the country's economy. During the campaign, he had called for combating unemployment first, which pleased traditional Democratic constituencies, including labor unions and African Americans. But Carter's fiscal conservatism kicked in after his victory. He now decided that large-scale programs aimed at promoting employment would be too costly and increase inflation; therefore, he said he would focus initially on reducing prices. Unions and minority workers were angered by what they considered a broken promise.

In an effort to jump-start the economy, Carter proposed a $50 rebate for taxpayers and tax cuts for businesses. To provide jobs, he offered to spend some money on public works, but not as much as favored by labor unions. Then, in April 1977, the president suddenly changed his mind and decided to forego the rebate, asserting that the economy had shown signs of rebounding. Members of Congress, many of whom had supported the tax refund reluctantly, were upset. Carter further irritated Capitol Hill when he announced he would cut a number of dam and water projects. His decision had the endorsement of environmentalists and reflected the president's own fiscal inclinations, but the projects had had strong backing in Congress.

Nor were the president's proposals to reform the welfare, Social Security, or tax systems going well. Once again, the administration had to try to figure out how to do all of this without angering traditional Democratic constituencies. In May 1977, Carter suggested giving a boost to Social Security by raising taxes. To talk about taking money out of people's pockets at the same time prices were rising did not meet with much approval. While reform programs languished, the president could point to success insofar as the energy crisis was concerned. Americans' dependence on foreign sources of fuel had increased since World War II; by the time of Carter's election, the United States imported 50 percent of its petroleum. Oil prices, meanwhile, had risen, due in part to a 1973 decision by the Organization of Petroleum Exporting Countries (OPEC) to impose a one-year embargo on oil shipments to the United States because of Washington's support for Israel. By 1975, a gallon of gasoline cost 60 cents, or nearly twice what it had been two years earlier. Causing additional frustration was the brutal winter of 1976–77, which saw industrial facilities and schools close in different parts of the country because of a shortage of natural gas.

To confront the energy crisis, shortly after taking office Carter asked for, and Congress passed, emergency legislation that permitted the shipment of natural gas to states in need of it. Most significant, however, was a massive piece of legislation proposed by the White House. Its more than 110 provisions included taxes on domestic oil production and on gas-guzzling cars, a standby tax that would raise domestic gas prices if consumer use of gasoline went beyond certain levels, and incentives to promote the conservation of energy and the development of alternate energy sources. The administration submitted this legislation without first vetting it with Congress. When they saw it, lawmakers launched various criticisms, including that the bill was too complex or that the taxes could increase inflation. But in August 1977 the Speaker of the House of Representatives, Tip O'Neill (D-Massachusetts), got the legislation through the Lower House, with the exception of the standby tax.

Carter was not able to rest on his laurels for long, though. The same month the energy bill passed the House, the administration had to confront a scandal. At the center was Bert Lance, a close friend of Jimmy and Rosalynn Carter and the director of the White House's Office of Management and Budget (OMB). Lance had had investments in the National Bank of Georgia (NBG) and, upon his appointment to OMB, had promised to divest himself of them to avoid a conflict of interest. A congressional investigation not only raised questions as to whether Lance had cut ties to NBG but found that the OMB head had used an NBG plane for personal reasons. Carter stood by his friend. Not until September, when it became clear that Lance had become a public relations liability, did the president ask for his OMB director's resignation. For a president who had promised a government that was open and honest, the Lance affair did not do him well.

More bad news followed as 1977 turned into 1978. Inflation and unemployment continued unabated, and the White House forecast prices to increase 7.5 percent in 1979. To check inflation, the president in 1978 curtailed pay raises for federal workers and urged private-sector employers and employees to voluntarily impose controls on wages and prices. Corporations balked, asserting that the proposed controls did not do enough to combat inflation. So did union workers, who again argued that Carter's first priority should be reducing unemployment. A welfare reform program proposed by the administration had stalled on Capitol Hill, and Carter's aides were so divided over whether Congress would pass tax reform that the administration decided to delay sending anything to lawmakers. Energy legislation was stuck in the Senate, where there was stronger opposition than in the House to the taxes proposed by the administration.

Carter's foreign policy also faced severe problems. The president in his inaugural address had called for an "absolute" human rights policy, implying that any government that violated the rights of its people could anticipate some form of retribution from Washington. Within a month, though, the White House retreated to a more pragmatic stance, fearful that absolutism could threaten economically, militarily, or politically important countries, among them South Korea, the Philippines, Egypt, communist China, and Saudi Arabia. Rhodesia, Argentina, Brazil, Chile, and Uruguay, which suffered various forms of economic and military sanctions because of the treatment of their people, were infuriated, as was the USSR. The White House cared little about the reaction in Latin America or southern Africa to its human rights initiative; the Kremlin's response was another matter, for Carter wanted to sign a SALT II agreement with the Soviet government, and Moscow threatened to be less accommodating on SALT if the president did not back off. Though Carter did not stop his criticism, he regarded SALT as important enough to tone down his rhetoric significantly. Some U.S. allies, among them West Germany and France, accused Carter of preachiness and of jeopardizing superpower ties.

Nor was the White House making much progress on curbing the proliferation of conventional or nuclear weapons technology. Here again, policies clashed. Whereas the State Department's Bureau of Human Rights wanted to punish nations that violated the rights of their people by cutting military aid to them, the State Department's regional bureaus and the Defense, Commerce, and Treasury departments argued that such sanctions would infuriate economically or geopolitically important U.S. allies. Carter sided with the latter group. As a result, Iran, South Korea, the Philippines, Saudi Arabia, and other human rights–violating nations received millions of dollars in conventional U.S. weaponry. In the hopes of preventing the spread of nuclear technology, Carter opposed West Germany's offer to help Brazil construct a nuclear power plant and Japan's desire to start up a facility at Tokai Mura to generate atomic energy. He also imposed military and economic aid sanctions upon Pakistan, not only because Pakistan wanted to acquire the power of the atom to protect it from India—which had tested a nuclear bomb in 1974—but also because Carter did not like Pakistan's repressive government.

The West Germans and Japanese protested on the grounds that their plans did not violate any international agreements regarding nuclear proliferation and that the president was interfering in their internal affairs. West Germany refused to budge, but the Japanese government, which had an agreement with the United States that affected its ability to start up its plant without Washington's approval, was stuck. Not until September 1977 were the United States and Japan able to work through their differences, thereby permitting the Tokai Mura plant to start operations. Pakistan was also angry. It historically had been a U.S. ally, and, despite his proclaimed desire to curb atomic technology, Carter in 1977 offered uranium to fuel a nuclear power plant in India. The president contended that he made the offer to India only after India promised to accept international safeguards aimed at stopping nuclear proliferation. To Pakistan, Carter was showing favoritism to its enemy.

Efforts to stimulate the world economy were proceeding little better. Carter wanted to reduce the U.S. trade deficit by getting America's friends, particularly Western Europeans and the Japanese, to increase the amount of U.S. goods they imported. Augmenting allied demand for U.S. products would require American firms to step up production, which would benefit the domestic economy. Simultaneously, Carter sought to convince Western Europe and Japan to curtail their use of oil, which would push down petroleum and gas prices and help him address the energy crisis. At a summit held in London in May 1977, West Germany and Japan said only that they hoped to reach their goals for economic growth; the question of oil consumption remained unresolved.

1978: YEAR OF SUCCESS

The year 1978 brought much better news, starting with the Senate's ratification of the Panama Canal Treaties. Negotiations between the United States and Panama over the waterway's future had gone on for over a decade. Knowing there was growing opposition in Panama to U.S. control of the canal, Carter believed it was morally right to turn the waterway over to Panama. Furthermore, such an act would receive a positive reception throughout Latin America. In September 1977, Washington and Panama signed two treaties. The first would turn the waterway over to Panama in 1999. The second would permit the United States to defend the canal from external threats. Despite strong opposition within the Senate and the American public at large to ratification of the treaties, the White House used intense lobbying to change minds and get the Upper House to endorse both agreements.

Even more noteworthy were the Camp David Accords of September 1978. Carter had wanted a comprehensive Middle East peace settlement that would address two matters. The first was Israel's control of territory it had captured from Egypt, Syria, and Jordan in a war in 1967. The second was the future of the Palestinian people, who had fled to the West Bank and the Gaza Strip, two areas of land Israel had won in that 1967 conflict. Without the Carter administration's knowledge, Egyptian president Anwar Sadat had begun secret talks with Israeli prime minister Menachem Begin. In July 1978, Sadat shocked the world when he announced his intention to travel to Israel to work out a bilateral agreement. When the two leaders proved unable to find common ground, Carter invited them to the presidential retreat at Camp David, Maryland. Following two weeks of intense negotiations, the accords were signed on 17 September. Israel agreed to return the Sinai Peninsula, which was one of the territories it had captured in 1967; Israel and Egypt would sign a peace treaty; and the two signatories, as well as the nation of Jordan, would seek an arrangement aimed at permitting Palestinian autonomy in the Gaza Strip and West Bank.

More good news followed the next month when Congress passed the National Energy Act and tax reform legislation. The energy bill did not represent as comprehensive a solution to the country's energy crisis as Carter had desired, for the standby tax and other provisions had been discarded. But it was still a significant achievement. The act improved the distribution of natural gas to prevent a repeat of the shortages seen in the winter of 1976–77 and encouraged both the conservation of energy and development of alternate fuel sources. While the legislation on taxes also had been altered, it reduced taxes by about $19 billion, with many of the provisions benefitting lower- and middle-class individuals.

The year ended with yet another noteworthy accomplishment, that of normalization of relations with the PRC. National Security Adviser Zbigniew Brzezinski had favored this move early on. Once allies, communist China and the USSR had become enemies, and Brzezinski felt that by playing the "China card," Moscow would become more obliging on SALT. Secretary of State Cyrus Vance demurred, insisting that such a move would have the opposite effect. Carter at first leaned in favor of Vance. But he had grown frustrated with the Soviet Union and its Cuban ally. Particularly annoying to the White House was Soviet and Cuban military support for Ethiopia, a nation in the strategically important Horn of Africa that was at the time in a war with its neighbor, Somalia. The president therefore decided to put an end to talk regarding normalization of relations with Cuba. He also took a harder line with the USSR and sided with Brzezinski on China. Normalization of relations with Beijing took place in December, and China's leader, Deng Xiaoping, visited Washington shortly thereafter.

These achievements, though, concealed some serious problems facing the White House and created new ones. The decision to normalize ties with China made the Soviet Union less willing to make concessions on SALT. On national health insurance, Carter had quarreled with a fellow Democrat, Senator Edward Kennedy of Massachusetts. Though both favored NHI, Kennedy wanted such a program implemented immediately, while Carter wanted to phase it in. Kennedy was infuriated when the president decided around mid-1978 that NHI was politically and economically impossible. The senator's anger represented a widening rift between fiscally conservative Democrats like Carter and more liberal-minded members of the party, including Kennedy.

Furthermore, minorities, labor unions, and women charged the president with ignoring issues important to them. Although Carter had done much for minorities and women—for instance, during his term in office he appointed more women, African Americans, and Hispanics to federal judgeships than any of his predecessors and was a strong supporter of the Equal Rights Amendment—these traditional constituencies felt that he was not doing enough. Blacks and union workers were upset that Carter refused to spend more money on programs aimed at creating jobs and eliminating urban blight. Hispanics were bothered by the president's talk of enforcing immigration laws. Although the president said he would not overturn the Supreme Court's 1973 *Roe v. Wade* decision that established a woman's right to an abortion, his personal abhorrence for abortion led feminists to conclude that he was not fully on their side.

Then there was the economy. With inflation at 9 percent and unemployment still hovering at about 6 percent, the momentum Carter had gained from his successes of the previous years had all but disappeared by early 1979. The state of the economy, in combination with the continued backlash against the liberalism of the 1960s, a feeling that the United States was losing ground to the USSR, and anger at both of the Panama Canal treaties, made themselves felt at the voting booth in the 1978 midterm election, with conservatives in both parties seeing gains in Congress.

1979–80: YEARS OF CRISIS

If anything, the administration's downward spiral continued through most of 1979. In Iran, Shah Mohammed Reza Pahlavi's repressive regime, an economic boom that did not benefit all Iranians, and an Islamic fundamentalist population upset by Pahlavi's support for Western ways had bred widespread protests in Iran. Fomenting the demonstrations was Ayatollah Ruhollah Khomeini. Forced into European exile by the shah, Khomeini sent cassette tapes to Iran calling for Pahlavi's overthrow. The instability in Iran affected the oil markets, as did a decision by OPEC to curtail petroleum production. In the United States, gas prices and the inflation rate continued to surge. The White House, which had hoped to reduce inflation to about 7.5 percent in 1979 and 6.5 percent in 1980 now questioned if it could achieve either goal. Most Americans agreed that inflation was enemy number one, but many Democratic constituencies continued to point to the president's need to do more about the lack of jobs. By May, almost two-thirds of Americans declared themselves pessimistic about the state of the nation. Pressure increased on Kennedy, particularly from the political left, to challenge the president in 1980 for the party's presidential nomination.

Carter could point to an achievement in southern Africa. In June 1979, the British government had convinced Rhodesia's prime minister, Ian Smith, to give up power and permit black majority rule. The president could claim that the sanctions he had imposed upon Rhodesia had helped in promoting human rights in southern Africa. But it mattered little as long as he could not solve the country's economic troubles, which continued to wear on Americans. In another attempt to come to grips with inflation and unemployment, Carter that same June traveled to Tokyo to attend an economic summit. On the one hand, the United States, Japan, and West Germany reached agreements to reduce both tariffs and their importation of oil. On the other, there was nothing to guarantee a sizeable lessening of duties, and the caps placed on oil imports were still larger than in 1978.

Mixed news as well came with the signing of SALT that same month. Its provisions reduced the number of launchers for ballistic missiles, limited the number of missiles with more than one warhead, and capped the destructive potential of each missile. While an important achievement, the agreement came under attack from senators in both parties. Some members of the Upper House charged that SALT did not go far enough. Others said it made too many concessions to the Soviets and questioned whether it was possible to verify Soviet compliance with the agreement. Still others feared that if they voted for SALT, they might lose their seats, as had happened in the 1978 midterm election, when a number of senators who had voted for the Panama Canal treaties failed to win another term.

"On the one hand and on the other" could apply as well to a nationally televised speech Carter gave the following month. In 1979, OPEC had increased the price of oil, only adding to the woes of Americans already paying a lot at the pump. In his address, the president blamed a national "crisis of spirit" for the unabated energy crisis. Though the "malaise" speech, as it became known, was well received, Carter undercut what support he had gained by asking for the resignation of each member of his cabinet. Among those he accepted was that of Health, Education, and Welfare Secretary Joseph Califano. Califano, a liberal Democrat, had clashed with the president's more conservative aides over such issues as welfare reform. While Carter had every right to ask his secretaries to quit, the wholesale resignations made Americans question the stability of the administration and further infuriated those on the political left.

Compounding matters were events in Nicaragua and Cuba. In July, a Marxist rebel group called the Sandinistas overthrew Nicaragua's repressive, but anticommunist, dictator, Anastasio Somoza Debayle. The Carter administration had given little support to Somoza because of human rights violations. Conservatives charged Carter with "losing" Nicaragua to communism. The following month, Democratic senator Frank Church of Idaho announced that he had "discovered" a brigade of Soviet combat troops in Cuba. Those troops, in fact, had been in Cuba since the 1960s as part of an agreement reached between President John F. Kennedy and the Soviet government.

Carter was able to put the issue behind him by increasing surveillance of Cuba, but Church's claim increased sentiment at home that the president was not doing enough to defend U.S. interests.

Far more serious were crises involving Iran and Afghanistan. In January, Pahlavi fled his homeland; shortly thereafter, Khomeini returned to Iran and assumed power. In the meantime, the shah sought refuge in another nation. Learning that Pahlavi was suffering from cancer, Carter in October allowed him to come to the United States for treatment. The Iranian government demanded the shah's return so he could be tried, but Carter refused. Incensed, militant Iranian students stormed the U.S. embassy in Tehran in November and took hostage several dozen Americans. A month later, the USSR sent nearly 100,000 troops, supported by heavy weapons, into Afghanistan to help that country's communist government crush an internal rebellion. Furious with the Kremlin, Carter told the Senate to shelve SALT II; signed Presidential Directive 59, which called for a U.S. military buildup; imposed an embargo of grain shipments to the Soviet Union; issued the "Carter Doctrine," in which he vowed to employ "any means necessary" to thwart a Soviet takeover of the Persian Gulf; and announced a U.S. boycott of the Summer Olympics, which were to be held in 1980 in Moscow.

The invasion of Afghanistan had far-reaching ramifications, beyond its effect on superpower relations. Abroad, every major U.S. ally in Western Europe, save Great Britain, denounced Carter's response to the invasion, calling it overkill and a greater threat to détente than the invasion itself. Believing now that the USSR was the main threat to the United States, Carter sought to improve ties with countries he had previously criticized, including Argentina and Pakistan. He found both nations less than prepared to cooperate. At home, the reception was different and helped Carter. Just after the hostages had been seized, Kennedy announced his intention to run for the Democratic nomination. But with U.S. nationals being held against their will in Iran and the Soviet Union invading a neighboring country, Americans felt they had to rally around their president. Carter saw his approval rating go up significantly.

Yet the president and his aides knew that support was soft. Of particular concern was the economy. The inflation rate reached 18 percent in February 1980, and by the spring, a recession had gripped the nation. Searching for a solution, Carter in March proposed an austerity program that included deep cuts in spending, a 10-cent-per-gallon tax on gas to encourage conservation, and limits on consumer credit. Congress did not accept all of these measures—the gas tax, for instance, was highly unpopular—but what it did enact served to reduce inflation. Even so, the inflation rate was still higher than in 1977, and the reduction in government spending caused unemployment to go up, reaching 7.5 percent by May. News in April of a failed attempt by U.S. commandos to rescue the hostages, which resulted in the death of eight American soldiers, caused the president additional political harm.

Despite all of these setbacks, Carter was able to use his incumbency to win enough delegates by June to guarantee himself the nomination. But Kennedy showed no sign of conceding, which risked splitting the Democratic Party. The hostage crisis continued unabated. Word in July that the president's brother, Billy, had accepted money from Libya and was asked by Mrs. Carter to use his Libyan connections to help get the hostages freed smacked of scandal and prompted a congressional investigation into whether Billy had tried to influence the president. While the inquiry turned up no evidence of malfeasance on Jimmy's part, the scandal, on top of the hostage crisis and the economy, did not help.

In August, Carter won the Democratic nomination for the presidency. Kennedy's unwillingness to shake hands with the president before the delegates gathered in the convention hall personified the division within the party. Double-digit inflation and an unemployment rate that had reached 8 percent by October took their toll. A week before the election, Carter had his only debate against the Republican nominee, former California governor Ronald Reagan. Although Carter performed well, Reagan played more effectively to the cameras. Moreover, he asked Americans whether they felt better in 1980 than they did in 1976. That question resonated, and voters, most of whom answered no, overwhelmingly selected Reagan as the country's next chief executive. Among those who voted for the Republican nominee were so-called "Reagan Democrats." This group included labor union workers, who felt the Democratic Party had abandoned them. While Hispanics and African Americans, who also tended to vote Democrat, gave the majority of their votes to Carter, it was a smaller percentage than in 1976.

Carter continued to pursue his agenda despite his loss. In November, Congress passed legislation that protected over 100 million acres of Alaskan land from development. In December, it voted for a bill that established a fund to clean up toxic waste. The negotiations to free the hostages continued, and on 20 January 1981, shortly after Reagan took the oath of office, Iran released them.

Since leaving office in January 1981, Carter has remained active. He is a member of Habitat for Humanity, which builds homes for low-income families. He and his wife established the Carter Center in Atlanta, which promotes human rights, the peaceful resolution of conflicts, disease eradication, and helping those with mental illness. In 2002, the former president won the Nobel Peace Prize for his work. He has publicly censured sitting presidents and the country of Israel for their policies, which has drawn him criticism in return. Today, polls are split over whether he was a good president or a poor one. But despite his detractors, many Americans see him as one of the, if not *the*, best ex-presidents in the country's history.

AARON, DAVID LAURENCE (1938–). Democrat. The deputy director of the National Security Council (NSC) from 1977 to 1981, David Laurence Aaron was born in Chicago. He graduated from Occidental College (B.A., 1960) and Princeton University (M.A., 1962). After Princeton, he joined the Foreign Service. He developed a reputation as a capable civil servant and was named to the U.S. delegation to hammer out the first **Strategic Arms Limitation Treaty** (SALT I). With the success of those talks in 1972, he joined the NSC as a senior member. He left that post two years later to accept a fellowship with the Council on Foreign Relations.

It was during his work for the Council on Foreign Relations that Aaron met Senator **Walter Mondale**. Mondale was considering a run for the presidency in 1976 but realized he needed to broaden his knowledge of **foreign policy**. He therefore asked Aaron to serve as his foreign policy adviser. Aaron agreed and was serving in that capacity when **Jimmy Carter** selected Mondale as his vice presidential running mate.

After Carter's victory, Mondale helped Aaron secure a position on the NSC as deputy to National Security Adviser **Zbigniew Brzezinski**. Aaron's main responsibilities were arms control and consultations with Europe. In 1977 he helped convince Carter to ask the **Union of Soviet Socialist Republics (USSR)** to join the United States in significantly cutting their arsenals of nuclear weapons. The following year, Carter sent him to Europe to determine whether America's European allies favored developing and deploying the **neutron bomb**. That same year Aaron traveled with Mondale to China as part of the Carter administration's plan to normalize relations with Beijing. Aaron was also a key player in both the White House's effort to find an alternative to the **Sandinistas**, who had recently overthrown **Nicaraguan** dictator **Anastasio Somoza Debayle**, and administration discussions over what to do should the shah of **Iran, Mohammed Reza Pahlavi**, lose power.

After Carter lost to **Ronald Reagan** in the **1980 election**, Aaron returned to private life, writing spy novels. He reentered government service when he accepted President Bill Clinton's request to serve as undersecretary of commerce for international trade. After Clinton's second term, Aaron left the public sector to work for a law firm. He is currently a senior fellow at the RAND Corporation.

AARON, HANK (1934–). Considered one of **baseball**'s greatest players, **African American** Henry Lewis Aaron was born in Mobile, Alabama. Too poor to afford baseball equipment, he hit bottle caps with sticks. At Central High School he excelled in both **football** and baseball. Offered scholarships to play football in college, he turned them down to pursue a major league baseball career. In 1949 he failed at his first attempt to secure a place on the Brooklyn Dodgers and so began to play for the Negro League, where he helped the Indianapolis Clowns win the 1952 Negro League World Series.

In 1953, Aaron was picked up by the major league's Boston Braves. He started with the Braves' minor league affiliates in Eau Claire, Wisconsin, and Jacksonville, Florida. He and fellow African Americans on those teams found themselves the target of racism, particularly in the South: they were rarely permitted to eat or stay with white players while on the road; instead, they had to have their meals on the team bus and spend nights with African American families willing to host them. Though upset with this treatment, Aaron believed it his duty to show Americans what a black player could accomplish. He did just that, hitting numerous home runs and maintaining a high batting average.

In 1954, the same year the Braves relocated to Milwaukee, Aaron achieved his dream when he signed a major league contract. He set numerous records in his 23 seasons of baseball. The most notable among them took place in 1974, when he broke Babe Ruth's long-standing record of 714 home runs. In 1976, his final season, he hit his 755th home run. He retired from baseball after that season and was inducted into the Baseball Hall of Fame in 1982. In 1999, *The Sporting News* named Aaron the fifth greatest baseball player to ever play the game.

See also SPORTS.

ABBA. Formed in 1970 in Sweden, ABBA was made up of two men and two women. Benny Andersson (1946–) and Bjorn Ulvaeus (1945–) met in 1966; each was at that time singing for another group. In 1969 they met the women who became their wives and the other half of ABBA. Both Agnetha Faltskog (1950–) and Anni-Frid Lyngstad (1945–) had released recordings. The four singers had their first hit in Sweden in 1972. In 1974 they sang "Waterloo" in the Eurovision Song Contest and won over the international juries with their entry. Using the initials of their first names, ABBA became known worldwide with the release of "Waterloo." That was followed by the hit "SOS."

In 1976, ABBA released the song "Dancing Queen," which reached number one on the U.S. *Billboard* chart. By this time, the group was one of the most popular in the world. The following year, ABBA toured Europe and Australia, playing to sold-out audiences. Between 1979 and 1981, both couples divorced, having found performing together too difficult. In 1982, the group dissolved, having seen 14 of its songs reach *Billboard*'s top 100. Yet ABBA's popularity continued unabated. In 1999 the musical comedy *Mamma Mia!* (based on the group's songs) opened in London, then in Broadway two years later. By 2012, more than 30 million people had seen the play. A movie by the same name appeared on American theaters in 2008 to mixed reviews. In 2009, ABBA the Museum opened in Stockholm.

See also DISCO; MUSIC; THEATER.

ABDUL-JABBAR, KAREEM (1947–). Born Lewis Ferdinand Alcindor Jr. in New York City, **African American** Abdul-Jabbar is still considered by many **sports** commentators to be one of the greatest **basketball** players in the sport's history. While attending the University of California at Los Angeles (B.A., 1969), he led the team to three national championships. In 1969, Alcindor left the Catholic Church, converted to Islam, and took the name for which he is known today. That same year he was the top draftee of the National Basketball Association (NBA) and became a member of the Milwaukee Bucks. In 1975 he was traded to the Los Angeles Lakers. At the end of the 1989–90 season he retired from basketball. Since then, he has appeared in movies, including the 1980 spoof *Airplane*, and several **television** shows. During the Gulf War he traveled to Saudi Arabia and appeared on an exhibition team that entertained the troops. In 1995 he was inducted into the Basketball Hall of Fame.

ABORTION. Though abortion had been legal in the early history of the United States, it became illegal during the 1800s. In the late 1950s, however, a European drug company produced thalidomide to combat morning sickness during pregnancy. Wealthy American women acquired the drug from Europe where thalidomide was legal; many of those same **women** gave birth to deformed children. Some American women, who were taking thalidomide, learned that their unborn children were deformed in the womb and sought an abortion. The thalidomide controversy led the courts to become involved in the abortion question and created a clash between pro-life and pro-choice groups. Formed in 1967, the **National Organization for Women (NOW)** placed the right to an abortion at the top of its priorities. In 1969 NOW was followed by the National Abortion and Reproductive Rights Action League (NARAL), the United States' first national pro-choice organization.

Even when a woman was raped, laws had prevented the termination of her pregnancy. In 1969, Norma McCorvey (aka Jane Roe), a rape victim who was pregnant, went to court to fight a Texas law making an abortion illegal. Her case was decided in 1973 by the **Supreme Court** in *Roe v. Wade*, which granted women the right to terminate a pregnancy. The Court's ruling has spurred many legal questions concerning an abortion, including when life begins. For instance, the **Moral Majority**, led by Reverend **Jerry Falwell**, stated that life began at conception. *Roe* also made abortion a political issue. **Jimmy Carter** tried to take a middle ground, declaring that while he personally opposed abortion, he would not endorse a constitutional amendment banning it; his position pleased neither side in the debate. To the present, presidential nominees include the controversy over abortion in their campaigns.

See also BLACKMUN, HARRY ANDREW (1908–1999); BRENNAN, WILLIAM JOSEPH, JR. (1906–1997); BURGER, WARREN EARL (1907–1995); CARTER, ELEANOR ROSALYNN SMITH (1927–); COMIC STRIPS AND CARTOONS; COSTANZA, MIDGE (MARGARET) (1932–2010); HEALTH; HELMS, JESSE ALEXANDER, JR. (1921–2008); MARSHALL, THURGOOD (1908–1993); REHNQUIST, WILLIAM HUBBS (1924–2005); RELIGION; STEWART, POTTER (1915–1985); WEDDINGTON, SARAH RAGLE (1945–); WHITE, BYRON RAYMOND (1917–2002).

ABSCAM. In 1978 the Federal Bureau of Investigation (FBI) formed a bogus company named Abdul Enterprises Ltd. The bureau was investigating reports of corruption in the U.S. government. FBI agents posed as businessmen representing a fictional sheik. Videotaping their interaction with members of Congress, the FBI was able to prove that several congressmen had bribed businessmen in order to receive special favors from the sheik. One senator and six representatives were indicted. Senator Harrison A. Williams, a **Democrat** from New Jersey, was the first senator to go to prison in 80 years. All of the representatives resigned except Michael Myers (D-Pennsylvania). Refusing to vacate his seat, Myers was expelled from Congress.

ABZUG, BELLA SAVITSKY (1920–1998). Democrat. A member of the House of Representatives from 1971 to 1977 and one of the leaders of the **women**'s movement, Bella Abzug was born in New York City. A graduate of Hunter College (B.A., 1942) and Columbia University Law School (LL.B., 1947), she was a lawyer for the American Civil Liberties Union (ACLU). Elected to the House of Representatives in 1970, she introduced the first **gay rights** bill in 1974. Although she tried to get her bill passed, she failed. In 1976 she was unsuccessful in her bid to become a senator from New York.

Outspoken and brash, Abzug was a constant problem for President **Jimmy Carter**. He had appointed her as cochair of the National Advisory Committee on Women (NACW). She believed hikes in **defense** spending took funds away from domestic programs, including initiatives beneficial to women. Fed up with her criticisms, Carter fired her. Some women endorsed Carter's decision, believing Abzug would hurt the administration's effort to see the **Equal Rights Amendment (ERA)** added to the Constitution, but others were infuriated. Abzug continued to fight for both women's and gay rights and for the protection of the **environment**. She died in 1998 from complications after heart surgery.

ACTION FOR CHILDREN'S TELEVISION. A children's advocacy group formed in 1968, Action for Children's Television was concerned with children's programs on **television**. It lobbied for more educational programs, less advertisements and cartoons, and more diversity in programming, especially on Saturday mornings. Action for Children's Television moved the Federal Communications Commission (FCC) in 1970 to launch better children's programs on the major networks with fewer commercial interruptions. In addition, during prime time, the FCC's rules stated that one hour every night must offer family-friendly programs.

ADAMS, BROCK (BROCKMAN) (1927–2004). Democrat. The secretary of transportation from 1977 to 1979, Brock Adams was born in Atlanta, Georgia, and raised on the West Coast. He received his B.S. in 1949 from the University of Washington and his LL.B. from Harvard University Law School in 1952. From 1954 to 1960 he taught law at the American Institute of Banking. In 1961 President John F. Kennedy appointed Adams U.S. attorney for the western district of Washington State. In 1964, he won the first of his six terms in the U.S. House of Representatives. He became well respected among his fellow lawmakers on Capitol Hill and developed a reputation as an expert in the fields of both finance and transportation.

It was because of his record and connections on Capitol Hill that **Jimmy Carter** selected Adams for the transportation secretaryship. Adams found his new post difficult. He faced opposition from the Big Three **automobile** companies over new safety regulations for cars. He believed Carter had acted too hastily in signing the **Airline Deregulation Act** (1978) and had not given proper consideration to the legislation's consequences. By 1979 Adams worried about his place in the administration. His concerns were justified when the president forced him to resign. He then returned to Washington State to practice law. Beginning in 1986 he represented Washington in the U.S. Senate; however, he withdrew from a bid for reelection in 1992 after being accused of misconduct with female workers. He died in 2004 of Parkinson's disease.

See also GOLDSCHMIDT, NEIL EDWARD (1940–).

ADVERTISEMENTS. The **women**'s movement led many married women to join the workforce. Advertisers focused on changing their ads to meet the newly acquired position of women in the country. Owning their own **automobiles** meant women needed to know both where to buy gas and where to repair their cars. The military stepped up its recruiting of females. For many families, the spending of household money was now in the woman's hands.

Advertisers responded to the challenging roles women faced by making them feel empowered to accomplish anything. Appliances, diet sodas, deodorants, toothpaste, and even feminine products were advertised on **television**. Enjoli perfume presented one of the most memorable ads of the 1970s. A woman in the ad sang, "I can bring home the bacon . . . fry it up in a pan . . . and never, ever let you forget you're a man . . . 'cause I'm a woman . . . with Enjoli." Singer Helen Reddy recorded a similar song in which she sang, "I am woman, hear me roar." Philip Morris created Virginia Slims and stressed that women showed their independence with a cigarette. Their catchy slogan was "You've come a long way, Baby." Women, however, were offended when a Continental Airlines ad showed its stewardesses and stated, "We move our tails for you." This advertisement was short-lived due to the campaign against it.

If Continental Airlines' catchphrase had unintended consequences, such was not the case for American Telephone & Telegraph's (AT&T) "Reach out and touch someone." A Polaroid camera ad stated simply, "It's so simple." Clever ads were memorable and were used for several years. Life cereal showed three young boys with a box of the product. Two of the boys were afraid to try the cereal, so they called to a third boy, "Hey, Mikey!" After Mikey continued to shovel the cereal into his mouth, the others chimed in, "He likes it!" Chiffon margarine was so buttery that even Mother Nature (played by a woman in the ad) was fooled. The ad ended with an explosion, followed by the woman stating, "It's not nice to fool Mother Nature." Budweiser told the audience, "This Bud's for you," while Miller Lite beer tasted great and was less filling. Burger King said, "Have it your way." Barry Manilow wrote several of the decade's most memorable jingles, including "Like a good neighbor, State Farm is there," and Band-Aid's "I am stuck on Band-Aids cause Band-Aid's stuck on me." He also wrote McDonalds's "You deserve a break today." **Sports** figures were used in two popular ads. **O. J. Simpson** used his running ability to get to his Hertz rental car, while a haggard **"Mean Joe" Greene** was offered a Coke by a young boy. "Have a

Coke and a smile" became a catchphrase for the cola. American Express also used famous people in its ad, who asked, "Do you know me?" BMW from the 1970s to the present continues to claim its cars as "the ultimate driving machine," while the U.S. Army still encourages people to sign up so they can "Be all you can be."

Some women became very wealthy not just because of their products but the advertisements used to sell them. Helena Rubinstein, Elizabeth Arden, and Mary Kay Ash were three women who became millionaires because of their perfumes and cosmetics. **African American** women had Madam C. J. Walker to thank for the many products that were best for use by women of color.

See also INFOMERCIALS.

AFFIRMATIVE ACTION. Though the term *affirmative action* was first used by President John F. Kennedy, President Lyndon B. Johnson was inspired by the **African American civil rights** and **women**'s rights movements and signed executive orders prohibiting racial, gender, ethnic, and religious discrimination in hiring and employment practices.

See also ALASKA PIPELINE; BAKKE, ALLEN PAUL (1940–); BLACKMUN, HARRY ANDREW (1908–1999); CONGRESSIONAL BLACK CAUCUS; LIPSHUTZ, ROBERT JEROME (1921–2010); MARSHALL, THURGOOD (1908–1993); POWELL, LEWIS FRANKLIN, JR. (1907–1998); STEVENS, JOHN PAUL (1920–); SUPREME COURT; *UNITED STEELWORKERS OF AMERICA V. WEBER*; YOUNG, ANDREW JACKSON, JR. (1932–).

AFGHANISTAN, RELATIONS WITH. Jimmy Carter entered the presidency with a desire to build close ties between the United States and the **Union of Soviet Socialist Republics (USSR)**. However, in 1979 **Afghanistan**'s procommunist government leader was killed by his second in command. Fearing that Afghanistan might become pro-American, Moscow invaded the country to establish a procommunist government. The Soviet Union's invasion infuriated Carter, who was seeking the Senate's ratification of the **Strategic Arms Limitation Treaty (SALT II)**. In response to Moscow's invasion of Afghanistan, Carter made three decisions: he withheld any decision on the SALT II agreement; he imposed a grain embargo against the Soviet Union; and he boycotted the 1980 Summer **Olympics** to be held in Moscow. In addition he issued his **"Carter Doctrine,"** by which the president threatened to use whatever means necessary to prevent a Soviet takeover of the Persian Gulf. Finally, he increased **defense** spending and sought to develop closer military ties with **China**, the Soviets' communist rival.

See also BREZHNEV, LEONID ILYICH (1906–1982); BRZEZINSKI, ZBIGNIEW KAZIMIERZ (1928–); CENTRAL INTELLIGENCE AGENCY (CIA); DONOVAN, HEDLEY WILLIAMS (1914–1990); FOLEY, THOMAS STEPHEN (1929–); FOREIGN POLICY; GISCARD D'ESTAING, VALERY (1926–); GREAT BRITAIN, RELATIONS WITH; HOCKEY; HORN OF AFRICA; KENNEDY, EDWARD MOORE "TED" (1932–2009); KLUTZNICK, PHILIP MORRIS (1907–1999); SCHMIDT, HELMUT HEINRICH (1918–); THATCHER, MARGARET (1925–); TURNER, STANSFIELD (1923–).

AFRICAN AMERICANS. The **civil rights** movement of the 1950s and 1960s produced great changes in the lives of African Americans in the 1970s. They starred in **sports**, **advertisements**, the **cinema**, and politics. Shirley Chisholm (1924–2005) was the first African American **woman** to serve in the U.S. House of Representatives. She also ran for president in the 1972 election. **Andrew Young**, born and raised in Georgia, was the first African American from the South since 1898 to serve in the U.S. House of Representatives. **Affirmative action** laws had opened housing, travel, restaurants, **education**, and employment to all Americans. The next great change came on the **television** screen where, in shows such as *All in the Family*, *The Jeffersons*, and *Good Times* viewers were challenged by language and characters unthinkable only a few years before.

See also AARON, HANK (1934–); ABDUL-JABBAR, KAREEM (1947–); ALI, MUHAMMAD (1942–); BAKER, JAMES ADDISON, III (1930–); BELL, GRIFFIN BOYETTE (1918–2009); CARTER, JAMES EARL, JR. (JIMMY) (1924–); CARTER, LILLIAN GORDY (1898–1983); CINEMA; CONGRESSIONAL BLACK CAUCUS; DANCES; DERIAN, PATRICIA MURPHY (1929–); DISCO; ECONOMY; FOREIGN POLICY; HALEY, ALEX (1921–1992); HARRIS, PATRICIA ROBERTS (1924–1985); HISPANIC AMERICANS; HUMAN RIGHTS; JACKSON, JESSE LOUIS (1941–); JACKSON, MAYNARD HOLBROOK, JR. (1938–2003); JACKSON, MICHAEL (1958–2009); JORDAN, BARBARA (1936–1996); JORDAN, VERNON EULION, JR. (1935–); LABOR; LANDRIEU, MOON (MAURICE EDWIN) (1930–); LEAR, NORMAN MILTON (1922–); MADDOX, LESTER GARFIELD (1915–2003); MARSHALL, THURGOOD (1908–1993); MUSIC; NATIVE AMERICANS; OPERA; PRESLEY, ELVIS (1935–1977); PRYOR, RICHARD (1940–2005); ROBINSON, FRANK (1935–); *ROOTS*; THURMOND, (JAMES) STROM (1902–2003); *UNITED STEELWORKERS OF AMERICA V. WEBER*; WALLACE, GEORGE CORLEY (1919–1998); WILSON, FLIP (CLEROW WILSON JR.) (1933–1998); YOUNG, COLEMAN ALEXANDER (1918–1997).

Carter meeting with the Congressional Black Caucus. The caucus criticized the president for not doing more for African Americans. Courtesy of the Jimmy Carter Library.

AGRICULTURE. In 1974 the U.S. **economy** was in the worst state it had been in in 40 years, and farmers were especially affected. Oil prices were at a record high, which made operating machinery difficult. With the steadily decreasing number of farm families, in 1977 farmers in Colorado formed the American Agriculture Movement (AAM). The following year the AAM held a convention in the nation's capital. Meeting with President **Jimmy Carter**, the AAM asked him to give government subsidies to farmers; the president refused to meet its demands. On 9 September 1977, Congress passed the Food and Agriculture Act of 1977, which increased both price and income supports as well as a farmer-owned reserve for grain. Poundage quotas were allotted to peanut farmers. Even with this new act, farmers still faced financial problems. In January 1978, farmers held a protest rally on the streets of Washington, D.C., in which about 3,000 tractors traveled down streets and highways. A moratorium was imposed on all farm foreclosures. Still problems continued, and the following year, more AAM members went to Washington to continue protesting the farm crisis. No one in the federal government would meet with the AAM. Within a few years farmers who had taken out loans went bankrupt when they were unable to pay them back while meeting higher living expenses. For migrant workers, the 1970s were also difficult. **Cesar Chavez**, who had moved to California in the 1960s, worked to improve the lives of migrant workers, most of whom were Mexican Americans. He organized them and demanded **health** insurance, better wages, and other benefits.

See also BAYH, BIRCH EVANS, JR. (1928–); BERGLAND, ROBERT SELMER (1928–); WEDDINGTON, SARAH RAGLE (1945–).

AIRLINE DEREGULATION ACT OF 1978. *See* DEREGULATION POLICIES.

ALASKA PIPELINE. In 1967 the largest oil field in North America was discovered in Prudhoe Bay, Alaska. U.S. oil companies wanted to pipe the oil from Alaska to the continental United States. Alaska was a pristine state, and the thought of a pipeline crossing its territory caused an outcry not only in Alaska among the native peoples of the state but also from conservation groups. However, when the **Organization of Petroleum Exporting Countries (OPEC)** limited the amount of oil shipped to the United States in response to Washington's support of **Israel** during the 1973 Yom Kippur War, Americans realized the importance of the Alaska pipeline.

Construction of the pipeline required the builders to comply with the National Environmental Policy Act, which demanded submission of a statement demonstrating that the project would not cause undue harm to the **environment**. After extensive hearings in Congress and court challenges by environmental groups, construction began in 1975 and lasted two years. The route laid out was carefully planned, and some parts had to be laid above ground due to the unstable soil. Numerous people were helped by the project. **Affirmative action** laws opened jobs on the pipeline to **women**. Roads were created in Alaska in order to bring in supplies, and the state benefitted financially from petroleum revenue. Workers' pay was many times the normal wage, which made many of them wealthy. Some of the people who came to work on the pipeline remained in Alaska. Approximately 15 percent of all oil produced in the United States travels through the pipeline.

ALBRIGHT, MADELEINE KORBEL (1937–). Democrat. Madeline Albright has had a long and prestigious career in government, serving on the National Security Council (NSC) from 1978 to 1981, as ambassador to the United Nations from 1993 to 1997, and then as secretary of state from 1997 to 2001. Born in Czechoslovakia, Albright's family fled from the Nazis during World War II. The family finally came to the United States and settled in Colorado. She received her political science degree from Wellesley College (1959) and her master's degree and doctorate from Columbia University in 1968 and 1976, respectively. She was a member of President **Jimmy Carter**'s NSC and White House staff from 1978 to 1981. In 1993 President

Bill Clinton named her the U.S. ambassador to the United Nations; three years later, he nominated her as secretary of state. After her confirmation in 1997, she became the first **woman** to serve in that capacity. She currently serves on the Board of Directors for the Council on Foreign Relations.

ALI, MUHAMMAD (1942–). Born Cassius Marcellus Clay in Louisville, Kentucky, Ali is a retired boxer who won his first professional fight in 1960. In 1964 he joined the Black Muslim sect and changed his name to Muhammad Ali. That same year he won the world heavyweight **boxing** title after beating Sonny Liston. During his career Ali became a close friend of **television sports** commentator **Howard Cosell**. Ali was famous for composing ditties, which delighted audiences. In 1967, during the Vietnam War, he refused to serve in the military. In response the government stripped Ali of his title and sent him to prison; however, in 1970 the **Supreme Court** overturned his conviction. Ali regained his heavyweight title twice but retired from boxing in 1981. He currently fights his own personal battle with Parkinson's disease.

See also AFRICAN AMERICANS.

ALL IN THE FAMILY. In 1971, **television** producer **Norman Lear** introduced Archie Bunker to viewers in the groundbreaking sitcom *All in the Family*. Bunker, typical of many lower-class workingmen, was outspoken and prejudiced toward any group who was not white, American, or Protestant. The **African American** couple next door, George and Louise Jefferson, would eventually star in their own television program (*The Jeffersons*) produced by Lear. Bunker's racism provided audiences with language they had never heard on television. His terms for various minorities included "chinks" for the Chinese and "jungle bunnies" for African Americans. Puerto Ricans were "spics" and Jews were "Heebs." Bunker's wife, daughter, and son-in-law, whom Archie called "meathead," found life with Archie very difficult; however, tolerating Archie's comments made the program that much funnier. When the Jeffersons came to visit the Bunkers, Archie, George, and Louise provided a half hour of laughter, which was strengthened by Archie's family's comments. Only during one of its nine seasons on the air was *All in the Family* not among the top ten most popular television shows.

See also GOOD TIMES.

ALLEN, IRWIN (1916–1991). The best disaster movies of the 1970s were directed by Irwin Allen. Born in New York City, Allen studied journalism and **advertising** at Columbia University (B.A., 1938). Although he began working at a **magazine**, he moved to **television** in the 1950s. In 1953 his documentary *The Sea around Us* won an Academy Award. In the 1960s he produced a successful **science fiction** series, which led to Hollywood. After recognizing the popularity of the 1970 disaster film *Airport*, he decided to concentrate on the genre. *The Poseidon Adventure* (1972) was a box office hit followed by *The Towering Inferno* (1974), which grossed more money than any film that year. Until 1979, his movies were top box office draws. However, in 1980, *Airplane!*, with its very funny cast and absurd script, ended the popularity of disaster films. Allen attempted to produce other motion pictures but never succeeded as before and lost a great deal of his wealth.

See also CINEMA.

ALLEN, WOODY (1935–). Born in New York City, Allen Stewart Konigsberg began his career as a stand-up comic at the age of 15. He starred in his first **cinematic** role in the 1965 comedy *What's New, Pussycat?* He was also involved in writing the script. Throughout the 1960s and 1970s Allen directed several highly successful movies focusing on city life. In 1977 he won three Academy Awards for his film *Annie Hall*, which he wrote and directed. His movies continued to win awards for both Allen and his stars, including *Hannah and Her Sisters* (1986), *Crimes and Misdemeanors* (1989), *Mighty Aphrodite* (1995), and *Vicky Cristina Barcelona* (2008). Allen continues to write, direct, and produce motion pictures.

See also FADS AND FASHIONS.

ALLON, YIGAL (1918–1980). Yigal Allon (Paicovitch) was born in Palestine. In 1948, after the birth of **Israel**, in which he played a part, he was involved in Israeli politics. In 1961, however, he left Israel to study at Oxford University but returned a year later for political reasons. After the Six Day War in 1967, Allon served in various positions in the Israeli government, including minister of foreign affairs from 1974 to 1977 and chair of the Knesset's (Israel's parliament) Committee on Foreign Affairs from 1977 to 1980. He believed in a Palestinian state, but not at the expense of Israel's security.

AMERICAN AGRICULTURE MOVEMENT (AAM). *See* AGRICULTURE.

AMERICAN FEDERATION OF LABOR AND CONGRESS OF INDUSTRIAL ORGANIZATIONS (AFL-CIO). For purely political reasons the American Federation of **Labor** (AFL) and the Congress of Industrial Organizations (CIO) merged in 1955, becoming the nation's largest labor organization. The main purpose of the merger was to unify organized labor behind repealing or amending the Taft-Hartley Act. Congressional passage of the Landrum-Griffith Act removed some of the objectionable features of that legislation. In the late 1950s the Teamsters were expelled from the AFL-CIO for corruption and nondemocratic union governance. The AFL-CIO supported both the 1957 and 1960 **Civil Rights** acts. It boycotted Coors beer after the company, known for being antiunion, replaced union workers who had gone on strike in 1977 with nonunion employees. The boycott ended in 1987.

During **Jimmy Carter**'s term in office, the AFL-CIO had two presidents. **George Meany**, who was also the union's first president, resigned in 1979; his vice president, Lane Kirkland, took his place. The relationship between the union and Carter was difficult, with the AFL-CIO believing that the president did not devote enough attention to cutting unemployment and stimulating the **economy**. In 1980 Joyce Miller became the first **woman** to serve on the union's executive board.

See also CHAVEZ, CESAR ESTRADA (1927–1993); MILLER, G. (GEORGE) WILLIAM (1925–2006); WALESA, LECH (1943–); WOODCOCK, LEONARD FREEL (1911–2001).

AMIN, IDI (1925–2003). President of Uganda from 1971 to 1979. Nicknamed the "Butcher of Uganda," Idi Amin was born in Uganda, where he received a rudimentary **education**. Although he was the son of peasants, in 1966, his military career quickly led to his becoming commander of Uganda's army and air force. On 25 January 1971, he staged a coup against Prime Minister Milton Obote and established himself as leader of Uganda. Establishing a military dictatorship, Amin killed thousands of his opponents, expelled both Asians who held British passports and **Israelis**, and seized foreign-owned companies and properties. In June 1976 Amin, a supporter of the **Palestine Liberation Organization (PLO)**, allowed a hijacked Air France plane, which had originated in Israel, to land in Uganda. The hijackers wanted imprisoned Palestinians freed in return for the hostages. In what became known as the **Entebbe Air Raid**, Israeli paratroopers stormed the plane and freed most of the detainees.

In 1978, Amin attempted to annex a portion of Tanzania but was thwarted by the Tanzanian military and troops of the anti-Amin Uganda National Liberation Army. Launching a counterattack, they invaded Uganda and forced Amin to flee. The ex-dictator tried to settle in several countries but was expelled from each. Finally, in 1980, he took refuge in Saudi Arabia, where he died in 2003. He fathered 43 children.

ANDERSON, JACK (JACKSON NORTHMAN) (1922–2005). A Pulitzer Prize–winning syndicated columnist and investigative reporter, Jack Anderson was born in California but raised near Salt Lake City, Utah. He began his reporting for the *Murray Eagle* followed by a job at the *Salt Lake Tribune*. In 1941 he went on a two-year Mormon mission in the Deep South. During World War II he was in the Merchant Marine and became a war correspondent. After the war he joined forces with noted reporter Drew Pearson's investigations of Washington insiders, including President Dwight D. Eisenhower's staff. After Pearson's death in 1969, Anderson continued to investigate President **Richard Nixon**'s administration and later President **Jimmy Carter**'s. Although Anderson respected Carter's religious convictions, he criticized both **Billy Carter**'s relationship with **Libya** and the president's relationship with Saudi Arabia. Carter considered Anderson a habitual liar, and **Jody Powell**, Carter's press secretary, viewed Anderson as a shameless and biased reporter during the president's term. Although Anderson voted for Carter in the **1976 election**, he later stated that he believed Carter was a hypocrite who wore his **religion** on his sleeve.

ANDERSON, JOHN BAYARD (1922–). Republican. A member of the House of Representatives from 1961 to 1981 and a candidate for the presidency in the **1980 election**, John Anderson was born in Ohio. He saw service in World War II, received a bachelor's in law from the University of Illinois in 1946, a master's in law from Harvard University in 1949, and then a position teaching at Northeastern University in Boston. He entered politics in 1956 when he became the state's attorney for Winnebago County, Illinois. In 1960 he was elected to the U.S. House of Representatives.

Concerned about Republican **Ronald Reagan**'s conservative stance during the 1980 election, Anderson entered the race as an independent on the National Unity Party ticket. He charged Reagan with wanting to spend too much on **defense** and President **Jimmy Carter** for not doing enough to strengthen the **economy**. Able to get on the ballot in all 50 states, he cut into Carter's **Democratic** base. Further hurting Carter was his refusal to debate Anderson and Reagan on the same stage. Though Anderson did not win any electoral votes in 1980, he got enough of the popular vote in two dozen states to prevent either of the other candidates from winning a majority. Following his defeat, Anderson became an active lecturer and appeared on various news programs as a commentator. He considered running on the Reform Party ticket in the 2000 election but decided against becoming a candidate.

ANDRUS, CECIL DALE (1931–). Democrat. The secretary of the interior from 1977 to 1981, Cecil Andrus was born in Oregon and attended Oregon State University for two years before leaving to serve in the U.S. Navy during the Korean War. In 1960 he was inspired to enter politics by President John F. Kennedy. In 1966 he ran for governor of Idaho but lost. In 1971 he was elected the 26th governor of Idaho. He was serving in that capacity when

President **Jimmy Carter** named Andrus secretary of the interior, a position he held throughout the president's term. He became best known for getting Congress to approve the Alaska National Interest Lands Conservation Act, which declared over 100 million acres off-limits to developers. After Carter's loss in the **1980 election**, Andrus returned to Idaho where he continued his political career. In 1987 he was again elected governor of Idaho, a position he held until 1995. He remains active in Idaho's Democratic Party.

See also ENVIRONMENT.

"ANN LANDERS" AND "DEAR ABBY". Twin sisters Esther Pauline Friedman (1918–2002) and Pauline Esther Friedman (1918–) became rival journalists in the 1950s when each was offered the position of writing an advice column at two different newspapers. Esther Pauline became "Ann Landers" and Pauline Esther became "Dear Abby." Their competing columns led to a clash in their personal lives, and they did not speak to each other from the mid-1950s until their reconciliation in 1964. "Ann Landers" published several books giving advice on everything from etiquette to cancer. She died of cancer in 2002. "Dear Abby" ended in the 1980s when Pauline Esther developed Alzheimer's disease, but her daughter has continued her mother's column under the name "Abigail Van Buren."

See also WOMEN.

APPLE COMPUTER. Steven Jobs (1955–2011) and Stephen Wozniak (1950–), two friends who met through a computer club in California's Silicon Valley, realized the value of making an easy-to-use personal computer. In 1976 they used their knowledge to create the first Apple computer. Wozniak was the **technological** genius while Jobs was the marketing guru. The success of their first Apple computer made them two of the country's richest men.

ARAFAT, YASSER (1929–2004). Chairman of the **Palestine Liberation Organization (PLO)** from 1969 to 2004, Yasser Arafat was born in Jerusalem and educated at Cairo University (1952–56). While at the university he was the leader of the Palestinian Students' Union. For many years Palestinians had been ignored by various Arabic leaders, and Arafat wanted them to have a permanent home in the Middle East. His main problem was the many factions in the Arab states, but the newly formed PLO brought Palestinians together to fight for a home of their own. **Israel**'s victory over its Arab neighbors during the 1967 Six Day War forced Arafat and many of his followers to settle in **Jordan**. That country's king, **Hussein I**, came to see the PLO as a threat and attacked them in 1970. Arafat and his supporters fled to **Syria** and then Lebanon, where they set up bases and launched attacks against Israel and Israelis. That the Arab League in 1973 recognized the PLO as the only legitimate Palestinian group gave Arafat additional reason to continue his assaults upon his sworn enemy.

Arafat hoped to capitalize on President **Jimmy Carter**'s desire to achieve a comprehensive Middle East peace settlement. He believed Carter favored the creation of a Palestinian state. However, after **Egypt**'s president, **Anwar el-Sadat**, spoke to the Israeli Knesset, Arafat felt betrayed and decided to continue his attacks upon Israel. Following one assault in March 1978 that left 35 people dead, Israel launched an invasion of Lebanon, during which 1,000 people died and another 100,000 were left homeless. Arafat joined with most Arab leaders in rejecting the **Camp David Accords** of 1978. In 1979, after the press revealed that **Andrew Young** had been secretly meeting with a PLO operative, Young was forced to resign his position as the U.S. ambassador to the United Nations.

For five decades Arafat led the PLO. The organization was involved in the intifada, an uprising of Palestinians against Israel in the late 1980s marked by violent protests. In the early 1990s, Palestinian militants began using suicide bombs. A possibility of peace came in 1994, when Arafat and Israeli prime minister Yitzhak Rabin tried to broker a peace deal between the two sides. But Rabin's assassination in 1995, the election of hard-liner Binyamin Netanyahu as the Israeli prime minister, and differences between Palestinians and Israelis thwarted an Israeli-Palestinian settlement.

See also FOREIGN POLICY.

ARCHITECTURE. In the 1970s architects designed buildings for the people who would use them. They were open, with a lot of glass, and often used geometric shapes. William L. Pereira designed San Francisco's Transamerica Building. I. M. Pei was the architect for the Dallas City Hall and the East Wing of the National Gallery in Washington, D.C. Louis I. Kahn's design of the Kimball Art Museum in Fort Worth has been referred to as timeless. New York's Twin Towers, Chicago's Sears Tower, and Boston's John Hancock Building were 1970s structures that reached new heights. The downward-spiraling **economy** of the 1970s forced architects to devise more economical materials to offset the cost of a structure. Solar panels were employed for heating and use was made of recycled materials. Another cost-saving measure was to use historic buildings. This not only saved the beauty of the outside of the building, but the public purchased items in a beautiful setting of a time gone by. Some of the most recognizable structures saved from destruction for their historic value are New York's Grand Central Station, San Francisco's Ghirardelli Square, and Boston's Quincy Market.

See also ART.

ART. Although the 1970s was not a notable decade for artists, it was unique in some odd ways. Graffiti art became popular; it was no longer considered vandalism. In 1975 the United Graffiti Artists displayed their artwork in an exhibition in New York. Andy Warhol, Roy Lichtenstein, and other pop artists continued to display their works. Abstract artist and sculptor Alexander Calder used bright colors. In the 1970s Braniff Airlines commissioned Calder to decorate their planes with his artwork. The 1970s also witnessed a conscious effort to save the earth. Earth Day was first celebrated in 1970 and has been recognized each year since. In honor of this movement, some artists used mud, salt, and other materials from the earth in their artwork. One of the most notable artists of earthworks was Robert Smithson. The **women**'s movement influenced Judy Chicago and Lynda Benglis, whose works have been exhibited throughout the world. In 1972 women and minorities joined forces to create the Women's Caucus for Art to promote their artwork. Perhaps one of the most famous artists to come out of the 1970s was Andrew Wyeth. His paintings were more authentic and realistic than the works of others in the decade.

See also ARCHITECTURE; HENSON, JIM (1936–1990).

ASSAD, HAFEZ AL- (1930–2000). The president of **Syria** from 1971 to 2000, Hafez al-Assad was born into a poor family in Syria. He attended local schools after which he pursued a career in the military. He studied in the **Union of Soviet Socialist Republics (USSR)** as part of his military training. A member of the Ba'ath Party since the age of 16, Assad took part in several coups that finally overthrew the government. Assad was made minister of **defense**. He strengthened ties with Moscow and blamed **Egypt**'s **Anwar el-Sadat** for losing the Yom Kippur War in 1973.

After assuming the U.S. presidency, **Jimmy Carter** tried to establish diplomatic ties with Assad, believing that Assad, **Jordan**'s King **Hussein I**, and Sadat were the most approachable leaders in the Middle East. However, Sadat's inclusion in the **Camp David Accords** alongside **Israel**'s **Menachem Begin** dampened any ties with Syria. To Assad, the accords meant that Israel no longer had to fear Egypt, which increased the possibility of Israel attacking Syria. In his remaining years, Assad tightened his control over the neighboring country of Lebanon, where Syria had military forces in 1976, and denounced a peace agreement reached between the **Palestinian Liberation Organization** and Israel in 1993. He died of a heart attack in June 2000.

See also FOREIGN POLICY.

AUTOMOBILES. The 1970s changed the American automobile industry forever. The decade began with a strike by the United Auto Workers (UAW), which affected General Motors (GM), Ford Motor Company, Chrysler, and the American Motors Corporation (AMC). The strike closed down the production of new vehicles, which permitted foreign automakers to obtain a niche in car sales.

Adding to American automakers' woes was the oil embargo by the **Organization of Petroleum Exporting Countries (OPEC)** in the early 1970s. Americans loved their big, roomy, and powerful cars, but these gas-guzzlers were expensive to fill at the pump. One of the most popular cars of the early 1970s was the Pontiac Trans Am, which averaged 10 miles on a gallon of gas. With the price of fuel rising, Americans shied away from vehicles like the Trans Am in favor of smaller cars such as the Ford Pinto, the AMC Gremlin, and the Chevrolet Vega. The Pinto, however, had an unprotected gas tank in its rear. By 1978 there had been so many fiery crashes and fatalities involving the Pinto that Ford discontinued the model.

Foreign cars had an impact as well. Desirous to avoid tariffs on imported automobiles, foreign automakers built plants in the United States; as an example, the first American-made Volkswagen rolled off a Pennsylvania assembly line in 1978. Foreign automakers had already gained a foothold in the American market as a result of the UAW strike, and their models, which were smaller and more fuel efficient than those of their U.S. competitors, attracted cost-conscious Americans. Moreover, the quality of foreign-made cars improved during the decade while that of American-produced vehicles did not. President **Jimmy Carter**'s secretary of transportation, **Brock Adams**, talked with the heads of the U.S. automakers, but found them unwilling to change their manufacturing plans.

Government policy also affected American-made cars. Washington set fuel efficiency standards, and the switch to lead-free fuel required automakers to alter engine design. To meet regulations established by the **Environmental** Protection Agency, U.S. automakers had to install catalytic converters on their products. Invented in the mid-1970s, the catalytic converter changed carbon monoxide, hydrocarbons, and nitrogen oxide into harmless compounds in the car's exhaust.

The OPEC embargo, foreign competition, federal directives, and their own errors meant that by the end of the decade, American automakers had a glut of large cars that they could not sell. Chrysler had produced an excess of three months of cars by the mid-1970s and had to shut down five of its six plants. Chrysler was hemorrhaging so much money that it had to get a government bailout in 1980. It was not until later in the 1980s that Lee Iacocca, the former president of Ford who became Chrysler's CEO, was able to turn the failing company around. The American Motors Corporation, producer of the ugly but fuel-efficient Gremlin, lost so much money in the 1970s that it was sold to Renault in 1981.

The DeLorean, a unique car that used stainless steel and gull-wing doors, and which became a centerpiece of the *Back to the Future* trilogy of the 1980s, suffered a similar fate as AMC. The vision of former GM executive John DeLorean, its $25,000 price tag—over $15,000 more than the average cost of a 1970s automobile—and poor sales, combined with the DeLorean Motor Company's financial problems, doomed it. In 1982, the company filed for bankruptcy.

Not all the news was bad for American automakers. The Trans Am saw a rise in sales after the movie *Smokey and the Bandit* was released in 1977. Starring Burt Reynolds and his Trans Am, the film was one of the biggest hits that year. (It also caused a phenomenal sale of **CB radios** in cars.) Yet for the most part, the decade was not a good one for U.S. car manufacturers. By the 1980s, foreign car sales outpaced those of American-produced vehicles.

See also CINEMA; DINGELL, JOHN DAVID, JR. (1926–); ENERGY CRISIS; FADS AND FASHIONS; GRIFFIN, ROBERT PAUL (1923–).

B

B-1 BOMBER. In the 1970s the U.S. Air Force was concerned about the continued use of the B-52 bomber, which it believed was outdated. North American Rockwell Corporation, headquartered in California, had acquired a contract for a replacement, called the B-1. President **Jimmy Carter**'s secretary of **defense**, **Harold Brown**, regarded the aircraft as too costly, and Carter, determined to rein in government spending, agreed. His decision to veto the B-1's production angered numerous members of Congress, including many senators whose support Carter needed if he hoped to get the **Strategic Arms Limitation Treaty (SALT II)** ratified, and played a part in his failure to win California in the **1980 election**.

See also McGOVERN, GEORGE STANLEY (1922–2012); NUNN, SAM (SAMUEL AUGUSTUS) (1938–); O'NEILL, TIP (THOMAS PHILLIP O'NEILL JR.) (1912–1994); TECHNOLOGICAL ADVANCES; WRIGHT, JIM (JAMES CLAUDE WRIGHT JR.) (1922–).

BAKER, HOWARD HENRY, JR. (1925–). Republican. A U.S. senator from 1967 to 1985, and the son of congressman Howard Baker Sr., Howard Baker Jr. was born and raised in Tennessee. The younger Baker received his law degree in 1949 from the University of Tennessee Law College. He made an unsuccessful run for a seat in the U.S. Senate in 1964 but was elected two years later. For almost 20 years he represented Tennessee in the Senate. He and President **Jimmy Carter** had a difficult working relationship. Part of it was a clash of personality. But there was also a clash of policy. While Baker, who was the Senate's minority leader, proved key to passage of the **Panama Canal treaties**, he opposed the president's decisions to cancel production of both the **B-1 bomber** and the **neutron bomb**, and to withdraw U.S. military forces from **South Korea**, arguing that all of these moves endangered America's defense. Because his support for the Panama Canal treaties cost him politically, Baker became an even stronger critic of the White House during Carter's last two years in office, challenging the president's management of the **Iran hostage crisis** and charging that the **Strategic Arms Limitation Treaty (SALT II)** made too many concessions to the **Union of Soviet Socialist Republics (USSR)**.

Baker hoped to receive the Republican nomination for the presidency in 1980, but he did poorly in the Republican primaries and withdrew his name. That year, the Republicans gained control of not just the White House but the Senate; consequently, Baker became Senate majority leader. He retired from the Upper House in 1985 and planned to run for president in 1988; however, he chose to accept President **Ronald Reagan**'s request that he serve as the president's chief of staff. He currently works for a law firm in Washington, D.C.

See also GRIFFIN, ROBERT PAUL (1923–).

BAKER, JAMES ADDISON, III (1930–). A **Republican** who worked as the campaign manager for President **Gerald Ford**, James A. Baker had never run for political office himself, yet he was one of the most politically savvy people in the 1970s. Born in Houston, Texas, Baker graduated from Princeton University (B.A., 1952) and the University of Texas Law School (LL.B., 1957). He practiced law in Austin and became active in the Texas Republican Party. In 1975 Ford appointed Baker undersecretary of commerce; the following year, Ford named Baker his campaign manager for the **1976 election**. During the campaign, Baker erred by suggesting to 400 **African American** ministers that the **Democrats**' presidential nominee, **Jimmy Carter**, had failed as a leader because he had failed to integrate the church he attended in Plains, Georgia. Rather than rally behind Ford, black leaders, among them **Jesse Jackson** and **Andrew Young**, defended Carter and pointed to Carter's support for African Americans during his term as Georgia's governor. Although Ford lost the election, Baker received high praise for his ability to run a political campaign. He headed **George H. W. Bush**'s campaign to become the Republicans' nominee, but the party gave the nod instead to **Ronald Reagan**. After Reagan defeated Carter in the **1980 election**, Baker became Reagan's chief of staff and managed Reagan's bid for reelection in 1984. At present, he serves as an honorary chair of the World Justice Project.

BAKKE, ALLEN PAUL (1940–). The litigant in the **Supreme Court** case of the ***Regents of the University of California v. Bakke***, Allen Bakke was born in Minnesota. He graduated from the University of Minnesota with a degree in engineering (1962) and a grade point average of 3.5 on a 4-point scale. After serving in the U.S. Marine Corps for four years, he returned to civilian life and obtained a degree in engineering from Stanford University in 1970.

In 1972 Bakke sought a medical degree and applied to Northwestern University and the University of Southern California but was denied entrance to both. The following year he applied to a dozen medical schools, among them the University of California at Davis (UC-Davis), which, to meet an **affirmative action** mandate, set aside a certain number of slots for minority students. Again Bakke was turned down by every medical school, even though his score on the Medical College Admission Test (MCAT) was high and he performed well in his interviews at the colleges. Threatening a lawsuit, Bakke was encouraged to apply again to UC-Davis, but he received another letter of rejection. He therefore took his case to court, maintaining that his rights under the equal protection provision of the 14th Amendment and Title VI of the **Civil Rights** Act of 1964 had been violated. He stressed that he had been denied admission even though his test scores were higher than those individuals admitted under a special program that reserved 16 of the 100 spaces each year for minority students. After the California Supreme Court found in Bakke's favor, the Board of Regents appealed to the U.S. Supreme Court.

The Bakke case put President **Jimmy Carter** in a difficult position. He disliked quotas but realized minorities had faced discrimination in the past in **education**. In June 1978 the Supreme Court reaffirmed its commitment to affirmative action but ruled 5–4 that Bakke should be admitted to UC-Davis. According to the Court, the university's policy employed an unconstitutional quota, and Bakke should be admitted to the medical school's next class. At the age of 38 Allen Bakke entered the medical school at UC-Davis and graduated four years later. He completed his residency at the Mayo Clinic in Rochester, Minnesota, in anesthesiology. He remains a practicing anesthesiologist in Minnesota.

BALL, GEORGE WILDMAN (1909–1994). Democrat. An adviser to President **Jimmy Carter**, George Ball was born in Iowa. He received both his undergraduate and law degrees (B.A., 1930; LL.B., 1993) from Northwestern University. Ball worked in a law firm run by Adlai Stevenson, who later became governor of Illinois, and volunteered for Stevenson's unsuccessful 1952 and 1956 bids for the presidency. He served as undersecretary of state for President John F. Kennedy but left Washington in 1966 to join the investment banking firm of Lehman Brothers. He retired in 1982.

George Ball was always concerned about U.S. policy toward the Middle East and sent Carter, then **Democratic** presidential candidate, a copy of his recently published book, *Diplomacy for a Crowded World: An American Foreign Policy*. Impressed, Carter asked **Zbigniew Brzezinski** whether Ball should be part of the transition team should Carter win the **1976 election**; Brzezinski, who became Carter's national security adviser, advised against it because Ball seemed to be anti-**Israel**. After Carter became president, Ball and other members of the **foreign policy** establishment questioned whether the new president was up to the job.

In 1978 Ball was asked to join Carter's advisers concerning the growing opposition to Iran's leader, **Mohammed Reza Pahlavi**. Ball was hired as a consultant to the National Security Council (NSC), headed by Brzezinski, and the two men clashed immediately over whether the United States should encourage the shah immediately toward establishing a civilian government. After presenting his findings to Carter, Ball left the administration and returned to private life. He passed away in 1994 at age 83.

BANKRUPTCY REFORM ACT (1978). This act was the first major change in bankruptcy legislation in 40 years and made it easier for both individuals and corporations to reorganize under bankruptcy protection. It also expanded the jurisdiction of bankruptcy judges.

BARYSHNIKOV, MIKHAIL (1948–). Kirov Ballet **dancer** and choreographer, Mikhail Baryshnikov was born in Latvia to Russian parents. In 1974 while on tour in Canada, he defected to the West and finally moved to the United States. His career in the United States began in New York City with the American Ballet Theater. His grace and incredible leaps led to solo roles created for him. He appeared in several **cinematic** roles, including the 1977 film *The Turning Point*, for which he received an Academy Award nomination. He is still the most recognizable ballet dancer today and has appeared on many **television** programs through the years.

BASEBALL. The World Series in the 1970s were not dominated by one team; however, between 1974 and 1981, the New York Yankees and the Los Angeles Dodgers appeared in more series than any other professional baseball teams. Three of the most notable players during this period were Reggie Jackson, **Hank Aaron**, and **Pete Rose**. In 1975 Aaron broke Babe Ruth's homerun record. Reggie Jackson, who helped the Oakland Athletics win three World Series (1972–74), followed this record with the New York Yankees, whom he helped win the 1977 series against the Los Angeles Dodgers. He was nicknamed "Mr. October" for his postseason performance on the field. Rose was one of baseball's greats during his time with the Cincinnati Reds (1963–78). He was also one of the first free agents to garner an astonishing million-dollar contract in 1979. Nicknamed "Charlie Hustle" for his ability on the field, he has been denied admission to the Baseball Hall of Fame for gambling on baseball games. History was made in 1974 when **African American Frank Robinson** became manager of the Cleveland Indians. Robinson was the first black to hold that position.

See also ESPN (ENTERTAINMENT AND SPORTS PROGRAMMING NETWORK); SPORTS.

BASKETBALL. During the 1970s the New York Knicks and the Boston Celtics each won two National Basketball championships, but the other years were shared by various teams. **Kareem Abdul-Jabbar**, **Julius Erving**, Walt Frazier, and **Wilt "the Stilt" Chamberlain** were four of the National Basketball Association's (NBA) stars during the 1970s. Chamberlain was the only one to begin his career with the famous Harlem Globetrotters, and Erving's professional career began with the short-lived American Basketball Association (ABA), which was created in 1967. The ABA received little **television** coverage and was dissolved in 1976. Erving, whose nickname was "Dr. J," was credited with helping the ABA to survive as long as it did. He played for the New York Knicks but was traded in 1977 to the Cleveland Cavaliers, after which his prowess on the court began to decline. Frazier, like Erving, played for the Knicks. All four **African American** men are named on the list of the 50 greatest NBA players, but Chamberlain is the one whose name always seems to top basketball aficionados' lists. Both Chamberlain and Kareem Abdul-Jabbar had parts in Hollywood films, Chamberlain in *Conan the Barbarian* (1984) and Abdul-Jabbar in the 1980 **cinema**-spoof *Airplane!*

See also SPORTS.

BAYH, BIRCH EVANS, JR. (1928–). Democrat. A U.S. senator from 1962 to 1980, Birch Bayh was born in Terre Haute, Indiana. He received his B.S. in 1951 from Purdue University where he majored in **agriculture**. He began his political career in 1954 when he won a seat in the largely **Republican** Indiana House of Representatives. In 1958 while still in the Indiana legislature, he earned his law degree from Indiana University School of Law (J.D., 1960). Popular with the state **American Federation of Labor and Congress of Industrial Organizations (AFL-CIO)**, in 1962 he defeated the Republican incumbent for the U.S. Senate.

Bayh developed a reputation as an expert on constitutional law. He worked on the **Equal Rights Amendment (ERA)** and was the author of Title IX of the Higher **Education** Act (1972) that mandated equal opportunity for **women** in educational programs that received federal aid. In 1972 Bayh planned to run for the presidency, but when his wife was diagnosed with cancer, he put his political aspirations on hold. In the **1976 election** Bayh again threw his hat in the ring, but his late start hindered his fundraising. As time passed, Bayh found his candidacy floundering, and he ended his bid for president. When President **Jimmy Carter** entered the White House in 1977, Bayh and the Democrats wielded power in Congress. He continued his work for the

ERA. In the **1980 election** Bayh and his fellow Democrats fell victim to the conservative movement, and he lost his bid for reelection to the Senate. Afterward, Bayh returned to practice law in Washington, D.C.

THE BEE GEES. One of the most successful **musical** groups in rock-and-roll history, the Bee Gees were comprised of three brothers: Maurice, Barry, and Robin Gibb. The Brothers were born in Australia where they had their first hit single in 1963. In 1967 the Gibb family moved to London, England, where the brothers released their first international hit. Their popularity continued to soar as the brothers released "How Can You Mend a Broken Heart" in 1971 and followed that with another number-one hit, "Jive Talkin'." The Bee Gees' career skyrocketed when they wrote and performed the music for the incredibly popular 1977 movie *Saturday Night Fever*. The **disco dancing** beat was evident in much of their music for the film. The brothers have also written songs for other performers, including Barbra Streisand, Diana Ross, and Frankie Valli, who sang their hit theme song "Grease" for the movie with the same name. In 1997 the Bee Gees were inducted into the Rock and Roll Hall of Fame.

See also CINEMA; THEATER.

BEGIN, MENACHEM WOLFOVITCH (1913–1992). The prime minister of **Israel** from 1977 to 1983, Menachem Begin was born in Poland and studied law at Warsaw University. When the Nazis invaded Poland, Begin fled to Lithuania where he was arrested by the Russians. Imprisoned from 1939 to 1941, he joined the Free Polish Army upon his release. The army sent him to Palestine in 1942 where he remained until his discharge in 1943. He then became a member of an underground group committed to expelling **Great Britain** from Palestine and forming a Jewish state. When Israel became an independent country in 1948, Begin was one of the leaders of the Knesset (Israel's parliament).

After becoming Israel's prime minister in 1977, Begin was determined to meet with President **Jimmy Carter**. During their discussions, the president had assumed that the reputedly hawkish Begin would prove to be an impediment to Carter's desire to achieve a comprehensive Middle East peace settlement; he was surprised by Begin's flexibility. A year later, Begin and **Egypt**'s president **Anwar Sadat** came to Camp David to discuss peace in the Middle East. After 13 difficult days of negotiation, the two Middle East leaders signed the **Camp David Accords**. Begin and Sadat were both awarded the Nobel Peace Prize in 1978. In 1983 Begin resigned as prime minister. He died in 1992 of complications from a heart attack.

See also FOREIGN POLICY.

BELL, GRIFFIN BOYETTE (1918–2009). Democrat. A native of Georgia who served as attorney general of the United States from 1977 to 1979, Griffin Bell received his law degree from Mercer University Law School (LL.B., 1947). Bell, one of President **Jimmy Carter**'s closest friends, co-chaired the Georgia state presidential campaign for John F. Kennedy. In 1961 President Kennedy nominated Bell for a judgeship on the U.S. Fifth Circuit Court of Appeals, a position he held until 1976.

Carter nominated Bell as his attorney general, despite controversy surrounding Bell's membership in two segregated social clubs. In fact, Bell was a supporter of **civil rights** and as attorney general worked to increase the number of **African Americans**, *Hispanics*, and **women** appointed to the 152 vacant federal judgeships. The major U.S. **Supreme Court** case during Bell's term as attorney general was *Regents of the University of California v. Bakke*. Bell was disenchanted by the rifts the Bakke case revealed. He also felt that the actions of Vice President **Walter Mondale** and other liberals in the administration inhibited his ability to adequately do his job. In 1979 he resigned from the administration. He passed away from pancreatic cancer and kidney disease in 2009.

See also CIVILETTI, BENJAMIN RICHARD (1935–).

BERGLAND, ROBERT SELMER (1928–). Democrat. The secretary of **agriculture** from 1977 to 1981, Robert Bergland was born and raised in Minnesota, and attended the University of Minnesota for two years, where he majored in agriculture. He spent two years at the U.S. Department of Agriculture (USDA) before running unsuccessfully for Congress in 1968; two years later, he launched another, this time successful, bid for a seat on Capitol Hill. For the next 20 years, he represented his district of Minnesota in the House of Representatives.

Bergland had developed a reputation as a strong defender of agricultural interests at the time President **Jimmy Carter** nominated him as secretary of agriculture. The two did not get along. Bergland felt the president did not give him enough authority over farm policy and disliked administration infighting over price supports for farmers; Carter criticized Bergland for trying to keep the food stamp program under the purview of the Department of Agriculture rather than allowing the Department of **Health**, **Education**, and Welfare to oversee it.

After leaving office, Bergland served on the boards of numerous organizations. He is presently president of Communicating for Seniors, an advocacy group that has been supporting legislation for drug coverage under the Medicare program.

BICENTENNIAL. The U.S. Bicentennial was observed in 1976, 200 years after the signing of the Declaration of Independence. John Warner, who later was elected a U.S. senator from Virginia, was director of the government office that coordinated the Bicentennial events. The country's birthday was celebrated around the country with fireworks, parades, and special events. Official events actually began a year before when the American Freedom Train started a 21-month journey around the continental United States. President **Gerald Ford** began the 1975 events by journeying to Boston where he lit a third lantern in the Old North Church, which signified the beginning of the country's third century. Special memorabilia were created, including a Bicentennial Flag, postage stamps, and even a unique design for coins minted by the U.S. Treasury. The queen of England, Elizabeth II, and her husband, Prince Philip, traveled to the United States and were guests of President and Mrs. Ford. The royal couple traveled aboard the Royal Yacht *Britannia* and stopped in various cities along the eastern seaboard. Patriotism swept the country with red, white, and blue painted on mailboxes and fire hydrants. In New York Harbor, a fleet of tall ships gathered on July 4, and a week later this same fleet sailed into Boston's harbor. In 1977 President **Jimmy Carter** signed an executive order that instructed the Department of the Interior to continue events related to the Bicentennial until 31 December 1983.

BICYCLING. The 1970s witnessed a growing interest in physical fitness. Bicycle sales boomed, for they were good for one's health and offered an alternative form of transportation to the **automobile** at a time when gas prices were on the rise. Between 1960 and 1970 the number of bicycles sold in the United States doubled and doubled again between 1971 and 1975. Bicycle shops and bicycling clubs proliferated. The lighter European racing bikes with 10 speeds were the overwhelming choice of consumers. The **magazine** *Bike World* was introduced in 1972 and joined the already popular *Bicycling*, which began in the early 1960s.

See also SPORTS.

BIDEN, JOSEPH ROBINETTE, JR. (1942–). Democrat. The incumbent vice president of the United States, Joseph Biden served as a U.S. senator from 1973 to 2009 and ran for the presidency in both 1988 and 2008. One of the youngest men to be elected senator, he was born in Pennsylvania but grew up in Delaware. Politically ambitious, the graduate of the University of Delaware (B.A., 1965) and the Syracuse University School of Law (J.D., 1968) used his law practice as a stepping-stone to the U.S. Senate. He won a seat in the Upper House on his first attempt in 1972 and developed a reputation for sincerity and debate.

At the time of **Jimmy Carter**'s accession to the presidency, Biden had a seat on several powerful committees: the Senate Committees on Foreign Relations and on the Judiciary, and the Select Committee on Intelligence. In 1979, he led a group of senators to **China** to speak with that country's leader, **Deng Xiaoping**, as part of Carter's effort to normalize relations with that communist nation. Later that same year, he took another group of senators to the **Union of Soviet Socialist Republics (USSR)** to discuss the **Strategic Arms Limitation Treaty (SALT II)**, which the Senate was considering for ratification.

Biden sought the Democratic Party's nomination for the presidency in both 1988 and 2008 but dropped out both times. When Senator Barack Obama became the party's nominee in 2008, he chose Biden as his running mate. Later that year, the Obama/Biden ticket was voted into the White House.

BILLYGATE. *See* CARTER, BILLY (WILLIAM ALTON, III) (1937–1988).

BITUMINOUS COAL STRIKE (1977–1978). For decades, the **United Mine Workers** of America (UMW) **labor** union had negotiated three-year contracts with the Bituminous Coal Operators Association (BCOA), which represented mine owners. The two sides had reached a collective bargaining agreement in 1974, which was set to expire in 1977. When the BCOA refused to meet the UMW's demand to stage wildcat strikes, the union struck on 6 December 1977. The UMW rank and file rejected tentative agreements reached between the union's leadership and the BCOA in February and March 1978.

As the nation's coal supply fell, forcing layoffs and school closings in parts of the United States, pressure grew on the White House to intervene. On 9 March 1978, President **Jimmy Carter** invoked the Taft-Hartley Act of 1947, which permitted him to intervene in strikes that caused a national emergency; however, he said he would hold off from taking over the mines, pending further negotiations between the miners and mine owners. Two weeks later, after 109 days, the two sides reached an agreement, ending the strike.

BLACKMUN, HARRY ANDREW (1908–1999). Harry Blackmun's 24-year service as an associate justice to the **Supreme Court** began in 1970 when he was appointed by President **Richard Nixon**. Born in Illinois, Blackmun graduated from Harvard University with a major in mathematics (B.A., 1929) and from Harvard University Law School (LL.B., 1932). He began his career in a prominent Minneapolis law firm and later became legal counsel for the Mayo Clinic and Mayo Foundation. In 1959 President Dwight D.

Eisenhower appointed him to the Eighth Circuit Court of Appeals. In 1970 Nixon nominated him to the U.S. Supreme Court. The president assumed Blackmun would prove a conservative justice; instead, Blackmun tended to side with his more liberal colleagues.

Blackmun strongly endorsed a person's right to privacy and protections for minorities. He joined the majority in *Roe v. Wade* (1973), which granted a woman the right to an **abortion**, and in *Regents of the University of California v. Bakke* (1978), which upheld **affirmative action** but struck down racial quotas. Once a proponent of the death penalty, he began to change his opinion later in his career, believing each case must be decided on its merits. Due to ill health, Blackmun retired from the Court in 1994. In 1997 he had a cameo appearance in director **Steven Spielberg**'s movie *Amistad*. He passed away from complications following hip replacement surgery.

BLUMENTHAL, WERNER MICHAEL (1926–). Democrat. The secretary of the treasury from 1977 to 1979, Michael Blumenthal had been born in Germany. He escaped with his family in 1939 from Nazi Germany to Shanghai, China. During World War II they were interned by the Japanese. In 1947 they came to the United States. In 1951 Blumenthal graduated from the University of California at Berkeley with a B.S. degree in international economics. He graduated from Princeton University with a master of arts and a master of public affairs (1953) and a Ph.D. in economics (1956).

Prior to being appointed to a cabinet position by President **Jimmy Carter**, Blumenthal had a successful career in business and public service. He held positions in the administrations of both President John F. Kennedy and President Lyndon B. Johnson. Blumenthal never believed he was part of Carter's inner circle. He continually clashed with others in the administration. As **inflation** increased, he suggested ways to combat the problem, only to be ignored. One example was the president's commitment to adjust domestic oil prices to world prices, which Blumenthal considered incompatible with the administration's goal to reduce inflation. Following a 1979 speech in which Carter cited a "crisis of confidence" as a cause of the country's weak **economy**, the president asked all of his cabinet secretaries to submit their resignations. Blumenthal was among several individuals whose resignations the president accepted. Since then, Blumenthal has written extensively on issues relating to finance and international business.

See also KREPS, JUANITA MORRIS (1921–2010); MILLER, G. (GEORGE) WILLIAM (1925–2006); SCHLESINGER, JAMES RODNEY (1929–).

BOMBECK, ERMA LOUISE (HARRIS) (1927–1996). Born in Dayton, Ohio, the humorist Erma Bombeck lost her father when she was nine years old. Without her father's salary to help the family pay their bills, the family was forced into near-poverty after a bank repossessed their home and furniture. When she was 20, Bombeck was diagnosed with a hereditary kidney condition. Although doctors told her she would suffer kidney failure at some point, she decided to live each day to its fullest. She attended Ohio University for a year and transferred to the University of Dayton in her sophomore year. Her professors told her she would never be successful as a writer; however, their comment simply made her more determined to be one.

In 1949 Erma married Bill Bombeck and also became a reporter for the *Ohio Journal Herald*. After five years with the paper, the Bombecks began their family. When their three children were in school, she contacted a local paper's editor with the idea of a daily humor column. Although not too impressed with her idea, the editor decided to give her a chance. In 1964 her first "At Wit's End" column appeared in the *Kettering-Oakwood Times*. The column was a success and within a year was nationally syndicated. "At Wit's End" appeared in 500 newspapers. For the next 30 years, Bombeck continued to make readers laugh. By the time she died in 1996 from complications after a kidney transplant, she had written 15 books, and her column was syndicated in 900 newspapers in the United States.

See also WOMEN.

BORDENKIRCHER V. HAYES. In 1978 the United States **Supreme Court** heard the case against Paul Lewis Hayes, a convicted forger with two prior convictions. The prosecution told Hayes that if he pled guilty he would receive less jail time. Hayes, who already had two felony convictions, rejected the idea and received a maximum life sentence. His lawyers appealed, charging that the prosecutor had violated the due-process clause of the 14th Amendment. In a 5–4 vote, the Court rejected the appeal, determining that a prosecutor could threaten a stiffer penalty if a defendant rejected a plea bargain.

BOURNE, PETER GEOFFREY (1939–). Democrat. The director of the Office of Drug Abuse Policy (ODAP) from 1977 to 1978, Peter Bourne was born in Oxford, Great Britain. He became a naturalized U.S. citizen and, by 1976, a close friend of both **Jimmy** and **Rosalynn Carter**. He had graduated from Emory University (M.D., 1962), interned in psychiatry, served in Vietnam, and won awards for valor during his tour of duty. In 1969 he received his M.A. in anthropology while also completing his residency in psychiatry at Stanford University. He returned to Atlanta to work with drug abusers and alcoholics. It was while he was in Atlanta that Jimmy Carter learned of Bourne's work and asked Bourne to advise him on health issues during Carter's second run for the Georgia governorship.

Bourne was one of the first persons to suggest that Carter run for president and, after the **1976 election**, worked in the president's administration as ODAP head. The other Georgians who worked for Carter did not like Bourne, finding his dress odd and angered by the amount of attention he received in the media. It was that same media attention, however, that would end Bourne's work for the White House. Stories began to circulate that Bourne had snorted cocaine at a party. Then, in mid-1978, the public learned that he had written a prescription for quaaludes for an aide and given her a false name to protect her identity. A year earlier, the president had come under intense scrutiny for supporting **Bert Lance**, his director of the Office of Management and Budget who had been accused of impropriety. Bourne realized that Carter did not want to have to face another scandal and offered his resignation, which the president accepted.

After leaving Washington, Bourne worked in the United Nations and held numerous academic positions at prestigious American universities. He has authored a number of books and articles. In 1996, he wrote a biography of Carter that was well received by reviewers.

See also JORDAN, HAMILTON (1944–2008).

BOXING. Boxing in the 1970s included several famous people; however, the strangest duo to come out of the decade were **Muhammad Ali** and **Howard Cosell**. Three times during the 1970s Ali held the title of World Heavyweight Champion. Cosell had studied to be a lawyer but became a well-known sportscaster. Ali loved to make up ditties, and Cosell delighted in talking with the reigning champion. Their relationship and continued friendship added a unique dimension to boxing. Other famous boxers during the 1970s were Joe Frazier, Larry Spinks, and George Foreman. George Foreman has had the most unusual career since leaving the ring. He advertises George Foreman grills in his **infomercials** and has become a successful businessman. He named all of his five sons George!

See also SPORTS.

BREAKDANCING. *See* DANCES.

BREAST CANCER. While President **Gerald Ford** was in office, First Lady **Betty Ford** was diagnosed with breast cancer. Mrs. Ford shared her illness with the American people and told them she had a mastectomy. Her honesty helped other **women** who had experienced the horror of breast cancer. It also made women aware of the need to care for their health. Vice

President **Nelson Rockefeller**'s wife, Margaretta, also had breast cancer, and, like the First Lady, let the public know. Prior to the openness of both women, the subject of breast cancer and women's health had not been discussed with such candor.

BRENNAN, WILLIAM JOSEPH, JR. (1906–1997). An associate justice of the **Supreme Court** from 1956 to 1990, William Brennan was considered one of the most influential justices in the Supreme Court's history. He was born in New Jersey to a Catholic family and was educated in both parochial and public schools. He received his undergraduate degree from the Wharton School at the University of Pennsylvania (B.A., 1928) and his law degree from Harvard University in 1931. After graduating Harvard, he returned home to practice labor law in one of New Jersey's most prestigious law firms.

Following service in World War II, Brennan returned to his New Jersey law firm. Although he became a partner in the firm, he left it in 1949 to become a superior court judge. In 1952 he was appointed to the state supreme court. Brennan's appointment to the United States Supreme Court was a political one by President Dwight D. Eisenhower. With the 1956 election in the offing, Eisenhower believed the appointment of a liberal northeastern Catholic would help him win a second term. Indeed, Brennan was one of the most liberal of the nine justices on the Supreme Court. He opposed the death penalty and took a pro-choice position on **abortion**. He had the gift of persuasion and was able to coax his fellow justices to follow his opinions. In his many years on the bench Justice Brennan listened to some of the most important cases in U.S. history, including free speech (*Roth v. United States*, 1957); abortion (***Roe v. Wade***, 1973); voting (*Baker v. Carr*, 1962); and **civil rights** (*Green v. New Kent County*, 1968). A stroke forced him to retire in 1990. He passed away during rehabilitation for a broken hip.

BREZHNEV, LEONID ILYICH (1906–1982). The general secretary of the **Union of Soviet Socialist Republics (USSR)** from 1964 to 1982, Leonid Brezhnev was born in the Ukraine. Taking a job as a factory worker, he rose from obscurity to a member of the Communist Party in 1931, a graduate degree in engineering in 1935, and party secretary overseeing the Ukrainian city of Dneproderzhinsk's defense industries. He continued to climb up the party ranks, attaining the post of second secretary of the Communist Party's Central Committee in 1959. After the party removed Nikita Khrushchev from power in 1964, Brezhnev shared leadership responsibilities with Alexi Kosygin but quickly became the USSR's undisputed head of state.

Although Brezhnev wanted to cooperate with President **Jimmy Carter** in curtailing the U.S.-Soviet arms race, Carter's public denunciations of the USSR's treatment of its people created difficulties between the two leaders. It was not until 1979 that they signed the **Strategic Arms Limitation Treaty (SALT II)**. But America's ratification of that agreement was far from certain, and Brezhnev's decision to order Soviet troops into **Afghanistan** moved Carter to tell the U.S. Senate to shelve further consideration of SALT. Furthermore, Carter had the United States boycott the 1980 Summer **Olympics**, which were held in Moscow; increased U.S. **defense** spending; and issued the **"Carter Doctrine,"** in which he warned that Washington would use any means necessary to protect the oil-rich Persian Gulf from foreign attack. For the remainder of Carter's term in office, there was little interest in improving Soviet-American relations.

See also FOREIGN POLICY; NIXON, RICHARD MILHOUS (1913–1994).

BROWN, HAROLD (1927–). Democrat. The secretary of **defense** from 1977 to 1981, Harold Brown was the first scientist to serve in that post. Born in New York City, he was a brilliant student, receiving his undergraduate degree from Columbia University at age 18. He then obtained a doctorate in physics, also from Columbia, in 1949. Between 1947 and 1960, Brown held positions at three educational institutions, including Columbia University, the Stevens Institute of Technology, and the University of California at Berkeley. At the latter he became director of the university's new Lawrence Livermore Radiation Laboratory. He worked in the Department of Defense in both the John F. Kennedy and Lyndon B. Johnson administrations, including a four-year stint as secretary of the air force. Following **Richard Nixon**'s victory in the 1968 presidential election, Brown left Washington to accept the presidency of the California Institute of Technology.

Brown was still in California when President **Jimmy Carter** nominated him as secretary of defense. Brown was an active participant in the **Strategic Arms Limitation Treaty (SALT II)** negotiations, was key in convincing Carter to forego production of the **B-1 bomber**, endorsed development of both the MX missile and stealth technology, approved the ill-fated attempt in 1980 to free the Americans being held hostage in the U.S. embassy in **Iran**, and worked alongside National Security Adviser **Zbigniew Brzezinski** in formulating PD 59 (1980). An attempt to escape the policy of mutual assured destruction, which assumed that in a nuclear exchange the United States and the Soviet Union would suffer widespread damage, PD 59 stated that U.S. retaliation would focus on the enemy's most important military and industrial targets.

After Carter left office, Brown taught at Johns Hopkins University, served on various corporation boards, and was affiliated with a number of research organizations. He is presently a member of the Board of Directors of Philip Morris International.

See also WARNKE, PAUL CULLITON (1920–2001).

BROWN, JERRY (EDMUND GERALD BROWN JR.) (1938–). Democrat. The sitting governor of California, Jerry Brown also served as governor of that state from 1975 to 1983 and ran for the presidency in both 1976 and 1980. Born and raised in California, he was the only son of one of California's most popular politicians, Edmund Gerald Sr., also called Pat Brown. The younger Brown received his B.A. in 1961 from the University of California at Berkeley and his law degree from Yale University (LL.B., 1964). In 1974, after holding other political offices in the state, Brown successfully ran for governor of California. An unconventional and liberal politician, he became known for innovation and fiscal conservatism. California developed an international reputation for developing wind and solar technology during Brown's tenure. Rather than reside in the governor's mansion and take a limousine to work, Brown lived in an apartment and drove his own car. By the end of 1975, he had an approval rating of 84 percent.

In March 1976 Brown entered the presidential race. Though his entry was late, Brown knew that **Jimmy Carter**, the front-runner for the Democratic nomination, had lost the Massachusetts primary and that liberals were not sure about Carter as a candidate. Brown even continued his campaign after Carter won enough delegates to secure the nomination. But reality set in, and Brown dropped out of the **1976 election**, returned to the California governorship, and easily won reelection in 1978. His political future, though, took a downward turn afterward. He was derided for his suggestion that California launch a space satellite into orbit. He ran in the **1980 election**, again hoping for the Democratic nomination, but his campaign had little traction, and he soon dropped out. In 1982, he ran for the U.S. Senate but lost to **Republican** Pete Wilson.

Brown disappeared from politics for over a decade. However, the late 1990s saw the start of his political revival. In 1998, he won a race for mayor of Oakland, California, and became popular for attracting jobs to the city and reducing crime. He was reelected in 2002. Four years later, he successfully ran for the state attorney generalship and then, in 2010, was again elected California's governor.

BRYANT, ANITA (1940–). Born in Oklahoma, singer Anita Bryant graduated from high school and entered the 1958 Miss Oklahoma pageant, which she won. In the 1959 Miss America pageant, Bryant was the second runner-up. The following year she married Bob Green, with whom she had four children. In 1969 she became the spokesperson for the Florida Citrus Commission.

In 1977, Bryant turned her attention to an ordinance passed in Dade County, Florida, which prohibited discrimination against anyone based upon that person's sexual orientation. Regarding the law as a violation of Christian values, she launched a campaign called "Save Our Children" that overturned it. In time Bryant was challenged by many who did not believe as she did. The Florida Citrus Commission realized that this publicity was not to its advantage and dropped her as spokesperson. To this day, Bryant's name is still reviled by **gay rights** activists. Although she has tried to revitalize her career as a singer, she has been unable to do so.

See also CIVIL RIGHTS.

BRZEZINSKI, ZBIGNIEW KAZIMIERZ (1928–). Democrat. The national security adviser from 1977 to 1981, Zbigniew Brzezinski was born in Poland but grew up in Canada. He received his B.A. and M.A. in 1949 and 1950, respectively, from McGill University, and his doctorate in 1953 from Harvard University. In 1958 he became a naturalized citizen of the United States. In 1961 he moved to New York, where he headed Columbia University's new Institute on Communist Affairs. Brzezinski advised officials in the administrations of Presidents John F. Kennedy and Lyndon B. Johnson. In 1973 he became director of the Trilateral Commission, the purpose of which was to bring together highly influential figures in government, business, finance, academia, and the media from North America, **Japan**, and Western Europe to promote mutual understanding and close cooperation among the world's major industrial democracies.

One of the original members of the Trilateral Commission was **Jimmy Carter**. After Carter won the **1976 election** he appointed Brzezinski as his national security adviser. Brzezinski and Secretary of State **Cyrus Vance** repeatedly clashed on numerous **foreign policy** topics, including the timing of normalizing relations with communist **China** and the **Horn of Africa**, how hard of a line to take with the **Union of Soviet Socialist Republics (USSR)**, how to handle the question of black majority rule in **Rhodesia**, and whether to launch a mission to rescue Americans being held hostage in **Iran**. More often than not, it was Brzezinski who came out on top. Both Carter and his wife, **Rosalynn**—whom the president regarded as a key adviser—were personally closer to the NSC adviser than to Vance. The president also increasingly came to agree with Brzezinski that the United States had to be firm with Moscow.

After leaving the White House, Brzezinski gave an interview in which he claimed that he and Carter initiated policies that increased the likelihood of the Soviet Union's 1979 invasion of **Afghanistan**. In so doing, he argued, the

Carter holding a breakfast meeting with National Security Adviser Zbigniew Brze-zinski (sitting next to the president), Vice President Walter Mondale, and Secre-tary of State Cyrus Vance (sitting across from Carter). Vance and Brzezinski were Carter's two main foreign policy advisers. Courtesy of the Jimmy Carter Library.

United States helped hasten the collapse of communism in the USSR. Brze-zinski continues to write, lecture, and appear on various **television** news programs.

See also AARON, DAVID LAURENCE (1938–); DONOVAN, HEDLEY WILLIAMS (1914–1990); FOREIGN POLICY; KISSINGER, HENRY AL-FRED (ALFRED HEINZ) (1923–); MARCOS, FERDINAND (EMMA-NUEL EDRALIN) (1917–1989); MUSKIE, EDMUND SIXTUS (1914–1996); STRAUSS, ROBERT SCHWARTZ (1918–); SULLIVAN, WILLIAM HEALY (1922–); TURNER, STANSFIELD (1923–); WALESA, LECH (1943–); WARNKE, PAUL CULLITON (1920–2001); WATSON, JACK HEARN, JR. (1938–).

BUCKLEY, WILLIAM FRANK, JR. (1925–2008). Author, talk show host, editor, and founder of the conservative **magazine** the *National Review*, Buckley was born into a wealthy New York family. He spoke Spanish and French before he learned to speak English, which resulted in his unusual pronunciation when speaking. He graduated from Yale University in 1950 where he excelled as a debater. In 1951 he published *God and Man at Yale: The Superstitions of "Academic Freedom,"* in which he criticized Yale for, in his opinion, losing its traditional values.

From 1952 until he founded the *National Review* in 1955, Buckley was a freelance writer. During that time, he published his second book, *McCarthy and His Enemies*, in which he defended Senator Joseph McCarthy. He used the *National Review* to defend those he believed were true "conservatives" and criticize those who were not; among the latter was **Republican** Dwight D. Eisenhower, whom the magazine only reluctantly endorsed for reelection in 1956.

In 1965, Buckley ran for the office of mayor of New York City. Although he lost, many historians believe his campaign was the beginning of the Republican Party's popularity with working-class people. Considered one of the founders of the modern conservative movement, Buckley became a popular figure on **television**. From 1966 to 1999 he hosted *Firing Line*, which ran longer than any other television program hosted by one person. One of the great intellects of the second part of the 20th century, he held his own with political figures, writers, and people in the news. With his boyish looks, gregarious personality, and wit, he had a commanding presence on his program or wherever he spoke.

In 1990 Buckley retired as editor of the magazine he founded but remained the *National Review*'s editor-at-large. He continued to make guest appearances on both radio and television shows and on the lecture circuit. An author in his own right, he penned 11 spy novels, finishing the final one in 2004. He also wrote on historical events, including a novel about the Nuremberg trials. He died peacefully at his desk in 2008.

See also LITERATURE.

BURGER, WARREN EARL (1907–1995). Chief justice of the **Supreme Court** from 1969 to 1986, Warren Burger was born in Saint Paul, Minnesota, and was president of his high school student council. He attended night classes at the University of Minnesota and sold life insurance during the day. In 1931 he received his law degree from the Saint Paul College of Law. He worked in a local law firm while teaching at Saint Paul. Burger's political career began in 1948 when he supported Minnesota governor Harold Stassen in his unsuccessful bid for the **Republican** nomination for the presidency. He also favored Stassen in 1952 but endorsed Dwight D. Eisenhower when it became clear the former general would win the party's nod. In 1955, President Eisenhower appointed Burger to the United States Court of Appeals of the Columbia Circuit, a position he held until 1969, when President **Richard Nixon** nominated Burger for chief justice of the Supreme Court.

Nixon had assumed Burger was a conservative, but once on the Court, the new chief justice demonstrated otherwise. Most notable was Burger's role in the case of ***Roe v. Wade*** (1973), in which he joined the majority in defending a **woman**'s right to an **abortion**. He also proved a strong proponent of **gay rights**. He led the Court in its unanimous decision in *United States v. Richard Milhous Nixon* (1974), which stated that the president had to relinquish his taped conversations during the Watergate scandal. Burger retired from the Supreme Court in 1986. He passed away from congestive heart failure.

BURNETT, CAROL (1933–). One of the most popular **television** variety programs in the 1970s was *The Carol Burnett Show*. Carol Burnett was born in San Antonio, Texas. Her parents were alcoholics, and Burnett was virtually raised by her grandmother. She attended the University of California at Los Angeles but moved to New York City before graduating. She began her career on a children's television program, which led to her appearing on Broadway. *Once Upon a Mattress* (1960) was her first theatrical presentation, and she was a success. She received her first Emmy Award while appearing on *The Gary Moore Show* (1959–62). In 1967 she starred in *The Carol Burnett Show*, which appeared on television until 1978; she was famous for ending the program by tugging her ear as a way to tell her grandmother hello. She appeared in several movies and has been a guest on various television programs.

See also CINEMA.

BURNS, ARTHUR FRANK (1904–1987). Democrat. The chairman of the Federal Reserve Board from 1970 to 1978, Arthur Burns was born in Austria. His family immigrated to the United States and settled in New Jersey. Burns received all three of his degrees from Columbia University: B.A., 1921; M.A., 1925; and Ph.D., 1934. Burns met Dwight D. Eisenhower when Eisenhower was Columbia's president. After the 1952 election, now-President Eisenhower named Burns as chair on his Council of Economic Advisers. Burns later took on temporary assignments with Presidents John F. Kennedy and Lyndon B. Johnson.

In 1970 President **Richard Nixon** appointed Burns as chair of the Federal Reserve Board, a position he held until he was fired by President **Jimmy Carter**. Carter and Burns clashed on a number of matters, particularly that of how to combat **inflation**. To the president and many of his advisers, Burns was too willing to criticize White House policies. Therefore, when Burns came up in January 1978 for another four-year term as Fed chair, Carter decided not to reappoint him. After leaving the Federal Reserve Board, Burns became a distinguished scholar at the American Enterprise Institute, a conservative think tank. He died from complications following heart surgery.

See also MILLER, G. (GEORGE) WILLIAM (1925–2006).

BUSH, GEORGE HERBERT WALKER (1924–). Republican. The vice president of the United States from 1981 to 1989, and president of the United States from 1989 to 1993, George H. W. Bush was born into a wealthy Massachusetts family. He attended the exclusive Phillips Andover Academy and, after graduating, entered the military during World War II. Following the war, he enrolled at Yale University (B.A., 1948). He moved to Texas in the early 1950s and by 1953 had cofounded his own oil and gas-drilling company. He entered politics in Texas in the 1960s and developed a national reputation. Consequently, he received a number of governmental appointments, culminating in his appointment by President **Gerald Ford** as director of the **Central Intelligence Agency (CIA)**. After Ford's loss in the **1976 election**, Bush resigned from the CIA.

Bush considered entering the **1980 election**, but after several primaries he realized that **Ronald Reagan** would be the Republican nominee. To the surprise of many observers, Reagan chose Bush as his running mate. Bush ran on Reagan's coattails in 1988, winning both the Republican nomination and the presidency. However, in 1992 he lost his bid for a second term to Bill Clinton. Bush's oldest son, George Walker, won the presidency in 2000 and served two terms in the White House. The elder Bush continues to make public appearances, including a series of ads in 2005 with Clinton, encouraging aid to help victims of both the 2004 tsunami in Asia and 2005's Hurricane Katrina.

See also MOYNIHAN, DANIEL PATRICK (1927–2003); STRAUSS, ROBERT SCHWARTZ (1918–).

BYRD, ROBERT CARLYLE (1917–2010). Democrat. A member of the House of Representatives from 1953 to 1958, a U.S. senator from 1959 to 2010, and Senate majority leader from 1977 to 1980 and from 1987 to 1988, Robert Byrd was born in North Carolina but raised in West Virginia. He is the only member of Congress to receive his law (American University, 1963) and bachelor's (Marshall University, 1984) degrees while serving on Capitol Hill. Beginning his career in West Virginia politics in 1946, Byrd was elected to the U.S. House of Representatives in 1952. Six years later, he began his career in the U.S. Senate. In 1977 Byrd replaced Mike Mansfield, who decided to retire from Congress, as Senate majority leader.

Byrd and President **Jimmy Carter** had a rocky relationship. The West Virginia senator was angry that Carter did not keep him or Speaker of the House **Tip O'Neill** adequately informed about decisions. Nor did he like Carter's decision to veto 19 water projects the president considered unnecessary. Byrd supported ratification of the **Panama Canal treaties** and the

Strategic Arms Limitation Treaty (SALT II), as well as many White House anti-**inflation** initiatives. However, the president's unwillingness to accept his advice on legislation made Byrd both angry and less prepared to cooperate with the White House on such matters as a comprehensive **energy** program or offering sophisticated military aircraft to **Iran**. Privately, he endorsed **Edward Kennedy** in the **1980 election**.

In June 2010, while serving in the Senate, Byrd died from natural causes. His tenure was the longest of any member of Congress or of the Senate in the history of the legislative branch.

C

CABLE NEWS NETWORK (CNN). *See* TURNER, TED (ROBERT EDWARD, III) (1938–).

CADDELL, PATRICK H. (1950–). Democrat. A political consultant and pollster for President **Jimmy Carter**, "Pat" Caddell was one of the architects of Carter's **1976 election**. Born in South Carolina, Caddell entered Harvard University but did not graduate. At the age of 22 he had become a pollster for Democratic presidential candidate **George McGovern** in the 1972 election. Caddell was one of Carter's inner circle of friends during the latter's term as president and sometimes had an easier time getting the president's ear than did Vice President **Walter Mondale** or special assistant **Stuart Eizenstat**. After Carter's loss in the **1980 election**, Caddell turned to screenwriting and occasionally appeared on some political programs on **television**.

CALIFANO, JOSEPH ANTHONY, JR. (1931–). Democrat. The secretary of **health**, **education**, and welfare (HEW) from 1977 to 1979, Joseph Califano was born in New York City. He graduated from Holy Cross College (B.A., 1952) and Harvard University Law School (LL.B., 1955), where he edited the *Harvard Law Review*. Califano worked in President Lyndon B. Johnson's administration on domestic legislation. He was strongly supportive of Johnson's Great Society programs and impressed by the president's work ethic. He returned to private life following **Richard Nixon**'s victory in the 1968 election but accepted **Jimmy Carter**'s request to join his administration as HEW secretary.

At first, Califano and Carter got along. The president liked Califano's desire to reorganize his department, which corresponded with Carter's own determination to streamline the federal government. But differences between them appeared, starting with Carter's call in 1977 for a welfare reform program. Because of his fiscal conservatism, the president insisted that such a program entail no new spending, which Califano considered unrealistic. The secretary also did not approve of Carter's decision to create a separate Department of Education, believing it unnecessary. Califano then announced an

Carter and his pollster Pat Caddell. Caddell had serious concerns about Carter's debate with Ronald Reagan because of Reagan's reputation as "the Great Debater." Courtesy of the Jimmy Carter Library.

antismoking campaign without first conferring with the White House, and at the cost of angering lawmakers from tobacco-producing states. Most important, his liberal views tended not to mesh with those of the majority of Carter's advisers, who were more conservative in orientation. With the administration facing criticism for its handling of the **energy** crisis and the **economy**, and having to engage in damage control because of leaks to the press, Carter decided he needed to guarantee the loyalty of those around him. Therefore, in July 1979, the president requested that his secretaries and senior staff submit their resignations; among those he accepted was Califano's. Since leaving the administration, Califano has continued his effort to improve health care in the United States.

See also HARRIS, PATRICIA ROBERTS (1924–1985); LABOR; MARSHALL, (FREDDIE) RAY (1928–); McINTYRE, JAMES TALMADGE, JR. (1940–).

CALLAGHAN, JAMES LEONARD (1912–2005). The prime minister of **Great Britain** from 1976 to 1979, James Callaghan was born into a poor family in Portsmouth, England. He was never able to get a college degree. He worked for the British Internal Revenue Service, then for the intelligence wing of the Royal Navy during World War II, and began rising up the ranks of the Labour Party following the war. Prime Minister Harold Wilson appointed Callaghan foreign secretary in 1974. When Wilson resigned in 1976, Callaghan assumed the prime ministership.

President **Jimmy Carter** was more at ease with Callaghan than with any other European leader. The United Kingdom faced economic difficulties similar to the United States. Though Irish-Americans urged Carter to pressure Callaghan over British treatment of Catholics in Northern Ireland, the two Western leaders finessed the matter to avoid an Anglo-American rift. Carter and Callaghan agreed to use sanctions to pressure **Rhodesia**'s government to end apartheid, and the prime minister endorsed the president's decision to forego production of the **neutron bomb**.

In 1979, Callaghan lost the prime ministership following a vote of no confidence in his leadership. Elections later that year brought **Margaret Thatcher** and the Conservative Party to power. Callaghan continued to serve in Parliament, joining the House of Lords in the late 1980s. He passed away one day short of his 93rd birthday.

See also FOREIGN POLICY.

CAMBODIA, RELATIONS WITH. *See* POL POT (1928–1998).

CAMP DAVID ACCORDS. From its independence in 1948, the state of **Israel** fought a series of military conflicts with its Arab neighbors. In the Six Day War of 1967, Israel captured the Gaza Strip and Sinai Peninsula from **Egypt**, the West Bank and East Jerusalem from **Jordan**, and the Golan Heights from **Syria**. The war displaced hundreds of thousands of Palestinians, many of whom had fled into Syria or Jordan; many others, who already lived in the West Bank and Gaza, now found themselves under Israeli rule. Though the United Nations demanded Israel withdraw from the territories it had occupied, Israel refused.

Upon assuming the presidency, **Jimmy Carter** sought to achieve a comprehensive Middle East peace settlement, one that would convince Israel to return the occupied territories and grant the Palestinians living on the West Bank and Gaza Strip autonomy. Unbeknownst to him, **Anwar Sadat**, the president of Egypt, had begun secret negotiations with Israeli prime minister **Menachem Begin** to resolve their differences. In 1977, Sadat announced he would travel to Israel. His trip failed to find a solution to the difficulties between the two countries.

For Carter, Sadat's junket created a serious problem. The U.S. president wanted a comprehensive Middle East peace settlement, but Sadat clearly favored focusing on Egyptian-Israeli matters. Still, Carter realized he had an

The Camp David Accords, signed by the leaders of Israel and Egypt, were one of Carter's greatest successes. From left, Egyptian president Anwar Sadat, President Carter, and Israeli prime minister Menachem Begin. Courtesy of the Jimmy Carter Library.

opportunity to bring peace between two enemies, and so he invited Sadat and Begin to come to the presidential retreat at Camp David, Maryland, for a series of talks aimed at a settlement.

The negotiations took place in September 1978 and were intense; they nearly broke down at one point. But after two weeks, Begin and Sadat signed the Camp David Accords. Probably the greatest **foreign policy** achievement of Carter's presidency, the Camp David Accords established the foundation for a peace treaty between Israel and Egypt, starting with Israel returning the Sinai Peninsula. In addition, the accords sought to settle the Palestinian issue: during a five-year transition period, Israel, Egypt, and Jordan would determine the status of the Gaza Strip and West Bank, with the Palestinians to receive "full autonomy" and the right to govern those territories.

The Camp David Accords were lacking in some respects. Nothing was said about the Golan Heights. The agreement did not prohibit Israel from building settlements in either the Gaza Strip or the West Bank, which was something the Palestinians wanted. There was no guarantee that the Palestinians or Jordan would take part in negotiations over the future of the occupied territories; in fact, King **Hussein I** of Jordan had made clear that he would not participate in such talks until Israel returned East Jerusalem, a demand Israel refused.

Despite these shortcomings, the Camp David Accords had established a foundation for future talks and had brought peace between two warring neighbors. In March 1979, Sadat and Begin signed a formal peace treaty, normalizing relations between their nations. Israel subsequently began withdrawing its troops from the Sinai, a process it completed in 1982.

See also KISSINGER, HENRY ALFRED (ALFRED HEINZ) (1923–); LIPSHUTZ, ROBERT JEROME (1921–2010); McGOVERN, GEORGE STANLEY (1922–2012); MONDALE, WALTER FREDERICK (FRITZ) (1928–); NIXON, RICHARD MILHOUS (1913–1994); PALESTINE LIBERATION ORGANIZATION (PLO); STRAUSS, ROBERT SCHWARTZ (1918–); TALMADGE, HERMAN EUGENE (1913–2002).

CARLIN, GEORGE (1937–2008). A comedian and social satirist, George Carlin was born in New York City. He dropped out of high school and joined the air force. He did not complete his enlistment, choosing instead to become a radio disc jockey. His popularity on the radio led to a career in stand-up comedy. He excelled at one-liners, exposing hypocrisy and questioning conventional wisdom. In 1972 Carlin did a routine on a New York radio station called "Seven Words You Can Never Say on **Television**." The program was heard by a small child, whose father brought the broadcast to the attention of the Federal Communications Commission (FCC). The radio station was fined for allowing the words to be heard on a public broadcast. The question over whether Carlin's routine was obscene went all the way to the United States **Supreme Court**. In the 1978 case of *F.C.C. v. Pacifica Foundation*, the Court ruled the broadcast was indecent. In the 1970s Carlin, however, was a hit on college campuses and was the first host of *Saturday Night Live*. Carlin was a drug user and openly admitted to this fact. From the 1960s, when his career began, until his death, Carlin's monologues constantly tackled taboo subjects.

CARRERAS, JOSÉ (JOSEP CARRERAS I COLL) (1946–). One of the "Three Tenors" who performed during the 1990s and into the 21st century, José Carreras was born in Barcelona, Spain. He studied voice at the University of Barcelona and debuted in that city in 1970. In 1974 he appeared for the first time at the Metropolitan **Opera**. Before he was 30 he had sung in 24 different operas in Europe and North America. Carreras has performed in **theater** productions, including *West Side Story* and *South Pacific*. His bout with leukemia, from which he recovered, moved him to find a cure. In 1988 he established the Jose Carreras International Leukemia Foundation. In 1990

Carreras, **Luciano Pavarotti**, and **Placido Domingo** sang together for the first time. The trio's initial performance led to many successful appearances of the Three Tenors.

CARSON, JOHNNY (1925–2005). Considered the "king of late-night **television**," John William Carson was the host of *The Tonight Show* for 30 years. He was born in Nebraska and graduated from the University of Nebraska (B.A., 1949). Although he studied journalism, Carson began working on an Omaha radio station as an announcer.

In 1951 he was living in Los Angeles, where he had a local television show called *Carson's Cellar*. He wrote for Red Skelton and was a guest host on Skelton's television program. In 1962 he replaced Jack Paar as host of *The Tonight Show* and in time became television's highest-paid performer. He was able to make guests comfortable and introduced many budding comedians, including Jay Leno, David Letterman, and Jerry Seinfeld. He retired in 1992, after which Leno became host of *The Tonight Show*.

See also McMAHON, ED(WARD) (1923–2009); SILLS, BEVERLY (1929–2007).

CARTER, BILLY (WILLIAM ALTON, III) (1937–1988). The younger brother of President **Jimmy Carter**, Billy Carter often proved an embarrassment during his elder sibling's tenure in the White House. The younger Carter was not as strong a student as Jimmy, and he was upset when their father turned the family peanut warehouse business over to Jimmy rather than him. However, he became something of a celebrity following the **1976 election**. He came to be seen as a beer-drinking redneck whose name became famous with the brewing of Billy Beer. He could be funny and showed this as a guest on various talk shows. However, after he visited Libya, from which he received a $220,000 loan, questions arose as to why the president's brother was interacting with a renegade nation. The White House's clumsy reaction and handling of the situation, which the media and **Republicans** called "Billygate," only added fuel to the fire. After Jimmy Carter lost the **1980 election**, Billy remained out of the limelight. His financial situation forced him to auction off most of his property. He died of pancreatic cancer, the same illness that killed his father and two sisters.

See also ANDERSON, JACK (JACKSON NORTHMAN) (1922–2005); CIVILETTI, BENJAMIN RICHARD (1935–); CUTLER, LLOYD NORTON (1917–2005); DOLE, ROBERT JOSEPH (1923–); FOREIGN POLICY.

Jimmy and Billy Carter. The president's younger brother's ties to Libya embar-rassed the administration. Courtesy of the Jimmy Carter Library.

CARTER, ELEANOR ROSALYNN SMITH (1927–). First lady and wife of President **Jimmy Carter**, Rosalynn Carter was born in Plains, Georgia, the oldest of four children. She was valedictorian of her high school graduat-ing class and attended Georgia Southwestern College for two years. She planned to continue her education in interior design at Georgia State College for **Women** but left school to marry Jimmy. While the future president was in the navy, they had their three sons. Rosalynn loved the life of a navy wife. When Jimmy learned that his father was dying, though, he made the decision to return to Plains to run the family farm. His decision led to a crisis within their marriage, but the Carters returned to Plains. Rosalynn quickly learned to be a partner with her husband as they ran the family's peanut business. During this time, she gave birth to a fourth child, Amy.

Mrs. Carter was an avid campaigner for her husband when he successfully ran for governor of Georgia and again in the **1976 election** for president. She became one of the most influential first ladies in U.S. history. She attended cabinet meetings and was her husband's confidant and adviser. She fought for women's rights and the improvement of mental health care facilities. She was most proud of the passage of the Mental Health Systems Act and was disappointed that the **Equal Rights Amendment (ERA)** was not ratified. Women, however, were upset that Rosalynn always appeared to side with her husband and opposed a woman's right to have an **abortion**. After President

Carter lost the **1980 election**, the Carters returned to Plains. She joined her husband in founding the **Carter Center** in Atlanta, Georgia, works with **Habitat for Humanity**, and advocates care for those with mental illnesses.

See also FOREIGN POLICY; STEINEM, GLORIA (1934–); WALESA, LECH (1943–).

CARTER, GLORIA (1926–1990). The oldest of **Jimmy Carter**'s three siblings, Gloria Carter married Walter Spann in 1953 and participated in Jimmy's 1962 campaign to win a seat in the Georgia state senate. A lover of motorcycles, she joined the Georgia Motorcycle Rights Organization in the 1970s. In 1977, she and her mother, **Lillian Carter**, published *Away from Home: Letters to My Family*, a collection of letters Lillian had mailed while serving with the Peace Corps in India. She was the last of Jimmy's siblings to pass away and, like them, lost her life to pancreatic cancer.

CARTER, JAMES EARL, JR. (JIMMY) (1924–). Democrat. Jimmy Carter was the 39th president of the United States, serving from 1977 to 1981. His political career began in 1962; however, he found the road to the White House an uneasy one. He was born in Plains, Georgia, on 1 October 1924. His father, **James Earl Carter Sr.**, was a successful peanut farmer; his mother, **Lillian Gordy Carter**, was a nurse. He grew up in Archer, Georgia, about five miles outside of Plains, in a house without indoor plumbing or electricity. Yet his childhood memories were fond ones and included hunting and fishing trips with his father. By the time he was a teenager, the family had grown to four children, two boys and two girls.

Carter's father believed in the southern practice of segregation, but he treated his **African American** workers with respect. His more liberal-minded mother was more defiant of southern mores. She helped those in need of medical care, no matter who they were. Watching his parents' treatment of African Americans set the stage for Carter's genuine concern for others. He even remembered going to the movies with his best friend, who was black; however, they were not permitted to sit together. Church services at the Plains Baptist Church, which the Carters attended, were also segregated, but once a year the Carters participated in services at a local all-black Methodist church. When Carter was in high school, he did not question why his black friends were not in the school. Instead he grew closer to his white high school friends even as he retained ties with his black friends in activities after school.

In 1941 Carter finished high school. A good student, he continued his **education** at Georgia Southwestern College in Americus and then the Georgia Institute of Technology in Atlanta. After two years of studying science he was admitted to the U.S. Naval Academy, a lifelong dream. He excelled in his studies at the academy, graduating in 1946 59th out of a class of 820. Shortly thereafter, he married **Rosalynn Smith**, who was also from Plains.

Carter's first assignment was as a radar officer, but he really wanted to be a submariner. In 1951 he was interviewed by Admiral **Hyman Rickover**, who oversaw construction of the first nuclear submarine. The interview ended with Rickover asking Carter if he had done his best at the Naval Academy. Answering that he had not, Rickover asked, "Why not?" The question stayed with Carter for the rest of his life and became the theme of his campaign for president in 1976. Under Rickover's command Carter strove to be the best. Even as president, Rickover always remained a larger-than-life figure for Carter. He broke out in a sweat if his former naval commander phoned.

Although Carter planned to be a career naval officer, his father's terminal illness from cancer forced the Carters to return to Plains in 1953. Rosalynn had resisted going back to her birthplace, for she loved the role of a naval officer's wife. Carter, on the other hand, believed it was his duty to run his father's business. Returning to the farm, the couple found the business faltering, and it took several years before they were able to show a profit from their hard work. By the 1960s, however, Carter had become one of Plains' most successful businessmen. He was also chairman of the Sumter County school board.

In 1962, Carter ran for a seat in the Georgia state senate. He lost by 139 votes to the candidate of a county political machine, Homer Moore. But with the help of two lawyers, **Griffin Bell** and **Charles Kirbo**, both of whom would figure prominently in Carter's later political career, he was able to go to court and prove that widespread voter fraud had been committed. In the regular election, he won by a comfortable margin. He served two terms in the senate, where he gained a reputation as a hardworking, honest legislator. He fought for the poor and against lobbyists representing special interest groups. In 1965, he was named one of the most influential legislators by a Georgia newspaper.

Having made a name for himself in Georgia, Carter in 1966 decided to run for governor. In the primary he narrowly came in third behind the eventual winner in the runoff, Lester Maddox. Depressed, Carter found solace in religion and declared himself a born-again Christian. In the meantime, he prepared for another try at the governor's mansion in 1970. He concluded that his surest path to victory necessitated appealing to segregationists. Although many of his supporters regretted the racist nature of his campaign, he won the election.

As governor, Carter surprised many political observers by establishing a reputation as a racial moderate and reformer. He increased the number of black state employees from 4,850 to 6,684. He signed a law providing equal

The Carters at the inauguration. Courtesy of the Jimmy Carter Library.

distribution of state aid to all areas of the state, whether rich or poor. He worked for tax, welfare, and judicial reform, as well as for **environmental** protection. He had help from **Bert Lance**, whom he had met during the 1966 campaign and who became part of Carter's inner circle. Appointed by Carter as director of the Georgia Department of Transportation, Lance helped plan political and budgetary strategy and lobbied state legislators on controversial matters. Though Carter succeeded in streamlining the state government, he did so at the cost of angering lawmakers, who believed he did not consult them adequately. It was a mistake he would repeat as president.

In 1974, Carter decided to make a bid for the presidency. No one from the South had sat in the White House for over a century. Unknown outside of Georgia, Carter realized he had to gain national recognition. His most trusted adviser, **Hamilton Jordan**, provided a strategic plan that called for Carter to enter as many primaries as possible. The idea worked brilliantly. Wherever he went, the candidate promised to restore dignity to the presidential office. He took advantage of the fact that President **Gerald Ford** had pardoned President **Richard Nixon**, who had resigned from office as a result of the Watergate scandal. Ford's actions had angered many voters. Positioning himself as the most moderate of the Democratic candidates running for the president, Carter gained broad appeal. Winning several key primaries, he picked up delegates even in states he did not win. One by one, his challengers, among them Representative **Morris Udall**, Senators **Birch Bayh** and

Henry Jackson, California governor **Jerry Brown**, and Alabama governor **George Wallace**, dropped out of the race. By the time the Democratic Convention was held in July in New York, Carter was assured a first-ballot majority.

As his running mate, Carter selected Minnesota senator **Walter Mondale**. Carter believed Mondale could draw him votes from the Midwest, and the senator's congressional experience could prove useful as the White House sought to get legislation passed. Additionally, Mondale insisted on having an active role in the administration, which Carter favored.

With the Democratic nomination in hand, Carter turned his attention to his **Republican** opponent, President Ford. As the **1976 election** headed into its final weeks, Carter made some mistakes, including an interview in *Playboy* **magazine** in which he admitted that he had "committed adultery in [his] heart many times." That an individual who declared himself highly religious would make such a statement, let alone in a pornographic magazine, angered many religious conservatives. Furthermore, Ford began to cut into Carter's lead in the polls by charging his Democratic rival with not giving specific answers to questions. During one of two televised debates, however, Ford made a fatal error, declaring that Eastern Europe was not under Soviet control and would never be during his administration. In November, Carter narrowly defeated Ford, receiving 40.8 million votes to Ford's 39.1 million.

Though he had, like most newly inaugurated presidents, a high approval rating in the early weeks of his administration, Carter quickly became a target of criticism. For one thing, most of his key advisory positions were filled with fellow Georgians, or the "Georgia mafia," as the group became known. Furthermore, he began to alienate Congress. He made legislators pay for their meals at the White House, cut pork barrel water projects strongly supported on Capitol Hill, canceled production of the **B-1 bomber**, and failed in the minds of lawmakers to consult them. He presented Congress with an overly ambitious domestic agenda, which included welfare reform, a comprehensive energy program, hospital cost-containment legislation, tax reform, and Social Security reform. By August 1977, every one of these initiatives had become stalled on Capitol Hill. Finally, he alienated many traditional Democratic constituencies. The **economy** at the time of Carter's victory was lethargic, with **inflation** hovering around 6 percent and unemployment about two points higher. Carter promised during the campaign that he would make combating unemployment his top priority, which pleased liberal Democrats, **labor** unions, and African Americans. But after securing the White House, the president made reducing inflation his number-one concern.

Complicating matters for the president was his management style. In addition to his domestic policy proposals, Carter proposed numerous **foreign policy** initiatives, including a comprehensive Middle East peace settlement, promotion of **human rights**, stimulating the world economy, normalizing relations with **China**, turning the Panama Canal over to Panama, removing U.S. troops from **South Korea**, and signing a second **Strategic Arms Limitation Treaty (SALT II)** with the **Union of Soviet Socialist Republics (USSR)**. Carter failed to prioritize these initiatives, which forced the administration to try to work on them all at once. Moreover, one policy could sometimes interfere with another; as an example, the USSR was furious with Carter's criticism of its human rights record, which made it less willing to cooperate on SALT. Finally, the president's top foreign policy aides, Secretary of State **Cyrus Vance** and National Security Adviser **Zbigniew Brzezinski**, jostled over the extent to which Soviet machinations were responsible for trouble spots around the world. Carter did a poor job in making clear whether Vance or Brzezinski spoke for the administration, which confused observers within and outside the United States.

Scandal also affected the White House, namely questions surrounding Bert Lance. Appointed by Carter as director of the Office of Management and Budget, questions began to arise regarding Lance's banking practices while he served as chairman of the board of Calhoun National Bank. Carter, who had promised to reestablish honesty in the White House, was devastated by the accusations. The resulting scandal forced Carter to ask for Lance's resignation. In September 1977 Lance resigned his position on the Carter cabinet.

Despite these problems, Carter registered successes. Determined to protect the environment, the president in August 1977 signed both the **Surface Mining Control and Reclamation Act** and the **Clean Air Act Amendments**. That same month, he established a new Department of Energy via the **Department of Energy Organization Act**. In March 1978, the Senate ratified the **Panama Canal treaties**. Signed by Carter and Panama's leader, **Omar Torrijos**, the treaties turned the waterway over to Panama in the year 2000. Six months later Carter brokered a peace agreement between **Israel**'s prime minister, **Menachem Begin**, and **Egypt**'s president, **Anwar Sadat**, whom he had brought together at Camp David. The signing of the **Camp David Accords** was a major achievement for the president, who received accolades from around the world. Believing **deregulation policies** would benefit consumers, Carter in October signed into law the **Airline Deregulation Act**. That same month, Congress passed the **National Energy Act**, which established programs aimed at solving the country's **energy crisis**. At the end of the year, the president normalized relations with China. Though Vance had opposed this move, believing it would irritate the Soviet Union and make Moscow less willing to offer concessions at the SALT negotiations, Brzezinski believed the "China card" would have the opposite effect. Though Carter had at first agreed with Vance, he had grown upset with Soviet activities in the **Horn of Africa** and sided with his national security adviser.

The acclaim Carter received for these achievements proved short-lived. In early 1979, Carter decided to forego withdrawing U.S. troops from South Korea. Not only did South Korea and **Japan** oppose such a move, insisting that the American presence was vital for their **defense**, but the proposal had generated intense opposition in Congress. The president and Soviet general secretary **Leonid Brezhnev** signed SALT II in June, but there was a clear lack of enthusiasm in the Senate to ratify it. While some members of the Upper House, among them **Jacob Javits**, **Frank Church**, and **Abraham Ribicoff**, endorsed SALT, most, including **Bob Dole**, **William Proxmire**, **Howard Baker**, **Jesse Helms**, **Sam Nunn**, **John Stennis**, and **Daniel Patrick Moynihan**, either rejected it or had serious reservations regarding some of its provisions.

Even more troublesome was the economy, which remained weak. Unemployment and inflation were high, and a decision by the **Organization of Petroleum Exporting Countries (OPEC)** to raise the price of oil did not help matters. Gas shortages and long lines at the pump became a common sight. Labor unions such as the **American Federation of Labor and Congress of Industrial Organizations (AFL-CIO)** complained that Carter was not doing enough to create jobs. Although Carter had done much for African Americans, **Hispanic Americans**, and **women**, including supporting the **Equal Rights Amendment (ERA)** and naming **Andrew Young**, **Anne Wexler**, **Patricia Derian**, **Midge Costanza**, **Sarah Weddington**, **Juanita Kreps**, **Shirley Hufstedler**, and **Patricia Harris** to important government posts, women and minorities believed he had not done enough to support their interests. Many feminists disliked what they regarded as Carter's tepid support for **abortion** rights, and both African Americans and women agreed with labor on the need for the White House to reduce unemployment.

Americans' anger was reflected in polls in mid-1979 that showed less than one-quarter of voters believed the country was doing well economically. Carter received a slight bump in his approval rating that July when he blamed a "crisis of the spirit" for the nation's economic troubles. Yet Carter lost what goodwill he had gained from the **"malaise" speech**—as it became known—when he requested his cabinet secretaries submit their resignations. Among those whose resignations Carter accepted were Health, Education, and Welfare Secretary **Joseph Califano**; Treasury Secretary **Michael Blumenthal**; and Secretary of Energy **James Schlesinger**. The president's signing in October 1979 of the **Department of Education Organization Act** was overshadowed by growing dissatisfaction with an administration that appeared divided and unable to find solutions to serious national problems.

Adding to Carter's woes was a series of foreign policy crises. In January 1979, the shah of **Iran, Mohammed Reza Pahlavi,** fled his country and eventually came to the United States for medical treatment. The new Iranian government, led by **Ayatollah Ruhollah Khomeini,** demanded the shah's return to Iran, but Carter refused. That July, **Anastasio Somoza Debayle**, **Nicaragua**'s dictator, fled his nation before a revolt led by the leftist **Sandinistas**. The loss of two foreign leaders who had been allies of the United States drew criticism of the White House, particularly from conservatives. In November, militant Iranian students, furious with Carter's unwillingness to send Pahlavi back to Iran, took hostage dozens of Americans in the U.S. embassy in Tehran. A month later, the USSR invaded **Afghanistan**. In response to the invasion, the president imposed a grain embargo on the Soviet Union, announced that the United States would not participate in the Summer **Olympic** Games in Moscow, and told the Senate to shelve SALT II.

The chancellor of **West Germany**, **Helmut Schmidt**, and French president **Valery Giscard d'Estaing** regarded Carter's reaction to the invasion of Afghanistan as overkill. At home, however, the invasion of Afghanistan, coming on top of the **Iran hostage crisis**, actually helped the president. Shortly after the hostage crisis began, Senator **Edward Kennedy** of Massachusetts announced his intent to challenge Carter for the Democratic Party's presidential nomination. With Soviet troops in Afghanistan and Americans being held captive against their will, U.S. voters felt they had to rally around their nation's leader.

Again, Carter's boost in the polls did not last. The hostage crisis continued unabated, and an attempt by the U.S. military to free the captive Americans failed in April, with the loss of eight American servicemen. Vance, who had opposed such an operation, resigned in protest; Senator **Edmund Muskie** succeeded Vance. Carter was able to win enough delegates by June 1980 to guarantee him the party's endorsement, yet the president's inability to extricate the hostages and the weak economy took their toll on the president's approval rating. News that **Billy Carter**, the president's younger brother, had received a $220,000 "loan" from Libya but had refused to register as a Libyan foreign agent only added to Carter's woes. It appeared the Republican nominee, **Ronald Reagan**, was a shoo-in to win the **1980 election**.

Carter, though, began to close the gap. He charged that Reagan's harsh anti-Soviet views could lead the United States into a war, and Reagan himself made a number of gaffes. However, at their only presidential debate, held a week before the election, Reagan turned the tide in his favor when he questioned Carter's handling of the economy, a topic of great importance with voters. Reagan received 51 percent of the popular vote, Carter 41 percent, and third-party candidate **John Anderson** won 7 percent.

For a couple of years, Democrats regarded Carter as a political pariah. In 1982, though, the ex-president's image began to change. He helped build homes with the Christian charity **Habitat for Humanity**. In 1988 the **Carter Center** opened in Atlanta as part of the Carter Presidential Library. It became a locus for international meetings aimed at promoting human rights, resolving international conflict, eradicating disease, and eliminating the stigma associated with mental illness—the last goal of particular interest to Mrs. Carter.

The Carter Center's accomplishments are impressive. Through the International Task Force for Disease Eradication, which the center established in 1988, Guinea worm has been all but eliminated. Additionally, the center has taken the lead in making sure the drug Mectizan is provided to people in Africa to combat river blindness. Meanwhile, observers have monitored elections in over three dozen countries. While the Center cannot take full credit for improved health care for those with mental illness, its efforts certainly have played a role. In 2002 Jimmy Carter was awarded the **Nobel Peace Prize** for his humanitarian work around the world.

Carter has not shied from controversy, though. He has met with leaders who have been criticized by U.S. officials, such North Korea's Kim Il Sung and Cuba's**Fidel Castro**. He has written over two dozen books, some of which have caused anger in the United States and abroad. The one that has received the most criticism was *Palestine: Peace Not Apartheid*, published in 2006. In this monograph, Carter focused on the treatment by the Israeli government of Palestinians living within Israel's borders, which he referred to as apartheid. The Israeli government was furious. When Carter visited Israel in 2008, the Israeli government would not provide him with protection.

Notwithstanding the criticism he has received, Jimmy Carter continues to be guided by his own deeply held views, which are often in conflict with U.S. policy. His records as a president and ex-president have generated a dichotomy, with the same poll sometimes ranking him among both the best and the worst presidents in the country's history. Yet many Americans believe that as an ex-president, he is one of the nation's best.

See also AARON, DAVID LAURENCE (1938–); ABZUG, BELLA SAVITSKY (1920–1998); ADAMS, BROCK (BROCKMAN) (1927–2004); AGRICULTURE; AUTOMOBILES; BERGLAND, ROBERT SELMER (1928–); BOURNE, PETER GEOFFREY (1939–); BROWN, HAROLD (1927–); BURNS, ARTHUR FRANK (1904–1987); CADDELL, PATRICK H. (1950–); CARTER FAMILY; CARTER, GLORIA (1926–1990); CARTER, RUTH (1929–1983); CENTRAL INTELLIGENCE AGENCY (CIA); CHRISTOPHER, WARREN MINOR (1925–2011); CIVIL RIGHTS; CIVILETTI, BENJAMIN RICHARD (1935–); CUTLER, LLOYD NORTON (1917–2005); DONOVAN, HEDLEY WILLIAMS (1914–1990); EIZENSTAT, STUART ELLIOTT (1943–); GOLDSCHMIDT, NEIL EDWARD (1940–); GRIFFIN, ROBERT PAUL (1923–); HEALTH; KAHN, ALFRED EDWARD (1917–2010); KLUTZNICK, PHILIP MORRIS (1907–1999); KRAFT, TIMOTHY E. (1941–); LINOWITZ, SOL MYRON (1913–2005); LIPSHUTZ, ROBERT JEROME (1921–2010); MARSHALL, (FREDDIE) RAY (1928–); McDONALD, AL (ALONZO LOWRY) (1928–); MILLER,

G. (GEORGE) WILLIAM (1925–2006); MOORE, FRANK (1935–); NEU-
TRON BOMB; PASTOR, ROBERT A. (1947–); PETERSON, ESTHER
EGGERTSON (1906–1997); POWELL, JODY (JOSEPH LESTER POW-
ELL JR.) (1943–2009); RAFSHOON, GERALD (1934–); RELIGION;
SCHULTZE, CHARLES LOUIS (1924–); SICK, GARY GORDON
(1935–); STRAUSS, ROBERT SCHWARTZ (1918–); SULLIVAN,
WILLIAM HEALY (1922–); SUPREME COURT; TURNER, STANS-
FIELD (1923–); VOLCKER, PAUL ADOLPH (1927–); WARNKE, PAUL
CULLITON (1920–2001); WATSON, JACK HEARN, JR. (1938–);
WOODCOCK, LEONARD FREEL (1911–2001).

CARTER, JAMES EARL, SR. (1894–1953). Born in 1894 in Cuthbert,
Georgia, James Earl Carter Sr. was the fourth of five children born to Billy
and Nina Carter. Billy owned over 400 acres of land, several sawmills, and a
vineyard. Following his father's murder in 1903, Nina moved the family to
Plains, Georgia. After graduating high school, Earl went to Riverside Military Academy in Gainesville, Georgia; spent time in Texas as a salesman;
and served in the U.S. Army in World War I. Returning to Plains after the
war, he made a small fortune, first by buying and selling peanuts and then
investing that money into land, a peanut warehouse, and a grocery. In 1923,
he married **Bessie Lillian Gordy**. The two had four children, the oldest of
them James Earl "Jimmy" Jr., who later became president of the United
States.

Earl was a fiscal conservative who opposed the New Deal. He was also
more prepared than Lillian to accept the system of segregation that was
prevalent in the South. Though Jimmy's mother influenced him more than
his father insofar as race relations, Earl instilled in his oldest son attributes
that he carried with him throughout his life and presidency, including a
commitment to hard work, a love of the outdoors, and a determination to
check federal spending. In 1953, Earl passed away from terminal pancreatic
cancer, a disease that later took the lives of each of Jimmy's siblings.

CARTER, LILLIAN GORDY (1898–1983). Bessie Lillian Gordy Carter,
mother of President **Jimmy Carter**, was born in Richland, Georgia. She
trained as a nurse and cared for **African Americans** in the area at a time
when this was simply not done by a white **woman**. Her liberal views rubbed
off on Jimmy. She received her nursing degree in 1923 from the Grady
Memorial Hospital School of Nursing in Atlanta and soon thereafter married
James Earl Carter Sr. After his death she worked at Auburn University but
left to enter the Peace Corps in 1966 at the age 68. "Miss Lillian," as she was
known following the **1976 election**, was surprised that her son would want to
be president but helped him during his campaign. She also participated in his

bid for reelection in 1980. After Carter left the White House, Lillian Carter was diagnosed with **breast cancer**. She died the same year as her daughter **Ruth**.

CARTER, RUTH (1929–1983). Ruth Carter was the third child of **James Earl Carter Sr.** and **Lillian Gordy Carter**. She married Robert T. Stapleton, and together they had four children. Ruth suffered periods of deep depression that involved group therapy sessions to help her. In time she converted to the Pentecostal faith, believing in its healing powers. She began to preach the healing power of prayer. In 1977 Ruth and **Larry Flynt**, publisher of the erotic **magazine** *Hustler*, were in the news. She claimed she had brought God into Flynt's life. He, however, did not change his ways and continued to publish his pornographic materials. Ruth Stapleton, like her father, brother, and sister, died of pancreatic cancer.

CARTER CENTER. Opened in 1982 and founded by **Jimmy** and **Rosalynn Carter**, the Carter Center, located in Atlanta, Georgia, seeks to promote human rights, peaceful resolution of conflicts, and eradication of disease worldwide. As part of this mandate, officials from the center since its founding have monitored elections, sought to improve sanitation, and held negotiations with leaders throughout the world. The Carter Center also devotes attention to the subject of mental health, a matter of particular interest to Mrs. Carter.

See also PASTOR, ROBERT A. (1947–).

"CARTER DOCTRINE". *See* AFGHANISTAN, RELATIONS WITH.

CARTER FAMILY. President **Jimmy Carter** was the oldest child of **James Earl Carter Sr.** (1894–1954) and **Lillian Gordy Carter** (1898–1983). His three siblings were **Gloria Carter** (Mrs. Walter G. Spann) (1926–1990), **Ruth Carter** (Mrs. Robert T. Stapleton) (1929–1983), and **Billy Carter** (1937–1988). President Carter's father was a peanut farmer and a storekeeper, and his mother was a nurse. Although Gloria was considered the smartest of the four, she was not close to Jimmy until later in her life. Gloria had eloped with a man her parents did not like and who brutally beat her. The marriage was annulled, and she married Walter Spann. After her brother became president, Gloria was not in the news to the extent of her mother and other siblings. James Earl Carter Sr., as well as Ruth, Gloria, and Billy, died from pancreatic cancer.

In 1946, Jimmy married **Eleanor Rosalynn Smith**. The two had four children: John "Jack" William (1947–), James Earl III "Chip" (1950–), Donnel Jeffrey (1952–), and Amy (1967–). Of the children, the two who have received the most attention are Jack and Amy. In 2006, Jack tried but failed to win a seat in the U.S. Senate representing Nevada. Amy became known for her opposition to South Africa's policy of apartheid and was arrested in 1986 during an antiapartheid protest in Massachusetts. She attended Brown University but failed to complete her degree. She eventually obtained a degree in fine arts from the Memphis College of Art.

Jimmy and Rosalynn have eleven grandchildren and two great-grandchildren. Most notable among them is Jack's oldest son, Jason, who won a seat in the Georgia state senate in 2010. He is the first Carter to win an elected office since Jimmy's victory in the **1976 election**.

CASTRO, FIDEL (1926–). The president of **Cuba** from 1959 to 2008, Fidel Castro was born Fidel Alejandro Castro Ruz in Birán, Cuba. It was while he was studying at the University of Havana that he became politically active, joining a number of student protests. He earned a law degree in 1950. In 1959, he led a successful revolution against the American-supported and corrupt government of Fulgencio Batista. After taking control of the government, Castro prohibited foreign-owned property, signed an agreement to purchase oil from the **Union of Soviet Socialist Republics (USSR)**, and took control of American oil refineries. The latter act led to President Dwight D. Eisenhower's decision to break diplomatic relations with Cuba and impose an embargo on trade with Havana. Castro then declared he was a communist. In 1961 the failed Bay of Pigs invasion only solidified Castro's position in Cuba and his ties with the USSR. President **Jimmy Carter** considered normalizing relations with Cuba but changed his mind because of Castro's unwillingness to remove Cuban troops from the African nation of Angola.

In 2008, Castro decided to resign as president due to ill health, thus ending a tenure longer than any other head of state. His younger brother, Raúl, became Cuba's president. In 2011, former president Carter visited Cuba, during which he called for ending the American embargo.

See also CUTLER, LLOYD NORTON (1917–2005); FOREIGN POLICY.

CENTRAL INTELLIGENCE AGENCY (CIA). Created after World War II, the Central Intelligence Agency (CIA) gathers foreign intelligence information for the president of the United States. Over time, however, the agency engaged in covert activities, including the overthrow (or attempted overthrow) of foreign governments and efforts to assassinate the leaders of other nations. These activities, though, were largely secret, and even members of Congress charged with overseeing the agency's activities did not want to know all it was doing.

That changed in the 1970s. Reports that President **Richard Nixon** had used the CIA to conduct domestic espionage and had tried to convince the agency to interfere with the investigation into the Watergate scandal precipitated congressional and media inquiries into the CIA's history. Having learned about the agency's dark history, lawmakers and President **Gerald Ford** took steps to rein it in, banning foreign assassinations and improving oversight.

President **Jimmy Carter** sought to restore the CIA's reputation by nominating Admiral **Stansfield Turner** as its new director. From top to bottom, however, Turner's tenure proved problematic. He had not served in the agency previously, so CIA agents viewed him as an interloper. Placing his faith in **technological advances**, he relieved numerous agents, depriving the CIA of expertise and on-the-spot intelligence. Carter found Turner's briefings uninteresting and therefore met with the CIA director more infrequently. As a result, neither Turner nor the agency was prepared for the revolution in **Iran** or the **Union of Soviet Socialist Republics' (USSR)** invasion of **Afghanistan**.

See also BUSH, GEORGE HERBERT WALKER (1924–); PAHLAVI, MOHAMMED REZA (1919–1980); SCHLESINGER, JAMES RODNEY (1929–).

CHAMBERLAIN, WILT (1936–1999). Born Wilton Norman Chamberlain in Philadelphia, Pennsylvania, Wilt "the Stilt" was seven feet one inch tall and played **basketball** for the University of Kansas Jayhawks. Chamberlain led the Jayhawks to national prominence in basketball. He did not graduate but left Kansas in his senior year to play professionally. As National Basketball Association (NBA) rules prohibited his playing professional basketball, Chamberlain joined the famous Harlem Globetrotters for one year. In 1959 he was drafted by the Philadelphia Warriors, which relocated to San Francisco in 1962. He was traded to the Philadelphia 76ers in 1965 and ended his professional career with the Los Angeles Lakers in 1968. He was named Rookie of the Year in 1960 and was honored for his ability on the court almost every year until his retirement at the end of the 1972–73 season. Although Chamberlain hated nicknames, especially "the Stilt," he always had to duck his head to go through any door. He was inducted into the Naismith Memorial Basketball Hall of Fame in 1978, his first year of eligibility. He died at the age of 63 from heart failure.

CHARLIE'S ANGELS. An overnight **television** hit, *Charlie's Angels* premiered in the fall of 1976. The premise of the show was three beautiful private eyes, played by Jaclyn Smith, Kate Jackson, and **Farrah Fawcett**, who worked for Charlie, a man viewers never saw but only heard. Of the three, it was Fawcett who received the most attention; millions of women copied her long, blond haircut, while many men purchased posters of her. *Charlie's Angels* ended in 1981.

See also WOMEN.

CHAVEZ, CESAR ESTRADA (1927–1993). Born in Yuma, Arizona, Cesar Chavez's parents were migrant workers. Chavez spent his youth in the fields with his family. After serving in the U.S. Navy during World War II, he returned to Arizona to work to improve the lives of migrant workers. In the early 1960s he began to organize the farmworkers into a union. He moved to California where he established the National Farm Workers Association (NFW). In time the farmworkers had become strong enough to affiliate themselves with the **American Federation of Labor and Congress of Industrial Organizations (AFL-CIO)**. Chavez led a successful boycott against grape growers in California but did not do as well in an effort to help migrant workers in Texas. Chavez was admired by Mexican Americans, and this admiration continued until his death in 1993.

See also AGRICULTURE; HISPANIC AMERICANS.

CHINA, RELATIONS WITH. Prior to 1949, China had been under the control of a pro-U.S. noncommunist government. However, that year the Chinese Communist Party seized control of the mainland, renamed the country the People's Republic of China (PRC), and forced the noncommunist leadership to flee to the island of **Taiwan**. Afterward, the United States refused to recognize the new government in Beijing, imposed an embargo on trade with the PRC, successfully fought to have Taiwan represent China in the United Nations, and signed a security treaty with Taipei. President **Richard Nixon** and his national security adviser, **Henry Kissinger**, succeeded in developing a rapprochement with China that included easing the embargo and allowing the PRC to represent China in the UN. However, he failed to normalize relations with Beijing in part because he refused to end the security pact with Taiwan. As such, the two countries were unable to exchange ambassadors or to develop a closer economic or military relationship.

Upon becoming president, **Jimmy Carter** sought to normalize relations with China, but the question was at what pace. His national security adviser, **Zbigniew Brzezinski**, wanted to move quickly, believing a close Sino-American relationship offered a bulwark against Soviet expansionism and would force Moscow to make concessions at the **Strategic Arms Limitation Treaty (SALT II)** talks. Secretary of State **Cyrus Vance**, however, argued that early normalization of relations with China would infuriate the **Union of Soviet Socialist Republics (USSR)** and threaten progress at the SALT negotiations. While Carter at first leaned in favor of Vance, Soviet machinations

CHRISTOPHER, WARREN MINOR (1925–2011) • 75

in places like Africa changed his mind. In December 1978, after intense negotiations—during which the White House promised to abrogate the Taiwan security treaty—Washington and Beijing agreed to normalize their relationship. Normalization became formalized the following month, with **Leonard Woodcock** appointed the first U.S. ambassador to the PRC since China turned to communism. Shortly thereafter, Chinese leader **Deng Xiaoping** visited the United States. In January 1980, the United States granted the PRC most-favored-nation status, permitting an increase in trade between the two countries. Likewise, as a result of the Soviet invasion of **Afghanistan** in December 1979, the United States and China began to develop closer military ties.

See also CHRISTOPHER, WARREN MINOR (1925–2011); DEFENSE; FOREIGN POLICY; INDOCHINESE IMMIGRANTS; POL POT (1928–1998).

THE CHINA SYNDROME. See CINEMA; THREE MILE ISLAND.

A CHORUS LINE. Prior to *Cats*, the show to see the longest run on Broadway had been *A Chorus Line*. The musical was nominated for many Tony Awards and won nine in 1976, the year after it opened to audiences. Playwright and actor James Kirkwood received a Pulitzer Prize for Drama for the play. The **music** was written by composer **Marvin Frederick Hamlisch**. The play was adapted for the big screen in 1985 but received only fair reviews. *A Chorus Line* ended its run in 1990.

See also THEATER.

CHRISTOPHER, WARREN MINOR (1925–2011). Democrat. The deputy secretary of state from 1977 to 1981, Warren Christopher was born in Scranton, North Dakota, and served with the naval reserves during World War II. Following the war he attended the University of Southern California (B.A., 1945) and the Stanford University School of Law (LL.B., 1949). After graduating from Stanford with honors, he became clerk to U.S. **Supreme Court** justice William O. Douglas. During President Lyndon B. Johnson's administration, Christopher worked under Attorney General Ramsey Clark and later with **Cyrus Vance**, who became his boss during the **Jimmy Carter** administration. As Vance's deputy, Christopher worked to see Senate ratification of the **Panama Canal treaties**, was a key player in the effort to normalize relations with the People's Republic of **China**, and worked to negotiate an end to the **Iran hostage crisis**. He had hoped to become secretary of state upon Vance's resignation and was disappointed when Carter chose instead **Edmund Muskie**.

Upon Carter's defeat in the **1980 election**, Christopher returned to a private law practice. He became U.S. secretary of state in the Bill Clinton administration but resigned after Clinton's first term. He passed away from bladder and kidney cancer.

See also FOREIGN POLICY; IRAN HOSTAGE CRISIS; MARCOS, FERDINAND (EMMANUEL EDRALIN) (1917–1989).

CHURCH, FRANK FORRESTER (1924–1984). Democrat. A U.S. senator from 1957 to 1980, Frank Church was born in Boise, Idaho, and served as an intelligence officer during World War II. After the war, he graduated from Stanford University (B.A., 1947) and then obtained a law degree from Stanford University Law School (LL.B., 1950). Active in the Democratic Party in Idaho, he won his first term as U.S. senator in 1956. During his tenure in the Senate (1956–1980), Church was an outspoken critic of the Vietnam War and an environmental activist. During the **1976 election** Church made an unsuccessful bid for the Democratic nomination.

As the ranking member of the Senate Foreign Relations Committee, Church supported ratification of both the **Panama Canal treaties** and the **Strategic Arms Limitation Treaty (SALT II)**. But he shared the sentiment of many leaders on Capitol Hill that President **Jimmy Carter** and his staff were distant, if not uncooperative. Church then created a crisis for the White House when he announced the "discovery" of a brigade of Soviet troops in **Cuba**. The fact was that those soldiers had been in Cuba since 1962, and to the knowledge of U.S. officials. But Church, fearful of losing a bid for reelection in 1980, decided he had to raise the matter to garner votes. In so doing, he made SALT's ratification, which was already in doubt, even more unlikely. Church lost his bid for reelection by a slim margin. He stayed in Washington to practice law. He died of cancer in April 1984.

See also FOREIGN CORRUPT PRACTICES ACT; LOCKHEED SCANDAL.

CINEMA. In 1976 **Studio 54**, a nightclub in New York City, opened. It provided **dancing** and freedom from the cares of the day. No other movie of the 1970s better reflected that life in the 1970s than *Saturday Night Fever* (1977). The humdrum life of a young man in New York during the day was followed by a night of dancing, where he was king of the dance floor. The **disco** music provided by the **Bee Gees** and the popular **fads and fashions** of the decade capped off this extremely popular film.

The motion picture industry also began to focus on movies with larger budgets, more special effects, and greater box office appeal. Four young directors began to take center stage in the world of cinema: **Woody Allen**, **George Lucas**, **Steven Spielberg**, and **Martin Scorsese**. Lucas and Spielberg used special effects that enthralled audiences. *Star Wars* (1977) was Lucas's **science fiction** blockbuster hit, which catapulted both young Harrison Ford and **African American** actor James Earl Jones to stardom. Spielberg frightened audiences with *Jaws* (1975), about a great white shark that terrorized beachgoers. He followed his box office success with the visually stunning special effects of *Close Encounters of the Third Kind* (1977). Scorsese introduced **Robert De Niro** in two hard-hitting movies about the Vietnam War: *Taxi Driver* (1976), in which De Niro played a mentally unstable war vet, and *The Deer Hunter* (1978), which concentrated on the war's effect on a small industrial town. Meryl Streep received her first Academy Award for her role in *The Deer Hunter*. Woody Allen wrote and directed comedies set mainly in New York. Many centered around a neurotic man, usually played by Allen, and the **women** in his life. *Annie Hall* (1977) was voted best picture that year. Other popular Allen films during the decade were *Interiors* (1978), *Manhattan* (1979), and *Stardust Memories*.

The Academy Award–winning films during the second half of the 1970s were often hard-hitting stories. *One Flew Over the Cuckoo's Nest* (1975) was set in a mental institution starring newcomer Jack Nicholson as a rebellious patient. *Rocky* (1976) introduced Sylvester Stallone to audiences as a boxer who succeeded in the ring against impossible odds, while *Network* (1976) warned of the impending dangers of **television** news reporting. The incidents leading to the resignation of President **Richard Nixon** were the basis of *All the President's Men* (1976). *Norma Rae* (1979) was based on a true story of the fight to unionize textile mills. *Kramer versus Kramer* (1979) focused on divorce when a child was involved, while the death of a child was the theme of *Ordinary People* (1980) and a mother's inability to overcome the loss of her oldest son at the expense of his younger brother. One of the highest-grossing comedies of the 1970s was *Smokey and the Bandit* (1977). It revitalized Jackie Gleason's career and made **citizens band radios (CB radios)** popular in **automobiles**. College life was the focus of *National Lampoon's Animal House* (1978), a comedy about a fraternity of misfits starring John Belushi, who was one of *Saturday Night Live*'s funniest cast members.

Disaster movies, with big budgets and numerous major actors, were also very popular during the 1970s. No one made more profitable films of this genre than **Irwin Allen**. *The Poseidon Adventure* (1972) horrified viewers as passengers tired to survive disaster at sea on their sinking ship. As cities increased the height of their skyscrapers, *The Towering Inferno* (1974) terrified audiences as the occupants of the building sought to escape a fire. *The Swarm* (1978) scared viewers with African bees invading American cities, killing many people. An active volcano provided the action in *When Time Ran Out* (1980), and the sequel *Beyond the Poseidon Adventure* (1979) provided more high-seas action. Although Irwin was not involved in the movie *Earthquake* (1974), it was also a hit at the box office. California was the setting of this disaster feature film. *The China Syndrome*, the story of serious safety violations at a nuclear power plant, was released on 16 March 1979; ironically, this was only 12 days prior to the disaster at the Pennsylvania nuclear power plant **Three Mile Island**. *Airplane!* (1980), a spoof of disaster movies, probably did more than any other film to end the genre. Some of the decade's films, including *Superman* (1978), *Rocky, Star Wars*, and the frightening *Alien* (1979) were followed by sequels and continued their popularity into the new millennium.

Perhaps the most unusual movie was *The Rocky Horror Picture Show* (1975), which is now a cult classic and often shown at midnight. The story involves a transvestite and other unusual characters in strange costumes. Audiences began to attend the movie in outfits comparable to ones worn in the film, a tradition that continues to this day.

See also ALLEN, WOODY (1935–); EASTWOOD, CLINTON, JR. (1930–); HAMLISCH, MARVIN FREDERICK (1944–2012); *HAPPY DAYS*; KING, STEPHEN EDWIN (1947–); McMURTRY, LARRY (1936–); PRYOR, RICHARD (1940–2005); SIMPSON, "O. J." (ORENTHAL JAMES) (1947–); *SISKEL AND EBERT*; WOMEN.

CITIZENS BAND RADIO (CB RADIO). After the release of the 1977 **cinematic** blockbuster *Smokey and the Bandit*, the use of CB radios became a hit with **automobile** drivers. Whereas truckers used their CB radios to warn other truckers of speed traps or to get aid on the road, the average driver used his or hers to talk to others. The majority of CB radios were made by Midland Radio of Kansas City, Missouri. During the 1970s, over 70 million CB radios were sold at an average cost of $1,100 each. Drivers of both cars and trucks used a nickname and a sort of slang, often called "slangage." The CB radio was replaced by the car phone and later by the cell phone.

See also FADS AND FASHIONS; TELEVISION.

CIVIL RIGHTS. Though the civil rights movement is generally dated to the 1950s and 1960s, **African Americans** continued their long fight for equal rights and recognition for their accomplishments. The year 1976 saw the founding of Black History Month, which is celebrated each year in February. President **Jimmy Carter** sought to increase the number of African Americans working in the federal government and named more blacks to federal judgeships than any of his predecessors. He also named **Andrew Young** as the U.S. ambassador to the United Nations. In the 1978 **Supreme Court** decision *University of California Board of Regents v. Bakke*, civil rights groups fought to protect both **affirmative action** and the use of quotas in determining admissions to universities.

The civil rights movement influenced other movements, including those fighting for **women's**, **Native American**, and **gay rights**. By the mid-1970s women were working in greater numbers outside of the home and seeking equal acceptance in a world dominated by men. Many women, including members of the **National Organization for Women**, campaigned for passage of the **Equal Rights Amendment (ERA)**, which President Carter favored. Native Americans became increasingly outspoken and saw both legislation and **Supreme Court** decisions that favored their interests. For gays and lesbians, the fight for equal rights was thwarted by ultraconservative **religious** leaders, such as **Jerry Falwell**, and antigay activists, including **Anita Bryant**.

See also AMERICAN FEDERATION OF LABOR AND CONGRESS OF INDUSTRIAL ORGANIZATIONS (AFL-CIO); BAKKE, ALLEN PAUL (1940–); BELL, GRIFFIN BOYETTE (1918–2009); BRENNAN, WILLIAM JOSEPH, JR. (1906–1997); DERIAN, PATRICIA MURPHY (1929–); ELECTION, 1976; HARRIS, PATRICIA ROBERTS (1924–1985); HUMPHREY, HUBERT HORATIO (1911–1978); JACKSON, HENRY MARTIN "SCOOP" (1912–1983); JACKSON, JESSE LOUIS (1941–); JORDAN, HAMILTON (1944–2008); JORDAN, VERNON EULION, JR. (1935–); KENNEDY, EDWARD MOORE "TED" (1932–2009); LANDRIEU, MOON (MAURICE EDWIN) (1930–); LITERATURE; MADDOX, LESTER GARFIELD (1915–2003); MARSHALL, THURGOOD (1908–1993); STENNIS, JOHN CORNELIUS (1901–1995); TELEVISION; THURMOND, (JAMES) STROM (1902–2003); *UNITED STEELWORKERS OF AMERICA V. WEBER*.

CIVIL SERVICE REFORM ACT. Passed into law in 1978, the Civil Service Reform Act was one of President **Jimmy Carter**'s major achievements. Creating a new merit system for civil service employees, it also gave managers the right to fire inept workers. New agencies were established, including the Office of Personnel Management, the Federal Labor Relations Authority (FLRA), and the Merit Systems Protection Board. All three agencies are dedicated to protecting the rights of federal civil servants.

CIVILETTI, BENJAMIN RICHARD (1935–). Democrat. Serving first as assistant attorney general from 1977 to 1979, and then as attorney general from 1979 to 1981, Benjamin Civiletti was born in Peekskill, New York. He received his B.A. in 1957 from Johns Hopkins University and his law degree from the University of Maryland Law School (LL.B., 1961). Specializing in criminal and civil trial litigation, **Griffin Bell**, President **Jimmy Carter**'s attorney general, chose Civiletti as his immediate subordinate. After Bell resigned in 1979, Civiletti became the new attorney general.

During his tenure at the Justice Department, Civiletti had to address a number of legal matters, many involving administration officials. One was **Hamilton Jordan**, who had been accused in 1978 of using cocaine while at New York's famous **Studio 54**; the charges were later dropped. An investigation into **Bert Lance**, who had been forced to resign as Carter's director of the Office of Management and Budget, ended with Lance's acquittal. Civiletti participated in an investigation of **Billy Carter**'s relationship with Libya and in the negotiations aimed at ending the **Iran hostage crisis**. Presently he is a trial lawyer in a Maryland law firm.

CLAY, CASSIUS MARCELLUS. *See* ALI, MUHAMMAD (1942–).

CLEAN AIR ACT AMENDMENTS. President **Jimmy Carter** was a strong supporter of the **environment**. He sought to prevent possible deterioration of air quality in places such as the national parks and wanted stronger fines for factories that polluted too much. The Clean Air Act Amendments of 1977 required those areas that met air quality standards not to allow that air quality to deteriorate significantly and added obligations for those locales that did not meet such standards.

CLEAN WATER ACT. Better known as the 1972 Clean Water Pollution Control Act, the Clean Water Act received its shorter name following an amendment in 1977. The act prohibits companies from adding pollutants to American waters without a permit.
See also ENVIRONMENT.

COMANECI, NADIA (1962–). Olympic gymnast and standout at the 1976 Olympic Games in Montreal, Nadia Comaneci was born near Bucharest, Romania. Her athletic ability was evident at a young age. Romania was part of the Communist bloc, with communist superiority measured in athletic ability. Comaneci was taken from her family and raised in a sports camp. During the 1976 Olympics, Comaneci became one of the most famous athletes in the world. In the four gymnastic events she received seven perfect scores and won three gold medals. In 1989 she defected to the United States.

COMIC STRIPS AND CARTOONS. The 1970s introduced four famous comic strips and cartoons, beginning in 1975 with the Kliban Cat. Bernard "Hap" Kliban (1935–1990) loved cats. He began drawing cartoons for *Playboy*, and, while doodling, he drew some outrageous cat cartoons. His editor loved the pictures and published them in 1975 in the first of several cartoon books, all featuring the famous striped cat. Kliban's cartoons led the way for other cartoonists, including Jim Davis's *Garfield the Cat*, introduced in 1978, and Gary Larson's *The Far Side*, which appeared the following year. Each introduced his own outlandish animals and people. The success of all three cartoonists led to calendars, T-shirts, and other merchandise featuring their characters. Unlike the other three, cartoonist Garry Trudeau's **Doonesbury** focused on politics. The first comic strip artist to win a Pulitzer Prize (1975), Trudeau began his career by spoofing fellow students in cartoons while he was a student at Yale. *Doonesbury* appeared as a daily strip nationally in 1970 and since has featured a variety of characters, many based on political figures. Trudeau has also tackled controversial topics, including **abortion**, which has led some newspapers to ban the strip for periods of time.

COMPREHENSIVE ENVIRONMENTAL RESPONSE, COMPENSA-TION, AND LIABILITY ACT (CERCLA). *See* LOVE CANAL.

COMPUTERS. Some of the most innovative ideas in the world of computers began in the 1970s. Apple personal computers appeared on the market, and **Microsoft** developed its first software ideas. The public shopped for the latest electronics at Radio Shack, and Texas Instruments entered the electronics market, as did Intel, Novell, and Oracle. Atari's *Pong* was one of the earliest computer games, and the floppy disk was introduced. Epson's dot matrix printers were reasonably priced in comparison to the price of computers. As the 1970s came to an end, the 1980s saw an explosion in the field of electronics and advancements in computer software.

See also GATES, BILL (WILLIAM HENRY III) (1955–); TECHNO-LOGICAL ADVANCES.

CONGRESSIONAL BLACK CAUCUS. In 1971, 13 member of Congress formed the Congressional Black Caucus to bring attention to the plight of **African Americans** worldwide. During the administration of President **Jimmy Carter** the newly established group focused its attention on apartheid in South Africa and, at home, urban housing problems, substance abuse, and **affirmative action**.

COSELL, HOWARD (1918–1995). Lawyer turned **sports** announcer, Howard Cosell was born in North Carolina. Educated at New York University (B.A., 1938), he received his law degree at the same in 1941; his specialty was union law. Many of his clients were athletes, including Willie Mays and the Little League of New York. In 1953 he was asked to host a radio program featuring Little League players. The popularity of his show led to a career as a sportscaster. When the American Broadcasting Company (ABC) launched its **television** program *Monday Night Football* (1970), Cosell was chosen as the commentator. Cosell's distinctive voice and command of the English language were part of his appeal. During the Vietnam War, boxer **Muhammad Ali** refused to fight and was stripped of his championship title. Cosell, who was a friend and supporter of Ali's, came to the boxer's defense. In declining health for several years, Cosell passed away from a heart embolism.

COSTANZA, MIDGE (MARGARET) (1932–2010). Democrat. The special assistant to President **Jimmy Carter**, Midge Costanza was the only one of Carter's top White House aides not from Georgia. She had been born in LeRoy, New York, and grew up in nearby Rochester. Although she did not attend college, she was active in many community organizations. In 1954 she began her political career campaigning for Governor Averell Harriman and later serving as county executive director of Robert Kennedy's Senate campaign (1965). From 1972 until her appointment as Carter's special assistant for public liaison, she served on the National Democratic Committee.

Costanza worked for one year in the Carter White House. Her liberal politics blurred her understanding of the president's intentions for the nation. He wanted to improve communication with groups that previously had had little access to the Oval Office, with particular emphasis on the disabled, poor, and elderly. She, though, added to that list more divisive groups, such as those who believed in giving amnesty to draft evaders and proponents of **women**'s right to an **abortion**. The president's chief aide, **Hamilton Jordan**, was not happy that Costanza used her post to advance abortion rights, while the president grew angry that despite his effort to give women high-level positions in Washington, he continued to receive criticism from women's rights advocates that he was not doing enough. Jordan essentially cut off Costanza from the Oval Office, prompting her to resign in September 1978 and angering women's rights groups. She passed away after a bout with cancer.

See also WEXLER, ANNE LEVY (1930–2009).

CRONKITE, WALTER (1916–2009). One of journalism's most respected **television** news anchors for over four decades, Walter Cronkite was born in Missouri. He attended the University of Texas for two years (1933–35). In 1939 he joined United Press (UP) and covered World War II, as well as the Nuremberg trials after the end of the war. In 1950 he joined the Columbia Broadcasting System (CBS), where he impressed viewers with his coverage of the 1952 presidential conventions. Cronkite became anchor of the CBS Evening News in 1962 and soon gained a reputation for reporting the news accurately and without bias. He ended each newscast with, "And that's the way it is." Although he retired from CBS in 1981, Cronkite continued to host various programs on cable networks. He died in July 2009 from complications caused by dementia.

C-SPAN (CABLE SATELLITE PUBLIC AFFAIRS NETWORK). In 1979 C-SPAN debuted on cable **television**. C-SPAN is actually three networks. C-SPAN is dedicated to uninterrupted coverage of the U.S. House of Representatives. C-SPAN2 focuses on the U.S. Senate. C-SPAN3 broadcasts live political events as well as historical ones.

CRUDE OIL WINDFALL PROFIT TAX. In an effort to combat the country's **energy crisis**, President **Jimmy Carter** made several proposals, one of which would remove controls on oil prices in the United States. Realizing this would mean larger profits for petroleum companies, he called for a crude oil windfall profits tax that would take approximately 50 percent of those profits and use the money to help low-income families pay for higher fuel prices, as well as to fund mass transit systems and develop alternative energy sources. Passed in 1980, the windfall profits tax was repealed in 1988.

CUBA, RELATIONS WITH. Following independence in 1902, Cuba went through a number of governments prior to 1959, when a communist rebel, **Fidel Castro**, seized power. The United States' response included the severing of diplomatic relations with, and the imposition of a trade embargo upon, Cuba. Following his victory in the 1976 U.S. presidential election, **Jimmy Carter** considered relaxation of the embargo and normalizing relations with Castro's government. However, Cuban military support for communist-allied movements and governments in Africa convinced Carter to forego improving ties.

Cuba continued to pose difficulties for Carter during the remainder of his term in office. In 1979, Idaho senator **Frank Church** announced the "discovery" of a brigade of troops from the **Union of Soviet Socialist Republics (USSR)** on Cuba. Church's proclamation jeopardized ratification of the **Strategic Arms Limitation Treaty (SALT II)**. In the spring of 1980, Castro decided to get rid of all disaffected Cubans by allowing any of them to leave their homeland from the port of Mariel. On their own or with the help of friends or family, thousands of Cubans left for Florida in what became known as the Mariel Boatlift. By September, when Castro closed Mariel harbor, 125,000 Cubans had landed in the United States. Coming on top of the recent influx of **Indochinese immigrants**, the sudden arrival of so many Cubans angered a majority of Americans and hurt Carter's 1980 reelection bid.

See also FOREIGN POLICY; PASTOR, ROBERT A. (1947–); REFU-GEE ACT; YOUNG, ANDREW JACKSON, JR. (1932–).

CURRENCY. *See* SUSAN B. ANTHONY DOLLAR COIN.

CUTLER, LLOYD NORTON (1917–2005). Democrat. The counsel to President **Jimmy Carter** from 1979 to 1980, Lloyd Cutler was born in New York City and earned both his B.A. and LL.B. (1936 and 1939, respectively) from Yale University. Although employed at one of New York's prestigious law firms, he left in 1941 after the attack on Pearl Harbor. He served in the army as a code breaker and an intelligence analyst. After the war he opened his own law firm in Washington, D.C., and by the 1970s it was one of the most renowned practices in the country. Cutler was active in the administrations of Presidents John F. Kennedy and Lyndon B. Johnson, including helping to free Cubans captured by the **Fidel Castro** government following the 1961 Bay of Pigs fiasco.

Cutler met Carter for the first time in 1974, during which the future president told Cutler of his decision to run for president in the **1976 election**. In 1979 Cutler held a part-time position in the Carter administration; however, his advice became a full-time job as a result of the **Strategic Arms Limitation Treaty (SALT II)** negotiations, questions about **Billy Carter**'s activities in Libya, and the **Iran hostage crisis**. After Carter's loss in the **1980 election**, Cutler returned to his law firm in Washington, D.C. He passed away in May 2005 after breaking his hip.

See also LIPSHUTZ, ROBERT JEROME (1921–2010).

D

DANCES. The 1970s will be remembered as the decade of **disco**, which became popular after the release of the 1977 **cinema** hit *Saturday Night Fever*. Other popular dances were the hustle and the electric slide. Breakdancing began in New York City when **African Americans** used the athletic onstage moves of singer James Brown and added difficult maneuvers such as head spins and spinning on one's hand. Breakdancing was done without a partner. The 1980 movie *Urban Cowboy* introduced moves that became a dance favorite of the 1980s and beyond, the Texas two-step.

See also STUDIO 54.

DE NIRO, ROBERT MARIO, JR. (1943–). Considered one of **cinema**'s greatest actors, Robert De Niro was born in New York City. He studied acting at the Stella Adler Conservatory and Lee Strassberg's Actors Studio. His first major cinematic role was in *Bang the Drum Slowly* (1973). His performance caught the attention of director **Martin Scorsese**, and the two men formed a close working relationship. Often De Niro played violent men or a mobster. He won Academy Awards for *The Godfather II* (1974) and *Raging Bull* (1980). In *Analyze This* (1999) and the sequel *Analyze That* (2002), he played a comedy role as a neurotic mobster. De Niro is one of the three founders of the Tribeca Film Festival.

DEFENSE. President **Jimmy Carter** came into office determined to rein in U.S. defense spending. A fiscal conservative, he insisted on keeping annual appropriations for the U.S. military to only 3 percent beyond the rate of inflation. He also believed there was too much financial waste in America's defense programs. During his first year in office, he sought to convince the **Union of Soviet Socialist Republics (USSR)** to join the United States in signing a **Strategic Arms Limitation Treaty (SALT II)** and curbing their conventional arms sales to other countries, canceled production of the **B-1 bomber**, vetoed legislation that provided $2 billion for a new aircraft carrier, and proposed withdrawing U.S. troops from **South Korea**. The following year, he canceled plans to produce and deploy the **neutron bomb**. By making these moves, the president hoped to save money, prevent sophisticated weaponry from getting into the hands of rogue states or terrorists, and reduce tensions with the USSR and the possibility of a nuclear exchange between the superpowers. Spending on the military for fiscal year (FY) 1977 was held to $95 billion and $102 billion in FY 1978 (or about $360 billion in current U.S. dollars for both years).

Carter's decisions regarding the B-1 bomber, the aircraft carrier, U.S. troops in South Korea, and the neutron bomb caused consternation at home and abroad. Members of Congress, including both **Republicans** and **Democrats**, charged that Carter was making the United States increasingly weak and unable to defend its allies. Lawmakers in whose districts the B-1 and aircraft carrier were to be built were enraged. The South Korean government worried about its ability to protect itself from communist North Korea, while **Japan** insisted that the presence of U.S. troops in South Korea was important to Tokyo's security. Chancellor **Helmut Schmidt** of West Germany charged that the president's cancelation of the neutron bomb was tantamount to abandoning Western Europe.

Curtailing conventional arms sales and getting SALT II signed also ran into trouble. One problem was trying to decide what types of conventional weapons should be covered in any treaty prohibiting their sale. Even U.S. officials were not sure how to address this conundrum. Furthermore, the Carter administration made clear that it wanted the right to sell sophisticated conventional weapons to key allies, such as South Korea, **Iran**, and Saudi Arabia. By the middle of 1978, any hope of progress with the Soviets on curbing conventional arms transfers had disappeared. Nor were the SALT negotiations going well. Angered at Carter's charges that it was violating the **human rights** of its people, the Soviet government became less willing to compromise with the United States. The president's decision in late 1978 to normalize relations with communist **China**, a country the Kremlin viewed as a threat, further slowed progress on SALT.

In January 1979, the U.S. military reported that North Korea's armed forces were stronger than originally thought. The uproar that ensued forced Carter to give up his plan to withdraw U.S. troops from South Korea. The president could point to success in June of that year, however, when he and Soviet general secretary **Leonid Brezhnev** signed SALT II.

Getting SALT ratified, however, was another matter. Some liberal members of the Senate charged that the treaty did not go far enough in reducing the superpowers' nuclear arsenals. Conservatives said the treaty gave away too much to the Soviets. Senators **Sam Nunn** of Georgia and **Henry Jackson** of Texas declared they would not vote for the treaty if the president did not increase defense spending by at least 5 percent the following year. Abroad,

Great Britain, France, and West Germany raised their own qualms about SALT, sharing the sentiment of some U.S. lawmakers that the treaty made too many concessions to Moscow.

Hoping to get past these reservations, Carter made concessions. He approved development of the Missile-eXperimental (or MX missile), which could be moved from location to location and, in turn, would be less vulnerable to a Soviet nuclear strike. He announced the formation of a Rapid Deployment Force that could respond to crises outside of Western Europe. Finally, he agreed to deploy Pershing and cruise missiles in Western Europe to assure America's allies that the United States would defend them. While ratification still appeared unlikely, the debate over SALT became moot following the USSR's invasion of **Afghanistan** in December 1979. Angered, Carter told the Upper House to shelve further consideration of the treaty. Furthermore, he signed Presidential Directive (PD) 59, which called for a large-scale U.S. military buildup. By the end of his term in office, Carter's defense policy was similar to those of his predecessors, with the focus on containing the threat posed by the USSR to the United States and its allies. This determination to contain the Soviet Union was reflected in a military budget that reached $130 billion in FY 1980 (or $362 billion in current dollars), and a proposed budget for FY 1982 of $196 billion (equivalent to $546 billion in 2012).

See also ABZUG, BELLA SAVITSKY (1920–1998); FOREIGN POLICY; RICKOVER, HYMAN GEORGE (1900–1986); STENNIS, JOHN CORNELIUS (1901–1995); TECHNOLOGICAL ADVANCES.

DEMOCRATIC PARTY. The pardoning of President **Richard Nixon** by President **Gerald Ford** angered many Americans. The Watergate scandal and the Vietnam War led Americans to feel betrayed by their government. When **Jimmy Carter** entered the **1976 election** for president, he campaigned on the theme of bringing honesty back to the White House. With **Walter Mondale** as his running mate and the help of a campaign staff that included **Patricia Derian**, **Charles Kirbo**, **Jody Powell**, and **Hamilton Jordan**, Carter won. Moreover, Democrats held on to their control of both houses on Capitol Hill.

That the legislative and executive branches were controlled by Democrats hid differences within the party. Carter had campaigned as a Washington outsider, which made him believe he did not owe lawmakers, including fellow Democrats, anything, or vice versa. The result was a relationship that was often antagonistic. Moreover, more conservative-minded individuals within the party began to contest liberals over policy. That Carter, a fiscal conservative, would have to overcome a strong challenge for the party's nomination in the **1980 election** from the more liberal Senator **Edward**

Kennedy of Massachusetts personified this latter intraparty split. The inability of Democrats to find unity played a part in Carter's failure to win his bid for reelection.

See also AARON, DAVID LAURENCE (1938–); ABZUG, BELLA SAVITSKY (1920–1998); ADAMS, BROCK (BROCKMAN) (1927–2004); ALBRIGHT, MADELEINE KORBEL (1937–); ANDRUS, CECIL DALE (1931–); BALL, GEORGE WILDMAN (1909–1994); BAYH, BIRCH EVANS, JR. (1928–); BIDEN, JOSEPH ROBINETTE, JR. (1942–); BLUMENTHAL, WERNER MICHAEL (1926–); BOURNE, PETER GEOFFREY (1939–); BROWN, HAROLD (1927–); BROWN, JERRY (EDMUND GERALD BROWN JR.) (1938–); BRZEZINSKI, ZBIGNIEW KAZIMIERZ (1928–); BURNS, ARTHUR FRANK (1904–1987); BYRD, ROBERT CARLYLE (1917–2010); CADDELL, PATRICK H. (1950–); CALIFANO, JOSEPH ANTHONY, JR. (1931–); CHRISTOPHER, WARREN MINOR (1925–2011); CHURCH, FRANK FORRESTER (1924–1984); CIVILETTI, BENJAMIN RICHARD (1935–); COSTANZA, MIDGE (MARGARET) (1932–2010); CUTLER, LLOYD NORTON (1917–2005); DEFENSE; DINGELL, JOHN DAVID, JR. (1926–); ECONOMY; FOLEY, THOMAS STEPHEN (1929–); FOREIGN POLICY; GOLDSCHMIDT, NEIL EDWARD (1940–); HARRIS, PATRICIA ROBERTS (1924–1985); HUFSTEDLER, SHIRLEY MOUNT (1925–); HUMPHREY, HUBERT HORATIO (1911–1978); ISRAEL, RELATIONS WITH; JACKSON, HENRY MARTIN "SCOOP" (1912–1983); JACKSON, JESSE LOUIS (1941–); JACKSON, MAYNARD HOLBROOK, JR. (1938–2003); JORDAN, BARBARA (1936–1996); KLUTZNICK, PHILIP MORRIS (1907–1999); KRAFT, TIMOTHY E. (1941–); LABOR; LANCE, BERT (THOMAS BERTRAM) (1931–); LANDRIEU, MOON (MAURICE EDWIN) (1930–); LONG, RUSSELL BILLIU (1918–2003); MADDOX, LESTER GARFIELD (1915–2003); McGOVERN, GEORGE STANLEY (1922–2012); McINTYRE, JAMES TALMADGE, JR. (1940–); MEANY, GEORGE (1894–1980); MILLS, WILBUR DAIGH (1909–1992); MOYNIHAN, DANIEL PATRICK (1927–2003); MUSKIE, EDMUND SIXTUS (1914–1996); NELSON, GAYLORD ANTON (1916–2005); NUNN, SAM (SAMUEL AUGUSTUS) (1938–); PASTOR, ROBERT A. (1947–); PRECHT, HENRY (1932–); PROXMIRE, EDWARD WILLIAM (1915–2005); REAGAN, RONALD WILSON (1911–2004); RIBICOFF, ABRAHAM ALEXANDER (1910–1998); ROSTENKOWSKI, DANIEL DAVID (1928–2010); SCHULTZE, CHARLES LOUIS (1924–); STENNIS, JOHN CORNELIUS (1901–1995); STRAUSS, ROBERT SCHWARTZ (1918–); SULLIVAN, WILLIAM HEALY (1922–); TALMADGE, HERMAN EUGENE (1913–2002); THURMOND, (JAMES) STROM (1902–2003); TURNER, STANSFIELD (1923–); UDALL, MORRIS (MO) KING (1922–1998); ULLMAN, AL (ALBERT CONRAD) (1914–1986);

VANCE, CYRUS ROBERT (1917–2002); WALLACE, GEORGE COR-
LEY (1919–1998); WARNKE, PAUL CULLITON (1920–2001); WHITE,
BYRON RAYMOND (1917–2002); WOMEN; WOODCOCK, LEONARD
FREEL (1911–2001); WRIGHT, JIM (JAMES CLAUDE WRIGHT JR.)
(1922–); YOUNG, ANDREW JACKSON, JR. (1932–); YOUNG, COLE-
MAN ALEXANDER (1918–1997).

DENG XIAOPING (TENG HSIAO-PING) (1904–1997). The leader of
the People's Republic of **China** from 1976 to 1990, Deng Xiaoping was born
in Sichuan Province. Little is known about his childhood. He became a
member of the Chinese Communist Party (CCP) while studying in France.
During World War II he fought against the Japanese. After the war he helped
to overthrow the Nationalist regime of Chiang Kai-shek. During Mao Zedong's leadership, Deng criticized the ideas of the Cultural Revolution,
which led to his disgrace and his exile to work in a tractor factory. However,
in 1973, Zhou Enlai brought Deng back into the CCP's party leadership. Six
years later, Deng oversaw the normalization of relations with the United
States.
See also FOREIGN POLICY.

DENVER, JOHN (1943–1997). Singer and songwriter John Denver was
born Henry John Deutschendorf in Roswell, New Mexico. His father was in
the U.S. Air Force, which meant many moves during his childhood. After
graduating high school in Texas, he enrolled at Texas Tech University to
study engineering, but he dropped out to pursue a singing career. He changed
his last name to Denver in honor of his favorite city.

His first major hit was in 1971 with his million-selling "Take Me Home,
Country Roads." Many popular songs followed, making Denver one of the
most successful recording stars in the 1970s. He advocated a love of nature,
which was evident in many of his songs. Other performers recorded his
songs, including Peter, Paul, and Mary's rendition of "Leaving on a Jet
Plane." In 1977 he appeared with George Burns in the movie *Oh, God!* He
loved to fly and was killed in the crash of a small experimental airplane in
1997. Some of his still-popular songs are "Rocky Mountain High," "Sun-
shine on My Shoulders," and "Thank God I'm a Country Boy."
See also MUSIC.

DEPARTMENT OF EDUCATION ORGANIZATION ACT. Designed
both to meet President **Jimmy Carter**'s desire to improve educational opportunities nationwide and as a promise to establish a government agency to
oversee education in the country, this 1979 law established the Department
of **Education**. The department administers federal funding to schools, seeks

to ensure equal access to education, and works to enhance both the coordination of federal education initiatives and the quality of education throughout the country.

DEPARTMENT OF ENERGY ORGANIZATION ACT. Signed into law in 1977 by President **Jimmy Carter** as a response to the nation's **energy crisis**, this law created the Department of Energy. The president realized the need to respond to the increase in oil prices and energy-related concerns in the United States. The department oversees the development of energy technology and conservation, the production of nuclear weapons, and the collection of energy-related data.

DEPOSITORY INSTITUTIONS DEREGULATION AND MONETARY CONTROL ACT. During the 1970s, many banks that had been members of the Federal Reserve System declined because banks could not maintain the required percentage of reserves. Problems also existed for savings and loan institutions and banks that were not members of the Federal Reserve System. In 1980, Congress passed the Depository Institutions Deregulation and Monetary Control Act to alleviate the difficulties facing these institutions. Banks and savings and loan institutions were allowed to offer checking accounts. Equal percentages of reserves were required for all banks, and they had to report their information on a regular basis, which allowed the federal government to keep better track of the amount of deposits in the United States.

DEREGULATION POLICIES. President **Jimmy Carter** believed that deregulating government-controlled industries, including airlines, trucking, and railroads, benefited the consumer by allowing for greater competition and, in turn, lower prices. Thus, during his term in office, President Carter signed into law the following acts: the **Airline Deregulation Act** (1978), the **Motor Carrier Act** (1980), and the Staggers Rail Act of 1980.

See also DINGELL, JOHN DAVID, JR. (1926–); ECONOMY; FOLEY, THOMAS STEPHEN (1929–); GOLDSCHMIDT, NEIL EDWARD (1940–); KAHN, ALFRED EDWARD (1917–2010); KENNEDY, EDWARD MOORE "TED" (1932–2009); McGOVERN, GEORGE STANLEY (1922–2012); MOORE, FRANK (1935–); WEXLER, ANNE LEVY (1930–2009).

DERIAN, PATRICIA MURPHY (1929–). Democrat. Patricia Derian served as coordinator of the State Department's Bureau of **Human Rights** and Humanitarian Affairs (HA) in 1977 and then as assistant secretary of state for human rights from 1977 to 1981. Born in New York City, she was raised in Virginia and attended nursing school at the University of Virginia, where she met her husband, Paul. They moved to Mississippi, where, in 1959, she joined the **African American civil rights** movement. In 1964 she gathered enough signatures to get Lyndon B. Johnson's name on the ballot in Mississippi. She later helped form the biracial Democratic Freedom Party, which challenged the all-white delegation from Mississippi at the Democratic National Convention in Chicago.

In the **1976 election**, **Jimmy Carter** asked Derian to help with his campaign, and, after winning the election, to serve on his transition team. He then appointed her coordinator of HA and shortly thereafter elevated her status to that of assistant secretary. Using that position, Derian had intended to make her voice heard and to punish countries that violated the rights of their people. Her stance placed her at odds with others in the administration who believed that economic, national security, or political considerations mattered more than human rights in American **foreign policy**. In these intra-administration struggles, HA lost more often than it won, prompting Derian late in Carter's administration to consider resigning her post. After Carter's defeat in the **1980 election**, Derian became an outspoken critic of President **Ronald Reagan**'s human rights policy. She continues to seek to protect human rights abroad.

See also MARCOS, FERDINAND (EMMANUEL EDRALIN) (1917–1989); WOMEN.

DÉTENTE. *See* FOREIGN POLICY.

DINGELL, JOHN DAVID, JR. (1926–). Democrat. John Dingell is the longest-serving member of the House of Representatives, having held his seat since 1955. Born in Colorado Springs, he served in the U.S. Army during World War II and attended Georgetown University afterward, where he received both his bachelor's and law degrees (B.S., 1949; J.D., 1952). In 1955, after the death of his father, a congressman from Detroit, Dingell won a special election to fill his father's seat.

Dingell was (and is) a defender of Michigan's **automobile** industry, which created difficulties for President **Jimmy Carter**. Though Dingell agreed with Carter's call for comprehensive **energy** legislation, he opposed measures that could hurt the automakers, including a tax on gas-guzzling cars and **deregulation** of oil prices. He agreed with the president's desire to promote alternative sources of energy, has long called for a national health insurance program, and ardently supports what has become known as "ObamaCare."

In 1983, Dingell became chairman of the Committee on Energy and Commerce. He has become known for excluding from conference committees those people he considers disloyal. In addition to organized labor, Dingell has relied upon the backing of the National Rifle Association—of which he is a member—to keep his seat.

DISCO. A form of **music** that combined **African American** funk and soul with a beat that appealed to **women**, minorities, and **gays**, disco's popularity may have begun at New York City's integrated **Studio 54**. Disc jockeys played continuous music on two turntables; thus, the **dancing** continued without a break. **ABBA**, the Village People, and the **Bee Gees** were some of the most popular disco recording artists. *Saturday Night Fever*, one of the highest-grossing films of the 1970s, accurately portrayed the influence of the disco movement on people hoping to escape their economically depressed lives.

The discotheque provided an outlet for a wide range of individuals who used dancing as a way to meet and to share their experiences. By the end of the 1970s, disco had begun to lose its popularity, and Studio 54 had been closed down. No event better illustrated disco's decline than what has been called "disco demolition night." In the summer of 1979, a doubleheader between the Chicago White Sox and the Detroit Tigers was held in Chicago's Comiskey Park. A popular local disc jockey (DJ) had been fired after his station decided to play only disco music. The owner of the White Sox and others sympathetic to the fired DJ devised a promotional event to be held between the games of the doubleheader. If one brought unwanted disco records, in exchange, admission was only 98 cents. The number of people who attended far exceeded the promoters' expectations. The records were placed in a large container, and between the games they were blown up. Why disco lost its popularity remains a matter of debate, but suggested reasons include a declining economy, homophobia, racism, and the growing appeal of rock music.

See also CINEMA.

DOLE, ROBERT JOSEPH (1923–). Republican. Bob Dole served as a U.S. senator from 1969 to 1996 and was the GOP vice presidential candidate in 1976 and the party's presidential candidate in 1996. Born in Kansas, Dole had hoped to be a doctor; however, World War II interrupted his **education**. Wounded during the war, he lost the use of his right arm and regained limited feeling in his left hand. Upon recovering from his wounds, he was well enough to complete his education. He received both his undergraduate and law degrees (B.A., 1949; LL.B., 1952) from Washburn University in Topeka, Kansas.

Even before completing law school, Dole successfully ran as a Republican for the state legislature (1950–52). In 1960 he was elected to the U.S. House of Representatives and in 1968 became a U.S. senator. A fiscal conservative with a sharp wit and a biting tongue, he caught the attention of President **Richard Nixon**, who, in 1971, asked Dole to head the Republican National Committee. In the **1976 election**, **Gerald Ford** chose Dole as his running mate, who many later said hurt Ford's reelection. Dole came across as mean-spirited and nasty, characteristics that were unbecoming for a potential vice president.

After Ford's loss to **Jimmy Carter**, Dole returned to the Senate. He became a strong opponent of many of the president's initiatives, including the 1977 economic stimulus program, the **Panama Canal treaties**, and the **Strategic Arms Limitation Treaty (SALT II)**. He also insisted on the resignation of Office of Management and Budget director **Bert Lance**, who had been accused of financial impropriety, and questioned **Billy Carter**'s ties to Libya. After Carter's defeat in the **1980 election**, Dole remained in the Senate, where he was the Senate majority leader from 1985 to 1987. In both the 1988 and 1996 presidential elections, he ran unsuccessful campaigns. In 1996 he resigned from the Senate and currently practices law in Washington, D.C.

See also ROCKEFELLER, NELSON (1908–1979).

DOMINGO, PLACIDO (JOSE PLACIDO DOMINGO EMBIL) (1941–). One of the "Three Tenors" who performed during the 1990s and into the 21st century, Placido Domingo was born in Madrid, Spain. When he was five, the Domingo family moved to Mexico where they worked as traveling musicians. In 1959 he auditioned for the Mexican National **Opera**. By the mid-1960s, Domingo was performing in the United States. He became one of opera's most respected performers. He has performed in benefit concerts for various causes, including raising money for victims of Mexico City's devastating earthquake in 1985 and New Orleans victims of Hurricane Katrina in 2005.

Domingo, **José Carreras**, and **Luciano Pavarotti** made their debut as the Three Tenors during a fund-raising campaign for the José Carreras International Leukemia Foundation. Domingo sang in the 2001 film *Moulin Rouge* and in 2007 had a cameo role in the popular **television** show *The Simpsons*.

See also MUSIC.

DONOVAN, HEDLEY WILLIAMS (1914–1990). The senior adviser to President **Jimmy Carter** from 1979 to 1981, Hedley Donovan was born in Minnesota. He was both a graduate of the University of Minnesota (B.A., 1934) and a Rhodes scholar (B.A., 1937). He was a reporter for the *Washing-*

ton Post until 1942 and then served in World War II as a naval intelligence officer. After the war he settled in New York City where he began his career with Time Inc. When the founder of Time became ill, Donovan became the editor-in-chief, a position he held until he joined the Carter administration.

Donovan considered Carter an intelligent, decent man but thought the president lacked the ability to visualize problems caused by poor decisions. Two areas of concern to Donovan were the fall of the shah of **Iran, Mohammed Reza Pahlavi,** and the invasion of **Afghanistan** by the **Union of Soviet Socialist Republics (USSR)**; he believed in both cases the president did not adequately consider the possibility of either event occurring. He was also disappointed that Carter appeared unable to settle the differences between National Security Adviser **Zbigniew Brzezinski** and Secretary of State **Cyrus Vance**, and that the president had little interest in history (except biblical history). After Carter's defeat in the **1980 election**, Donovan returned to private life. He passed away in August 1990 as a result of a lung condition.

DOONESBURY. A **comic strip** that oftentimes has political overtones, *Doonesbury* first appeared in 1968 under the title *Bull Tales* in the student newspaper of Yale University, which the strip's creator, Garry Trudeau, was then attending. It began appearing nationally in 1970. *Doonesbury*'s characters ranged from average Americans to academics, businesspersons, and politicians. In 1975, the strip received a Pulitzer Prize for Editorial Cartooning. The following year, it became the first comic strip to depict premarital sex and to introduce a **gay** character, both times prompting some newspapers to refuse to run it. In 1977, Trudeau wrote *A Doonesbury Special*, which appeared on the National Broadcasting Corporation and later won an award at the Cannes Film Festival. Since then, Trudeau has received additional accolades, among them the National Cartoonist Society's Reuben Award in 1995. Today, the strip appears in 1,200 publications worldwide.

E

EASTWOOD, CLINTON, JR. (1930–). Actor, director, and Academy Award winner, Clint Eastwood was born in San Francisco. He began his career in Hollywood on **television** in the western series *Rawhide*. In the 1960s his **cinema** career began in Italian westerns, but his status as a star was realized in the 1971 film *Dirty Harry*. His tough on-screen persona was a hit with audiences. In 1986, Eastwood was elected mayor of Carmel, California, a position he held for two years. He continues to direct and star in films, including *Unforgiven* (1992), for which he received the Academy Award for best director, and *Million Dollar Baby*, which won Oscars for the three leading performers. Eastwood also wrote the **music** for *Million Dollar Baby*. Considered the iconic macho antihero, Eastwood shows no signs of slowing down.

ECONOMY. At the time of **Jimmy Carter**'s victory in the **1976 election**, the economy was reeling from **stagflation**, with **inflation** hovering around 6 percent, unemployment at about 8 percent, and the economy showing little growth. During the campaign for the White House, Carter had called for tackling unemployment, but following the election, he announced that the country's most serious economic problem was inflation. A fiscal conservative, Carter proposed a package aimed at stimulating the economy, including a small public works program and a onetime tax rebate of $50. He infuriated congressional **Democrats** when he decided against the tax rebate on the grounds that the economy had shown signs of improving. Even so, he convinced lawmakers to pass a number of proposals, including a $20 billion public works program. By the middle of 1978, unemployment had fallen to about 6 percent.

The president also hoped to give a spark to the economy through **deregulation**. He believed removing government controls over such industries as airlines, trucking, and railroads would allow for a growth of businesses in those sectors, generate more competition, and, to the benefit of consumers, lower prices. While he did enact laws to deregulate these sectors of corporate America, he had to face a growing number of American companies that moved their factories overseas or that faced such stiff competition that they went out of business. As examples, **television** and textile manufacturers moved their plants to countries where labor costs were cheaper. Other clothes producers as well as the steel industry were hard hit by lower-priced imports. The closure of factories made it difficult for Carter to force the rate of unemployment down.

Then there was inflation, against which the administration was waging a losing battle. The White House estimated that the inflation rate would climb to over 7 percent in 1978. To check higher consumer costs, Carter during 1978 announced he would restrict pay increases for federal workers, hold the deficit to $30 billion, and keep a close eye on corporate wage and price increases. These proposals angered liberal Democrats and **African Americans**, who believed that controlling the deficit would mean cuts for social programs; corporations, which contended that wage and price hikes were not the cause of inflation; and **labor** unions, which argued that Carter's desire to curtail inflation was less important than stimulating the economy and creating jobs. Making matters even more difficult for the White House was the 1979 revolution in **Iran** and a decision by the **Organization of Petroleum Exporting Countries (OPEC)** to increase the price of oil. The result was an annual inflation rate that reached 11 percent. To meet higher gas prices, businesses removed controls on wages, and even federal agencies refused to comply with White House calls to enact spending measures designed to curb inflation.

Hoping to escape inflation's grip, Carter in 1979 appointed **Paul Volcker** to chair the Federal Reserve Board. Volcker increased interest rates and restricted the money supply, yet prices continued to rise. By the spring of 1980, the inflation rate had reached nearly 20 percent, and the country had sunk into a recession. The White House therefore enacted further measures, including deep cuts in federal spending and restrictions on consumer credit. Inflation began to fall but remained high nonetheless. Moreover, with less money being pumped into the economy, the unemployment rate, which had hovered around 6 percent throughout 1979, increased to about 7.5 percent in May 1980 and 8 percent in October. Carter's inability to solve the country's economic troubles proved one of the reasons for his failure to defeat the **Republican Party** candidate, **Ronald Reagan**, in the **1980 election**.

See also AGRICULTURE; AMERICAN FEDERATION OF LABOR AND CONGRESS OF INDUSTRIAL ORGANIZATIONS (AFL-CIO); ANDERSON, JOHN BAYARD (1922–); BLUMENTHAL, WERNER MICHAEL (1926–); ENVIRONMENT; FORD, GERALD RUDOLPH (1913–2006); FOREIGN POLICY; GREAT BRITAIN, RELATIONS WITH; JAPAN, RELATIONS WITH; JORDAN, HAMILTON (1944–2008); KAHN, ALFRED EDWARD (1917–2010); KREPS, JUANITA MORRIS (1921–2010); LONG, RUSSELL BILLIU (1918–2003);

"MALAISE" SPEECH; McINTYRE, JAMES TALMADGE, JR. (1940–); MILLER, G. (GEORGE) WILLIAM (1925–2006); SCHULTZE, CHARLES LOUIS (1924–); TRADE AGREEMENTS ACT (TAA).

EDUCATION. Building upon previous statutes, the federal government during the 1970s implemented laws aimed at improving access to education, no matter one's race, ethnicity, gender, or physical handicap. As examples, the Education Amendments of 1972 provided grants and loans to allow students to obtain an education and established a new Office of Indian Education within the federal government. The Education for All Handicapped Children Act of 1975 requires a free education for children with disabilities.

Jimmy Carter had a strong interest in education. While living in Plains, Georgia, he had opposed those who insisted the U.S. Supreme Court reverse its 1954 *Brown v. Board of Education* decision that ended school segregation. He also served on the Sumter Country School Board, during which he called for consolidating several schools on the grounds that it would improve educational opportunities for local children; voters in the county rejected the suggestion. After winning a seat in 1962 in the Georgia state senate, he served on the governor's Commission to Improve Education, which sought to consolidate small schools, expand vocational training programs, and increase enrollment in institutions of higher education. As both the governor of Georgia and president of the United States, he took steps to combat racial discrimination in education and to provide educational opportunities for individuals with special needs.

Possibly Carter's most significant contribution to education was the creation of a new Department of Education. The National Education Association had long called for such an agency and had endorsed presidential candidate Carter following his promise to establish it. The proposal engendered resistance from **Joseph Califano**, the secretary of the Department of **Health**, Education, and Welfare, who did not want to see his department lose some of its authority. Some members of Congress also disputed the need for such an agency, considering it costly and a threat to local and state oversight of education. However, in 1979, lawmakers passed the **Department of Education Organization Act**, establishing the new bureau. Its first secretary was **Shirley Mount Hufstedler**.

See also BAYH, BIRCH EVANS, JR. (1928–); HISPANIC AMERICANS; KENNEDY, EDWARD MOORE "TED" (1932–2009); SPORTS; WOMEN.

EGYPT, RELATIONS WITH. U.S. relations with Egypt had been strained throughout much of the post–World War II era, in part because of America's close ties to **Israel**—against which Egypt fought several wars—and in part because of Egypt's preparedness to side with the **Union of Soviet Socialist Republics (USSR)**. But in the mid-1970s, Egyptian president **Anwar Sadat** began to distance his country from the USSR and to seek an accommodation with Israel. Using that opening, President **Jimmy Carter** succeeded in bringing Sadat and Israeli prime minister **Menachem Begin** to the United States, where the two Middle Eastern leaders signed the **Camp David Accords** in September 1978. A year later, Israel and Egypt normalized relations and exchanged ambassadors.

See also FOREIGN POLICY; HUSSEIN I (HUSSEIN IBN TALAN IBAN HUSSEIN) (1935–1999); KLUTZNICK, PHILIP MORRIS (1907–1999); PALESTINE LIBERATION ORGANIZATION (PLO).

EIZENSTAT, STUART ELLIOTT (1943–). Stuart Eizenstat was the executive director of the White House domestic policy staff from 1977 to 1981. Considered one of the so-called Georgia Mafia who came to Washington with President **Jimmy Carter**, he became one of the most respected members of the administration, both within and outside of the White House. Born in Chicago but raised in Atlanta, Eizenstat graduated with honors from the University of North Carolina at Chapel Hill (B.A., 1964), and then attained his law degree in 1967 from Harvard University. Political work began for him in President Lyndon B. Johnson's administration, writing domestic policy papers. During the 1968 election, **Democrat** presidential nominee Hubert Humphrey asked Eizenstat to do the same work for him.

In 1969 Eizenstat met then–Georgia gubernatorial candidate Carter and was impressed by Carter's ability to appeal to rural and urban Georgians. When Carter decided to run for president in 1976, Eizenstat helped, which required him to take a leave of absence from the law firm for which he worked. Following his victory, Carter appointed Eizenstat as his director of policy planning. With an **energy crisis** facing the country, Eizenstat urged the president to seek passage of a plan that would appeal to both the executive and legislative branches; the policy planning director regretted the complex proposal the White House later sent to Congress, believing a simpler package would have stood a better chance of success. Not until the fall of 1978 did lawmakers pass an energy plan, one that lacked provisions favored by the Oval Office. Eizenstat also was involved in the ultimately fruitless discussions between Carter and Massachusetts senator **Edward Kennedy** over national **health** insurance. He was displeased with both Carter's July 1979 speech that blamed a "crisis of confidence" among the American people as a cause of the energy crisis and the subsequent shakeup of the cabinet. A member of the Jewish faith, he urged the construction of a memorial for Holocaust victims. After the **1980 election**, Eizenstat returned to practicing law and is active on the boards of several Jewish organizations.

See also SCHLESINGER, JAMES RODNEY (1929–); WATSON, JACK HEARN, JR. (1938–).

ELECTION, 1976. In 1974, **Jimmy Carter** announced his intention to seek the **Democratic Party**'s nomination for the presidency. Little-known outside of the South, Carter was certain he could win. The Democrats' poor showing in 1972 demonstrated to him the need for new blood; more states had begun using primaries, which increased the power of the average voter to determine the party's candidate; the Vietnam War and the Watergate scandal had increased Americans' distrust of their elected officials; and there was a sense among many in the country that the movements of the 1960s, such as those promoting **women**'s, **gay**, and **civil rights** had encouraged immorality and misuse of taxpayer money. Encouraged by friends, among them **Peter Bourne** and **Hamilton Jordan**, to throw his hat in the ring, Carter announced his candidacy in 1974, portraying himself as a Washington outsider who would bring honesty, morality, and fiscal responsibility to the capital. Assisted by a campaign staff whose members included Jordan, **Charles Kirbo**, **Jody Powell**, and **Patricia Derian**, as well as numerous volunteers throughout the country, Carter received the party's endorsement.

Carter's **Republican Party** opponent was the incumbent president, **Gerald Ford**. Ford, who had become president following **Richard Nixon**'s resignation, had faced a serious challenge from former California governor **Ronald Reagan** for his party's nomination. The sharp divide within his own party did not bode well for Ford. But the president also made a number of errors that cost him politically. Shortly after entering the Oval Office, Ford had pardoned Nixon, which angered many Americans. Possibly the most important reason for Carter's victory, though, was Ford's performance during the **televised** presidential debates. In an answer to a question, Ford insisted that the **Union of Soviet Socialist Republics (USSR)** did not dominate Eastern Europe. Clearly untrue, that statement led to Ford's downfall in the polls.

See also BAYH, BIRCH EVANS, JR. (1928–); BROWN, JERRY (EDMUND GERALD BROWN JR.) (1938–); CADDELL, PATRICK H. (1950–); CARTER, ELEANOR ROSALYNN SMITH (1927–); CHURCH, FRANK FORRESTER (1924–1984); DOLE, ROBERT JOSEPH (1923–); ECONOMY; FALLOWS, JAMES MACKENZIE (1949–); FOLEY, THOMAS STEPHEN (1929–); GOLDSCHMIDT, NEIL EDWARD (1940–); GOLDWATER, BARRY MORRIS (1909–1998); GRIFFIN, ROBERT PAUL (1923–); HISPANIC AMERICANS; JACKSON, HENRY MARTIN "SCOOP" (1912–1983); JACKSON, JESSE LOUIS (1941–); JORDAN, BARBARA (1936–1996); LIPSHUTZ, ROBERT JEROME

(1921–2010); RELIGION; SAFIRE, WILLIAM (1929–2009); SOUTH KO-REA, RELATIONS WITH; WALTERS, BARBARA (1929–); WOOD-COCK, LEONARD FREEL (1911–2001).

ELECTION, 1980. Jimmy Carter's presidency has led many historians to name him one of the country's worst presidents. The mishandling of the **Iran hostage crisis**, the failed attempt to free the hostages, and the United States' weak **economy** militated against the president's reelection. The president also faced a divided party, with Senator **Edward Kennedy** of Massachusetts challenging him for the party's nomination. Carter's opponent, former **Republican** governor of California **Ronald Reagan**, was skilled at using the **television** and performed well in the single debate held between the two candidates. The question Reagan posed to viewers, "Are you better off now than you were four years ago?" was easy for most voters to answer since the answer was clearly no. Reagan easily defeated Carter.

See also ANDERSON, JOHN BAYARD (1922–); BROWN, JERRY (ED-MUND GERALD BROWN JR.) (1938–); BUSH, GEORGE HERBERT WALKER (1924–); BYRD, ROBERT CARLYLE (1917–2010); CARTER, ELEANOR ROSALYNN SMITH (1927–); HISPANIC AMERICANS; IS-RAEL, RELATIONS WITH; JACKSON, JESSE LOUIS (1941–); KRAFT, TIMOTHY E. (1941–); LABOR; RELIGION; SICK, GARY GORDON (1935–); STAGFLATION; STRAUSS, ROBERT SCHWARTZ (1918–); WRIGHT, JIM (JAMES CLAUDE WRIGHT JR.) (1922–).

ENERGY CONSERVATION POLICY ACT. Passed in 1975 in response to the **energy crisis**, the Energy Conservation Policy Act established the Strategic Petroleum Reserve (SPR). The SPR provides the United States with an emergency supply of oil in the event of a shortage.

ENERGY CRISIS. Despite proclamations by numerous post–World War II presidents to achieve energy independence, U.S. dependence on foreign sources of fuel had increased, rising from over 12.5 percent in the early 1950s to more than 50 percent by 1976. The implications of this reliance on foreign sources of fuel became evident in 1973, when the **Organization of Petroleum Exporting Countries (OPEC)** imposed a yearlong embargo on petroleum shipments to the United States. The price of oil rose 400 percent, to $8 a barrel, and the country witnessed long lines of automobiles outside gasoline stations. The price per gallon of gasoline increased from 35 cents in 1973 to almost 60 cents by 1975. Adding to the country's woes was the harsh winter of 1976–77, which saw schools and industrial plants throughout the nation close because of a lack of natural gas.

Following his inauguration as president, **Jimmy Carter** took steps to deregulate natural gas to make sure it could get where needed. But he remained concerned about the nation's dependence on foreign fuel. Therefore, in 1977 he asked his secretary of energy, **James Schlesinger**, to put together a comprehensive program aimed at curbing the use of fossil fuels and promoting sources of alternative energy. What Schlesinger and his aides presented later that year had over 110 provisions, including taxes on domestic oil production and gas-guzzling **automobiles**; a "wellhead tax" on domestically produced petroleum, which would increase the cost of oil to world levels; and a variety of incentives, among them tax credits, to encourage Americans to conserve energy.

The administration, however, failed to vet these proposals with Congress. In the House of Representatives, Speaker **Tip O'Neill** succeeded in getting much of the proposed legislation passed, despite intense opposition. At about the same time, the president signed into law the **Department of Energy Organization Act**, which established a new Department of Energy to oversee the country's energy policy. In the Senate, though, the administration's comprehensive energy plan ran headlong into **Russell Long** of Louisiana, the chair of the powerful Finance Committee, who said the tax on domestic oil production would hurt his home state. Not until the fall of 1978 did the president see passage of what became the National Energy Act. While lawmakers removed the wellhead tax and the tax on gas-guzzling automobiles, they did provide incentives to promote alternative energy sources and improved the nationwide distribution of natural gas.

Yet the country remained dependent on foreign sources of fuel. Moreover, the 1979 revolution in **Iran** and a decision by OPEC that same year to increase oil prices caused the cost of fuel and the rate of **inflation** to go up. Therefore, in April 1979 Carter offered another energy plan, the centerpiece of which called for removing controls on oil prices. The president realized his suggestion would mean greater profits for petroleum companies and would anger Americans. Accordingly, he proposed a windfall profits tax that would impose a duty on oil firms' profits; that money would help low-income families handle their higher gas bills, increase federal appropriations for mass transit systems, and establish a federal fund to develop sources of alternative fuels. Three months later, he gave a national speech citing a "crisis of spirit" affecting the country and making further recommendations to handle the energy crisis. This address, which later became known as the **"malaise" speech**, was well received. But it did not resolve the energy crisis. Nor did it convince Congress to endorse immediately any of his proposals to reduce dependence on foreign sources of energy. Not until 1980 did lawmakers pass the **Crude Oil Windfall Profit Tax Act** and the **Energy Security**

Act, the latter of which established the proposed federal fund to develop alternative energy sources. Despite these measures, it was not until 1997 that the United States imported less than 50 percent of its oil.

See also BYRD, ROBERT CARLYLE (1917–2010); DINGELL, JOHN DAVID, JR. (1926–); EIZENSTAT, STUART ELLIOTT (1943–); ENERGY REORGANIZATION ACT; FADS AND FASHIONS; FOLEY, THOMAS STEPHEN (1929–); FOREIGN POLICY; JAPAN, RELATIONS WITH; MONDALE, WALTER FREDERICK (FRITZ) (1928–); SURFACE MINING CONTROL AND RECLAMATION ACT; ULLMAN, AL (ALBERT CONRAD) (1914–1986); WRIGHT, JIM (JAMES CLAUDE WRIGHT JR.) (1922–).

ENERGY REORGANIZATION ACT. After World War II, government regulation of atomic power rested in the hands of the Atomic Energy Commission (AEC). However, as the Cold War progressed, the AEC came under growing criticism for its handling of matters related to nuclear power and energy. Accordingly, in 1974 Congress passed the Energy Reorganization Act, which abolished the AEC and replaced it with two new agencies, the Nuclear Regulatory Commission (NRC) and the Energy Research and Development Administration (ERDA). The NRC regulates civilian applications of nuclear power. This includes overseeing atomic power plants, the licensing of nuclear materials, and managing atomic waste. The ERDA assumed all of the AEC's functions not assigned to the NRC, including research and development in nuclear and alternative power sources, and management of the nation's nuclear weapon and naval reactor programs.

ENERGY RESEARCH AND DEVELOPMENT ADMINISTRATION (ERDA). *See* ENERGY REORGANIZATION ACT.

ENERGY SECURITY ACT. As part of his effort to combat America's **energy crisis**, President **Jimmy Carter** on 30 June 1980 signed the Energy Security Act. It established a Synthetic Fuels Corporation with the authority to spend up to $88 billion over the next 10 years to develop alternative energy sources.

ENTEBBE AIR RAID. On 27 June 1976, Air France flight 139 left **Israel**'s Ben Gurion Airport for Paris. When the plane stopped to refuel in Athens, Greece, Arab terrorists boarded it and ordered the pilot to fly to Libya. After the stop in Libya, the plane flew to Entebbe, Uganda. The collaboration of **Idi Amin**, dictator of Uganda, and members of a branch of the **Palestine Liberation Organization** led to the successful hijacking of the Air France plane. On 4 July, Israeli commandos landed at Entebbe and rescued the majority of the hostages. The Air France plane took off with its remaining passengers and landed in Israel to the delight of their families and friends.

ENVIRONMENT. In the years following World War II, concerns about the health effects of nuclear testing, pesticides, and dumping of waste had generated a movement aimed at protecting the environment. During the 1960s and 1970s, the U.S. government had joined this effort through passage of such legislation as the **Clean Air Act** and the **Clean Water Act**, and the establishment of the Environmental Protection Agency (EPA).

Himself a lover of the outdoors, **Jimmy Carter** had worked to protect the environment as Georgia governor and promised during the 1976 presidential campaign to continue that effort. Yet as president his record was mixed. On the one hand, he sometimes acted in ways that displeased environmentalists. For instance, in 1977 lawmakers forced him to fund several dams by attaching appropriations for those dams to legislation favored by Carter aimed at stimulating the **economy**. In 1979, the president proposed establishing an Energy Mobilization Board, which would expedite construction of new power plants by freeing them from environmental controls. On the other hand, in 1977 Carter endorsed both the **Surface Mining Control and Reclamation Act**, which restricted mining, and amendments designed to strengthen both the Clean Air and Clean Water acts. In a major speech in 1979, the president declared it necessary to balance the nation's energy requirements with the need to protect the environment. In 1980, he signed legislation designed to clean up toxic waste at **Love Canal**, New York. That same year, following two years of lobbying efforts on Capitol Hill, he saw passage of a bill to protect over 100 million acres of wilderness in Alaska. Thus, while the environment was not one of the Carter administration's top priorities, the administration did take important steps aimed at protecting it.

See also ABZUG, BELLA SAVITSKY (1920–1998); ALASKA PIPELINE; CLEAN AIR ACT AMENDMENTS; MOORE, FRANK (1935–); MUSKIE, EDMUND SIXTUS (1914–1996); NELSON, GAYLORD ANTON (1916–2005); THREE MILE ISLAND; UDALL, MORRIS (MO) KING (1922–1998).

EQUAL RIGHTS AMENDMENT (ERA). First proposed in 1923, the Equal Rights Amendment called for giving **women** the same rights as men. Under the Constitution, adding an amendment required approval of two-thirds of both houses of Congress and ratification by two-thirds of the states. By the time of **Jimmy Carter**'s election, Capitol Hill had approved the amendment, but the ERA was four states short of the requisite 38. With the amendment facing a ratification deadline of 1979, the **National Organiza-**

tion for Women (NOW), joined by First Lady **Rosalynn Carter**, began an intense lobbying effort in several states. However, NOW, Mrs. Carter, and the amendment faced strong grassroots opposition led by **Phyllis Schlafly**. Realizing she would not meet the deadline, Mrs. Carter, with the support of her husband, got Congress to extend it until 1982. Yet the amendment still failed to pass and to this day is not part of the U.S. Constitution.

See also ABZUG, BELLA SAVITSKY (1920–1998); BAYH, BIRCH EVANS, JR. (1928–); CIVIL RIGHTS; FALWELL, JERRY (1933–2007); WEDDINGTON, SARAH RAGLE (1945–).

ERVING, JULIUS (1950–). Nicknamed "Dr. J.," Julius Erving was one of **basketball**'s greatest players. He was born in Roosevelt, New York, and attended the University of Massachusetts from 1968 until 1971, when he left to play for the American Basketball Association's (ABA) Virginia Squires. Prior to the 1973–74 season, Erving was traded to the New York Nets. Outstanding on the court, he was the ABA's most valuable player three times. The National Basketball Association (NBA) wanted Erving, but in order to have him, the NBA and the ABA had to merge into the NBA; that merger took place in 1976. Erving completed his professional career playing for the Philadelphia 76ers. In 1987 he retired to become an NBA goodwill ambassador. The fifth-highest scorer in professional basketball now has a successful business career, including ownership of the Celebrity Golf Club near Atlanta, which is a popular club for basketball players.

See also SPORTS.

ESPN (ENTERTAINMENT AND SPORTS PROGRAMMING NETWORK). In 1979 ESPN covered a limited number of athletic events on cable **television**, but by 1980 the new cable station was covering **sports** 24 hours a day. In 1984 the American Broadcasting Company (ABC) purchased ESPN. In 1987 ESPN began broadcasting National **Football** League (NFL) games, followed by major league **baseball** starting in 1989. Since then ESPN has become an international cable television station and has expanded into other operating units, including ESPN 2, ESPNews, ESPN Classic, ESPN Deportes, and *ESPN: The Magazine*.

See also MONDAY NIGHT FOOTBALL.

ETHICS IN GOVERNMENT ACT. The Watergate scandal during President **Richard Nixon**'s second term led to the Ethics in Government Act (1978). The act requires public officials to disclose their finances and restricts former government employees from becoming lobbyists.

ETHIOPIA, RELATIONS WITH. *See* HORN OF AFRICA.

F

FADS AND FASHIONS. The 1970s are remembered for some of the strangest fads and ugliest fashions ever conceived. In the home, two of the new colors for major appliances were avocado green and harvest gold. New small appliances were toaster ovens and Crock-Pots. Fondue pots were introduced with special long-handled forks for dipping food into the mixture. Shag carpeting was popular, and a special rake was introduced to keep the carpet from matting. Fashions included bell-bottom pants and platform shoes for men and **women**. Paisley was a popular material for ties and clothing. Men wore leisure suits. T-shirts began to advertise stores and products. Shorts had fringes, and headbands were worn by men and women. Jeans with sequins were a must, and many Americans drank **Billy** Beer, named for President **Jimmy Carter**'s brother. **Woody Allen**'s movie *Annie Hall* popularized men's clothing for women, and mustaches and facial hair became all the rage. The movie *Smokey and the Bandit* generated an increase in the use of **CB radios** in **automobiles**. Bumper stickers and buttons publicized one's opinions about the Vietnam War, women's rights, and the **environment**. Streaking (running in the nude), owning a pet rock, and riding a moped were all part of the 1970s. One of the unique icons of the decade, which is still popular, is the round, yellow smiley face. The face symbolized happiness and was put on everything from shirts to toilet seats. Military surplus stores sold clothing, which many hippies and others liked to wear. Many of the fads and fashions began in California, and spread rapidly and widely. The popularity of hot tubs and saunas became part of homes. Drugs that caused psychedelic dreams were common.

See also CINEMA.

FALLOWS, JAMES MACKENZIE (1949–). The chief speechwriter for President **Jimmy Carter** from 1977 to 1978, James Fallows was born in Philadelphia but raised in southern California. He graduated from Harvard University (B.A., 1970). A Rhodes scholar who had been president of Harvard's daily newspaper, Fallows admired Carter during the **1976 election**, seeing in the former Georgia governor a presidential candidate unlike the others running for the White House. He joined the Carter campaign as a speechwriter and became Carter's chief speechwriter shortly after the 1976 election. By 1979, however, he had become disenchanted with the president: he liked Carter as a person but believed he did not understand how to govern. Fallows accepted a job with the *Atlantic Monthly* and wrote an article for that magazine criticizing Carter and his administration. Published in 1979, at a time when the administration was already facing public criticism, the article caused further damage to Carter's political standing. Fallows presently continues to work for the *Atlantic Monthly*, where he is a national correspondent.

FALWELL, JERRY (1933–2007). Founder of the **Moral Majority** in 1979, **television** evangelist Jerry Falwell was born in Lynchburg, Virginia. Although he planned to be an engineer, he attended Baptist Bible College in Springfield, Missouri, where he had a religious awakening. After completing his education in Missouri, Falwell returned to Lynchburg, Virginia, where he founded Liberty Baptist College. In the 1970s the Moral Majority spoke out against **gays**, the **Equal Rights Amendment (ERA)**, and **abortion**. In declining health, he passed away in May 2007.

See also CIVIL RIGHTS; FLYNT, LARRY (1942–); RELIGION.

FAWCETT, FARRAH (1947–2009). Born in Corpus Christi, Texas, Farrah Fawcett became in the 1970s among the most recognizable and emulated of women, with men adoring her beauty and women copying her hairstyle. Fawcett attended the University of Texas from 1966 to 1969. She dropped out after being discovered by a Hollywood agent who saw her in a photo of the university's 10 most beautiful coeds. Her stardom began when she appeared in a poster wearing a red bathing suit, her blonde hair styled to perfection. No other poster has sold more copies to date. From 1976 to 1977 she appeared in the **television** series *Charlie's Angels*, which debuted with the highest rating in history.

The two other women who starred with Fawcett were billed as athletic, which coincided with the **women**'s movement of the 1970s. Farrah left the show after one year to appear in films and received accolades for her performance in *The Burning Bed* (1984). The television film's theme was spousal abuse, which women faced but was never discussed. In 2006 she was diagnosed with cancer. In 2009 she wanted cameras to document her battle with the disease, which she lost in June of that year.

FIXX, JAMES (1932–1984). Jim Fixx lived in New York City and graduated from Oberlin College in 1957. A member of Mensa, he published three books of puzzles for the superintelligent. More significantly, he is credited with beginning the fitness revolution. Fixx's father had died of a heart attack, and Fixx, who weighed over 200 pounds by the late 1960s, decided he should take up jogging to lose weight. His best-selling book *The Complete Book of Running* (1977) sold over a million copies. Ironically, Fixx died while running, apparently from a combination of stress and a genetic predisposition to heart problems.

See also LITERATURE.

FLYNT, LARRY (1942–). Born in Kentucky, Larry Flynt's family was very poor. He enlisted in the U.S. Army but was discharged due to poor test scores. He turned to the navy, where he served for five years. Upon leaving the navy, Flynt moved to Dayton, Ohio, to be with his mother. In Dayton he opened a strip club, which was so successful that he launched similar establishments in other Ohio cities. In 1974 Flynt decided to publish a **magazine** that would compete with other popular magazines for men. *Hustler*'s audience was working-class men, and the issues included hard-core pornography. In 1977 Flynt met **Jimmy Carter**'s sister **Ruth Carter Stapleton** on *60 Minutes*. Stapleton, an evangelist, and Flynt became close friends. The following year he was shot by a white supremacist, which paralyzed his legs and affected his speaking. He was sued by Reverend **Jerry Falwell** in 1996 for publishing a cartoon implying that Falwell and his mother had an incestuous relationship. A jury decided to award Falwell $200,000. Currently, Flynt lives in Beverly Hills, California. His life was the subject of the 1996 film *The People vs. Larry Flynt*.

FOLEY, THOMAS STEPHEN (1929–). Democrat. Tom Foley had a long political career, serving as a member of the House of Representatives from 1965 to 1995, as Speaker of the House of Representatives from 1989 to 1995, and as ambassador to **Japan** from 1998 to 2001. Foley was born in Spokane, Washington. He attended Gonzaga University but later transferred to the University of Washington in Seattle (B.A., 1951). He received his law degree from the University of Washington in 1957 and entered private practice. In 1961 he moved to Washington, D.C., where he joined the staff of the Senate Committee on Interior and Insular Affairs. In 1964 he was elected to Congress from Washington State. In the **1976 election**, he endorsed the campaign of his fellow Washingtonian, Senator **Henry Jackson**.

During the **Jimmy Carter** administration, Foley championed subsidies for farmers and achieved a compromise with the president, who wanted lower price supports. He supported the White House's positions on confronting the **energy crisis**, containing hospital costs, and **deregulation**. He disapproved, however, of the embargo on grain shipments to the **Union of Soviet Socialist Republics (USSR)** following its invasion of **Afghanistan** on the grounds that the embargo hurt farmers in his state.

Foley became speaker of the House in 1989, but in 1992, he lost a bid for reelection. He thus became the first Speaker to fail to win another term since the Civil War. He became ambassador to Japan during President Bill Clinton's second term.

FOOTBALL. Two professional football teams were added to the National Football League in 1976: the Seattle Seahawks and the Tampa Bay Buccaneers. Of the ten Super Bowl games in the 1970s, the Dallas Cowboys played in five of them and won two. Tom Landry, legendary coach of the Cowboys for 29 seasons, made the Cowboys a winning team. The Pittsburgh Steelers, led by Coach Chuck Noll, was the other powerhouse of the 1970s, winning all three Super Bowls in which they played. *Monday Night Football*, which debuted in 1970, has been one of **television**'s most popular weekly **sports** programs. Announcers, including **Howard Cosell**, have added to the program's popularity. Aside from the game, professional football has included the ongoing legal problems of **O. J. Simpson** and the hitting of one of the Ohio State Buckeye players by Woody Hayes, the Buckeyes' coach.

See also ESPN (ENTERTAINMENT AND SPORTS PROGRAMMING NETWORK); FORD, GERALD RUDOLPH (1913–2006); GREENE, "MEAN JOE" (CHARLES EDWARD) (1946–).

FORD, BETTY (1918–2011). Wife of President **Gerald Ford**, Elizabeth Ann Bloomer was born in Chicago. A dancer and model, she had married William Warren in 1942 but divorced him five years later. Not long thereafter, she began dating Gerald Ford, whom she wed in 1948. Outspoken, pro-choice, and pro-**Equal Rights Amendment (ERA)**, she brought both **breast cancer** and alcoholism into the open by sharing her battles with both. She was the primary founder in 1982 of the Betty Ford Center, which has helped her and others combat their addictions.

FORD, GERALD RUDOLPH (1913–2006). Republican. The president of the United States from 1974 to 1977, Gerald Ford had previously served as a member of the House of Representatives from 1948 to 1973 and as vice president of the United States from 1973 to 1974. Born in Omaha, Nebraska, but raised in Grand Rapids, Michigan, Ford attended the University of Michigan on a **football** scholarship (B.A., 1935). In 1938 he entered Yale University Law School where he received his law degree in 1941. After serving in the navy during World War II, he returned to Michigan where he was re-elected to the U.S. House of Representatives 12 times. After Vice President Spiro Agnew resigned in 1973, President **Richard Nixon** chose Ford to be his new vice president. In 1974 Nixon resigned as a result of the Watergate scandal, making Ford America's first and only unelected president.

Ford served only two years in office. His decision to pardon Nixon for crimes committed during Watergate infuriated many voters, and his inability to rescue the country from a weak **economy** made them even more upset. In the **1976 election**, Ford first had to face a serious challenge to his bid for the Republican Party nomination from **Ronald Reagan**. Securing the party's nod, he competed against former Georgia governor **Jimmy Carter** for the White House. Though it was a close race, Carter won. Afterward, Ford became a popular guest lecturer as well as a business consultant. An avid golfer and skier, his final years were spent in California and Vail, Colorado.

See also DOLE, ROBERT JOSEPH (1923–); GOLDWATER, BARRY MORRIS (1909–1998); GRIFFIN, ROBERT PAUL (1923–); KISSINGER, HENRY ALFRED (ALFRED HEINZ) (1923–); MOYNIHAN, DANIEL PATRICK (1927–2003); ROCKEFELLER, NELSON (1908–1979); ROOSEVELT, ALICE LONGWORTH (1884–1980); SCHLESINGER, JAMES RODNEY (1929–); SOUTH KOREA, RELATIONS WITH; SPACE PROGRAM; TRADE AGREEMENTS ACT (TAA).

FOREIGN CORRUPT PRACTICES ACT. Between 1975 and 1976, a series of investigations led by the U.S. Securities and Exchange Commission and Senator **Frank Church** discovered that starting in the 1950s, officials from the U.S.-based Lockheed Corporation had bribed foreign officials to win contracts in foreign countries. The scandal led to the investigation, resignation, or imprisonment of a number of foreign government officials as well as the resignation of Lockheed's chairman of the board and president. This and several similar events led to the passage in 1977 of the Foreign Corrupt Practices Act, which prohibits Americans from using bribes to acquire or retain business abroad.

See also LOCKHEED SCANDAL.

FOREIGN INTELLIGENCE SURVEILLANCE ACT (FISA). During the 1970s, the Senate learned from its investigation into the Watergate scandal that the **Richard Nixon** administration had used U.S. intelligence agencies to spy on Americans. In an attempt to protect U.S. security while precluding Nixon's abuses, in 1977 Senator **Edward Kennedy** of Massachusetts submitted legislation that became the Foreign Intelligence Surveillance Act, or FISA. Signed into law in 1978, FISA permits the federal government, without a court order, to spend up to a year conducting electronic information gathering, except in those cases where the communications might involve those of a U.S. citizen. It further established the Foreign Intelligence Service Court, from which U.S. government officials can request warrants to investigate possible activities by foreign agents within the nation.

FOREIGN POLICY. By the mid-1970s, U.S. foreign policy had undergone a transformation. For much of the period after World War II, America's diplomacy was based upon a Cold War consensus, with the **Union of Soviet Socialist Republics (USSR)** as the main U.S. enemy. The goal of Washington's foreign policy was to contain the spread of communism, which Americans believed was directed from Moscow. But the Vietnam War, U.S. support for repressive governments, and the worsening relationship between the USSR and communist **China** led to a breakdown of the Cold War consensus. By the early 1970s, an improvement in relations between Washington and Moscow—better known as **détente**—had emerged. The best example of détente was the **Strategic Arms Limitation Treaty** (SALT I), signed between the two superpowers in 1972.

By the mid-1970s, U.S.-Soviet relations appeared headed to a new phase, marked by confrontation. One problem was that the superpowers defined détente differently. The Soviets believed it permitted them the right to aid communist nations and movements; to American officials, détente meant the Soviet Union should not try to change the status quo. Additionally, the United States began to emphasize the importance of **human rights** in its foreign policy, which meant criticizing the Kremlin for abusing its people. Moscow angrily responded that Washington was interfering in its internal affairs.

President **Jimmy Carter** hoped to revive détente. At the same time, he wanted to redirect American diplomacy. Rather than have the USSR continue to play a central role in American foreign policy making, he sought to give greater emphasis to U.S. relations with **Japan**, Western Europe, and the Third World. As such, he proposed a laundry list of diplomatic initiatives. While he intended to continue promoting human rights, his goals also included signing a SALT II agreement with the Soviet Union, turning the Panama Canal over to Panama, achieving a comprehensive peace agreement in the Middle East, normalizing relations with communist China, stopping the proliferation of nuclear weapons, and stimulating the world **economy**.

Trying to do so much proved problematic for several reasons. First, because Carter did not make clear which of these goals was most important, the administration tried to work on them all at once, which proved overly burdensome. Second, individuals and agencies within the government found themselves at odds. National Security Adviser **Zbigniew Brzezinski** favored normalizing relations with China quickly. Secretary of State **Cyrus Vance** believed such a move would anger the USSR and endanger SALT. Meanwhile, the Bureau of Human Rights and Humanitarian Affairs, which was to oversee implementation of the human rights policy, found itself at odds with the Departments of Commerce, Treasury, and Defense, which feared that an aggressive human rights policy would upset economically or militarily important, though repressive, U.S. allies. Indeed, within two weeks of Carter's inauguration, the White House made clear it would not take a hard line toward such nations as **South Korea**, **Iran**, and the **Philippines**, despite those countries' authoritarian regimes.

Finally, and possibly most important, policies could and did interfere with one another. The best example was the human rights initiative. Carter berated the Soviet Union for the treatment of its people, moving the Kremlin to become less willing to cooperate with him on SALT. Believing arms control was more important, Carter toned down his criticism. Though he considered the Cambodian government of **Pol Pot** one of the worst human rights violators in the world, the president refused to put much pressure on Pol Pot because the Cambodian leader was a close ally of China's, a nation with which the president wanted to improve ties.

By early 1978, the human rights policy had become so watered down that the list of countries targeted for violations had become substantially reduced. The African countries of **Rhodesia** and South Africa were condemned because of their apartheid systems; moreover, the president imposed trade sanctions upon the Rhodesian government, led by Prime Minister **Ian Smith**. Additionally, criticizing those two nations appealed to **African Americans**, who were upset with the treatment of black Africans. But more than any part of the world, it was Latin America that became the focus of the human rights initiative. Argentina, Brazil, Chile, and Uruguay were among those countries in the region facing economic and military sanctions because of their repressive governments. Despite U.S. pressure, none of these nations showed a willingness to change their ways.

The president also ran into difficulties insofar as nuclear nonproliferation and stimulating the world economy. Carter opposed **West Germany**'s proposal to help Brazil build a nuclear power plant and Japan's desire to start up a new atomic plant. Both West Germany and Japan insisted they had not violated international law and that any effort to stop them amounted to interference in their internal policies. The president proved unable to stop the West Germans but was able to work out an agreement with the Japanese that allowed their plant to begin operations. Nor did he find the help for which he had hoped to stimulate the world economy. With the United States facing higher unemployment and **inflation**, an **energy crisis**, and a growing trade deficit, Carter urged Japan and Western Europe to curb their use of oil and import more American-made goods. At a summit held in July 1978, both the West Germans and Japanese agreed to take measures to stimulate their economies and increase their imports, but other matters, particularly that of petroleum use, remained unresolved.

Despite all of the problems he encountered, Carter could point to foreign policy successes as 1978 came to an end. He had convinced Bonn and Tokyo to do more to help Washington on the economic front. Four months earlier, and as a result of intense lobbying on the part of the White House, the Senate ratified the **Panama Canal treaties**, which turned the Panama Canal over to Panama. In September 1978, **Israeli** prime minister **Menachem Begin** and **Egyptian** president **Anwar Sadat** signed the **Camp David Accords**, which brought peace between the two former enemies. Though not the comprehensive Middle East settlement Carter had wanted, it was a significant step forward. In December, the president announced the normalization of relations with China.

In June 1979, Carter scored another major success when he and Soviet general secretary **Leonid Brezhnev** signed SALT II. Good news came out of Africa later that year. With U.S. ambassador to the United Nations **Andrew Young** forced to resign after meeting with a member of the **Palestine Liberation Organization**, and with Carter's attention turning more toward other issues, including the economy and a crisis in Iran, the White House was devoting less time to ending apartheid. Such was not the case for the new British prime minister, **Margaret Thatcher**. Facing a military revolt by blacks against his leadership, and with the economic sanctions wreaking havoc on the Rhodesian economy, Smith accepted a plan in December 1979 put together by Thatcher and British foreign secretary Peter Carrington that gave blacks majority rule in Rhodesia. The apartheid system in South Africa, however, would continue for another decade.

These auspicious events could not hide some serious problems facing the White House. The timing of the SALT agreement was poor. Continuing to define détente differently than the United States, the USSR had continued to give aid to communists elsewhere. Particularly frustrating to the White House was the Kremlin's decision to offer military assistance to the African nation of **Ethiopia**, which was in a war with its neighbor, **Somalia**. That frustration was shared by Americans in general, who had elected in 1978 a Congress that was decidedly more conservative, and therefore more anti-Soviet, than its predecessor. Moreover, some members of the U.S. Senate had risked their seats by agreeing to the Panama Canal treaties and did not want to guarantee their failure to win reelection by accepting an unpopular SALT agreement.

Making matters worse for Carter was a series of crises with which his administration had to contend in 1979. The first was in January, when the shah of Iran, **Mohammed Reza Pahlavi**, fled in the face of intense opposition to his rule. The president came under criticism, particularly from the political right, for not doing more to help a longtime U.S. ally. Similar words of censure were heard when **Anastasio Somoza Debayle**, the leader of Nicaragua, fell from power before a revolution led by the leftist **Sandinistas**. Carter was charged not only for "losing" Nicaragua but losing it to a group viewed by many Americans as communistic. In November 1979 the **Iran hostage crisis** began when Iranian militants seized U.S. nationals working in the American embassy in Tehran. A month later, the USSR invaded **Afghan-**

istan to prop up that country's communist government. An infuriated Carter declared that the United States would not attend the Summer **Olympics**, which were to be held in Moscow; announced what became known as the **"Carter Doctrine"**; imposed an embargo on grain shipments to the Soviet Union; told the Senate to shelve SALT II; and authorized a U.S. military buildup. Moreover, to contain the threat posed by the USSR, Carter sought to improve ties with countries he previously had condemned. As examples, Argentina, once cited for human rights violations, now received offers of economic aid in return for its cooperation. In 1977, Carter, citing Pakistan's repressive government and its determination to get nuclear weapons—which constituted a violation of the president's desire to stop the proliferation of atomic technology—suspended military and economic aid to that country. Now the United States wanted Pakistan on its side and, in 1980, presented that country with a $400 million economic and military assistance package. Both Argentina and Pakistan proved unwilling to accommodate the White House.

The hostage crisis and invasion of Afghanistan led Americans to rally around the president they had criticized a few months earlier. The timing could not have been better for Carter. In June 1979, he had attended a summit in Tokyo where Japan, West Germany, and the United States agreed to reduce both their tariffs and petroleum imports. But there was nothing to guarantee a permanent reduction of duties, and the settlement regarding oil was not terribly significant. The revolution in Iran and a decision by the **Organization of Petroleum Exporting Countries (OPEC)** in June—and while Carter was in Tokyo—to increase petroleum prices had caused inflation in the United States to continue to rise. Upset Americans had begun to look for an alternative to Carter. One possibility was Massachusetts senator **Edward Kennedy**, who in November 1979 had decided to challenge the president for the **Democratic Party**'s nomination. With the American people now rallying around the president, it appeared Carter had a good chance of overcoming both the general frustrations directed at his leadership and the threat posed by Kennedy to his hope for another term in office.

By June 1980, Carter had won enough delegates to guarantee himself the Democrats' nomination. Yet his fortunes by then had begun to wane and continued to do so. The hostage crisis appeared unending, angering Americans, who questioned whether the president was doing all he could to free those being held against their will in Iran. An attempt in April 1980 to rescue the hostages not only failed, with the loss of eight American servicemen, but led Secretary of State Vance, who had opposed such an effort, to resign. Another international economic summit, held in June, was only partially successful. West German chancellor **Helmut Schmidt**, who had criticized Carter's human rights policy for angering the USSR, and who believed the U.S. president's response to the invasion of Afghanistan went too far, agreed to join Carter in taking further steps to control oil imports. But the two Western leaders remained far apart on other matters, including the U.S. president's request that West Germany follow America's lead and increase its spending on **defense**. The following month, news that Carter's brother, **Billy**, had accepted a "loan" from Libya, and that Billy, at the request of First Lady **Rosalynn Carter**, had tried to use his Libyan contacts to free the hostages being held in Iran, embarrassed the White House. Inflation and unemployment continued to rise. On Election Day, the American people, having reached the conclusion that their president seemed either unable or unwilling to do enough to rescue the hostages or to solve their country's economic problems, chose the **Republican Party** candidate, **Ronald Reagan**, as their next president.

See also AARON, DAVID LAURENCE (1938–); ARAFAT, YASSER (1929–2004); ASSAD, HAFEZ AL- (1930–2000); CASTRO, FIDEL (1926–); CHRISTOPHER, WARREN MINOR (1925–2011); CUBA, RELATIONS WITH; DENG XIAOPING (TENG HSIAO-PING) (1904–1997); DERIAN, PATRICIA MURPHY (1929–); GISCARD D'ESTAING, VALERY (1926–); KISSINGER, HENRY ALFRED (ALFRED HEINZ) (1923–); KLUTZNICK, PHILIP MORRIS (1907–1999); MARCOS, FERDINAND (EMMANUEL EDRALIN) (1917–1989); MUSKIE, EDMUND SIXTUS (1914–1996); NEUTRON BOMB; O'NEILL, TIP (THOMAS PHILLIP O'NEILL JR.) (1912–1994); RELIGION; SOUTH KOREA, RELATIONS WITH.

FRANCE, RELATIONS WITH. See GISCARD D'ESTAING, VALERY (1926–).

FRANCHISES. A franchise is a store, restaurant, or other business that operates under a license granted to it by a company or the government. Franchises quickly expanded in the 1960s and 1970s. Some founded in the 1970s include such national chains as Fuddruckers, Century 21, Starbucks Coffee Company, Schlotzsky's, and Ruby Tuesday. Others went bankrupt due to poor management and left owners in financial trouble. The Franchise Rule of 1979 was passed to protect franchisees. Too, the International Franchise Association (IFA) and the Federal Trade Commission (FTC) have worked together to improve relations with franchisees.

FULL EMPLOYMENT AND BALANCED GROWTH ACT. In order to stop the **stagflation** of the 1970s, the Full Employment and Balanced Growth Act was passed in 1978. The act contained four goals: economic growth, full employment, a balanced budget, and the elimination of **inflation**. It is also called the Humphrey-Hawkins Act.

See also ECONOMY.

FULLER, MILLARD (1935–2009). The founder of **Habitat for Humanity**, Millard Fuller was born in Alabama. He received his bachelor's degree from Auburn University in 1957, married Linda Caldwell in 1959, and a year later earned his law degree from the University of Alabama. By the mid-1960s, he had made a fortune running a mail-order catalog company. The long hours he spent at work strained his marriage, with Linda claiming he cared more about earning money than her. Not wanting his marriage to fall apart, he convinced Linda to stay with him by promising to give his wealth to charity and adopt a simpler lifestyle.

In 1965, the Fullers and their children moved to Koinonia Farm, an interracial Christian commune established by the theologian Clarence Jordan, one of **Hamilton Jordan**'s uncles. Inspired by Clarence to combat racial injustice, the Fullers headed to Africa to do missionary work. There, they met other missionaries who suggested creating a nonprofit organization to build homes for the poor. Inspired, the Fullers in 1969 took over the Fund for Humanity, a group established by Clarence Jordan that relied upon donations and no-interest loans to construct homes for low-income families. The Fullers returned to Africa in 1973 to build houses in Zaire, and, upon returning to the United States in 1976, announced the formation of Habitat for Humanity. Today, this organization builds homes for poorer families worldwide. Its work has attracted numerous celebrities, **sports** figures, and politicians, among them **Jimmy** and **Rosalynn Carter**, who each year participate in Habitat's Jimmy and Rosalynn Carter Work Project.

G

GATES, BILL (WILLIAM HENRY III) (1955–). One of the richest men in the world, Bill Gates was born in Seattle. He attended Harvard University but did not graduate. Instead, in 1975, at the age of 19, he founded the Microsoft Corporation with his friend Paul Allen. Allen and Gates licensed their operating system to International Business Machines (IBM) in 1980. By 1987 Bill Gates was a billionaire. The Microsoft Corporation has continually updated its system for use by personal **computer** companies worldwide. In 1995 Gates bought the Bettman Archives, which houses historical photographs, and Microsoft transformed the materials in the Bettman Archives into digital images for use online. Today his company is the biggest producer of computer software in the world. Gates and his wife, Melinda, whom he married in 1994, have given millions of dollars to other countries to help eradicate illnesses.

See also TECHNOLOGICAL ADVANCES.

GAY RIGHTS MOVEMENT. During the 1970s the gay rights movement gained strength and became influential in local, state, and national politics. In 1977, in San Francisco, where many gays lived, **Harvey Milk**, an openly gay man, won an election to serve on the city council. Many people, including **Anita Bryant**, openly frowned upon gays and lesbians. Bryant and her followers saw people in the gay rights movement as having a mental disorder. When the number of AIDS cases grew among gay men, discrimination became more evident. People feared contagion from the illness and wanted to keep gays and lesbians far from everyone else.

See also ABZUG, BELLA SAVITSKY (1920–1998); BURGER, WARREN EARL (1907–1995); CIVIL RIGHTS; DISCO; *DOONESBURY*; ELECTION, 1976; FALWELL, JERRY (1933–2007); TELEVISION; WOMEN.

GISCARD D'ESTAING, VALERY (1926–). The president of **France** from 1974 to 1981, Valery Giscard d'Estaing was born in Germany and educated in Paris. He fought with the French resistance against the Germans during World War II. He developed a successful political career after the war, spent a year at Harvard Business School, and was elected to the French parliament in 1956. From 1969 to 1974 he served as finance minister during the presidency of Georges Pompidou. Follow Pompidou's death in 1974, Giscard ran a successful campaign to succeed him.

Giscard, like **West Germany**'s **Helmut Schmidt**, did not get along well with President **Jimmy Carter**. He believed Carter's support for **human rights** risked poor relations with the **Union of Soviet Socialist Republics (USSR)**, he disagreed with the White House on policy toward the Middle East and the international economy, and he regarded the U.S. president's response to the Soviet invasion of **Afghanistan** as excessive. Giscard lost a bid for reelection in 1981 but has remained active in French politics.

See also FOREIGN POLICY; GREAT BRITAIN, RELATIONS WITH.

GOLDSCHMIDT, NEIL EDWARD (1940–). Democrat. The secretary of transportation from 1979 to 1981, Neil Goldschmidt was born in Oregon. He received degrees from the University of Oregon (B.A., 1963) and the University of California, Berkeley School of Law (J.D., 1967). His political career began in 1971 after he was elected to the city commission of Portland, Oregon. Two years later, he was elected Portland's mayor, making him the country's youngest large-city mayor. He revitalized the downtown area; the creation of a light-rail system for the city became a model for other metropolises. During the **1976 election**, Goldschmidt campaigned for **Jimmy Carter**. In 1979 Carter named Goldschmidt to replace **Brock Adams** as secretary of transportation. During his tenure, Goldschmidt oversaw **deregulation** of the railroad and trucking industries.

After President Carter lost reelection in 1980, Goldschmidt returned to Oregon where he campaigned for and won the governorship of that state. He left politics in the 1990s when rumors spread that he had been involved with a 14-year-old girl while he was Portland's mayor. Goldschmidt had tried to keep the affair, which would make him guilty of a felony, quiet, telling only his second wife. But when he learned in 2004 that the matter was going to be published, he voluntarily gave up his license to practice law and withdrew to private life with his second wife. Because the statute of limitations had expired, he was not tried. However, the scandal continues to reverberate to the present.

GOLDWATER, BARRY MORRIS (1909–1998). Republican. A U.S. senator from 1953 to 1965 and from 1969 to 1987, and the Republican Party's presidential candidate in 1964, Barry Goldwater was known as "Mr. Conservative." Born in Phoenix, his father was a wealthy businessman who directed his son's education. Goldwater had wanted to attend West Point, but his father made his son enroll at the University of Arizona. During his time at the university, Goldwater's father died, and Goldwater withdrew from school to run his father's business. He was a good businessman and became the president of the family-owned department stores his father had owned.

Goldwater's political career began in 1949 when he successfully won a seat on the Phoenix City Council. During the presidency of Dwight D. Eisenhower, Goldwater began to notice the popularity of the Republican Party, whose views corresponded more closely with his own than the **Democratic Party**. Although Arizona was a Democratic state at the time, Goldwater decided to run for the U.S. Senate as a Republican. His opinions of the federal government's decisions during the presidencies of both Franklin D. Roosevelt and Eisenhower appealed to many in his state, and he won his bid for the Senate.

In the **1976 election**, Goldwater campaigned for **Gerald Ford** against **Jimmy Carter**. He opposed ratification of the **Panama Canal treaties** and Carter's decision to abrogate the U.S. alliance with **Taiwan**. After **Ronald Reagan** won the **1980 election**, Goldwater became disillusioned with the Republican Party, which he concluded had become too conservative socially and culturally; to him, political conservatism mattered most. In 1987 Goldwater retired from the U.S. Senate. Nine years later, he suffered a stroke after which Alzheimer's disease set in. He passed away in May 1998 in Phoenix.

See also NUNN, SAM (SAMUEL AUGUSTUS) (1938–); WALLACE, GEORGE CORLEY (1919–1998).

GOLF. During the 1970s the most notable golfers were Jack Nicklaus and Gary Player, both of whom won the Masters twice in the decade. Tom Watson won the Masters in 1977 and was considered a top player from 1978 to 1982 by *Golf World*.

See also SPORTS.

GOOD TIMES. A groundbreaking sitcom that aired on **television** from 1974 to 1979, *Good Times* depicted the lives of the Evans family who resided in the projects of Chicago. It was the first weekly comedy program to focus on an **African American** family living in abject poverty. Yet despite their struggles, including the death of the father, the Evanses persevered. In addition to tackling poverty, the program also addressed such powerful topics as class differences within the African American community, political corruption, racism, **religion**, and child abuse. *Good Times*, like *All in the Family*, was created by **Norman Lear**.

GRATEFUL DEAD. The most popular psychedelic rock band in American **music** history, the Grateful Dead was formed in 1965 in San Francisco. Its members, Jerry Garcia, Phil Lesh, Bob Weir, Ron McKernan, and Bill Kreutzmann combined rock, blues, country, **jazz**, and folk to create a sound that drew them a large audience, who became known as "deadheads." Unlike most musical groups, they allowed their audience to tape their concerts, and they kept ticket prices very low. Following Garcia's death in 1995, the group disbanded, though the surviving members have held periodic reunion tours under different band names. The Grateful Dead was popular for almost three decades.

GREAT BRITAIN, RELATIONS WITH. Scholars have written of the so-called special relationshipthat has existed between the United States and Great Britain, particularly in the years since the end of World War II. This relationship continued during the **Jimmy Carter** administration. President Carter and British prime minister **James Callaghan** were personally close, and in the name of Anglo-American harmony, Callaghan tended not to side with his European colleagues on decisions made by the U.S. president. Whereas West German chancellor **Helmut Schmidt** and French president **Valery Giscard d'Estaing** blamed the United States for many of the problems in the world **economy**, Callaghan was less critical. He was more reluctant than Schmidt and d'Estaing to charge that Carter's **human rights** policy made the **Union of Soviet Socialist Republics (USSR)** more unwilling to sign a **Strategic Arms Limitation Treaty (SALT II)**. Carter and Callaghan also agreed on the need for **Rhodesia**'s prime minister, **Ian Smith**, to end apartheid.

One issue that offered to pose a major problem for U.S.-British relations during the Carter years was London's control of Northern Ireland. There, fighting took place between Protestants, who tended to side with Great Britain, and Catholics, who leaned toward the Republic of Ireland. The Republic of Ireland insisted that London relinquish its authority over Northern Ireland, while a militant organization called the Irish Republican Army used acts of terrorism to force the British out. Carter himself faced strong pressure from Irish Americans to do something. In August 1977, the president publicly called upon Ireland and Great Britain to resolve their differences and offered to have the United States act as a mediator. But in the name of Anglo-American friendship, he refused to go further.

Carter was not as close to Callaghan's successor, **Margaret Thatcher**. Thatcher liked the U.S. president as a decent person but regarded him as a poor politician. Yet for all practical purposes, the "special relationship" continued. Indeed, it was Thatcher who, alongside her foreign secretary, Peter Carrington, reached an arrangement to end apartheid in Rhodesia, a goal of

Carter's since he took office. Thatcher also endorsed the U.S. president's call for an international boycott of the 1980 **Olympics**, which were to be held in the USSR, following the Soviet invasion of **Afghanistan**.

See also FOREIGN POLICY.

GREENE, "MEAN JOE" (CHARLES EDWARD) (1946–). One of the National **Football** League's greatest defensive linemen, Charles Edward Greene was born in Temple, Texas. He attended North Texas State University for two years (1966–68), where his amazing career on the college football team led to his becoming a member of the Pittsburg Steelers in 1969. He remained on that team from 1969 to 1981. In 1979, one of the most famous **television advertisements** starred Greene and a small boy, who offered the football player a Coca-Cola; in return, Greene gave the child his jersey. According to *TV Guide*, it is still considered one of the top ten commercials ever produced. The North Texas State mascot is the Mean Greene, in honor of "Mean Joe" Greene. He was elected into the College Football Hall of Fame in 1984 and the Pro Football Hall of Fame in 1988.

GRIFFIN, ROBERT PAUL (1923–). Republican. A member of the House of Representatives from Michigan from 1957 to 1964 and a U.S. senator from 1965 to 1978, Robert Griffin was known as a "giant killer." Born in Dearborn, Michigan, he graduated from Central Michigan College (B.A., 1947), received his law degree in 1950 from the University of Michigan Law School, and ran a successful bid for the U.S. House in 1956. He became a senator when he was appointed by Governor George Romney upon the death of **Democratic** senator Patrick V. McNamara. Griffin filibustered President Lyndon B. Johnson's choice of Abe Fortas to the United States **Supreme Court**, which forced Fortas to withdraw his name. He worked to elect **Gerald Ford** in the **1976 election**.

Griffin consistently opposed President **Jimmy Carter**'s initiatives, including the nomination of **Paul Warnke** as the administration's chief arms negotiator, ratification of the **Panama Canal treaties**, and stricter controls on **automobile** fuel emissions. He had hoped to become Senate minority leader following the 1976 election but lost out to **Howard Baker** of Tennessee; discouraged, he decided not to run for reelection in 1978. Afterward, he joined the conservative American Enterprise Institute, was a Michigan Supreme Court justice from 1987 to 1994, and presently sits on the U.S. Court of Appeals for the Sixth Circuit.

HABITAT FOR HUMANITY. In 1976 **Millard Fuller** and his wife, Linda, founded Habitat for Humanity, a nonprofit organization, the volunteers for which build homes for poor families. The group has built over 300,000 homes worldwide. In 1984 President **Jimmy Carter** and his wife, **Rosalynn Carter**, became volunteers in the organization.

HALEY, ALEX (1921–1992). One of the most successful **television** miniseries in the 1970s was *Roots*, which was based upon a book by **African American** author Alex Haley. The central figure in the program was Kunta Kinte, a young African who was captured by slave traders and forced into slavery in the United States. Kunta's treatment was harsh, and he came to realize that he was never to be free. The audience watched as Kunta married, had a family, lived through historic events in American history, and was freed after the Civil War. The program is still one of the highest rated in television history.

See also LITERATURE.

HAMLISCH, MARVIN FREDERICK (1944–2012). Composer of Broadway and **cinema music**, Marvin Hamlisch was born in New York City. His father was a musician and bandleader and greatly influenced his son. One of the youngest people to be admitted to the Juilliard School of Music, Hamlisch later graduated from Queens College (B.A., 1967). In the 1970s, while at a party, he learned of the upcoming film *The Swimmer* (1968), for which he was hired to compose the music. His success led to more compositions, including writing songs for Barbra Streisand. Perhaps Hamlisch's best-known work is Broadway's 1975 hit *A Chorus Line*. Hamlisch continued to compose music for films, winning Academy Awards for *The Sting* and *The Way We Were*. He passed away following a brief illness.

HAPPY DAYS. **Norman Lear**'s **television** program *Happy Days* began in 1974, appearing on the Columbia Broadcasting System (CBS). The episodes revolved around a family of four in the 1950s. The **music** was familiar as were the problems they faced each week. Of course, each episode ended happily. The program featured Ron Howard, who had been a child star on the popular *Andy Griffith Show*. Henry Winkler's character, Fonzie, was the highlight of *Happy Days*. When the program finished a 10-year run (1974–84), it opened the door for Howard to begin a successful career as a director. *Happy Days* introduced several actors who went on to star in their own Norman Lear programs. Two of these popular spin-offs were *Laverne and Shirley* and *Mork and Mindy*. Robin Williams, star of *Mork and Mindy*, became a major **cinematic** star. In 2011, the stars of *Happy Days* sued CBS over merchandising revenue and settled out of court the following year.

HARRIS, PATRICIA ROBERTS (1924–1985). Democrat. Patricia Harris worked as secretary of housing and urban development from 1977 to 1979 and as secretary of health and human services from 1979 to 1981. Born in Illinois, Harris's life was one of firsts. She was first in her graduating class from George Washington Law School (LL.B., 1960), and the first **African American woman** to serve as a U.S. ambassador; head a major U.S. corporation (IBM, 1971); and hold a cabinet position. She had had an interest in politics prior to getting her bachelor's degree from Harvard University. Her husband, William Harris, whom she married in 1955, encouraged her to get her degree in law. A defender of **civil rights**, she garnered the attention of President Lyndon B. Johnson, who appointed her as ambassador to Luxembourg (1965–67). Afterward, she taught for a time at Howard University before joining a private law practice.

President-elect **Jimmy Carter**, who wanted to see more minorities and women hold high positions in the federal government, named Harris as the secretary of housing and urban development (HUD). She had hoped to draw the president's attention to the plight of urban areas and was dismayed with what she regarded as his lack of interest. She also found that her priorities conflicted with those of **Health**, **Education**, and Welfare Secretary **Joseph Califano**, who wanted to direct some of HUD's housing subsidies toward reform of the country's welfare system. After Califano's forced resignation in mid-1979, Harris accepted Carter's request that she take over the HEW secretaryship. In her new post she failed to see any significant accomplishments. After Carter's defeat in the **1980 election**, Harris got a position teaching law at George Washington University. She passed away in March 1985 from cancer.

See also LANDRIEU, MOON (MAURICE EDWIN) (1930–).

HARVEY, PAUL (1918–2009). A radio personality for over 60 years, Paul Harvey Aurandt was born in Tulsa, Oklahoma. While in high school, one of his teachers recognized his speaking ability and urged a local radio station to hire Harvey. He dropped his last name upon starting his new job. Moving to Chicago, Harvey's audience grew. His program, *News and Comment*, debuted on American Broadcasting Company (ABC) News radio in 1951; in 1976 he began the famous "Rest of the Story" portion of his broadcast. He proved able to keep his listeners interested by leaving the answer to his program until the end. His political views were very conservative, but he shocked listeners when he told his radio audience that President **Richard Nixon** was wrong to invade Cambodia. Though ABC radio planned to keep *News and Comment* going after Harvey's death, the program was pulled from the air after only one week.

HEALTH. The 1970s witnessed a growing trend toward individualism and a desire to improve one's health. Americans began exercising more and eating healthier meals. Bicycling became increasingly popular, both as a form of training and to escape increasing gas prices. More Americans took up jogging; the development of waffle soles and air cushions made shoes lighter and gave them improved traction. Health food stores and restaurants grew in number, among them Whole Foods, which opened its first store in Texas in 1978. The invention of artificial sweeteners, starting with sucralose in 1975, allowed Americans to avoid overindulgence in sugar. A 1972 report by the U.S. surgeon general on the danger of smoking proved critical to the decline in smoking and cigarette sales during the decade. Commercial airlines established nonsmoking sections on their planes, though they had limited success in curtailing secondhand smoke from spreading throughout the cabin. Both President **Jimmy Carter** and officials within his administration joined the new emphasis on health. The president personified the popularity of jogging by himself running about 40 miles a week. **Joseph Califano**, himself a former smoker who became Carter's secretary of the Department of Health, **Education**, and Welfare, instituted an antismoking campaign.

These years also witnessed medical discoveries and advancements. Scientists identified Lyme disease in 1975 and determined in 1978 that it was spread by ticks. The year 1976 saw the discovery of both a form of pneumonia that became known as Legionnaires' disease and the far-deadlier Ebola virus, which is spread by human contact with the bodily fluid of live or dead animals. Reports in the **Union of Soviet Socialist Republics (USSR)** and United States that red dye number 2 caused cancer led Washington in 1976 to ban its use. The year 1977 witnessed construction of the first Medical Resonance Imaging, or MRI, machine, which uses a magnetic field to take detailed pictures of the human body's internal structure. In July 1978, Louise Joy Brown became the first "test tube baby" through a process referred to as in vitro fertilization. Two years later, French biochemist Étienne-Émile Baulieu invented RU-486; better known as the **"abortion** pill," RU-486 can induce an abortion in the early months of a woman's pregnancy. By that same year, scientists had found a connection between tampon use and toxic shock syndrome.

The interest in health and improvements in medical technology could not hide the sobering cost of medical care. By the time of Carter's inauguration, hospital costs were increasing annually by 15 to 16 percent. The president hoped to cut that number by 4 or 5 percent, but he could not overcome opposition from the health care industry and members of Congress. Carter also sought to institute a program of comprehensive national health insurance (NHI). This proposal brought him in conflict with Senator **Edward Kennedy** of Massachusetts; though both Carter and Kennedy favored NHI, the latter wanted such a program implemented immediately, whereas the former favored enacting it in a series of phases. To Kennedy's consternation, the White House by mid-1978 had decided that it was both politically and economically inexpedient to pursue a national health insurance initiative.

See also EIZENSTAT, STUART ELLIOTT (1943–); LITERATURE; MOYNIHAN, DANIEL PATRICK (1927–2003); SILKWOOD, KAREN (1946–1974); TALMADGE, HERMAN EUGENE (1913–2002).

HEARST, PATRICIA (1954–). Granddaughter of newspaper tycoon William Randolph Hearst, Patricia Hearst made headlines when she was kidnapped by members of the Symbionese Liberation Army (SLA), a Marxist group in California. The SLA demanded $400 million in ransom to give to the poor in California. Hearst's family met the kidnappers' demands, but the SLA refused to release her. Moreover, when the SLA held up several businesses, Hearst was photographed holding weapons to aid her kidnappers. After the leader of the SLA was killed, Hearst fled from her kidnappers. The Federal Bureau of Investigation (FBI) finally captured Hearst, and she was tried as a criminal. Her trial was a major story of the decade. In 1976 she was found guilty for taking part in SLA's armed robberies and sent to prison. After she had served 23 months, President **Jimmy Carter** commuted her sentence. Since her release, she has married, had two children, and periodically gives interviews on the SLA. In 2008, she made news again when her bulldog won an award at the Westminster Dog Show.

HELMS, JESSE ALEXANDER, JR. (1921–2008). Republican. One of the most conservative senators during his years in office (1973–2003), Jesse Helms was often called "Dr. No" by others in Congress. He was born in Monroe, North Carolina, and attended Wake Forest College, though he did not graduate. He served in the U.S. Navy from 1942 to 1945. After the war, he entered politics, working as an adviser to U.S. Senator Willis Smith. He then served on the city council for Raleigh, North Carolina, followed by 12 years as a vice president for Capital Broadcasting Company. Though a member of the **Democratic Party**, he denounced the Civil Rights Act of 1964 and welfare programs. In 1972, he switched his party affiliation to the Republican Party and ran for and won a seat in the U.S. Senate.

Helms and President **Jimmy Carter** repeatedly clashed. The senator was more conservative than Carter on **abortion** rights, opposed ratification of the **Panama Canal treaties** and the **Strategic Arms Limitation Treaty (SALT II)**, and fought to lift U.S. economic sanctions imposed against the apartheid government of **Rhodesia**. Helms's influence during these years and afterward grew. In 2003, he retired from the Senate as a result of ill health. He published a memoir in 2005 and passed away three years later from dementia.

HELSINKI ACCORDS. On 1 August 1975, 35 nations, including the United States and every European country (minus Albania and Andorra), sent representatives to Helsinki, Finland, for the Conference on Security and Cooperation in Europe. The final act of the conference was the Helsinki Accords. Regarded as an important step in the improvement of relations between the West and the Soviet bloc, the document called upon the signatories to forego the use of force, resolve disputes between themselves peacefully, respect one another's internal affairs, and uphold **human rights**. A follow-up meeting was held in Belgrade in 1978.

See also FOREIGN POLICY.

HENSON, JIM (1936–1990). James Maury Henson was born in Greenville, Mississippi. He graduated from the University of Maryland (B.A., 1960). His interest in commercial **art** led to his work on a **television** program in Washington, D.C. The program, *Sam and Friends* (1955–61), became very popular; it offered a way for Henson to introduce some of his popular puppets and characters on other programs, and finally to his work on *Sesame Street*. *The Muppet Show* (1976–81) was an extremely popular television program, which featured Miss Piggy and Kermit the Frog, as well as well-known guests. After becoming ill in 1990, Jim Henson died in New York City. His imaginative creations continue to delight all ages.

HISPANIC AMERICANS. By the time of **Jimmy Carter**'s election, Hispanic Americans were poised to become the largest racial or ethnic minority in the country. As was the case with **African Americans** and **women**, Carter took notice of the status of Latinos in the United States. That he spoke Spanish added to his interest in Latin America and in those who traced their lineage to that part of the world. He named about 200 Hispanic Americans to his administration, including Secretary of the Navy Edward Hidalgo. Among his appointees to federal judgeships was Reynaldo Garza, who in 1979 joined the U.S. Court of Appeals, Fifth District. Additionally, he sought to strengthen bilingual **education** programs.

A key issue with which Carter had to contend, and which administrations since have tried to solve, was illegal immigration, a topic of intense interest to the Hispanic population in the United States. The president faced competing interests here. **Labor** unions wanted to restrict illegal immigration, believing that doing so would open more jobs in the United States and reduce unemployment. Agricultural firms, particularly those in the Southwest, contended that because of a lack of domestic workers, they had to rely on immigrants, including illegal ones, to conduct their business. Carter tried to find a middle ground. In August 1977, he proposed granting amnesty to aliens who had been in the United States for at least seven years while strengthening the enforcement of immigrations laws. Many in Congress charged him with making illegal activity legal, while Carter's aides warned that tougher enforcement would cost him Latino votes.

By the time Carter left office, the problem of illegal immigration had not been resolved. In the **1980 election**, a majority of Hispanics (56 percent) voted for Carter, though by a significantly smaller margin than in the **1976 election** (82 percent).

See also CHAVEZ, CESAR ESTRADA (1927–1993); KRAFT, TIMOTHY E. (1941–).

HOCKEY. While hockey has not had the same following as **football, baseball**, or **basketball** in the United States, it took center stage at the 1980 Winter **Olympics**. There, the U.S. hockey team not only reached the medal round but defeated the favored squad from the **Union of Soviet Socialist Republics (USSR)**. With U.S.-Soviet relations deteriorating as a result of Moscow's invasion of **Afghanistan** the previous year, the "Miracle on Ice," as it became known, was seen by Americans not just as a major accomplishment in **sport** but as a symbolic victory over communism. The U.S. team would then go on to defeat the Finnish squad and capture the gold medal.

HOFFA, JAMES "JIMMY" (1913–1975). Republican. Declared legally dead in 1983, **labor** leader Jimmy Hoffa was born in Brazil, Indiana. Living in Detroit, he quit school at the age of 15 to work in a department store. In the 1930s he was a member of the Teamsters Union, of which he became president in 1957. Hoffa was investigated by the government and in 1964 was convicted on charges of racketeering, jury tampering, and labor union corruption. In 1967 he was sent to a federal penitentiary but was pardoned by President **Richard Nixon**. He disappeared in 1975.

HORN OF AFRICA. A strategically located region of Africa that borders the Red and Arabian Seas, as well as the Indian Ocean, the Horn of Africa today includes the nations of Ethiopia, Somalia, Eritrea, and Djibouti. This region is just across from the oil-rich Arabian Peninsula. In 1977, Somalia and Ethiopia engaged in the Ogaden War, a one-year conflict that erupted over a border dispute. The war was significant for both the **Union of Soviet Socialist Republics (USSR)** and the United States. The USSR was an ally of both countries and tried to mediate an end to the conflict. When that failed, Moscow abandoned Somalia in favor of aiding Ethiopia. That aid included weaponry, advisers, and about 15,000 troops from **Cuba**. With that help, Ethiopia was able to force a Somali retreat, and the war ended in March 1978.

Soviet and Cuban involvement in the Ogaden conflict caused a debate within the **Jimmy Carter** administration. Carter had hoped to revive **détente** with the USSR and was not sure how to react to USSR-Cuban aid to Ethiopia. Secretary of State **Cyrus Vance** preferred to view the situation in the Horn as a regional matter unrelated to U.S.-Soviet relations. National Security Adviser **Zbigniew Brzezinski**, however, saw Soviet and Cuban involvement in the Horn as evidence of Moscow's untrustworthiness and called for linking the Kremlin's activities to other issues, such as U.S. willingness to sign the **Strategic Arms Limitation Treaty (SALT II)**. Though not prepared to give up on détente, Carter leaned in favor of Brzezinski and began to make statements suggestive of his own frustration with the USSR. The United States even considered offering military aid to Somalia, but Somalia's refusal to give up its designs on the Ogaden convinced the Carter administration to forego such assistance. Meanwhile, the president decided not to move forward with his original plan of trying to normalize relations with Cuba.

The United States developed a closer relationship with Somalia as the decade came to an end. The fall of the shah of **Iran, Mohammed Reza Pahlavi**, in early 1979 meant the loss of a key U.S. ally in the Middle East, and the Soviet invasion of **Afghanistan** late that year was taken by Washington as clear evidence that Moscow could not be trusted. Therefore, in 1980, the Carter administration signed an agreement with Somalia by which it would supply arms to that country in return for the right to use Somali military bases.

See also FOREIGN POLICY.

HUFSTEDLER, SHIRLEY MOUNT (1925–). Democrat. The secretary of **education** from 1979 to 1981, Shirley Hufstedler was born in Denver, Colorado. Getting her undergraduate degree from the University of New Mexico (B.B.A., 1945) in two and half years, she earned a law degree at Stanford University (LL.B., 1949), becoming the first **woman** elected to the *Stanford*

Law Review. Hufstedler then practiced law before California governor Edmund Brown appointed her to the Los Angeles Superior Court. In 1968 President Lyndon B. Johnson named her to the U.S. Ninth Court of Appeals.

In 1979 President **Jimmy Carter** selected Hufstedler as secretary of the new Department of Education. Carter chose her in part because she had no background in education, believing she could bring new insights to the field. Appointed in November 1979, she had only six months to get the department operating by its mandated date of 4 May 1980. She foresaw a proactive department, one that would promote bilingual education and seek to apply successful local educational models throughout the country. After Carter lost the **1980 election**, she returned to practicing law and is presently a member of a law firm in Los Angeles.

HUMAN RIGHTS. Though it had long dubbed itself a champion of freedom and basic rights, the United States has been criticized for being anything but. During the 1950s, U.S. officials found themselves on the defensive when they accused the **Union of Soviet Socialist Republics (USSR)** of violating the rights of Soviet nationals, only to have Moscow point to treatment within the United States of **African Americans**. America's record on human rights became even more central in the early 1970s, when Congress began to criticize the executive branch for giving aid to nations known for having repressive governments. Evidence that former presidents, including John F. Kennedy and **Richard Nixon**, had ordered the leaders of foreign nations thrown out of power or killed added to the uproar regarding America's apparent lack of morality.

Jimmy Carter ran on a platform promising to restore America's moral stance in the world by making human rights a top priority of his **foreign policy**. In his inaugural address, he referred to his human rights initiative as "absolute," giving the impression that both friends and enemies of the United States could expect public denunciation and even economic or military sanctions if they violated the rights of their people. Furthermore, he appointed **Patricia Derian**, an outspoken supporter of human rights, as head of the State Department's Bureau of Human Rights and Humanitarian Affairs (HA).

Within two weeks of the inauguration, however, the Carter administration began to backtrack on the grounds that despite their repressive governments, nations such as **South Korea**, **Iran**, and the **Philippines** deserved U.S. economic and military aid, for they were strategically important to the United States. Infighting among bureaucratic departments further watered down the human rights initiative and HA's influence. The White House also became the target of critics at home and abroad. Conservatives charged Carter with focusing his attacks largely on friendly, anticommunist governments. Liberals disliked the fact that he offered military aid to repressive right-wing governments. European allies, among them **West Germany**, charged Carter with preachiness and endangering **détente** with the USSR.

As tensions with the Kremlin increased, human rights were pushed even more into the background in favor of developing and maintaining close ties with noncommunist countries. By 1980, the human rights initiative had become a shell of its original self. Even so, Carter has been praised for symbolically restoring America's moral position in the world, and some political prisoners have credited his human rights initiative for their release.

See also DEFENSE; GISCARD D'ESTAING, VALERY (1926–); GREAT BRITAIN, RELATIONS WITH; HELSINKI ACCORDS; JACKSON, HENRY MARTIN "SCOOP" (1912–1983); JONES, JAMES WARREN "JIM" (1931–1978); KISSINGER, HENRY ALFRED (ALFRED HEINZ) (1923–); MARCOS, FERDINAND (EMMANUEL EDRALIN) (1917–1989); NEUTRON BOMB; PASTOR, ROBERT A. (1947–); POL POT (1928–1998); RELIGION; RICKOVER, HYMAN GEORGE (1900–1986); SMITH, IAN (1919–2007); SOMOZA DEBAYLE, ANASTASIO (1925–1980); TALMADGE, HERMAN EUGENE (1913–2002); THURMOND, (JAMES) STROM (1902–2003); WOMEN; YOUNG, ANDREW JACKSON, JR. (1932–).

HUMPHREY, HUBERT HORATIO (1911–1978). Democrat. Hubert Humphrey served as a U.S. senator from 1949 to 1964 and as vice president of the United States from 1964 to 1969, and ran as the Democratic candidate for the presidency in 1968. Born in South Dakota, Humphrey graduated from the University of Minnesota (B.A., 1939) and Louisiana State University (M.A., 1940). He taught at Louisiana State University and the University of Minnesota before deciding to enter politics. In 1945 he was elected mayor of Minneapolis after narrowly losing the mayoral race two years earlier. He quickly became one of the rising stars of the Democratic Party. In 1948 he was elected to the United States Senate where he championed tax reform, **civil rights**, and pro-**labor** legislation. He also formed a close relationship with then-Senator Lyndon B. Johnson. After trying unsuccessfully to gain the Democratic nomination for president in 1956, he ran for president in 1960 but lost after a bitter primary struggle to the more organized and younger John F. Kennedy. In 1964, Johnson, now president, selected Humphrey as his running mate.

Humphrey had a difficult vice presidency. His relationship with Johnson was not good. He publicly supported the U.S. war effort in Vietnam, though privately he believed it was a lost cause. In 1968, he won a hard-fought campaign for the Democratic nomination for the presidency but lost in the general election to **Richard Nixon**.

Humphrey ran again for the party's nomination in 1972 but failed to get its endorsement. In 1976, liberal Democrats hoped he would run against **Jimmy Carter** and seek the party's nomination, but he decided against doing so. Despite their divergent political views, Humphrey and President Carter got along well, with the senator helping the White House on a number of pieces of legislation. Suffering from cancer, Humphrey passed away in Minnesota in January 1978.

See also MEANY, GEORGE (1894–1980); MONDALE, WALTER FREDERICK (FRITZ) (1928–); MUSKIE, EDMUND SIXTUS (1914–1996).

HUSSEIN I (HUSSEIN IBN TALAN IBAN HUSSEIN) (1935–1999). Hussein I was the king of Jordan from 1953 to 1999. Born in Amman, Hussein's father had to abdicate the throne when Hussein was only 15 years old. As the younger Hussein was not of age to rule, several regents actually ran the nation until he reached age 18. In 1967, Hussein ordered his military to join **Egypt** and **Syria** in the Six Day War against **Israel**, losing both East Jerusalem and the West Bank. Seeking to retrieve that territory, he helped prepare United Nations Resolution 242, which called for Israel to return the territories it had seized. When Egypt and Syria attacked Israel again in 1973, Hussein, not wanting to suffer another defeat, offered his Arab allies limited support.

President **Jimmy Carter** hoped to enlist Hussein in his effort to achieve a comprehensive Middle East peace settlement. Carter had reason to believe he would get the Jordanian monarch's cooperation, for Hussein had been educated in the West, understood Western culture, and realized Israel had significant support in the United States and Europe. Yet Hussein was also the leader of an Arab nation that had lost territory to Israel. Hussein, therefore, refused to negotiate with Israel or to endorse the **Camp David Accords** until Israel complied with Resolution 242. This remained his position through the remainder of Carter's term in office. Even so, he remained highly popular in the United States, in part because of his marriage to an American, Lisa Halaby (Queen Noor), in 1978.

During the 1990s, Hussein demonstrated a moderation of his position. While at first he publicly defended Iraq's invasion of Kuwait in 1990, in 1992, he declared that Iraqi leader **Saddam Hussein** should step aside and allow democracy to take hold. Two years later, he signed a peace treaty with Israel. Four years later, the world learned that he was suffering from non-Hodgkin's lymphoma. He passed away in February 1999.

See also FOREIGN POLICY.

HUSSEIN, SADDAM (1937–2006). The president of Iraq from 1979 to 2003, Saddam Hussein was born in Al-Awja, Iraq. He joined the Ba'ath Party and became its secretary. In 1968, he partook in a coup that overthrew the Iraqi government and became deputy to the new president, Ahmad Hassan al-Bakr. With the help of money from oil exports, Hussein modernized Iraq's **economy** and developed a powerful security force. By the end of 1976, he had become a general in the Iraqi military, and, with al-Bakr in failing health, the de facto leader of Iraq.

In 1979, Hussein officially became Iraq's president. That same year, the Ayatollah **Ruhollah Khomeini** assumed the leadership of **Iran**. Hussein distrusted Khomeini: the ayatollah had lived in exile in Iraq for several years, during which he demanded Hussein's ouster. In 1980, therefore, Hussein ordered an invasion of Iran, precipitating the eight-year war between the two countries. Although the United States supported Hussein during the **Iran-Iraq War**, relations between the two countries quickly deteriorated after Iraq's invasion of Kuwait in 1990. This convinced U.S. officials that Hussein posed a serious threat to the oil-rich Middle East, which led to the Persian Gulf War of 1990–91. For several reasons, including reports that Hussein was developing weapons of mass destruction and violating the rights of his people, a largely U.S. military force invaded Iraq in March 2003 and overthrew the Iraqi leader. American troops captured Hussein later that year and turned him over to the new Iraqi government, which put him on trial for crimes against humanity. He was found guilty in 2006 and executed later that year.

See also FOREIGN POLICY.

I

INDOCHINESE IMMIGRANTS. North Vietnam's attack upon, and eventual conquest of, South Vietnam in 1975 convinced tens of thousands of Vietnamese to flee their homeland to escape possible persecution (or worse) by the North's communist leadership. Four years later, **China** attacked Vietnam, prompting thousands of ethnic Chinese who had lived in Vietnam to leave as well. Thailand, which accepted at least 150,000 of these refugees during 1979, announced it could not receive any more, and China insisted it was doing all it could. To address this humanitarian crisis, President **Jimmy Carter** admitted many of these refugees into the United States; by July 1979, 17,000 refugees per month were arriving on U.S. soil. With the nation already facing rising unemployment, many Americans criticized Carter for allowing so many immigrants into the country.

See also CUBA, RELATIONS WITH.

INFLATION. *See* ECONOMY; STAGFLATION.

INFOMERCIALS. Generally referring to commercials at least five minutes long, the first infomercial appeared in the 1970s on a San Diego TV station, XETV, which each Sunday devoted an hour to infomercials for homes available for purchase. Infomercials have since proliferated and appear regularly on **television**.

See also ADVERTISEMENTS.

IRAN, RELATIONS WITH. The United States had had a close relationship with Iran and its leader, Shah **Mohammed Reza Pahlavi**, for a generation prior to **Jimmy Carter**'s election. U.S. oil companies had interests in Iran. Tehran was one of the largest purchasers of American military hardware, and the **Central Intelligence Agency (CIA)** helped Pahlavi train a secret police called the National Information and Security Organization (SAVAK). Yet the shah's hold on power had begun to show signs of cracking. His willingness to permit the secularization of Iranian society had upset Islamic fundamentalists, his economic programs and corruption among Iran's elite had left many Iranians disenfranchised, and his repressive policies had upset many sections of the population. A growing number of Iranians thus rallied around an Islamic cleric, Ayatollah **Ruhollah Khomeini**, who was then living in exile.

By the time Carter came into office, the shah had made some political reforms, including greater freedom of the press, in an effort to meet criticism within and outside Iran for violating the human rights of his people. Though Carter himself had made **human rights** a key component of both his campaign promises and, following his election, his **foreign policy**, the new president was prepared to make exceptions to the rule. One was Iran, which was seen as vital to American economic and strategic interests in the Middle East. Consequently, Carter refused to publicly criticize the shah for continuing human rights violations. Moreover, during Carter's tenure, about one-third of American foreign arms sales went to Iran, despite the president's call to curb the sale of conventional weaponry. The unwillingness of the U.S. government to pressure the shah to institute further reforms, combined with the ability of Iranians to speak more freely than in the past, served to keep alive the fires of anger against Pahlavi and to generate criticism of Carter.

In December 1977, Carter visited Iran and praised the shah, which only added to the anger and frustration in Iran. During 1978, the unrest in Iran grew, with protests taking place in a number of cities. The shah responded with a combination of reforms and force. To Iranians, the reforms were too little, too late, while the use of force was to them further proof that the shah had every intention of staying in power. In the fall, U.S. ambassador to Iran, **William Sullivan**, who throughout had claimed Pahlavi had a firm hold on power, now reported that the shah's position was precarious. The White House began to give contradictory advice to the shah, declaring that it stood behind him while rejecting proposals for a military crackdown. Not certain where he stood, in December the shah appointed Shahpour Bakhtiar as prime minister. Bakhtiar insisted the shah leave Iran, which Pahlavi did in January 1979. Shortly thereafter, Khomeini returned to Iran. Bakhtiar realized Khomeini did not like him, and Iran's armed forces declared themselves unwilling to stop Khomeini from consolidating his power. Bakhtiar therefore resigned, and Khomeini established a new government.

In the meantime, the shah moved from country to country, eventually winding up in the United States to receive treatment for cancer. Carter refused Tehran's demands that the shah be sent home to face trial. Frustrated with the U.S. president, in November 1979 a group of Iranian militants stormed the U.S. embassy in Tehran, precipitating the **Iran hostage crisis**. That crisis, which would continue through the remainder of Carter's presidency, played a key part in the U.S. president's failure to win reelection.

See also AARON, DAVID LAURENCE (1938–); BYRD, ROBERT CARLYLE (1917–2010); DEFENSE; DONOVAN, HEDLEY WILLIAMS (1914–1990); ECONOMY; ENERGY CRISIS; HORN OF AFRICA; HUSSEIN, SADDAM (1937–2006); JAVITS, JACOB KOPPEL (1904–1986); KISSINGER, HENRY ALFRED (ALFRED HEINZ) (1923–); LAINGEN, (LOWELL) BRUCE (1922–); NIXON, RICHARD MILHOUS (1913–1994); ORGANIZATION OF PETROLEUM EXPORTING COUNTRIES (OPEC); PRECHT, HENRY (1932–); ROCKEFELLER, DAVID (1915–); SICK, GARY GORDON (1935–); TURNER, STANSFIELD (1923–); VANCE, CYRUS ROBERT (1917–2002).

IRAN HOSTAGE CRISIS. On 4 November 1979, a group of about 150 student militants who called themselves the Muslim Students Following the Line of Imam, seized the U.S. embassy in Tehran, **Iran**, and took 63 Americans hostage. These students based their action upon long-standing U.S. support for the shah of Iran, **Mohammed Reza Pahlavi**. Under his rule, Iran had witnessed economic troubles, political repression, and the admission of Western culture, all of which had served to upset both secular and religious elements. In the face of widespread, violent protests to his rule, Pahlavi fled in January 1979. After bouncing from one country to another, Pahlavi in October 1979 received permission from President **Jimmy Carter** to come to the United States so he could receive cancer treatment. Iranians demanded that Carter return the shah to be put on trial, but the American president refused. Infuriated, the students struck. Ayatollah **Ruhollah Khomeini**, who had assumed control following the shah's departure, did not encourage the takeover of the embassy, but he quickly endorsed the students' action.

At first, Americans rallied around Carter. But the continuation of the crisis bred frustration and saw his approval rating decline. The decision of the hostage takers to release about a dozen of their captives did not help him, and a mission in April 1980 by the U.S. military to rescue the remaining Americans failed, which only increased his discomfiture. The hostage crisis ultimately proved one reason for Carter's failure to win the **1980 election**. Not until 20 January 1981, after holding them in captivity for 444 days, did the Iranians release the hostages.

See also BROWN, HAROLD (1927–); BRZEZINSKI, ZBIGNIEW KAZIMIERZ (1928–); CHRISTOPHER, WARREN MINOR (1925–2011); CIVILETTI, BENJAMIN RICHARD (1935–); CUTLER, LLOYD NORTON (1917–2005); FOREIGN POLICY; JORDAN, HAMILTON (1944–2008); KENNEDY, EDWARD MOORE "TED" (1932–2009); KISSINGER, HENRY ALFRED (ALFRED HEINZ) (1923–); MILLER, G. (GEORGE) WILLIAM (1925–2006); PRECHT, HENRY (1932–); TURNER, STANSFIELD (1923–).

IRAN-IRAQ WAR. An eight-year conflict that began in 1980, the **Iran**-Iraq War was the result of economic, political, religious, and personality disputes involving these two Arab countries. One dispute was over control of the Shatt al-Arab waterway, an important shipping route into the Persian Gulf. Another was the growing military might of Iran, which Iraq saw as a challenge to its predominance in the region. **Religion** also divided the two nations, for, whereas Iraqi president **Saddam Hussein** and the members of his Ba'ath Party were Sunni Muslims, Iran had a predominantly Shi'ite population. A final factor was the Ayatollah **Ruhollah Khomeini**'s accession to power in Iran. Khomeini had spent several years in the 1970s living in exile in Iraq, during which time he had demanded Hussein's ouster. Now leader of Iran, Khomeini renewed his call. With Iran posing more than ever a threat to him and his nation, Hussein ordered an attack on Iran. It appears the war played a role in the decision of the Iranian government to end the **Iran hostage crisis**. When the war ended, anywhere from 800,000 to 1.3 million civilians and soldiers had been killed or wounded.

See also FOREIGN POLICY.

ISRAEL, RELATIONS WITH. The United States had been Israel's closest ally since the founding of the Jewish state in 1948. Between 1948 and 1973, Israel fought four wars with its Arab neighbors. Of particular importance was the Six Day War of 1967, during which Israel captured the Golan Heights from **Syria**, the West Bank and East Jerusalem from **Jordan**, and the Gaza Strip and Sinai Peninsula from **Egypt**. Later that year, the United Nations passed Resolution 242, calling upon Israel to return what became known as the "occupied territories."

As a presidential candidate, **Jimmy Carter** had taken an ambivalent stand with regard to Israel. He called upon that nation to return most of the land it had taken in 1967 and asserted that Israel needed, as he put it, "defensible borders." Additionally, he criticized the **Palestine Liberation Organization (PLO)**, an organization formed in 1964 and which had begun a campaign of violence to destroy the Jewish state. Upon becoming president, however, Carter determined to achieve a comprehensive Middle East peace settlement, including finding a home for Palestinians who had become refugees because of the earlier wars Israel had fought with its neighbors. Carter's preparedness to consider a peace agreement, which could require Israel to give up the occupied territories and provide the Palestinians with a state of their own, infuriated Israel and its allies within the United States.

The election in May 1977 of Israel's new prime minister, **Menachem Begin**, increased Carter's uncertainty of achieving a peace settlement, as Begin was known to oppose relinquishing any of the occupied territories. Without America's knowledge, Egyptian president **Anwar Sadat** had been holding secret talks with Israeli officials. Not long after taking power, Begin invited Sadat to Israel; that one of Israel's former enemies would come for a visit became a major news story. Begin offered to withdraw Israeli forces from the Sinai Peninsula but rejected Sadat's request to give the Palestinians living in the West Bank autonomy. With the Egyptians and Israelis seemingly unable to come to terms, Carter invited Begin and Sadat to Camp David. During a tense 13 days of meetings, the three leaders and their aides hammered out the **Camp David Accords**. There was still much to be worked out, including formalizing a peace treaty between Egypt and Israel. Following further discussions, Sadat and Begin signed that peace agreement in March 1979; the following year, the two nations exchanged ambassadors, and Israel withdrew its forces from the Sinai Peninsula.

These indications of harmony in U.S.-Israeli relations, however, were deceiving. The president himself found Begin far harder to work with than Sadat. News in 1979 that U.S. ambassador to the United Nations **Andrew Young** had had an unauthorized meeting with a PLO representative infuriated Israel and American Jews. In 1980, the failure of the White House to remove from a UN resolution language calling upon Israel to withdraw from Jerusalem caused additional outrage and cost the president in **Democratic Party** primaries held in Connecticut and New York. By the time of the **1980 election**, U.S.-Israeli relations, which had been tense throughout Carter's term in office, were even more so.

See also ENTEBBE AIR RAID; FOREIGN POLICY; HUSSEIN I (HUSSEIN IBN TALAN IBAN HUSSEIN) (1935–1999); JACKSON, HENRY MARTIN "SCOOP" (1912–1983); JAVITS, JACOB KOPPEL (1904–1986); KLUTZNICK, PHILIP MORRIS (1907–1999); LINOWITZ, SOL MYRON (1913–2005); ORGANIZATION OF PETROLEUM EXPORTING COUNTRIES (OPEC); STRAUSS, ROBERT SCHWARTZ (1918–).

J

JACKSON FIVE. *See* JACKSON, MICHAEL (1958–2009).

JACKSON, HENRY MARTIN "SCOOP" (1912–1983). Democrat. A member of the House of Representatives from 1941 to 1953 and then U.S. senator from 1953 to 1983, Henry Jackson was born in Everett, Washington. He received a bachelor's and law degree from the University of Washington, worked as an attorney, and then, in 1940, won election to the U.S. House of Representatives. He quickly demonstrated an interest in the power of the atom, both for weaponry and for peaceful purposes, and, following a visit to a Nazi concentration camp, became a staunch defender of **Israel** and an equally strong opponent of totalitarianism. As such, he came to see the **Union of Soviet Socialist Republics (USSR)** as posing a serious threat to the United States, one that necessitated the maintenance by America of a powerful nuclear arsenal.

Elected to the Senate in 1952, Jackson developed a reputation as an expert on national security. He tended to side with conservatives on matters related to containing Soviet-inspired communism; hence, he supported U.S. involvement in Vietnam, opposed **détente** with the USSR, and refused to sign the **Strategic Arms Limitation Treaty** (SALT I) of 1972 until an amendment was added guaranteeing that the United States would acquire an equal number of land-based missiles as the Soviets. On social policy, however, he was more liberal, endorsing **civil rights** legislation during the 1960s. He ran for the Democratic Party's nomination for the presidency in both the 1972 and the **1976 election**, but did not come close either time to getting it.

Jackson's mix of liberal and conservative leanings set him apart from President **Jimmy Carter**. The result was constant clashes between the two. Jackson disliked the impact Carter's fiscal conservatism had upon social programs. He criticized the president for inconsistently applying the administration's **human rights** policy against other nations. Most important, he believed the White House did not give enough attention to national **defense**. On this score, he charged that the SALT II agreement placed overly stringent limits on U.S. missiles and gave the Soviet Union an unnecessary advantage in the number of land-based missiles with multiple warheads. Although Carter told the Senate to shelve consideration of SALT II following the Soviet invasion of **Afghanistan**, Jackson's reputation on Capitol Hill as an expert on national security had severely lessened the likelihood of the treaty's ratification.

In the **1980 election**, the **Republican Party** both won the presidency and gained a majority in the Senate. Additionally, while many Republicans accepted Jackson's views on national defense, they rejected his liberal position insofar as social programs. Taken together, Jackson's influence on Capitol Hill began to wane. In 1983, he passed away from a heart attack.

See also FOLEY, THOMAS STEPHEN (1929–); MEANY, GEORGE (1894–1980); NUNN, SAM (SAMUEL AUGUSTUS) (1938–); STENNIS, JOHN CORNELIUS (1901–1995).

JACKSON, JESSE LOUIS (1941–). A **civil rights** leader and founder of Operation PUSH (People United to Save Humanity), Jesse Jackson was born in Greenville, South Carolina. He received his bachelor's degree in 1964 from North Carolina Agricultural and Technical College (North Carolina A& T). This was the same school that had become famous in 1960 when four of its students launched the sit-in movement, the purpose of which was to break down segregation in the South. It was while he was at A&T that Jackson himself became involved in the civil rights movement. He took part in numerous protests and became one of Martin Luther King Jr.'s top aides. Alongside **Andrew Young**, Jackson was with King when King was shot and killed in Memphis. In 1970, Jackson received ordination as a Baptist minister and shortly thereafter founded PUSH, which sought to promote the employment of minorities. Five years later, he established PUSH Excel, designed to encourage teachers, clergy, and families to cooperate in promoting the **education** of minorities. By this time, Jackson had become one of the top leaders of the civil rights movement, and so his decision to endorse **Jimmy Carter**'s nomination in the **1976 election** was important for Carter to receive a large number of **African American** votes.

After Carter's defeat in the **1980 election**, Jackson continued to play a leading role in both American politics and the civil rights movement. In 1984, he founded the National Rainbow Coalition, which sought to provide all Americans with equal rights. That same year, and again in 1988, he campaigned for the **Democratic Party**'s nomination for the presidency; he did quite well, particularly among African Americans, but did not receive the nomination either time. He endorsed Bill Clinton's bid for the presidency in 1992. In 2000, Clinton awarded Jackson the Presidential Medal of Freedom. Yet Jackson had also been a lightning rod for controversy. He did not make clear the sources of what critics charged was his lavish income. During the 1988 campaign, he referred to Jews as "Hymies." In 2001, Jackson, who had been married since 1962 and had five children, admitted to an affair with a staffer, who had borne him a child. He called the 2004 presidential election results in Ohio "rigged." While he endorsed Illinois senator Barack Obama's bid for the Democratic nomination in the 2008 presidential campaign, he also charged Obama, who is of mixed-race ancestry, of "acting like he's white." Despite the controversies surrounding him, Jackson remains to the present one of the highest-profile civil rights leaders in the nation.

JACKSON, MAYNARD HOLBROOK, JR. (1938–2003). A **Democrat** and mayor of Atlanta, Georgia, from 1974 to 1982 and again from 1990 to 1994, Maynard Jackson was a native of Dallas, Texas. His family moved when he was a child to Atlanta, where his father became a minister in a local Baptist church. Highly intelligent, Jackson went to Morehouse College when he was only 14 years old, graduating in 1956. He worked for a time in Ohio before getting a law degree at the University of North Carolina in 1964. Jackson then headed back to Atlanta, where he became involved in politics. He challenged incumbent **Herman Talmadge** for the Democratic Party's nomination for U.S. Senate in 1968. Though he lost by a wide margin, Jackson got enough votes to convince him he could succeed in the world of Georgia politics. Therefore, in 1969 he ran for and won the post of vice mayor of Atlanta, defeating the white incumbent. Four years later, he ran against the white mayor of Atlanta and won again. In so doing, he became, alongside Tom Bradley of Los Angeles and **Coleman Young** of Detroit, one of three **African Americans** overseeing some of America's largest cities. As mayor, Jackson saw to it that black contractors were involved in city construction projects, oversaw development of Atlanta's rapid-transit system, and helped make the city a business and transportation hub.

Jackson was slow in supporting **Jimmy Carter**'s bid for the presidency, despite Carter's effort as governor to improve race relations. It was not until April 1976 that he publicly endorsed Carter's candidacy and went on the campaign trail stumping for him. Jackson was close to Carter's United Nations ambassador, **Andrew Young**, and **Vernon Jordan**, the head of the National Urban League and one of Carter's friends. Yet Jackson himself never developed the same type of relationship with the president as had Young and Jordan.

Unable to serve for more than two consecutive terms as mayor, the popular Jackson chose Young to run as his replacement. Young won and served until 1989, when Jackson once again became mayor. Though Jackson, alongside Young, helped bring the 1996 Summer **Olympics** to Atlanta, he no longer showed the same desire to lead the city as he had previously. This could be attributed in part to health problems that required heart surgery in 1992.

Deciding not to run for reelection, Jackson continued to work for the Democratic Party and unsuccessfully sought in 2001 the chairmanship of the party's national committee. He passed away two years later from a heart attack.

JACKSON, MICHAEL (1958–2009). Born in Gary, Indiana, Michael Jackson was the youngest of the Jackson Five, an **African American** group of singers made up of Michael and his four older brothers. From the beginning, Michael was the star of the group. In 1968 the Jackson Five was signed by Motown Records and had a series of hit records, including "ABC," "I'll Be There," and "I Want You Back." During the 1970s Michael Jackson began his solo performances, and in 1982 he released *Thriller*, which holds the record for most albums sold. Jackson broke the color barrier on **Music Television** (MTV) with his incredible dancing and music, which was different from any video seen before on that channel, and influenced future videos.

Jackson never had a real childhood since he was quite young when he began with the Jackson Five. His father was abusive, and Jackson never overcame the abuse. As his popularity increased, his behavior became more erratic and strange. He was accused of preying on young boys, which led to a highly publicized trial. He had many surgeries to change his skin color. Jackson died at the age of 50, only days before he was to begin a tour to recoup some of his financial losses as well as to restore his image. He was often referred to as the "King of Pop."

See also STUDIO 54.

JAPAN, RELATIONS WITH. Upon becoming president of the United States, **Jimmy Carter** sought to redirect U.S. **foreign policy** away from focusing upon the **Union of Soviet Socialist Republics (USSR)** and instead toward giving more attention to other countries, among them Japan. Carter understood that by the mid-1970s, Japan had become a major player in the world, particularly because of its economic might, which posed a challenge to U.S. economic predominance. Japan also was turning increasingly to the use of nuclear power for **energy**, which the president regarded as a threat to his effort to stop the proliferation of atomic technology.

Throughout his term in office, Carter's relationship with Japan was oftentimes marked by tension. He opposed Japan's effort to start operating a nuclear reprocessing plant at Tokai Mura, for the plant would produce plutonium, which could be used in weapons development. To function, Tokai Mura required uranium; Japan had no domestic source of uranium and therefore had turned to the United States. Furthermore, under an agreement with Washington, Tokyo could not reprocess uranium without U.S. approval. Not until September 1978 did the two countries work out their differences so that the plant could begin operations.

Japan was also bothered by Carter's proposal to withdraw U.S. troops from **South Korea**. To Tokyo, the presence of American forces in South Korea was important for Japan's **defense**. The Japanese government was relieved when, in early 1979, Carter decided against removing those soldiers.

Possibly the most pressing matter in U.S.-Japanese relations during the Carter years was the **economy**. With **inflation** and unemployment both high in the United States, Carter wanted other countries, including Japan, to stimulate their economies, accept more American imports, and curb their use of petroleum. In December 1977, Japanese prime minister Takeo Fukuda agreed to import more products, but he blamed much of the trade imbalance between his country and the United States on Americans' demands for foreign goods. In the middle of the following year, the Japanese announced further steps to increase imports. At a summit held in Tokyo in June 1979, Japan's new prime minister, Masayoshi Ohira, promised to restrict Japan's oil imports, but the limit he accepted was still higher than the year before. The ever-growing use of petroleum by industrialized nations, combined with the revolution in oil-rich **Iran**, meant gas prices and, in turn, inflation continued to go up in the United States.

In 1980, Masayoshi's government fell following a no-confidence vote, and his successor, Zenko Suzuki, promised to curb American imports. Suzuki also proved uncooperative on military affairs. Following the USSR's invasion of **Afghanistan**, Carter asked his allies, including Japan, to increase defense spending. Suzuki refused, declaring it would require him to cut appropriations for social programs on which his people relied. By the time Carter left office, the United States and Japan had been unable to find common ground on their trade or military relations.

See also KLUTZNICK, PHILIP MORRIS (1907–1999); KREPS, JUANITA MORRIS (1921–2010); LABOR; McDONALD, AL (ALONZO LOWRY) (1928–); MONDALE, WALTER FREDERICK (FRITZ) (1928–); STRAUSS, ROBERT SCHWARTZ (1918–).

JAVITS, JACOB KOPPEL (1904–1986). A **Republican** U.S. senator from 1957 to 1981, Jacob Javits's voting record was more in line with that of the **Democratic Party**. During his years in the Upper House, he was the only Jewish senator. A ranking member of the Foreign Relations Committee and a supporter of **Israel**, Javits was acutely aware of anti-Semitism.

The son of Jewish immigrants, Javits was born in New York City. He worked during the day and attended classes at night at Columbia University. In 1926 he obtained his law degree from New York University, after which he set up a law office with his brother, Benjamin. During World War II, he served in the army. After the war, he was nominated and won the election for U.S. representative from New York's highly Democratic Upper West Side.

His four terms in Congress were followed by winning the 1954 New York election for attorney general. He returned to Capitol Hill in 1956 when he won a race for the U.S. Senate.

As a U.S. senator, Javits became known for his liberal views. He was against the war in Vietnam and supported President **Jimmy Carter**'s **Strategic Arms Limitation Treaty (SALT II)**, but broke with the Carter administration's response to the 1979 revolution in **Iran**. Diagnosed with amyotrophic lateral sclerosis (ALS), Jacob Javits became an advocate for the disabled. He died in Florida in 1986 of complications from ALS.

JAZZ. Although the 1970s introduced various kinds of **music**, including **disco**, jazz was still popular. Some well-known jazz musicians were continuing to entertain and to perform, including Count Basie and Duke Ellington. Newer names in the world of jazz were Thelonious Monk, John Coltrane, trumpeter Thad Jones, and drummer Mel Lewis, all of whom were welcomed by jazz enthusiasts. Additionally, some educational institutes, including North Texas State University and the Berklee College of Music, offered degrees in the history of jazz and performance. In time, other educational institutions added the study of jazz to their curriculum.

See also GRATEFUL DEAD.

THE JEFFERSONS. A spin-off of the **television** sitcom *All in the Family*, *The Jeffersons* depicted an **African American** couple, George and Louise Jefferson, who had made enough money to leave a working-class neighborhood and move into a luxury apartment in New York City. While *The Jeffersons* had fewer political overtones than *All in the Family*, it was still groundbreaking. It was the first show about a black couple who had joined the ranks of the wealthy. Two of the Jeffersons' neighbors, Tom and Helen Willis, were a mixed-race couple who had two children. Finally, whereas *All in the Family*'s Archie Bunker was a white racist, George Jefferson tended to look at people who were not black with disdain, referring to the Willises' children as "zebras" and whites as "honkeys." The sitcom aired for 11 seasons, from 1975 to 1985. Like *All in the Family*, *The Jeffersons* was produced by **Norman Lear**.

JOHN, ELTON (1947–). Considered one of the greatest singers and songwriters of his generation, **musician** Elton John was born Reginald Kenneth Dwight in Pinner, Middlesex, England. He attended the Royal Academy of Music in London (1959–64), where he established himself as a singer, songwriter, and musician. In 1970–71 he toured the United States four times. One of his most famous songs, "Candle in the Wind," was written in memory of Marilyn Monroe. Others of his most popular songs were "Crocodile Rock,"

"Benny and the Jets," and "Rocket Man," and altogether he has had 40 top hits, selling more than a quarter million recordings since 1970. Although he began his onstage musical career wearing flamboyant costumes, John hid his bisexuality. He owned a flotilla of automobiles, a large estate, and a British soccer team. He entertained audiences with his vitality and unusual props. He continues to perform before sold-out audiences, and, in 1992, he established the Elton John AIDS Foundation, for which he was knighted by Queen Elizabeth of England. John and his partner, David, live in Atlanta, Georgia.

JONES, JAMES WARREN "JIM" (1931–1978). The founder of the Peoples Temple, Jim Jones was born in Indiana and developed a strong interest in **religion** early in his childhood. He was for a time a member of the U.S. Communist Party and strongly defended racial integration. Angered by the policy of segregation in the church he attended outside Indianapolis, in 1956 he founded what became known as the Peoples Temple Full Gospel Church, or Peoples Temple for short. Fearful of suffering from fallout that might take place should the United States and the **Union of Soviet Socialist Republics (USSR)** engage in a nuclear exchange, he moved his church to California in 1967. A decade later, he moved it again, this time to the nation of Guyana, following reports by former Temple members that they had suffered sexual and physical abuse. Several hundred followers went with him and established a new settlement that they called Jonestown.

In 1978, Representative Leo Ryan traveled to Jonestown to investigate claims of **human rights** abuses there. As Ryan and his entourage prepared to leave, some of Jones's armed guards opened fire, killing the congressman and four others. Believing Ryan was part of a larger conspiracy to destroy Jonestown, Jones's followers drank Flavor Aid laced with cyanide, with adults giving the poison to their children. Jones himself died from a gunshot wound, possibly at the hands of an aide. A total of 909 people died, making it the largest mass suicide/murder in history.

JONESTOWN MASS SUICIDE. *See* JONES, JAMES WARREN "JIM" (1931–1978).

JORDAN, BARBARA (1936–1996). Democrat. A member of the House of Representatives from 1973 to 1979, Barbara Jordan was a pathbreaker, becoming the first **African American woman** to serve in the Texas state senate since Reconstruction and the first African American woman elected to the U.S. House of Representatives. Born in Houston, she was unable to attend the University of Texas because of segregation and therefore went instead to Texas Southern University. After teaching for a year at Alabama's Tuskegee Institute, she returned to Texas to practice law.

Jordan originally had sought election to the Texas House of Representatives in both 1962 and 1964 but proved unable to get the necessary votes. She then made a bid for the Texas state senate in 1966 and won. She continued to serve in the state legislature until she won election to the U.S. House of Representatives in 1972. Winning an appointment to the House Judiciary Committee, she made an important and powerful speech that observers credit with convincing the committee to seek President **Richard Nixon**'s impeachment. During the **1976 election**, **Jimmy Carter** considered Jordan as a vice presidential candidate. Though he chose Senator **Walter Mondale** instead, it was Jordan who gave the keynote address at that year's Democratic National Convention, an honor she received again in 1992.

Jordan retired from the U.S. House in 1979 to take up an adjunct teaching position at the University of Texas at Austin. She was the recipient of numerous awards, including the Presidential Medal of Freedom. President Bill Clinton considered nominating her to the U.S. Supreme Court, but her fight with multiple sclerosis, ongoing since 1973, convinced him otherwise. A lesbian, her sexual orientation remained a well-kept secret until after her death. She continued to teach until she passed away, a result of pneumonia caused by leukemia.

JORDAN, HAMILTON (1944–2008). Hamilton Jordan served as chief of staff to President **Jimmy Carter** from 1979 to 1980 and was one of Carter's closest confidants. Jordan was born and raised in Georgia. He had come to question his state's segregationist policies after witnessing in 1961 a violent attack on peaceful **civil rights** demonstrators. In 1966, the same year he graduated from the University of Georgia, he met Carter; then running for governor, Carter's talk of enlightened government impressed Jordan. He therefore joined the Carter campaign, working as youth coordinator. After Carter failed to win the **Democratic** nomination for governor, Jordan decided to go to Vietnam. Unable to meet the physical requirements to serve in the U.S. military, he did volunteer work. Six months later, he was back in the United States to get treatment for a tropical illness called blackwater fever.

Still recovering from his ailment, Jordan contacted Carter and, learning that Carter planned to run for governor again in 1970, offered to help. Carter was taken with Jordan and appointed him his campaign manager. Emerging victorious, Carter picked Jordan to serve as his executive secretary. Jordan, only 26 years of age, now had a position and responsibilities similar to those of a chief of staff. His record as an administrator was mediocre and drew him significant criticism from the Georgia state legislature. He was, however, a superb strategist. Having successfully brought Carter to the top office in Georgia, and knowing that the state constitution prohibited Carter from running for consecutive terms, Jordan began preparing a plan aimed at securing for the governor the Democratic nomination for the U.S. presidency. Taking advantage of changes in how the party chose delegates, he believed Carter's lack of name recognition outside Georgia could actually prove beneficial, and having the governor portray himself as a moderate, concluded Jordan, offered an excellent chance for victory. Another Carter friend, **Peter Bourne**, had reached a similar conclusion. Meeting with Jordan, Bourne, and other aides, Carter, who on his own had begun to consider a run for the White House, agreed that he could win. Jordan put his ideas into a famous 72-page memo which he presented to Carter in November 1972. The strategy he developed helped the governor garner the Democratic nomination and then the presidency.

Having been so central to Carter's political fortunes, it was obvious that Jordan would receive a high post. Shortly after the election, Carter gave his friend the job of overseeing White House appointments. At this point, the president was reluctant to have a chief of staff, believing that such a person could curtail the access of cabinet members and top staff to the Oval Office. Yet Jordan was in essence a de facto chief of staff, one whose responsibilities ranged from managing the president's personal affairs to overseeing day-to-day business in the White House. He also oftentimes offered his own opinion on policy recommendations sent to Carter.

In 1979, Carter reached the conclusion that administrative efficiency and effectiveness necessitated a chief of staff, and he selected Jordan for the post. From the start, Jordan had been a controversial figure, one accused of having too much influence in the White House, and who engaged in indecent and even anti-Semitic behavior. While he proved himself an able chief of staff who worked to improve relations with Congress and set up task forces to oversee important administrative matters, in 1979 both he and Press Secretary **Jody Powell** were charged for using cocaine at **Studio 54** in New York City. Though the two men were cleared of all charges, the affair smacked of scandal and tainted the administration.

Later that year, Jordan found himself adding to his responsibilities an effort to bring an end to the **Iran hostage crisis**. He arranged a meeting in 1980 between two intermediaries and Iranian president Abolhassan Bani-Sadr, but the talks fell through. By then, he was also actively involved in overseeing Carter's bid for reelection. Ultimately, Carter lost to the **Republican** candidate, **Ronald Reagan**. While the hostage crisis hurt Carter, Jordan believed the key reasons for the president's defeat were the poor state of the U.S. **economy** and Massachusetts senator **Edward Kennedy**, whose own bid for the Democratic nomination for the presidency had split the party. After Reagan's inauguration, Jordan returned to private life. He wrote two memoirs, became involved in the **sports** industry, and made an unsuccessful run in 1986 for the U.S. Senate. During his life, he had repeated bouts with cancer, and it was that disease which took his life.

See also CIVILETTI, BENJAMIN RICHARD (1935–); COSTANZA, MIDGE (MARGARET) (1932–2010); FULLER, MILLARD (1935–2009); McDONALD, AL (ALONZO LOWRY) (1928–); MOORE, FRANK (1935–); WATSON, JACK HEARN, JR. (1938–).

JORDAN, RELATIONS WITH. *See* HUSSEIN I (HUSSEIN IBN TALAN IBAN HUSSEIN) (1935–1999).

JORDAN, VERNON EULION, JR. (1935–). Born in Atlanta, Vernon Jordan received a bachelor's degree from DePauw University (B.A., 1957) and a law degree from Howard University (J.D., 1960). He then returned to Atlanta, where he joined the **civil rights** movement. He helped integrate the University of Georgia in 1961, served as a field secretary for the National Association for the Advancement of Colored People (NAACP) from 1961 to 1963, became in 1970 the United Negro College Fund's (UNCF) executive director, and in 1971 assumed the position of executive director of the National Urban League.

A year before receiving the directorship of the UNCF, Jordan had met **Jimmy Carter**, who was then seeking the Georgia governorship. The two became close friends; indeed, Jordan was among the first **African American** leaders to endorse Carter's bid for the presidency. When Carter won, Jordan was hopeful the new president would endorse programs aimed at providing assistance to inner cities. However, Carter's fiscal conservatism kept him from offering the amount of aid Jordan desired. Frustrated, Jordan in July 1977 assailed Carter, prompting an angry retort from the president and a permanent weakening of their friendship. For the remainder of Carter's term, Jordan tried to avoid a complete break with the White House. He offered support (albeit tepid) for Carter's welfare reform program. Furthermore, he established the Black Leadership Forum, which included the heads of all the major African American organizations, and which held a number of meetings with the president. Yet the relationship between Jordan and Carter remained cool.

In May 1980, a white supremacist shot Jordan. After recovering, Jordan in 1981 resigned his position on the National Urban League and joined a Washington, D.C., law firm. Having been friends with Bill Clinton since the 1970s, he worked closely with Clinton's presidential bid in 1992 and served on Clinton's transition team. Jordan currently works for a law firm in New York City.

See also JACKSON, MAYNARD HOLBROOK, JR. (1938–2003).

K

KAHN, ALFRED EDWARD (1917–2010). A professor and an expert in the field of business **deregulation**, Alfred Kahn served as chair of the Civil Aeronautics Board (CAB) from 1977 to 1978 and then as chair of the Council of Wage and Price Stability (COWPS) from 1978 to 1981. A New Jersey native, he graduated high school at age 15, received a bachelor's degree from New York University in 1936, and then went on to complete his master's and Ph.D., the latter of which he obtained from Yale in 1942. Employed both in the public and private sectors during World War II, he focused particularly upon antitrust matters. Afterward, he taught at both Ripon College and Cornell University.

In 1970, Kahn published the influential book *The Economics of Regulation* and had the opportunity to put his conclusions into practice when he left Cornell in 1974 to take up the job as chair of the New York Public Service Commission (NYPSC). The NYPSC regulated over three dozen industries in the state, including buses, water utilities, and docks. Kahn changed the way the commission conducted business; for instance, he replaced the flat rate charged for use of electricity with one that was based upon the amount of electricity used. Consequently, electrical bills fell during off-peak periods. Impressed with Kahn, President **Jimmy Carter** asked him to oversee the CAB. Carter agreed with Kahn that deregulation of industry would mean less government red tape and increased competition, to the benefit of the consumer. Though he knew little about the airline industry, Kahn accepted the role in 1977. The airlines opposed deregulation, but many lawmakers seconded the need to take such a step and in 1978 passed the **Airline Deregulation Act**.

When **inflation** began to spin out of control, Carter asked Kahn to move from CAB to the COWPS. Here Kahn proved less successful. He eventually reached the conclusion that the best way to combat inflation was to reduce the nation's money supply, even though doing so likely would cause a recession. Federal Reserve chairman **Paul Volcker** implemented such a policy in 1979, which served to curb inflation but, as Kahn had anticipated, also caused a slowdown in the **economy**. After **Ronald Reagan**'s victory in the

1980 election, Kahn went back to Cornell. He served as a witness before several congressional commissions and continued to tout the benefits of deregulation. He passed away in 2010 from cancer.

See also MEANY, GEORGE (1894–1980).

KENNEDY, EDWARD MOORE "TED" (1932–2009). Democrat. Born in Brookline, Massachusetts, to one of the wealthiest, most famous, and most influential families of the 20th century, Edward Kennedy served in the U.S. Senate from 1962 to 2009. Kennedy's father, Joseph, had served as U.S. ambassador to **Great Britain**. Ted himself had managed his brother John's U.S. Senate campaign in 1958 and then John's successful bid for the presidency in 1960. In 1962, Ted won a special election to fill his brother's Senate seat, where he would remain until his death.

A member of the party's liberal wing, Kennedy supported initiatives aimed at improving **education** and **health** care, and defending **civil rights**. He actively participated in his brother Robert's presidential campaign in 1968; Robert might have won had he not been assassinated in June of that year. Ted could have been a candidate himself in 1972 and 1976 had he not been at the center of a controversy involving the death in 1969 of Mary Jo Kopechne, a **woman** who was with the senator when the **automobile** he was

Carter and Senator Edward Kennedy of Massachusetts. Upset with Carter's policies, Kennedy ran against him for the Democratic nomination in 1980. Courtesy of the Jimmy Carter Library.

driving went off a bridge near Martha's Vineyard, Massachusetts, and into a pond. Although he got out of the vehicle safely, she drowned. Kennedy pled guilty and received a two-month suspended sentence. With Kennedy out of the race in 1976, the liberal vote became divided among several candidates, allowing **Jimmy Carter** to assume the political center and win the party's nomination.

During his term in office, Carter's relationship with Kennedy became contentious. Although Kennedy supported the president's call for **deregulation** of industry, he and Carter developed a professional and personal antagonism over national health insurance (NHI). Both favored a comprehensive NHI program, but Kennedy wanted one implemented immediately, while Carter preferred one that was phased in. By mid-1978, the White House, to Kennedy's consternation, had determined that the economic and political winds made even a phased-in insurance plan infeasible. Furious, Kennedy began preparations to run against Carter for the Democratic nomination in 1980, and polls showed him winning. Kennedy formally entered the race on 7 November 1979. The timing could not have been worse for him. Americans had rallied around Carter as a result of the **Iran hostage crisis**, which had begun a few days earlier, and the invasion of **Afghanistan** by the **Union of Soviet Socialist Republics (USSR)** a month later brought more support for the president. Kennedy's poor response to a reporter's questions about Kopechne's death did not help matters. By June, Carter had won the nomination, but Kennedy continued to fight for the party's nod all the way until the convention that August. Some administration officials believed that the split in the Democratic Party between Carter and Kennedy played a part in the president's failure to win the **1980 election**.

Kennedy gave up any designs on the White House after 1980, instead focusing on his legislative career. Despite his liberal leanings, he became known as someone willing to reach out to conservatives on such matters as immigration and civil rights. He also continued his fight for universal health coverage. In 2008, Kennedy was diagnosed with a malignant brain tumor caused by cancer. Efforts to stop the tumor from spreading failed, and he passed away August 2009.

See also BYRD, ROBERT CARLYLE (1917–2010); EIZENSTAT, STUART ELLIOTT (1943–); FOREIGN INTELLIGENCE SURVEILLANCE ACT (FISA); FOREIGN POLICY; JORDAN, HAMILTON (1944–2008); MOYNIHAN, DANIEL PATRICK (1927–2003); O'NEILL, TIP (THOMAS PHILLIP O'NEILL JR.) (1912–1994).

KERR-McGHEE. *See* SILKWOOD, KAREN (1946–1974).

KHOMEINI, AYATOLLAH RUHOLLAH MUSSAUI (1900?–1989). The supreme leader of **Iran** from 1979 to 1989 and a Shi'ite Muslim spiritual leader, Ruhollah Khomeini was born in either 1900 or 1902 and began to study the Qu'ran when he was six years old. A landlord killed his father, and so his mother and aunt, and later his brother, Mortaza, raised him. Mortaza was himself an ayatollah and continued Khomeini's education in Islam, as did another ayatollah, Abdul Karim Haeri-ye Yazdi. Khomeini himself became an ayatollah in the 1950s and was proclaimed a grand ayatollah the following decade, making him one of the top religious leaders among Shi'ites in Iran.

Khomeini had long disliked the Pahlavi family that ruled Iran, whom he believed had accepted secularism at the expense of Islam. Around the same time he became a grand ayatollah, Khomeini began to call for the ouster of the shah (king), **Mohammed Reza Pahlavi**. In response, Pahlavi had him exiled to Iraq in 1964. Yet Khomeini's continued denunciations of the shah's government moved the Iranian leader to request Iraq to send Khomeini to some place farther away. Kicked out of Iraq in 1978, Khomeini traveled to Paris, where he made cassette tapes of his speeches and had them smuggled into Iran. By this time, Iran was going through convulsions as protests against the shah's government spread throughout the nation. Under intense pressure at home, and with the United States government unwilling to offer him unconditional support, the shah left Iran in 1979. Khomeini returned to his homeland shortly thereafter, where he established a strict theocratic government. While there is no evidence Khomeini planned what became the **Iran hostage crisis**, he endorsed the action of the hostage takers. He opposed a peaceful resolution of the **Iran-Iraq War** until 1988, when he accepted a cease-fire. Although Iran's **economy** remained weak under his leadership and Iran failed to win a victory over Iraq, Khomeini remained in firm control of the nation. A year after the end of the Iran-Iraq War, he passed away in a hospital.

See also FOREIGN POLICY; HUSSEIN, SADDAM (1937–2006); PRECHT, HENRY (1932–); SULLIVAN, WILLIAM HEALY (1922–).

KING, BILLIE JEAN (1943–). Tennis star Billie Jean King began playing her **sport** at an early age. In her career, she won a record 20 Wimbledon titles (singles, doubles, and mixed doubles) in the 1960s and 1970s. She also succeeded in winning several international titles. One of her goals was to obtain equal pay for **women** in sports. Perhaps one of her most remembered and unusual tennis matches was in 1973, when Bobby Riggs, a champion in men's tennis, challenged King to a competitive match. Riggs wanted to prove men were superior to women. Much publicity was given to this match, and many people watched it on **television**. King won every match the two played. She became the first president of the Women's Tennis Association

(WTA) in 1974. She was married to Lawrence King from 1965 to 1987. About 10 years later, however, while still married, she revealed that in the 1970s she had had an intimate relationship with her female secretary. Billie Jean King was one of the first athletes to admit to having had a **gay** relationship.

KING, STEPHEN EDWIN (1947–). A master in the genres of horror and **science fiction**, many of Stephen King's novels were made into movies. *Carrie* was the first of his many **cinema** successes. A 1970 graduate from the University of Maine, he and his family still reside in Maine. King continues to write fiction and anticipates that more of his books will make it to the big screen.

See also LITERATURE.

KIRBO, CHARLES HUGHES (1917–1996). A lawyer and unofficial adviser to President **Jimmy Carter**, Charles Kirbo was born in Bainbridge, Georgia. He received a law degree from the University of Georgia and then served in the army during World War II. Afterward, he returned to law. In 1962, Carter lost a bid for the **Democratic** nomination for the Georgia state senate. He believed the outcome had been rigged and, having received Kirbo's name from a relative, contacted him. Kirbo took the case to court, where a judge determined fraud had indeed taken place. Consequently, Carter received the nomination and went on to win the seat. From that point, Kirbo became one of Carter's top confidants, suggesting that Carter run the presidential campaign for the **1976 election** on a theme of restoring faith in government, and carefully interviewed possible vice presidential candidates.

Though he continued to practice law in Georgia, Kirbo traveled frequently to Washington, D.C., where he helped choose members of the president's cabinet. He suggested that Carter fire Office of Management and Budget director **Bert Lance**, who had been implicated in a scandal, and participated in meetings at Camp David in 1979, after which Carter shook up his cabinet. Kirbo and Carter remained close friends after the president lost the **1980 election**. He continued to practice law up to his retirement in 1987. He passed away following gall bladder surgery.

See also WATSON, JACK HEARN, JR. (1938–).

KISSINGER, HENRY ALFRED (ALFRED HEINZ) (1923–). Republican. A member of the administrations of Presidents **Richard Nixon** and **Gerald Ford**, Henry Kissinger served as National Security Council (NSC) adviser from 1969 to 1975 and as secretary of state from 1973 to 1977. Kissinger was born in Germany, but because of Nazi persecution of Jews, his family moved to the United States in 1938. Three years later, Kissinger was drafted into the U.S. Army, during which time he became a naturalized citizen. After the war, he entered Harvard College (later Harvard University), eventually receiving his Ph.D. in 1954. He joined the university faculty, where he remained for the next 15 years.

While teaching, Kissinger took on various duties outside Harvard, including sitting on the Council of Foreign Relations and acting as a consultant to both the Arms Control and Disarmament Agency and the State Department. Moreover, he served as an adviser to New York governor **Nelson Rockefeller,** who made several unsuccessful bids in the 1960s for the Republican Party's nomination for the presidency. It thus came as a surprise when Nixon, who ran against Rockefeller in 1968, appointed Kissinger as his NSC adviser.

After winning reelection in 1972, Nixon also named Kissinger secretary of state; Kissinger held both posts until President Ford named Brent Scowcroft as his national security adviser. Kissinger was a strong believer in realpolitik, the idea that **foreign policy** is driven by power and national self-interest rather than morality. That ideology increasingly generated a backlash, particularly from those who contended that realpolitik led the United States to give support to repressive regimes abroad. Among those individuals was **Jimmy Carter,** who in the **1976 election** promised to make the promotion of **human rights** a keystone of his foreign policy.

Although Kissinger returned to private life following Carter's victory, he remained very active politically. He used his influence to obtain ratification of the **Panama Canal treaties** and strongly endorsed the **Camp David Accords** and normalization of U.S. relations with **China**. In general, however, Kissinger tended to criticize rather than laud Carter's diplomacy. He believed that Carter's effort to achieve a comprehensive Middle East peace agreement stood less chance of success than a step-by-step approach. He was upset that Carter was reluctant to allow the shah of **Iran, Mohammed Reza Pahlavi,** to enter the United States for cancer treatment, and he joined National Security Adviser **Zbigniew Brzezinski** in lobbying the president to reconsider. On humanitarian grounds, Carter changed his mind, thereby setting the stage for the **Iran hostage crisis**.

In actuality, Kissinger has had little influence over U.S. diplomacy since leaving the White House. His moderate Republican views have been out of step with the conservatism that has dominated the party since **Ronald Reagan**'s presidency. Furthermore, his critics have accused him of war crimes related to the bombing of **Cambodia** during the Vietnam War, the overthrow of the Chilean government of Salvador Allende in 1973, and the support for repressive governments. Even so, he retains a high level of respect within and outside the diplomatic community. He appears on **television** programs to discuss international affairs and consults with officials in Washington on matters of U.S. diplomacy.

See also SADAT, (MUHAMMAD) ANWAR AL- (1918–1981).

KLUTZNICK, PHILIP MORRIS (1907–1999). Democrat. The secretary of commerce from 1980 to 1981, Klutznick was born in 1907 in Kansas City, Missouri. He came from an Orthodox Jewish family and was active in the American Jewish community. After receiving his law degree from Creighton University in 1930, Klutznick took a job as general counsel for the city of Omaha. He spent World War II working for the U.S. government to provide housing for defense workers but returned to private life a year after the war ended. He became a successful real estate developer in Chicago whose projects included Park Forest, one of the nation's first planned suburban communities. All the while, he continued his work for the Jewish community, serving as international president of B'nai B'rith from 1953 to 1959. While heading B'nai B'rith, Klutznick received an invitation from President Dwight D. Eisenhower's secretary of state, John Foster Dulles, to join the U.S. delegation to the United Nations (UN). Thus began a close association with the UN that continued during the 1960s and into the 1970s, including a stint as ambassador to the UN Economic and Social Council. He maintained his commitment to the welfare of American Jews and was elected in 1977 as president of the World Jewish Congress.

Klutznick's work for Jews drew him to the attention of President **Jimmy Carter**, who wanted to bring an end to the dispute between **Israel** and its Arab neighbors as part of a more comprehensive Middle East peace settlement. Indeed, Klutznick had come to know most of Israel's leaders, and his work for the UN had made him familiar with officials from other countries in the region, such as **Egypt**'s ambassador to the United States, Ashraf Ghorbal. Klutznick thus became an important consultant to Carter and Vice President **Walter Mondale** and made clear that the president's peace initiative would have the endorsement of American Jews. In 1979, Klutznick officially joined the Carter administration after accepting the president's nomination to succeed **Juanita Kreps** as secretary of commerce. To Carter, Klutznick had impressive credentials, including his success as a businessman and his extensive **foreign policy** experience. While Klutznick's work included trying to improve the competitiveness of U.S. industry at a time when it faced a growing challenge from **Japan**, most of his time focused on implementing the sanctions imposed against the **Union of Soviet Socialist Republics (USSR)** by the Carter administration following Moscow's invasion of **Afghanistan**. After Carter's term in office, Klutznick returned to private life, continuing his work for the American Jewish community and seeking to achieve a comprehensive Middle East peace settlement. In 1999, he passed away from Alzheimer's disease.

KRAFT, TIMOTHY E. (1941–). Democrat. The appointments secretary to President **Jimmy Carter** from 1977 to 1978, Tim Kraft was born in Nashville, Indiana. He graduated from Dartmouth College in 1963 with a degree in government, after which he spent two years with the Peace Corps in Guatemala. In 1966–67 he attended Georgetown University where he majored in Latin American Studies. Kraft moved to New Mexico but failed to achieve success in various political venues.

In 1975, presidential candidate **Jimmy Carter** visited New Mexico and met Kraft. The former Georgia governor was impressed by Kraft and hired him to run his campaign in the West. Proving himself highly capable, Kraft was given the job of overseeing Carter's campaign in Iowa. After Carter won the Iowa caucuses in January 1976, Kraft helped the candidate win more states, organizing volunteers to ring doorbells and pass out literature about the Democratic Party's presidential candidate. Pleased with Kraft's work, Carter appointed him national field coordinator. Following the **1976 election**, now-President Carter gave Kraft the job of appointments secretary. He excelled at his job, and Carter came to realize he needed to use Kraft's talents elsewhere. As the White House's relationship with Congress was shaky, the president appointed Kraft as liaison to Democratic Party lawmakers. He again proved himself capable, working also to improve relations between the party and **Hispanic Americans**.

Kraft left his job to work as Carter's campaign manager in the **1980 election**. But he was forced to resign after being accused of using cocaine. He traveled to South America, where he monitored elections and assisted in several presidential campaigns. Kraft returned to the United States and worked for Howard Dean, who in 2004 sought the Democratic Party's nomination for president. Retired, he lives in New Mexico where he writes opinion pieces for the *Albuquerque Journal*.

KREPS, JUANITA MORRIS (1921–2010). The secretary of commerce from 1977 to 1979, Juanita Kreps was born in Kentucky. She attended Berea College and then Duke University, receiving a degree in economics in 1948. The same year she graduated from Berea, she married Clifton Kreps, who received teaching positions at several universities, and she went with him. She then headed back to Duke University in 1958, rising from an instructor to professor and then, starting in 1973, vice president. She served as well on the boards of several companies. Additionally, in 1972, she became the first **woman** to sit on the New York Stock Exchange's board of directors.

Determined to place more women in high-level government positions, **Jimmy Carter** selected Kreps to head the Commerce Department, making her the first woman to hold that post. Kreps sought to be an active secretary. She established an interagency task force to increase the number of women who owned businesses, worked to keep industries from leaving major cities by offering grants and low-interest loans, and sought to increase U.S. foreign trade. She felt the administration tended to ignore her advice. Though she was an economist, she was cut out of weekly breakfasts led by Treasury Secretary **Michael Blumenthal** where the state of the **economy** was discussed. She believed the White House did a poor job of consulting with business officials. Finally, the president discarded her proposals to protect the U.S. steel industry, which was having trouble competing against steel imports from **Japan**. In 1979, she resigned, not out of anger with the White House but because her husband, a professor at the University of North Carolina, had grown severely depressed at not being able to be with her in the capital. Kreps returned to Duke, where she became vice president emeritus and served on various government committees. She passed away from Alzheimer's disease at age 89.

See also KLUTZNICK, PHILIP MORRIS (1907–1999).

L

LABOR. Labor unions, once a powerful force in the United States, had seen their influence wane by the 1970s. Countries such as **Japan** and **West Germany** had begun to challenge America's standing as the world's leading producer of manufactured goods, and U.S. corporations had increasingly outsourced jobs to Mexico and East Asia, where labor costs were cheaper. Meanwhile, more and more Americans got jobs in the service sector, with 70 percent of them working in service jobs by 1980; this was 10 percent higher than a decade earlier.

Unionized workers had tended to support the **Democratic Party** since the 1930s, for Franklin D. Roosevelt's New Deal programs had given them various protections. That backing continued into the 1976 presidential election. With **inflation** at about 6 percent and unemployment at approximately 8 percent, unions such as the **American Federation of Labor and Congress of Industrial Organizations (AFL-CIO)** hoped the Democratic nominee, **Jimmy Carter**, would take steps to create jobs by stimulating the **economy** and strengthening social welfare programs. That Carter identified unemployment as the country's prime threat further enthused organized labor. So did his choice of **Ray Marshall** as secretary of labor. While AFL-CIO president **George Meany** favored that post going to **Gerald Ford**'s labor secretary, John Dunlop, he believed Marshall would support unions' interests.

The relationship between the executive branch and labor quickly soured. Shortly after winning the White House, Carter declared combating inflation more important than defeating unemployment. His call for wage and price controls to rein in inflation upset labor leaders, including Meany. His fiscal conservatism moved him from enacting stimulus programs as large as favored by the trade federations. He created further anger among the ranks of industrial workers when he invoked the Taft-Hartley Act to compel the **United Mine Workers** to end a strike they had begun in December 1977. Finally, Carter's call for welfare reform pitted Marshall against **Joseph Califano**, the secretary of **health**, **education**, and welfare; whereas Marshall wanted to see such reform include steps to create jobs, Califano preferred to focus on guaranteeing families an income. By the time Califano and Marshall had worked through their differences and Carter sent a package of welfare reform proposals to Congress, it had virtually no support and received no consideration by lawmakers. Labor was pleased with the administration's decision to increase the minimum wage from $2.30 to $2.65, and then $3.35 by 1981, but this did not mitigate a feeling among unions that the president did not have their interests in mind.

Despite their anger with Carter, labor leaders tended to endorse him in the **1980 election**, determining that the Republican candidate, **Ronald Reagan**, was more of a threat to their interests. Yet there were many unionized workers who joined the ranks of the so-called Reagan Democrats. Though liberal on some issues, such as immigration, they believed the Democratic Party had abandoned them in favor of the well-being of other groups, including **African Americans**, **women**, and **Hispanic Americans**.

See also HOFFA, JAMES "JIMMY" (1913–1975); HUMPHREY, HUBERT HORATIO (1911–1978); PETERSON, ESTHER EGGERTSON (1906–1997); SILKWOOD, KAREN (1946–1974); WALESA, LECH (1943–); WOODCOCK, LEONARD FREEL (1911–2001).

LAINGEN, (LOWELL) BRUCE (1922–). The chargé d'affaires to **Iran** from 1979 to 1981, Bruce Laingen was born in Minnesota, attended St. Olaf College, and received a master's degree from the University of Minnesota in 1949. He began a career in the Foreign Service the same year he received his master's, holding posts in Europe and Asia, including ambassador to Malta. After the U.S. ambassador to Iran, **William Sullivan**, resigned in early 1979, Laingen agreed to a State Department request to become chargé d'affaires, making him the highest-ranking U.S. diplomatic official in that nation. Later that year, he became one of the Americans held in captivity during the **Iran hostage crisis**. Upon returning to the United States, Laingen accepted the vice presidency of the National Defense University, retiring from that post in 1986. A year later, he left the Foreign Service. From 1991 to 2006, he was president of the American Academy of Diplomacy. He continues to speak on and write about U.S. **foreign policy**, particularly relations with Iran.

LANCE, BERT (THOMAS BERTRAM) (1931–). Democrat. The director of the Office of Management and Budget (OMB) in 1977 and one of President **Jimmy Carter**'s closest confidants, Bert Lance was born in Gainesville, Georgia. He attended Emory University and the University of Georgia as an undergrad and then took graduate-level banking courses at both Louisiana State University and Rutgers University. He married LaBelle David in 1950, whose family owned Calhoun National Bank in Calhoun, Georgia. Starting off as a teller, he quickly rose up the bank's ranks, becoming its president by

1963 and its chairman of the board in 1974. A year later, he had bought enough stock in the National Bank of Georgia (NBG) to become its head as well.

It was during Carter's first bid for Georgia governor in 1966 that he met Lance, and the two quickly became good friends. After Carter won the 1970 gubernatorial race, he appointed Lance as head of the state's Department of Transportation. But Lance also helped on such matters as the budget and lobbying state lawmakers. Following his victory in the 1976 presidential election, Carter nominated Lance to head the OMB. In that role, Lance worked to curb government spending, deregulate private industry, and shrink the size of the federal government. Outside of their official duties, he and Carter continued their close personal friendship, with Lance acting almost as a sibling to the president.

It was that close relationship that caused Carter such grief when Lance became the center of a scandal. The "Lance Affair," as it became known, developed out of reports that he had met with officials from NBG and used his position at OMB to get a bank loan. Although a congressional inquiry found no evidence of legal wrongdoing, investigators uncovered additional evidence of malfeasance, including Lance's use of an NBG plane for personal purposes. There were also questions over whether Lance had fully di-

Carter with Bert and LaBelle Lance. Lance, the president's close friend and director of the Office of Management and Budget, was forced to resign because of alleged financial improprieties. Courtesy of the Jimmy Carter Library.

vulged his finances, as required by law. The scandal began to take its toll on Carter, who had promised an open and honest government during the campaign for the **1976 election**. Some people questioned whether, because of their friendship, Carter might also have acted unethically, if not illegally. Members of Congress, among them Republicans **Robert Dole** and **Charles Percy**, and Democrats **Abraham Ribicoff** and **William Proxmire**, called for Lance's resignation. Realizing that allowing Lance to remain at his post would cause serious problems for his administration, Carter in September 1977 convinced his OMB director to resign.

Returning to Georgia, Lance again became head of the Calhoun National Bank. He also continued his work with the Democratic Party, including service as chairman of **Walter Mondale**'s presidential campaign in 1984. However, Lance was never able to escape repeated charges of official wrongdoing. In 1979, he faced federal charges of conspiracy and banking irregularities involving his relationship with the Bank of Credit and Commerce International (BCCI) but was found innocent at trial. An investigation into BCCI in the 1980s found evidence that it had engaged in illegal activities ranging from money laundering to arms trafficking. Once again, Lance's name came up, though no charges were ever brought against him. Now retired, he lives with his wife in Calhoun.

See also CIVILETTI, BENJAMIN RICHARD (1935–); KIRBO, CHARLES HUGHES (1917–1996); McINTYRE, JAMES TALMADGE, JR. (1940–); SAFIRE, WILLIAM (1929–2009).

LANDRIEU, MOON (MAURICE EDWIN) (1930–). Democrat. The secretary of housing and urban development (HUD) from 1979 to 1981, Moon Landrieu was born in New Orleans and received both his undergraduate and law degrees from Loyola University. Afterward, he spent three years (1954–57) in the U.S. Army and then returned to New Orleans to work as an attorney and teach at Loyola. He joined the state legislature in 1960, where he proved himself a defender of **civil rights**; indeed, he was one of only a handful of white state legislators who fought to integrate schools. Six years later, he was elected to the city council of New Orleans, and he became mayor of that city in 1970. As mayor, he continued his commitment to civil rights, opening more positions in the city government to **African Americans** than had previously been the case.

When President **Jimmy Carter** moved his incumbent HUD secretary, **Patricia Harris**, to the Department of **Health, Education**, and Welfare, he named Landrieu as her replacement. While Landrieu was someone who could have helped Carter draw votes from southerners, southern mayors, and African Americans, the president had more interest in curbing spending than in devoting resources to the needs of cities. Consequently, Landrieu found himself acting as little more than a caretaker. Landrieu returned to New

Orleans in 1981. Ten years later, he received an appointment to the Fourth Circuit Court of Appeals, a post he held until he retired in 2001. His daughter, Mary, and son, Mitch, are currently a U.S. senator and mayor of New Orleans, respectively.

LAVERNE AND SHIRLEY. One of the most popular **television** programs in the 1970s, *Laverne and Shirley* premiered in 1976. A spinoff of *Happy Days*, the weekly show was unusual since it focused on two unmarried working **women** who lived together. Each week their quirky behavior, while pursuing eligible bachelors, made the half-hour show very funny.

LEAR, NORMAN MILTON (1922–). One of the most successful producers of **television** programs in the 1970s, and also one of the most innovative, Norman Lear starred **African Americans** in weekly programs. He began his television career with *All in the Family*, which included George Jefferson, played by African American actor Sherman Hemsley, as one of the main characters. *All in the Family* was followed by more groundbreaking comedies. A spinoff of *All in the Family* was *The Jeffersons*, in which George and his wife, Louise, had moved from their lower-class neighborhood to an upper-class, high-rise apartment building. Included in the cast of *The Jeffersons* was an interracial couple, Tom and Helen Willis. Like *All in the Family*'s Archie Bunker, George Jefferson had his own prejudices. Many of the weekly episodes involved George's inability to be civil, especially when he was with the Willises.

Lear continued to produce programs starring African Americans. Unlike *The Jeffersons*, the Evans family in *Good Times* lived in the projects. They were a struggling family who met many of the social and financial problems faced by poor African Americans. One of the dominant characters of this series was the Evanses' oldest son, J. J., who was known for his loud catchword, "Dyn-o-mite!" Lear continued his influential television career with *Sanford and Son*, which starred outspoken African American comedian Red Foxx. The sitcom featured a father (Foxx) and his son, who owned a junkyard. Their relationship presented audiences with many laughs. Foxx's character was comparable to Archie Bunker's, as both were bigots.

LED ZEPPELIN. One of the most influential **musical** groups of all time, Led Zeppelin was formed in 1968. Its members, vocalist Robert Plant, guitarist Jimmy Page, bass guitarist and keyboardist John Paul Jones, and percussionist John Bonham, combined blues and rock to create a sound oftentimes credited with giving birth to hard rock and heavy metal. By 1977, they were one of the most popular bands in the world, setting an attendance record during a concert in Detroit. In 1980, Bonham passed away following a drinking binge, and the band broke up. Since 1980, the surviving members have periodically reunited, sometimes joined by Bonham's son, Jason. In 1995, Led Zeppelin was inducted into the Rock and Roll Hall of Fame.

LENNON, JOHN (1940–1980). Born in Liverpool, England, John Lennon became famous as a member of the Beatles. After the Beatles broke up in 1970, he established himself as a successful singer and songwriter. In 1962, he wed Cynthia Powell, with whom he had his first son, Julian. Shortly after divorcing Powell in 1968, he married Yoko Ono and had a second son, Sean. His **music** reflected both his political and personal views, including opposition to the war in Vietnam, **women**'s rights, and his estranged relationship with former Beatle Paul McCartney. In December 1980, a security guard named Mark David Chapman, who suffered from mental delusions and an obsession with Lennon, shot and killed him outside Lennon's apartment building in New York City. Lennon has been posthumously inducted into the Songwriters Hall of Fame and the Rock and Roll Hall of Fame.

LINOWITZ, SOL MYRON (1913–2005). A native of New Jersey, Sol Linowitz was a negotiator to the **Panama Canal treaties** in 1977 and President **Jimmy Carter**'s Middle East negotiator in 1980. He graduated from Hamilton College in 1935 and then went on to get his law degree in 1938 from Cornell University. When the United States entered World War II, he hoped to join the military, but his poor eyesight and a previous leg injury prevented him from doing so. Accordingly, he worked for the Office of Price Administration and the Office of the General Counsel of the Navy. After the war ended, he returned to law, but he then encountered Joe Wilson, the president of Haloid, which sold paper used for copying. Alongside Wilson, Linowitz created what became the Xerox Corporation. He served as the company's chairman of the board from 1959 to 1966 and, starting in 1966, as its chief executive officer.

During this period with Xerox, Linowitz spent a significant amount of time involved in Latin American affairs. He established corporate offices in that part of the world and, in 1964, formed with **David Rockefeller** International Executive Service Corporation, which offered advice to companies in the developing world. Linowitz's work in Latin America brought him to the attention of President Lyndon B. Johnson, who, in 1966, convinced Linowitz to leave Xerox and become the U.S. ambassador to the Organization of American States (OAS).

Following **Richard Nixon**'s inauguration in 1969, Linowitz returned to practicing law. However, he continued his interest in Latin American affairs. Most notably, shortly before the **1976 election**, Linowitz chaired a commission arguing that the greatest problem facing Washington in the region was the conflict with Panama over U.S. control of the Panama Canal. The Lino-witz Commission report, issued in 1977, found favor from Jimmy Carter. The new president asked Linowitz to join Ellsworth Bunker, a diplomat who had been involved for some time in negotiations with Panama over the canal, to negotiate a new agreement on the waterway. After months of talks, Lino-witz and Bunker worked out with their Panamanian counterparts the Panama Canal treaties. Afterward, and at Carter's request, Linowitz lobbied members of the Senate to ratify the agreement.

In 1980, Linowitz again received Carter's request for help, this time to take over **Robert Strauss**'s position as Middle East negotiator. Linowitz had far less success here than he had had with Panama, as he lacked knowledge of the key issues in the Arab-**Israeli** dispute and found the quarreling parties unwilling to come to terms. Following **Ronald Reagan**'s election in 1980, Linowitz devoted his time to public service and writing books on his experiences and on the law profession. President Bill Clinton awarded him the Congressional Medal of Honor in 1998. He passed away at age 91.

See also PASTOR, ROBERT A. (1947–).

LIPSHUTZ, ROBERT JEROME (1921–2010). Counselor to President **Jimmy Carter** from 1977 to 1979, Robert Lipshutz was born in Atlanta. Receiving both his bachelor's and law degrees from the University of Geor-gia, he served in the U.S. Army during World War II and then opened his own law office in Atlanta. It was during Carter's first bid for the Georgia governorship that the two met. They became close, with Lipshutz working for Governor Carter and then serving as national campaign treasurer when Carter ran for the White House in the **1976 election**.

From almost the beginning, Lipshutz demonstrated his influence in the Carter administration. He convinced the president to commute the sentence of G. Gordon Liddy, the last of the Watergate conspirators still serving jail time. In the **Supreme Court** case *Regents of the University of California v. Bakke*, he persuaded the White House, over the objections of the Justice Department, to write a brief defending **affirmative action**. During the nego-tiations preceding the **Camp David Accords**, Lipshutz acted as a liaison between the administration and American Jewish groups. Finally, he encour-aged the president to increase the number of minority persons holding posi-tions in the administration and the judiciary.

While Carter was happy with Lipshutz's work, in 1979 he asked his coun-sel to resign as part of a larger administration shake-up. In actuality, Lipshutz was happy to do so, as he wished to return to his law practice in Atlanta. **Lloyd Cutler** took Lipshutz's place. In addition to his legal work, Lipshutz was an active member of Atlanta's Jewish community and served on the

Board of Directors of the Carter Center. It was he who wrote the presidential executive order that in 1993 established the Holocaust Memorial Museum. He died of a pulmonary embolism.

See also WATSON, JACK HEARN, JR. (1938–).

LITERATURE. By 1980 almost 70 percent of books were published in paperback, and anyone going to a bookstore would find numerous genres from which to choose. Though romances remained popular, the decade witnessed the rise of the modern romance, with greater emphasis on historical fiction and stronger female characters; the latter trend reflected the influence of the **women**'s rights movement. The **civil rights** movement made itself felt through works that focused on race or racism, among them Madison Jones's *A Cry of Absence* and **Alex Haley**'s *Roots: The Saga of an American Family*. Paranoia and horror became popular, with books by Thomas Pynchon, Kurt Vonnegut, and **Stephen King** selling in large numbers. The "new wave" of **science fiction** literature, which dated to the 1960s and had been heavily influenced by William Burroughs, remained active. Many of the leading authors of science fiction continued to write in the 1970s, including Isaac Asimov, Ray Bradbury, and Frank Herbert.

For those who preferred nonfiction, the exposé developed a large following. Best sellers included *All the President's Men*, a story of the Watergate scandal written by investigative journalists Carl Bernstein and Robert Woodward, and the sequel, *Final Days*. **Aleksandr Solzhenitsyn**'s *The Gulag Archipelago* told the story of life in a forced labor camp in the **Union of Soviet Socialist Republics (USSR)**. Books on self-help and **health** received a large audience, among them Thomas Anthony's *I'm OK, You're OK* and **James Fixx**'s *The Complete Book of Running*.

LOCKHEED SCANDAL. Between 1975 and 1976, a series of investigations led by the U.S. Securities and Exchange Commission and Senator **Frank Church** discovered that starting in the 1950s, officials from the U.S.-based Lockheed Corporation had bribed foreign officials to win contracts in foreign countries. The scandal led to the investigation, resignation, or imprisonment of a number of foreign government officials as well as the resignation of Lockheed's chairman of the board and president. It was also one of several similar events that led to passage in the United States of the **Foreign Corrupt Practices Act**.

LONG, RUSSELL BILLIU (1918–2003). Democrat. A U.S. senator from 1948 to 1987, Russell Long was born in Shreveport, Louisiana. He came from a political family, his famous father, Huey, and mother having both been U.S. senators. He received his bachelor's and law degrees from Louisiana State University (B.S., 1939; LL.B., 1942), served in the U.S. Navy in World War II, and won a seat in the U.S. Senate in 1948. There, he became a staunch defender of the oil and gas industries. In 1966, he assumed the chairmanship of the Finance Committee, where he developed a reputation as an expert on tax law.

Jimmy Carter's election pleased Long, for it brought to the White House a fellow southerner. The two, however, almost immediately began to butt heads. Long opposed Carter's proposal in early 1977 to provide a $50 tax credit to Americans to stimulate the **economy**. The president's decision to cancel numerous water projects, including several in Louisiana, frustrated the senator. Their biggest disagreement, however, was over Carter's plan to solve the country's **energy crisis**. The two men agreed that the nation needed to address Americans' heavy consumption of oil and gas. To Carter, the answer was a program that included taxes on oil production, on gas-guzzling cars, and on gasoline itself if gas consumption exceeded established limits. To Long, such proposals would cause severe harm to the nation's petroleum and gas producers. The senator used his position on the Finance Committee and his knowledge of parliamentary procedure to eliminate many of these provisions, including the taxes on petroleum production and gas-guzzling vehicles. Long then convinced the House to adopt much of the Senate's energy proposals. Thus, when sent to Carter's desk in October 1978, the **National Energy Act** offered a watered-down version of what the president had wanted.

This is not to say Long and Carter always disagreed. In 1977, Long's endorsement of the **Panama Canal treaties** had been vital to their passage. In 1979, Carter responded to a new energy crisis by eliminating price controls on oil established by the 1975 Energy Policy and Conservation Act. Realizing this would mean higher fuel prices and larger corporate profits, the president proposed a windfall profits tax, the money from which would go to low-income families. Long agreed to this measure, though he altered the legislation to reduce the tax below what Carter had favored. In the mid-1980s, Long considered, but decided not to seek, a bid for the Louisiana governorship. Rather, in 1986 he announced his decision not to run for another Senate term, choosing instead to work for a law firm in Washington, D.C. In 2003, he passed away from heart failure.

LOVE CANAL. A residential neighborhood near Niagara Falls, New York, Love Canal had been constructed on a waste dump formerly used by a chemical company. Although an investigation in the mid-1970s had found evidence of chemical contamination in some homes, it was not until 1978 that Love Canal made national news; that year, a local journalist reported an unusually high number of illnesses and birth defects among the residents. Angered, a local housewife, Lois Gibbs, rallied homeowners and called for an investigation. In 1978, both state and federal authorities declared an emergency at Love Canal. President **Jimmy Carter** announced he would provide federal aid to clean up the site; it was the first time in its history that the United States government had provided emergency money for something other than a natural disaster. Washington also began the process of relocating people in the neighborhood, eventually finding new homes for 800 families. The tragedy at Love Canal prompted the U.S. Congress to pass the **Comprehensive Environmental Response, Compensation, and Liability Act (CERCLA)** of 1980. Also known as the Superfund, CERCLA provides federal funding to clean up hazardous waste sites and declares that polluters can be held financially responsible for damage they cause. Much of Love Canal presently remains unsuitable for habitation.

See also ENVIRONMENT.

LUCAS, GEORGE (1944–). An American screenwriter, director, and producer, George Lucas was born in California. He attended a community college and then transferred to the University of Southern California's School of **Cinematic** Arts. His first full-length film, *THX 1138* (1971), based upon a short film he made while a student, did not do well. He then founded Lucasfilm Ltd. and directed *American Graffiti* (1973), which received five Oscar nominations, including Best Director. It was the *Star Wars* series of movies, however, that made Lucas a household name. To create the necessary visuals, he established Industrial Light and Magic. When released in 1977, *Star Wars* (officially titled *Star Wars: Episode IV—A New Hope*) received critical acclaim for its story of good versus evil and its groundbreaking special effects. It became one of the highest-grossing films in U.S. history and received seven Oscars, including Best Visual Effects, Best Film Editing, and Best **Musical** Score. Lucas's work as writer and producer of all four Indiana Jones films, starting with *Raiders of the Lost Ark* (1981), solidified his reputation as one of Hollywood's top producers and directors. With his first wife, Marcia Lou Griffin, whom he divorced in 1983, he adopted a child and since has adopted two more. He also continues to produce and direct, both for the big screen and **television**.

See also SCIENCE FICTION.

MADDOX, LESTER GARFIELD (1915–2003). Democrat. A defender of segregation, Lester Maddox served as governor of Georgia from 1967 to 1971. He was born in Atlanta, dropped out of high school, and opened what became a lucrative fast food restaurant in town. He became nationally famous when he refused to comply with the 1964 **Civil Rights** Act and allow three **African Americans** to enter his establishment. When told he had no choice, he closed the restaurant in 1965. A year later, he ran for and won the Georgia governorship, defeating both **Jimmy Carter** for the Democratic Party nomination and the incumbent **Republican** governor, Howard Callaway. It was Carter's failure to defeat a segregationist that convinced him to run a racist campaign in his successful 1970 bid for governor. Maddox could not succeed himself as governor but received enough votes to win the lieutenant governorship that year.

As Georgia's chief executive, Carter proved far more progressive on racial issues than his campaign had suggested. He also sought to reorganize the state government to make it more efficient. On both scores, he found himself at odds with Maddox, who had significant pull in the state legislature. Yet Maddox's views, particularly on race, did not reflect changes taking place in the South, and he failed to win another term as governor in 1974. In 1976, he ran for the U.S. presidency on the American Independent Party ticket but received few votes. Afterward, he dropped out of politics. He passed away from pneumonia in June 2003.

See also TALMADGE, HERMAN EUGENE (1913–2002).

MAGAZINES. Women's magazines had been published for many years with household hints, but the women's movement of the 1970s added more profound, realistic, and timely articles within their pages. One of the most influential publishers of women's magazines during the Carter era was **Gloria Steinem**. Her magazine *Ms.* was introduced in 1972. It was not filled with household hints but rather topics of interest to the modern woman. Other now-popular magazines, which began in the 1970s, included *Rolling Stone*, *Hustler*, and *People Weekly*, the last of which had Mia Farrow on the cover of its first issue (1974). *Playgirl*, *Playboy*'s sister magazine that aimed at a female audience, began in 1973. There were just two monthly **science fiction** magazines that found an audience, *Analog* and *The Magazine of Fantasy & Science Fiction.* A semiprofessional magazine, *Galileo*, was launched in 1976 but ceased production in 1980 after only 15 issues. *Isaac Asimov's Science Fiction Magazine* was launched in 1977. *New York* magazine, founded in 1968, was purchased in the 1970s by Rupert Murdock.

See also BUCKLEY, WILLIAM FRANK, JR. (1925–2008); CARTER, RUTH (1929–1983); FLYNT, LARRY (1942–); SCHMIDT, HELMUT HEINRICH (1918–).

"MALAISE" SPEECH. By the middle of 1979, President **Jimmy Carter** faced intense criticism at home, in part because of Americans' belief that he had done little to cure the nation's sick **economy**. Only adding to the country's woes was the decision by the **Organization of Petroleum Exporting Countries (OPEC)** to increase the price of oil. Shortly thereafter, Carter traveled to Camp David where he spent 11 days meeting with officials from the worlds of business, academia, **religion**, government, and **labor**. In the meantime, he had his aides work on a speech aimed at addressing the nation's economic troubles, particularly the **energy crisis**. On July 15, the president delivered his speech, in which he referred to a "crisis of spirit" facing the country and offered recommendations to confront the energy problem. While the president never spelled out what the "crisis of spirit" was, the media used the term "malaise" to describe the nation's temper. From that point, the speech became known as the "malaise" speech.

See also RAFSHOON, GERALD (1934–).

MARCOS, FERDINAND (EMMANUEL EDRALIN) (1917–1989). The president of the Philippines from 1965 to 1986, Ferdinand Marcos was born in the Philippines, received a law degree from the University of the Philippines, and fought against the Japanese during World War II. He was elected to the Philippine Congress after the war and climbed up his country's political ranks. In 1965, he was elected the Philippines' president. He became increasingly corrupt and dictatorial; in 1972, he imposed martial law and arrested numerous political opponents, claiming there was a communist conspiracy seeking to overthrow him. His wife, Imelda, became known for extravagant shopping trips—during one junket, she reportedly spent $2 million in a single day—and for her enormous collection of shoes.

Although President **Jimmy Carter** proclaimed he supported promoting **human rights** in his **foreign policy**, he sought to avoid pressuring countries too hard that were economically, politically, or militarily important to the United States. The Philippines was an example. Strategically located, it was the site of several important U.S. bases, including Clark Air Force Base and Subic Naval Bay. Moreover, Marcos wanted an increase in the amount of money the United States paid him for the land on which those bases were located. When Assistant Secretary for Human Rights **Patricia Derian** visited the Philippines in January 1978 and blasted Marcos for the treatment of his people, Secretary of State **Cyrus Vance**, National Security Adviser **Zbigniew Brzezinski**, and Deputy Secretary of State **Warren Christopher** asked Carter to have Vice President **Walter Mondale** travel to the Philippines to smooth things over. Mondale did just that. Furthermore, the White House accepted Marcos's demand for more monetary compensation. Carter's refusal to do more about Marcos's repressive policies was one reason why Derian considered resigning from the administration.

Marcos's downfall began in the early 1980s. A political opponent, Benigno Aquino Jr., returned to the Philippines in 1983, after spending years in exile, and was shot dead after getting off his plane. In 1985, a resolution signed by Filipino lawmakers charged Marcos with diverting U.S. aid for personal use. A year later, he engaged in fraud to win reelection, triggering condemnation from within and outside the Philippines. His health declining, his support at home fading, and his U.S. ally urging him to relinquish power, Marcos went into exile in Hawaii. An investigation found that he and his family had committed widespread fraud, and he and Imelda were charged with racketeering. He died before he could be tried. Imelda was acquitted and shortly thereafter returned to the Philippines.

MARIEL BOATLIFT. *See* CUBA, RELATIONS WITH; REFUGEE ACT.

MARSHALL, (FREDDIE) RAY (1928–). The secretary of **labor** from 1977 to 1981, Ray Marshall was a staunch defender of the rights of workers. Born in 1928 in Oak Grove, Louisiana, he lied about his age to join the U.S. Navy and saw action in World War II. After the war, he went to college, and in 1955, he received his Ph.D. in economics from the University of California at Berkeley. He had begun teaching at universities even before he received his doctorate and continued to do so until 1976, during which time he wrote numerous books on labor-related issues. He also served on a number of national committees and boards. Accordingly, when President-elect **Jimmy Carter** selected him to serve as secretary of labor, Marshall was already well connected nationally.

As secretary, Marshall convinced Carter to increase the number of public-service jobs, particularly for younger individuals, and to raise the national minimum wage. He joined **Health, Education**, and Welfare Secretary **Joseph Califano** in molding a program to reform the nation's welfare system, though it was never passed by Congress. While labor leaders grew frustrated with Carter's fiscal conservatism and unwillingness to give priority to combating unemployment rather than **inflation**, Marshall proved able to remain on friendly terms with both the president and workers. After leaving the White House, Marshall returned to academia and is presently Professor Emeritus of the Audre and Bernard Rapoport Centennial Chair in Economics and Public Affairs at the University of Texas at Austin.

MARSHALL, THURGOOD (1908–1993). An associate justice of the **Supreme Court** from 1967 to 1991, Thurgood Marshall was born in Baltimore and educated at Howard University Law School, where he graduated at the top of his class (1933). His first position was as legal counsel to the National Association for the Advancement of Colored People (NAACP). He then became the director of the NAACP Legal Defense and **Education** Fund. In this position he won a series of **civil rights** cases before the United States Supreme Court, including *Murray v. Pearson* (1936), his first case. Of the 32 cases he argued in front of the Court, he won 27. His greatest success was the Supreme Court's decision in *Brown v. Board of Education* (1954).

In 1961 President John F. Kennedy nominated Marshall for a judgeship on the Second Circuit Court of Appeals. He served on that court for four years, when he accepted President Lyndon B. Johnson's request that he serve as solicitor general. In 1967, Johnson nominated Marshall to the Supreme Court. Appointed by the Senate later that year, he became the first **African American** to sit on the country's highest bench. He joined the majority of justices in favoring the 1973 *Roe v. Wade* decision that granted **women** the right to an **abortion**. In the 1978 case *Regents of the University of California v. Bakke*, he strongly endorsed **affirmative action**. Marshall showed growing frustration as the Court moved increasingly to the political right during the **Ronald Reagan** administration. He resigned in 1991 and passed away two years later from heart failure.

THE MARY TYLER MOORE SHOW. One of the most watched **television** shows in the 1970s, the weekly comedy was unique for a couple of reasons. One was the star, Mary Tyler Moore, who had made a name for herself on *The Dick Van Dyke Show* in the 1960s. The other was that Mary was a single **woman** who had entered the world of men. Working at a local television news program, she always seemed to know just how to react to all situations commonly faced by single women in a male-dominated world.

M*A*S*H. Based upon a 1968 novel of the same name by Richard Hooker, *M*A*S*H* was one of the most popular **television** shows of all time. Focusing on the lives of doctors and staff at a mobile army surgical hospital during the Korean War, it aired from 1972 until 1983. The finale to this day holds the record for the most people who viewed a television episode. In its earlier seasons, many of the installments came from the stories of real MASH surgeons who served in the Korean War. *M*A*S*H* remains one of the most highly regarded television programs of all time.

MASTERS, WILLIAM HOWELL (1915–2001), AND JOHNSON, VIRGINIA ESHELMAN (1925–). William Masters and Virginia Johnson became well known for their work on human sexuality. Born in Cleveland, Masters received his bachelor's degree from Hamilton College. He then attended the University of Rochester Medical School where he became interested in human sexuality. Following a brief period of service with the U.S. Navy in World War II, in 1943 he completed his medical degree. Johnson, born in Missouri, attended Drury College in 1941 but did not finish her degree. Over the next 15 years, she took on several jobs, married and divorced three times, and had two children. In 1956, she went to St. Louis in the hopes of working at Washington University while trying to get a degree in sociology. It was there that she met Masters, who was seeking volunteers for a research project on sex.

Over the next 11 years, Masters and Johnson (who had kept the last name of her third husband) studied 700 people, ranging in age from 18 to 89, of whom just over half were **women**. Photographing their subjects, they determined that men and women went through four stages of sexual arousal. They published their findings in 1966 under the title *Human Sexual Response*, which became a national best seller. They married in 1971 and in 1973 founded the Masters and Johnson Institute to study human sexuality. Two years later, in their book *The Pleasure Bond: A New Look at Sexuality and Commitment*, Masters and Johnson argued that complete faithfulness to one's partner guaranteed a healthy, long-term sexual relationship. In 1979, in *Homosexuality in Perspective*, they claimed that homosexual behavior was learned rather than based upon genetics or emotion; they even asserted that they had helped **gays** and lesbians become heterosexuals. In 1992, Masters and Johnson divorced, and two years later the institute closed its doors. Johnson, who acquired most of the institute's records following her divorce, continues her research.

McDONALD, AL (ALONZO LOWRY) (1928–). An assistant to President **Jimmy Carter** from 1977 to 1981, Al McDonald was born in Atlanta, graduated from Emory University in 1948, worked for the *Atlanta Journal* from 1948 to 1950, served in the U.S. Marine Corps for the following two years, and then went to Harvard University, where he received a degree in business in 1956. Afterward, he began work with the consulting firm McKinsey and Co.

It was at a fund-raising dinner in New York in 1976 that McDonald first met Jimmy Carter. Following Carter's victory in that year's presidential election, **Robert Strauss**, appointed by Carter as special trade representative, asked McDonald to join him in trade negotiations to take place in **Japan**. Strauss and McDonald spent the next two years working closely together, during which time Strauss convinced Japan to open its market to U.S. imports.

While working with Strauss, McDonald came to the attention of **Hamilton Jordan**, one of President Carter's closest confidants and top aides. Learning in 1979 that Carter was about to appoint him chief of staff, Jordan contacted Strauss, who suggested that Jordan hire a deputy. After discussions with several people, Jordan offered the job to McDonald. McDonald worked to improve coordination in the West Wing. He had doors, walls, and offices moved. For instance, he brought together the offices of those involved in congressional liaison. He then placed his office between those offices and the offices of Jordan and the president to make sure the West Wing staff understood how the hierarchy functioned and, in turn, to improve discipline. To reinforce his authority, he made sure to be seen with Jordan as often as possible. He also began to oversee speechwriting and made sure speechwriters had improved access to the president, particularly when preparing major addresses. For the most part, his effort to centralize West Wing operations received praise from his colleagues.

Following Carter's term in office, McDonald became president of the Bendix Corporation. He stayed there until 1983, when he began working as counselor to the dean of the Harvard University Business School. That same year, he founded Avenir Group Inc., a private development bank. He stopped working with Harvard in 1987 but continues his work with Avenir, for which he is chief executive officer.

McGOVERN, GEORGE STANLEY (1922–2012). Democrat. A U.S. senator from 1963 to 1981 and three-time presidential candidate (1968, 1972, and 1984), George McGovern was born in Avon, South Dakota, in 1922. He had to put his college education on hold so he could join the U.S. Army Air Corps during World War II. After the war, he finished his degree at Dakota Wesleyan University in 1946 and then went to Northwestern University, where he received his master's in 1950 and his doctorate in history in 1953. While finishing his doctorate, he worked as a faculty member at Dakota Wesleyan.

McGovern had shown an interest in politics as early as high school, where he was elected class president twice. In 1948, he was a delegate to the Progressive Party Convention that nominated Henry Wallace for president. Four years later, he became a volunteer for Adlai Stevenson, who unsuccessfully ran as the Democratic Party's presidential nominee that year. Yet

McGovern did a good enough job to receive an appointment as the South Dakota Democratic Party's executive secretary, and his reputation helped him win a seat in the U.S. House of Representatives in 1956. There he served two terms before launching a failed bid for the U.S. Senate. In 1962, he ran for the state's other Senate post and won.

McGovern became among the chief liberals in Congress. He supported the Great Society and opposed the Vietnam War. He sought the Democratic Party's nomination for the presidency in 1968 and again in 1972; his efforts did not bear fruit in 1968, but he succeeded in getting the party's endorsement four years later. However, he ended up losing the 1972 election to the **Republican** nominee, **Richard Nixon**. McGovern's defeat in 1972 was one of the reasons why **Jimmy Carter** decided to seek the presidency in 1976. He believed that his qualifications were as strong as McGovern's. He made sure, however, to adopt a more moderate stance than McGovern had in the previous election.

Carter and McGovern often butted heads. On the one hand, the senator endorsed the president's decision to cancel production of the **B-1 bomber** and praised the **Camp David Accords**. On the other, he regarded Carter's fiscal policies as too conservative and too harmful to the poor, voted for the **Panama Canal treaties** only after the second treaty included a statement forbidding the United States from interfering in Panama's internal affairs, contended that the **Strategic Arms Limitation Treaty (SALT II)** of 1979 did not go far enough in curbing the threat posed by atomic weapons, and believed the White House's support for **deregulation** of the airline industry would lead airlines to stop flying to some South Dakota cities.

McGovern suffered politically and personally beginning in 1980. The nation had shifted to the political right, which did not bode well for a senator who remained wedded to a liberal agenda. Indeed, he lost a bid for reelection to the Republican nominee, James Abdnor. In 1984, McGovern made an abortive bid for the White House. In 1988, he purchased a hotel in Connecticut but had to declare bankruptcy two years later. His daughter, Terry, suffered from alcoholism and, after a drinking binge, froze to death in 1994.

Despite such setbacks and tragedies, McGovern refused to give up on politics. In the 1990s, he headed the Middle East Policy Council, the purpose of which was to teach Americans about various issues that affected U.S. interests in that part of the world. Considered an expert on world hunger, he spent three years (2000–2003) as U.S. Ambassador to the UN Food and Agricultural Organization. He criticized the decision of President George W. Bush to go to war with Iraq in 2003. In the 2008 presidential election, he first endorsed Senator Hillary Clinton, but, deciding after a time that Clinton could not win, backed Senator Barack Obama. In 2009, he published a biography of Abraham Lincoln. McGovern was hospitalized several times in 2011 and 2012. He passed away in October 2012.

See also MONDALE, WALTER FREDERICK (FRITZ) (1928–); RIBIC-OFF, ABRAHAM ALEXANDER (1910–1998); WARNKE, PAUL CULLI-TON (1920–2001); WEXLER, ANNE LEVY (1930–2009).

McINTYRE, JAMES TALMADGE, JR. (1940–). Democrat. James McIntyre was the successor to **Bert Lance**, serving as director of the Office of Management and Budget (OMB) from 1977 to 1981. Born in Vidalia, Georgia, McIntyre received both his bachelor and law degrees from the University of Georgia in 1963 and oversaw the Office of Planning and Budget for Governor **Jimmy Carter**. After Carter became president, McIntyre served as Lance's assistant.

Like Carter, McIntyre was a financial conservative. He believed the administration's top priority for the **economy** should be fighting **inflation** rather than unemployment. He also called for limited spending on social programs. As such, he found himself at odds with more liberal members of the administration, including Secretary of **Health**, **Education**, and Welfare **Joseph Califano** and Vice President **Walter Mondale**, as well as liberal Democrats in Congress. He became frustrated with opposition by such individuals to budget cuts that he felt were necessary but which would have affected programs favored by them. When Carter left office in 1981, McIntyre headed to Washington, D.C., where he opened the McIntyre Law Firm and then McIntyre and Lemon, PLLC. Additionally, he became a director of the Committee for a Responsible Budget.

McKAY, JIM (JAMES) (1921–2008). Born James McManus in Philadelphia, Pennsylvania, McKay served in the U.S. Navy during World War II. After the war he hosted a **sports** program in Baltimore. His personality led the American Broadcasting Company (ABC) to hire McKay to host their new *Wide World of Sports*, which became one of **television**'s most popular sports shows. McKay hosted the show from 1961 to 1998. One of his most outstanding programs appeared after the 1972 Munich **Olympics** where 11 **Israeli** athletes were murdered by Palestinian terrorists. McKay traveled the world to host various sports events. He used the last name "McKay" after hosting *The Real McKay*, a New York sports program.

McMAHON, ED(WARD) (1923–2009). Known primarily as **Johnny Carson**'s sidekick on **television**'s *The Tonight Show*, Ed McMahon was born in Michigan. He began his collegiate career in 1940 at Boston College but dropped out to fight during World War II in the U.S. Marine Corps. He joined flight school and trained pilots; he did not himself see combat, for shortly after he received his orders in 1945 to head to the Pacific, the war ended. With peace restored, McMahon finished his undergraduate studies at the Catholic University of America. Recalled to military duty when the Korean War began in 1950, he flew over 80 combat missions. After that conflict ended, he joined the Marine reserve, retiring with the rank of colonel in 1966.

In 1962, McMahon began a three-decade career as the announcer of *The Today Show*. He had known Carson from their work together on the game show *Who Do You Trust?*, which aired from 1957 to 1962. In addition, he cohosted the *Jerry Lewis Labor Day Telethon* from 1973 to 2008 and was one of several individuals who covered the Macy's Thanksgiving Day Parade. In 1992, both he and Carson retired from *The Tonight Show*. He passed away in 2009 from natural causes.

McMURTRY, LARRY (1936–). In the 1970s, author Larry McMurtry used contemporary Texas or the Old West as a setting for most of his popular stories. He was born and raised in Texas and received his degree from the University of North Texas (B.A., 1958) followed by his M.A. in 1960 from Rice University. He wrote the following stories, which all became successful movies: *The Last Picture Show* (1966); *Terms of Endearment* (1984), which won the Best Picture Award at the Academy Awards; and *Lonesome Dove*, which became a popular **television** movie.

See also CINEMA; LITERATURE.

MEANY, GEORGE (1894–1980). President of the **American Federation of Labor and Congress of Industrial Organizations (AFL-CIO)** from 1955 to 1979, Meany was born in New York City. His father headed a local plumber's union. Meany followed his father's lead, leaving school at age 16 to become a plumber's apprentice; he got his certificate in 1915. He rose rapidly up the union ranks, becoming business agent of the local union in 1922, president of the New York State Federation of **Labor** in 1934, and secretary-treasurer of the AFL in 1939. In 1952, Meany succeeded AFL president William Green when Green retired. Three years later, he unified the AFL and CIO, and the newly combined union named him president. Until his death in 1979, Meany fought for the workers he represented, seeking to provide them with better wages, benefits, and working conditions. He also strongly opposed communism and supported U.S. involvement in Vietnam.

A **Democrat** from the time he could vote, Meany favored in the 1976 presidential election individuals such as Senator **Henry Jackson** or former vice president **Hubert Humphrey**, whom he considered more in line with his values than **Jimmy Carter**. Yet he endorsed Carter when the Georgia governor won the party's nomination. With the help of organized labor, Carter went on to win the election. The goodwill did not last. Meany was upset that both Carter and some of the president's advisers, among them the chairman of the Council of Economic Advisers, **Charles Schultze**, and the head of the Council on Wage and Price Stability, **Alfred Kahn**, tended to give little time to union workers. To Carter, Schultze, and Kahn, union demands for higher salaries were partially responsible for what had become a serious problem with **inflation**. Furthermore, in Schultze's mind, the wages demanded by labor made it more difficult for the United States to compete in the global marketplace. To Meany, the White House was too willing to sacrifice workers' interests in the name of holding down prices. Even so, in September 1979, Carter announced that the AFL-CIO had agreed to join a pay advisory board. Two months later, Meany stepped down as AFL-CIO head because of deteriorating health and turned his responsibilities over to Lane Kirkland, who the administration found more amenable to its interests. Meany passed away in January 1980.

See also ECONOMY; MILLER, G. (GEORGE) WILLIAM (1925–2006).

METRIC CONVERSION ACT. Signed into law in 1975, the Metric Conversion Act declared that the United States would use the metric system for trade and commercial transactions but permit the customary system for activities unrelated to business. The act further created a United States Metric Board to teach the American people about the metric system and encourage that system's use. The conversion to metric was slow and partial.

MICROSOFT. *See* GATES, BILL (WILLIAM HENRY III) (1955–); COMPUTERS.

MILK, HARVEY (1930–1978). The first openly **gay** person elected to public office in California, and the first gay nonincumbent elected in the United States, Milk was born on Long Island, New York. He received a bachelor's degree from the New York State College for Teachers and, after graduating in 1951, spent four years serving in the U.S. Navy. He kept his homosexuality secret while carrying on several romances following his time in the military. In 1969, he moved with his partner to San Francisco, which by that time had developed a thriving gay community. He became politically active and, in 1976, won a seat on the city's board of supervisors. In November 1978, Dan White—a city supervisor who had quit his post, sought to get it back, and was refused by Mayor George Moscone—shot and killed both Moscone and Milk. In 2009, President Barack Obama posthumously awarded Milk the Presidential Medal of Freedom.

MILLER, G. (GEORGE) WILLIAM (1925–2006). The chair of the Federal Reserve Board (FRB) from 1978 to 1979 and secretary of the treasury from 1979 to 1981, G. William Miller was born in Sapulpa, Oklahoma. He attended Amarillo College, served with the U.S. Coast Guard from 1945 to

1949, and in 1951 went to the University of California, from which he obtained his law degree. After working for a time in a New York City law firm, he left in 1956 to work in the textile company Textron. Twelve years later, he became Textron's chief executive officer, a post he would hold for a decade.

When FRB chairman **Arthur Burns**'s term expired, President **Jimmy Carter** decided not to renew it and instead selected Miller to assume the post. The choice did not play well on Wall Street, for Miller did not have a background in economics or banking. To Carter, however, Miller was more likely than Burns to follow his lead on tackling the nation's troubled **economy**, including stabilizing the dollar and curbing **inflation**. Miller did just that, raising the rate the Federal Reserve charged banks on loans and making it easier for foreign nations to purchase U.S. dollars. Though his actions did indeed stabilize the dollar, Miller came under criticism for not doing enough on that score or on curbing inflation. Indeed, by mid-1979, inflation had hit double digits. Facing intense criticism from within and outside the United States regarding Miller's stewardship at the Fed, Carter appointed Miller to replace the recently fired treasury secretary, **Michael Blumenthal**.

As secretary of the treasury, Miller opposed the policies of his Fed successor, **Paul Volcker**, who believed that the best way to address the nation's economic troubles was to have the market determine interest rates rather than the Federal Reserve. He also seized Iranian assets in the United States during the **Iran hostage crisis**, attempted to smooth over the difficult relationship Carter had with **American Federation of Labor and Council for Industrial Organizations** president **George Meany**, and oversaw in 1980 the loan program aimed at preventing the Chrysler Corporation from going bankrupt. When Carter's tenure in office ended, Miller worked in the investment firm G. William Miller & Co. and for a time was chief executive of Federated Stores. He passed away from pulmonary fibrosis, a lung condition.

MILLS, WILBUR DAIGH (1909–1992). Democrat. A member of the House of Representatives from 1939 to 1977, Wilbur Mills was born in Arkansas. He attended Hendrix College in Conway, Arkansas, and then Harvard University, where he received his law degree. He served as a judge from 1935 to 1938 and, in 1939, was elected to represent Arkansas in the U.S. House. He was chair of the powerful Ways and Means Committee for 18 of the 36 years he spent in Congress. In 1972 he sought but did not receive the Democratic nomination for the presidency. Two incidents involving public intoxication led him to give up his Ways and Means post in 1975 and not seek reelection the following year. Afterward, he devoted his time to raising money and heightening awareness to fight alcoholism.

MINORITY SET-ASIDES. In 1977, the federal government passed legislation that required that 10 percent of federal monies used for public works programs go to companies owned by minorities. H. Earl Fullilove argued that this provision violated the Constitution. However, the U.S. **Supreme Court** ruling in the 1980 case of *Fullilove v. Klutznick* upheld the ruling of lower courts that the legislation was legal.

MONDALE, WALTER FREDERICK (FRITZ) (1928–). Democrat. The vice president of the United States from 1977 to 1981 and Democratic presidential candidate in 1984, Walter Mondale was born in Ceylon, Minnesota, to a Methodist minister who encouraged help for the needy. Mondale demonstrated a strong interest in politics during his freshman year at Macalester College, when he served as a volunteer for **Hubert Humphrey**, who was then running for mayor of Minneapolis. In 1948, he again worked for Humphrey, this time helping him win a seat in the U.S. Senate. After Mondale graduated from Macalester, he spent a year in Washington, D.C., and then returned to Minnesota, where he obtained his law degree in 1956 from the University of Minnesota.

While practicing law in Minneapolis, Mondale found time to continue his political work. In 1960, he managed Orville Freeman's gubernatorial campaign. After winning, Freeman appointed Mondale as state attorney general. When Humphrey became vice president in the Lyndon B. Johnson administration, the new governor, Karl Rolvaag, had Mondale take over Humphrey's Senate seat. There, Mondale developed a reputation as a liberal who supported Johnson's Great Society programs. He also garnered enough name recognition that Senator **George McGovern** considered naming Mondale as his running mate after McGovern won the Democratic Party's presidential nomination in 1972. Four years later, **Jimmy Carter** selected Mondale as his vice presidential running mate. In Mondale, Carter saw someone who could draw votes from the Midwest and from liberals. Moreover, the Minnesotan's extensive experience in the U.S. capital would prove useful as the White House pushed forward its legislative agenda. Finally, Carter had wanted an activist vice president and liked Mondale's insistence that he play more than a symbolic role in a Carter administration.

Mondale indeed became an active participant in the administration. He acted as the White House's representative on over a dozen foreign trips, oversaw the administration's Africa policy, was vital to Senate ratification of the **Panama Canal treaties** and congressional passage of legislation to combat the **energy crisis**, successfully fought to have Attorney General **Griffin Bell** rewrite the Justice Department's brief in the **Supreme Court** case *Regents of the University of California v. Bakke*, and took part in the negotiations that led to the **Camp David Accords**. He did have disagreements with the president. Aside from their ideological differences, he believed Carter's legislative agenda was too ambitious and later commented that the president's disdain for the political game of give-and-take made it difficult to get support on Capitol Hill for administration initiatives. Yet throughout he remained loyal to Carter.

After Carter's loss in the 1980 presidential election, Mondale took a job with a Washington law firm. But he could not resist the pull of politics and, by the end of 1981, had decided to run for the Democratic nomination for the presidency. He received the party's nod in 1984, only to lose in a landslide to **Ronald Reagan**. In 1987, he joined the Minneapolis law firm of Dorsey and Whitney. From 1993 to 1996, he served as President Bill Clinton's ambassador to **Japan**. After Minnesota senator Paul Wellstone died in a plane crash, Mondale ran for the seat but lost. He continues to practice law and lecture.

See also AARON, DAVID LAURENCE (1938–); JORDAN, BARBARA (1936–1996); KLUTZNICK, PHILIP MORRIS (1907–1999); LANCE, BERT (THOMAS BERTRAM) (1931–); MARCOS, FERDINAND (EMMANUEL EDRALIN) (1917–1989); McINTYRE, JAMES TALMADGE, JR. (1940–).

MONDAY NIGHT FOOTBALL. First aired in 1970, Monday Night Football has become one of the longest-running and highest-rated prime-time programs. Originally airing on the American Broadcasting Company (ABC), it was obtained by **ESPN (Entertainment and Sports Programming Network)** in 2005. Sportscaster **Howard Cosell** quickly became a favorite with viewers. Monday Night Football is still the most watched **television** series in U.S. history.

See also FOOTBALL.

MOORE, FRANK (1935–). President **Jimmy Carter**'s assistant for congressional liaison from 1977 to 1981, Frank Moore was born in Gainesville, Georgia. He received a bachelor's degree from the University of Georgia and later oversaw the Head Start program in the northeast part of his home state. It was while he was working for Head Start that he met Carter, who was then making his first bid for Georgia's governorship. Carter failed in this attempt to win the state's highest-elected post but made another run, this time successful, in 1970. Moore had volunteered during the 1970 campaign, and in return Carter offered him a post working for his chief of staff, **Hamilton Jordan**. In 1973, Moore took Jordan's place after Jordan began to work for the **Democratic** National Committee. Moore served as the Carter presidential campaign's national finance chairman during the **1976 election** and, at the governor's request, took time to get to know lawmakers on Capitol Hill.

It was because of Moore's experience working for him that following the election President Carter appointed Moore as his liaison to Congress. Moore had a difficult time in that role, for lawmakers believed the president tended to ignore them and placed much of the blame on Moore and his staff. There was some truth to that accusation, for Moore was known not to return the phone calls from members of Congress or meet with them in social gatherings. Still, Moore could take credit for playing an important part in many of the administration's achievements, including **deregulation policies**, the **Panama Canal treaties**, and **environmental** legislation. After Carter's defeat, Moore worked for Waste Management Incorporated and is presently vice president for government relations for the underwater-technology company Coda Octopus Group Inc.

MORAL MAJORITY. *See* FALWELL, JERRY (1933–2007); RELIGION.

MOTOR CARRIER ACT. *See* DEREGULATION POLICIES.

MOUNT SAINT HELENS. One of a number of active volcanoes that lines the U.S. West Coast, Mount Saint Helens is located in southwestern Washington State. In late March 1980, the 9,677-foot-tall volcano began to experience earthquakes, followed by a series of eruptions, prompting officials to order an evacuation of the area around the mountain. On 18 May, the volcano experienced a massive explosion that blew out its north side, flattened over 350 square miles of forest, killed 57 people—including scientists and at least one resident who refused the evacuation order—and reduced the mountain's height by 1,300 feet. The $1 billion in damage made it the most expensive volcanic disaster in U.S. history.

MOYNIHAN, DANIEL PATRICK (1927–2003). Democrat. A U.S. senator from 1977 to 2001, Daniel Patrick Moynihan had had a long career in the executive branch prior to entering the halls of Congress. Born in Tulsa, Oklahoma, he grew up in New York City, where he began taking college classes before joining the U.S. Navy to fight in World War II. After the war, he went to Tufts University (B.A., 1948; M.A., 1949; Ph.D., 1961). He then became active in politics. Though a Democrat, he served in both Democratic and **Republican** administrations, including as chief aide to New York State governor Averell Harriman, assistant secretary in the Department of Labor under Presidents John F. Kennedy and Lyndon B. Johnson, head of President **Richard Nixon**'s Urban Affairs Council, and permanent representative to the United Nations under President **Gerald Ford**.

In 1976, Moynihan left his UN post to make an ultimately successful bid for a seat in the U.S. Senate. That same year, **Jimmy Carter** won the U.S. presidential election. The relationship between the two men was not close. Moynihan declared that the Carter administration was too soft on the **Union of Soviet Socialist Republics (USSR)** and considered the **Strategic Arms Limitation Treaty (SALT II)** an example of appeasement. He called for doing more for social security and attacked Carter's call in 1979 to reduce welfare costs in the name of combating **inflation**. Moynihan came to dislike Carter enough that he openly endorsed Senator **Edward Kennedy** for the Democratic presidential nomination in 1980.

Moynihan was critical as well of Carter's successors. He blasted President **Ronald Reagan**'s cuts in social welfare programs, voted against giving President **George H. W. Bush** the authority to attack Iraq following Iraq's 1990 invasion of Kuwait, and insisted that President Bill Clinton's proposal for national **health** care insurance was not the proper way to address the nation's health care problems. While in the year 2000 he certainly would have won another Senate term had he decided to run, he chose instead to retire. He passed away in 2003 following surgery for a ruptured appendix.

THE MUPPET SHOW. See HENSON, JIM (1936–1990).

MUSIC. The 1970s offered music fans many different genres, groups, and singers. The decade saw the rise and decline of **disco**, a form of music that made groups like **ABBA**, the **Bee Gees**, and the Village People famous. Hard rock, featuring such bands as **Led Zeppelin**, Black Sabbath, KISS, and AC/DC, became popular. Punk rock, which was largely an underground movement in the 1960s, emerged thanks to the Ramones and Blondie (the latter of which would become one of the bigger pop music groups of the 1980s). Funk music, popular particularly among the **African American** community, bred James Brown, Sly and the Family Stone, Stevie Wonder, and others. **Michael Jackson**, who became one of the most popular artists in U.S. history, began his solo career. George Thorogood played a form that combined rock and blues, as did ZZ Top. Country and soft rock groups and singers popular in the decade included **John Denver**, Jim Croce, and Fleetwood Mac. The **Grateful Dead**, a band formed in the 1960s that fused rock, folk, **jazz**, and country, performed almost nonstop throughout the decade. Some of these bands, including AC/DC, George Thorogood, and KISS, continue to tour.

The 1970s also witnessed the breakup of groups and the death of musical artists. The Beatles disbanded at the beginning of the decade, though members Paul McCartney and **John Lennon** established lucrative solo careers. Rock music lost Jimi Hendrix and Janis Joplin, while jazz said good-bye to Louis Armstrong and Duke Ellington. The psychedelic rock group the Doors broke up shortly after the death of lead singer Jim Morrison in 1971. Jim Croce died in a plane crash in 1973. **Elvis Presley**, who became one of the great singers of the 1950s, passed away in 1977, as did the actor and crooner Bing Crosby. In 1980, Lennon lost his life to a deranged fan. That same year, Led Zeppelin broke up after the band's drummer, John Bonham, passed away.

See also A CHORUS LINE; DOMINGO, PLACIDO (JOSE PLACIDO DOMINGO EMBIL) (1941–); EASTWOOD, CLINTON, JR. (1930–); HAMLISCH, MARVIN FREDERICK (1944–2012); *HAPPY DAYS*; JOHN, ELTON (1947–); LUCAS, GEORGE (1944–); TECHNOLOGICAL ADVANCES; THEATER; WEBBER, ANDREW LLOYD (1948–); WILLIAMS, JOHN (1932–).

MUSKIE, EDMUND SIXTUS (1914–1996). Democrat. A U.S. senator from 1959 to 1980 and secretary of state from 1980 to 1981, Edmund Muskie was born in Rumford, Maine. He attended Bates College (B.A., 1936), received a law degree from Cornell University (LL.B., 1939), and then opened a legal practice in his home state. He served in the U.S. Navy during World War II. Afterward, he was elected to the Maine state legislature, where he spent eight years before voters chose him as the state's governor. In 1959, he ran for and won a seat in the U.S. Senate. In the Upper House, he became known for his hard work, his promotion of bipartisanship, and his support for **environmental** legislation. Yet Muskie had little national recognition until 1968, when Vice President **Hubert Humphrey**, who was then seeking the presidency, selected him as his vice presidential candidate. Humphrey lost, but Muskie achieved enough notoriety to become the Democrats' likely presidential candidate in 1972. His hope to receive his party's nod, however, unraveled after he appeared to cry while defending his wife against accusations made about her. The incident raised questions about Muskie's mental stability and prompted him to withdraw from the race.

In 1976, **Jimmy Carter** had considered Muskie as a possible vice presidential candidate but instead selected **Walter Mondale**, whom he found more in tune with the party's left wing. Personally, Muskie liked Carter, but politically, he was critical of many of the president's actions, including Carter's decisions not to fund a number of water projects and to forego a $50 tax rebate to Americans. It was thus a surprise to Muskie and many observers when Carter selected the senator to replace **Cyrus Vance** as secretary of state following Vance's resignation in 1980. Muskie knew that Vance had vied with National Security Adviser **Zbigniew Brzezinski** for control over the administration's **foreign policy** and hoped to achieve a better working relationship with Brzezinski. Here, he was only partially successful. Most notably, Brzezinski kept Muskie uninformed about Presidential Directive (PD) 59, which called for a major U.S. arms buildup, until the secretary of state read about it in a news story. Indeed, Carter had by this time come to rely so heavily upon Brzezinski for advice that Muskie found himself relegated largely to the role of an administration spokesman.

Following Carter's defeat in the **1980 election**, Muskie joined a law practice in Washington, D.C. He was also a member of the Tower Commission, which investigated the actions taken by the **Ronald Reagan** administration during the Iran-Contra affair. In 1993, he headed a delegation to Vietnam to consider lifting an embargo on trade with that nation dating back to the end of the Vietnam War. He passed away in 1996 from a heart attack.

See also CHRISTOPHER, WARREN MINOR (1925–2011); WARNKE, PAUL CULLITON (1920–2001).

N

NATIONAL ENERGY ACT. *See* ENERGY CRISIS.

NATIONAL LAMPOON'S ANIMAL HOUSE. This **cinema** comedy re-leased in 1978 is still one of the highest-grossing movies of all time. Set on a college campus, the story centered around two students who wanted to join a fraternity with little success. They were finally accepted into Delta Frater-nity, the worst fraternity at Faber College, on probation for its social conduct. The fraternity members feared they would be expelled and decided to enjoy their remaining time at Faber. Many of the actors were unknown, but their antics left audiences laughing hysterically. The film set the stage for other college movies as well as continued success for many of the actors, including Kevin Bacon and *Saturday Night Live*'s John Belushi.

NATIONAL ORGANIZATION FOR WOMEN (NOW). Founded in 1966, the National Organization for Women began to help women with their **civil rights**, their demand for equal pay, and their efforts to combat sexual harassment. In the 1970s, NOW worked to see Congress pass the **Equal Rights Amendment (ERA)**. The organization's greatest victory was the **Supreme Court**'s decision in the 1973 case of *Roe v Wade*, which upheld a woman's right to an **abortion**.
    See also WOMEN.

NATIVE AMERICANS. Inspired by the **African American civil rights** movement, Native Americans had begun in the 1960s to defend and expand their rights. This included the formation of the American Indian Movement (AIM) in 1968. In the early 1970s, members of AIM took part in protests in Washington, D.C., and at the site of the massacre at Wounded Knee, where in 1890 approximately 200 Sioux Indians had been killed. Some of these protests became violent. Recognizing that Native Americans had been stripped, oftentimes illegally, of their land, and not wanting further, poten-tially violent confrontations, the U.S. government began taking measures to protect the rights of the country's indigenous people. In 1977, the American

189

Indian Policy Review Commission called for rejecting long-standing policies aimed at assimilating Native Americans. In 1978, Congress passed the Indian Child Welfare Act, which gives Native American tribes a significant say regarding the adoption or foster care of American Indian children. That same year, the American Indian Religious Freedom Act guaranteed the right of Native Americans to practice their traditional faiths.

The **Supreme Court** also involved itself in Native American matters. In the case *U.S. v. Wheeler* (1978), the nation's highest bench recognized tribal sovereignty over the prosecution of Native Americans who broke the law, though the Court also gave Congress the final say over the extent to which that sovereignty existed. Two years later, in *U.S. v. Sioux Nation of Indians*, the Court ruled that the Sioux deserved over $100 million in compensation for the loss of the Black Hills, which, the Court stated, had been taken from the Sioux in 1877 in violation of a treaty.

In 1980, the Seminole Indians of Florida became the first to use bingo as a way to make money and become more economically self-sufficient. Today, many tribes run gambling casinos to generate income.

See also UDALL, MORRIS (MO) KING (1922–1998).

NATURAL GAS POLICY ACT. *See* ENERGY CRISIS.

NELSON, GAYLORD ANTON (1916–2005). Democrat. A. U.S. senator from 1963 to 1980, Gaylord Nelson was born in Clear Lake, Wisconsin. He received a law degree from the University of Wisconsin in 1942 and then served in the U.S. Army during World War II. Returning home, he established a law practice in Wisconsin and, in 1948, was elected to the state senate. Ten years later, he became the state's governor. In 1962, he won a seat in the U.S. Senate. A product of a rural family, Nelson had developed a strong interest in the **environment**. As governor he put a tax on cigarettes, the money from which went toward purchasing land for public recreation. As a senator, he proposed a bill to ban the deadly pesticide DDT. But he became best known in 1970 for promoting Earth Day, slated to take place on 22 April of that year. Inspired by the teach-ins of the Vietnam War, the purpose of Earth Day was to encourage similar discussion, but in this case on the environment. That approximately 20 million people took part shocked observers and demonstrated how important protection of the environment had become. The enormous outpouring of sentiment convinced President **Richard Nixon** and lawmakers to establish the Environmental Protection Agency.

Unlike many liberals in Congress, Nelson tended to work well with President **Jimmy Carter**. They fought industrial efforts to weaken the Clean Air Act, sought to impose a windfall profits tax on oil companies, and attempted to force hospitals to enact policies aimed at containing costs for patients.

Nelson's liberal leanings turned away voters as the nation moved in a more conservative direction, and in 1980 he failed to win a fourth Senate term. Afterward, he continued his efforts to protect the environment, becoming a counselor for the Wilderness Society and criticizing President George W. Bush's environmental policies. He died of cardiovascular failure in 2005.

NEUTRON BOMB. Known also as the enriched radiation weapon (ERW), the neutron bomb was designed to produce an enormous radioactive blast that killed people but did not damage buildings. U.S. officials had considered developing such a weapon as early as the 1950s, but it was not until 1976 that Congress passed legislation to fund and construct it. Almost immediately, the ERW generated a debate between the military and those members of Congress who believed it would prove a powerful addition to the U.S. nuclear arsenal, and others, including some lawmakers, who considered it an immoral weapon that violated President **Jimmy Carter**'s commitment to promote **human rights**. Carter's top **foreign policy** advisers endorsed development of the ERW, and the president himself at first appeared to join them. But in April 1978, and to the shock of those same advisers, Carter canceled the bomb's development and production. The ERW was to have been deployed in **West Germany**, and the president based his decision on that nation's refusal to commit itself to having the bomb on its soil. The ERW's defenders charged Carter with weakening America's nuclear deterrent.

See also AARON, DAVID LAURENCE (1938–); CALLAGHAN, JAMES LEONARD (1912–2005); DEFENSE; NUNN, SAM (SAMUEL AUGUSTUS) (1938–); SCHMIDT, HELMUT HEINRICH (1918–); TECHNOLOGICAL ADVANCES.

NICARAGUA, RELATIONS WITH. *See* SANDINISTAS; SOMOZA DEBAYLE, ANASTASIO (1925–1980).

NICKELODEON. Originally called Pinwheel, Nickelodeon began airing in April 1979 as the first cable **television** station to offer programming for children. It has since become the highest-rated cable network among preteens. Additionally, it has expanded to include Nicktoons, which offers animated programs; Nick Jr. for preschoolers; and Teen Nick for teenagers and young adults.

NIXON, RICHARD MILHOUS (1913–1994). Republican. The only president forced to resign, Richard Nixon was a member of the House of Representatives from 1947 to 1951, a U.S. senator from 1951 to 1953, vice president of the United States from 1953 to 1961, and president of the United States from 1969 to 1974. He was born in Yorba Linda, California; received his law degree from Duke University (1937); and returned to California to practice law. Nixon was a representative during the anticommunist witch hunts of the 1940s carried out by the House Un-American Activities Committee (HUAC). One of the most notable cases during the HUAC hearings involved a former United States Department of State official named Alger Hiss. After Hiss was accused by an editor of *Time* magazine of having been a member of the Communist Party, Nixon probed into Hiss's background and established that he had been a communist in the 1930s. His findings led to Hiss's conviction on perjury charges and made Nixon a nationally known figure.

In the 1952 election, Republican presidential nominee Dwight D. Eisenhower selected Nixon as his running mate. Nixon held the vice presidency for the next eight years and became acting president while Eisenhower was in the hospital in 1955, 1956, and 1957. The vice president showed his ability to take charge, all of the time hoping to become the president after Eisenhower left office in 1961. But Nixon lost the 1960 election to **Democrat** John F. Kennedy.

Nixon disappeared from the limelight afterward but returned to the political scene in 1968 when he sought and received the Republican Party's nomination for the presidency. He narrowly defeated his Democratic opponent, Vice President **Hubert Humphrey**. One of the reasons for Nixon's victory was his promise, if elected, to end the Vietnam War. He did so in 1973, but not before incurring heavy American losses. Working closely with his national security adviser, and later secretary of state, **Henry Kissinger**, Nixon became the first president to travel to communist **China** (1972). Because of his visit, Washington and Beijing reopened their relationship. Nixon also traveled to the **Union of Soviet Socialist Republics (USSR)** (1972) where he signed the first **Strategic Arms Limitation Treaty** (SALT I) with Moscow.

Nixon's political career, however, came to an ignominious end because of the Watergate scandal. In 1972, five burglars broke into the Democratic Party's headquarters, located in the Watergate hotel in Washington, D.C. When it became clear that at least one of the burglars had ties to the White House, Nixon involved himself in an effort to cover up any ties to the crime. Congressional hearings found evidence of Nixon's involvement; realizing he risked impeachment, he resigned.

Nixon, however, did not disappear. Pardoned by President **Gerald Ford**, Nixon tried to remain politically involved. He gave advice to Ford during the **1976 election**, endorsed ratification of the **Panama Canal treaties**, and praised the **Camp David Accords**. But he disliked the SALT II agreement signed by President **Jimmy Carter** and Soviet leader **Leonid Brezhnev**, and he was upset by the White House's treatment of the shah of **Iran, Mo-**

hammed **Reza Pahlavi**. In his later years, he wrote a number of books on **foreign policy** and, while unable to put Watergate behind him, saw his reputation somewhat revitalized. He died of a stroke in April 1994.

See also CENTRAL INTELLIGENCE AGENCY (CIA); CINEMA; DOLE, ROBERT JOSEPH (1923–); ETHICS IN GOVERNMENT ACT; FOREIGN INTELLIGENCE SURVEILLANCE ACT (FISA); HOFFA, JAMES "JIMMY" (1913–1975); HUMAN RIGHTS; McGOVERN, GEORGE STANLEY (1922–2012); MOYNIHAN, DANIEL PATRICK (1927–2003); NELSON, GAYLORD ANTON (1916–2005); PERCY, CHARLES HARTING (1919–2011); REHNQUIST, WILLIAM HUBBS (1924–2005); SAFIRE, WILLIAM (1929–2009); SCHLESINGER, JAMES RODNEY (1929–); SOUTH KOREA, RELATIONS WITH; SPACE PROGRAM; STEVENS, JOHN PAUL (1920–); VOLCKER, PAUL ADOLPH (1927–).

NOBEL PEACE PRIZE. In the 1890s, the Swedish industrialist Alfred Nobel established international prizes to recognize those who made advancements in the hard sciences, literature, and peace. The last of these prizes, awarded in December of each year, was given to **Jimmy Carter** in 2002 for his efforts to promote world peace. Some critics charged that the Nobel Prize committee awarded it to Carter as a way to denounce President George W. Bush. Bush had recently received congressional authorization to use force against the Iraqi government of **Saddam Hussein**; Carter had been critical of Bush's determination to take military action against Hussein.

NUCLEAR NONPROLIFERATION ACT. The effort to prevent the spread of atomic technology began shortly after World War II and had seen success in 1968 when the United Nations General Assembly endorsed the Nonproliferation Treaty (NPT). Numerous countries, including the United States, ratified the agreement soon thereafter. But some, among them India and Pakistan, refused to sign. India's successful test of a nuclear device in 1974 and the possibility of other countries following suit convinced members of Congress overwhelmingly to pass in 1978 the Nuclear Nonproliferation Act. The law requires Congress to approve nuclear assistance to any country that has refused to sign the NPT or to have its atomic facilities meet safeguards established by the International Atomic Energy Agency.

NUCLEAR REGULATORY COMMISSION (NRC). *See* ENERGY REORGANIZATION ACT.

NUNN, SAM (SAMUEL AUGUSTUS) (1938–). Democrat. Sam Nunn, who served in the U.S. Senate from 1971 to 1996, developed a reputation as one of the Upper House's experts on matters of national **defense**. Born in Perry, Georgia, to a well-off, politically connected family, Nunn started his undergraduate education at Georgia Tech University. However, in 1959 he dropped out to become a member of the U.S. Coast Guard. A year later, he joined the Coast Guard reserves and completed his undergraduate course work at Emory University. In 1962, he received a law degree, also from Emory. He worked for a time on the staff of the House Armed Services Committee and then returned to Perry, where he was elected in 1968 to the Georgia state legislature. He served on **Jimmy Carter**'s campaign team during Carter's run for the state governorship in 1970. After Carter won the state's highest office, he named Nunn head of the Goals for Georgia program, the purpose of which was to muster support among voters for the governor's agenda. Two years later, Nunn surprised observers by running for and winning a seat in the U.S. Senate. Nunn received a seat on the Armed Services Committee, where he became a close ally of Senator **Henry Jackson**. Like Jackson, Nunn favored sizeable appropriations for defense; otherwise, he tended to be a fiscal conservative.

After Carter won the presidency, he found in Nunn an ally on most issues, including welfare reform, cancelation of the **B-1 bomber**, and ratification of the **Panama Canal treaties**. But the two had a number of disagreements about defense policy. Nunn opposed Carter's call to withdraw U.S. troops from **South Korea** and the president's decision to halt production of the **neutron bomb**. Most significantly, Nunn joined Jackson in refusing to ratify the **Strategic Arms Limitation Treaty (SALT II)** without a promise of greater funding for national defense than favored by the White House.

After Carter's defeat in the **1980 election**, Nunn continued to focus on U.S. defense. Alongside Senator **Barry Goldwater**, he sponsored legislation that strengthened the role of the chairperson of the military's Joint Chiefs of Staff. In 1996, he decided to retire from the Senate and take up a position with a law firm in Atlanta. He no longer practices law but remains politically active. In 2008, some observers speculated that Democratic presidential Barack Obama might choose Nunn as his vice presidential candidate. Presently, Nunn is cochairman and chief executive officer of the Nuclear Threat Initiative, which seeks to curtail the threat posed to the world by weapons of mass destruction.

O

OLYMPICS. While supposedly apolitical, the Olympics oftentimes has political connotations to it, and such was the case in the 1970s. Between 1970 and 1972, the International Olympic Committee expelled both South Africa and **Rhodesia** for supporting apartheid. New Zealand's decision to have its national rugby team tour South Africa prompted two dozen African nations to boycott the Summer Games held in 1976 in Montreal, Canada. But possibly no year saw the Olympics affected by politics more than 1980. The **Union of Soviet Socialist Republics' (USSR)** invasion of **Afghanistan** in December 1979 caused extreme tension between the USSR and the United States. The Winter Games, held in Lake Placid, New York, witnessed the "Miracle on Ice," when the American **hockey** team defeated its heavily favored Soviet rival and then went on to win the gold medal. The Summer Games took place in Moscow, the first time the Olympics had taken place in Eastern Europe or the Soviet Union. Because the Kremlin would not withdraw its troops from Afghanistan, President **Jimmy Carter** refused to permit the U.S. Olympic team to compete in the Summer Games and urged other nations to join the American boycott. Ultimately, about 80 countries participated, the fewest to take part in the Olympics since 1956.

See also COMANECI, NADIA (1962–); FOREIGN POLICY; GREAT BRITAIN, RELATIONS WITH; JACKSON, MAYNARD HOLBROOK, JR. (1938–2003); McKAY, JIM (JAMES) (1921–2008); THATCHER, MARGARET (1925–); YOUNG, ANDREW JACKSON, JR. (1932–).

O'NEILL, TIP (THOMAS PHILLIP O'NEILL JR.) (1912–1994). Democrat. A member of the House of Representatives from 1953 to 1987, the majority leader of the House of Representatives from 1973 to 1977, and Speaker of the House of Representatives from 1977 to 1987, Tip O'Neill was born in Cambridge, Massachusetts. He had seen the effects of the Great Depression and saw in Franklin D. Roosevelt's New Deal programs proof of the good that government could do for those in need. He graduated from Boston College in 1936 and that same year ran for and won a seat in the Massachusetts State House of Representatives. When Representative John F.

Kennedy gave up his seat in the U.S. House of Representatives in 1952 so he could seek membership in the U.S. Senate, O'Neill successfully campaigned to replace him. He gradually rose up the ranks of the Lower House, becoming majority whip in 1971 and, two years later, House majority leader.

O'Neill became Speaker of the House the same year as **Jimmy Carter**'s inauguration as U.S. president. The representative was excited to have a fellow Democrat in the Oval Office, believing the two would endorse a similar agenda. As it turned out, O'Neill and Carter were far from the same both in terms of temperament and political beliefs. Having been elected on an antiestablishment platform, Carter believed he did not owe congressional members of his party anything. Whereas O'Neill understood that politics involved give-and-take, Carter sought to eschew politics altogether. At first, O'Neill tried to stand behind Carter, endorsing the president's program to address the country's **energy crisis** and Carter's decision to cancel the **B-1 bomber**. Yet the two had fundamental disagreements. O'Neill believed that Carter too often disregarded the concerns of Capitol Hill when making decisions, was too fiscally conservative, and was overly focused on **foreign policy** at the expense of the nation's domestic problems. Consequently, when Senator **Edward Kennedy** ran against Carter in 1980 for the Democratic

The president and Speaker of the House Thomas "Tip" O'Neill of Massachusetts. The relationship between Carter and O'Neill grew increasingly tense during the president's term in office. Courtesy of the Jimmy Carter Library.

nomination, O'Neill found himself torn between the incumbent leader of his party and a lawmaker who was from the same state and shared a similar ideology. Unwilling to choose, O'Neill decided it was best to remain neutral.

The **1980 election** saw a shift to the political right, with the Republican candidate, **Ronald Reagan**, capturing the White House and the Republicans assuming control of the Senate. As conservatism made its power felt in Washington through the decade, O'Neill fought to protect New Deal–style programs. Though he was able to shield Social Security, Medicare, and other entitlement programs from the chopping block, he failed to stop tax and budget cuts that, he argued, benefited the rich at the expense of those in need. In 1986, he decided not to seek reelection and retired from politics. He passed away from cancer in 1994.

See also WRIGHT, JIM (JAMES CLAUDE WRIGHT JR.) (1922–).

OPERA. In 1977 **Luciano Pavarotti** was heard for the first time by a national audience when he sang on the Texaco-sponsored Metropolitan Opera radio broadcast. The popularity of these broadcasts, begun in the 1930s, continues today. The voices of **Beverly Sills**, **Placido Domingo**, and **José Carreras**, as well as **African American** mezzo-soprano Grace Bumbry (1937–) and Australian coloratura soprano Joan Sutherland (1926–), delighted audiences during the 1970s and beyond. Pavarotti and Sills were able to cross the line from being opera singers to being engaging guests on talk shows. The 1990 appearance of Pavarotti, Carreras, and Domingo together for the first time led to their successful career as the "Three Tenors."

See also STUDIO 54.

ORGANIZATION OF PETROLEUM EXPORTING COUNTRIES (OPEC). OPEC was organized in Baghdad in September 1960 in response to a decline in prices for Mideast oil. The original members—Saudi Arabia, **Iran**, Iraq, Kuwait, and Venezuela—resolved to take as much power as possible from oil companies to control the cost of petroleum. OPEC did just that, taking advantage of the world's demand for oil and breaking the control over Middle Eastern petroleum that private companies had had since the 1920s. In 1973, OPEC embargoed petroleum exports to the United States because of U.S. support for **Israel**, causing an **energy crisis** in the United States that had serious repercussions for the American **economy**. That crisis would continue into the late 1970s, made worse in part by OPEC's decision in 1979 to raise the price of oil.

See also ALASKA PIPELINE; FOREIGN POLICY; "MALAISE" SPEECH.

P

PAHLAVI, MOHAMMED REZA (1919–1980). In 1941 Mohammed Reza Pahlavi succeeded his father as the shah of **Iran**. Pro-Western, he instituted many social reforms, which were nontraditional, and worked closely with U.S. oil companies to increase Iran's oil production. In 1951 Prime Minister Mohammad Mossadegh, leader of the National Front Movement, and supported by the Iranian Communist Party, nationalized the British-owned Anglo-Iranian Oil Company, the country's main source of income. In 1953 the shah was forced to flee the country, taking refuge in Italy. That same year a covert operation, called Operation Ajax, spearheaded by the **Central Intelligence Agency (CIA)**, forced Mossadegh from office.

Returning to Iran, the shah over time became increasingly unpopular. His effort to Westernize Iran, corruption within his government, economic programs that left many Iranians disenfranchised, and his repressive policies drew him opposition from both religious and secular elements alike. Protests against his regime grew increasingly violent. The shah's opponents rallied around Ayatollah **Ruhollah Khomeini**, one of Pahlavi's strongest opponents who was then living in exile. The **Jimmy Carter** administration was divided over how to handle the situation, and the shah, finding himself without guidance from the United States and having lost support at home, fled in January 1979. Shortly thereafter, Khomeini returned to Iran and assumed power. Later that year, the shah came to the United States for cancer treatment. The refusal of President Carter to accede to Iranian demands that the shah be returned home to face trial led to the **Iran hostage crisis**. The shah died the following year while in exile in **Egypt**.

See also AARON, DAVID LAURENCE (1938–); DONOVAN, HEDLEY WILLIAMS (1914–1990); FOREIGN POLICY; HORN OF AFRICA; KISSINGER, HENRY ALFRED (ALFRED HEINZ) (1923–); NIXON, RICHARD MILHOUS (1913–1994); PRECHT, HENRY (1932–); ROCKEFELLER, DAVID (1915–); SICK, GARY GORDON (1935–); SULLIVAN, WILLIAM HEALY (1922–); TORRIJOS, OMAR (1929–1981).

Carter and the shah of Iran, Mohammad Reza Pahlavi. The administration was divided over how to handle growing opposition in Iran to the shah's rule. Courtesy of the Jimmy Carter Library.

PALESTINE LIBERATION ORGANIZATION (PLO). Founded in 1964 by both **Egypt** and the Arab League, and chaired by **Yasser Arafat** starting in 1967, the Palestine Liberation Organization for much of its history sought the elimination of **Israel**, including through the use of armed force. The PLO denounced the **Camp David Accords** because they did not require Israel to withdraw from territory it had seized in the 1967 Six Day War. Following negotiations with Israel in the early 1990s, the PLO removed from its charter language calling for Israel's destruction. However, the relationship between it and Israel remains tense.

See also ENTEBBE AIR RAID; FOREIGN POLICY; YOUNG, ANDREW JACKSON, JR. (1932–).

PANAMA CANAL TREATIES. In 1903, the United States and Panama signed a treaty giving the United States "in perpetuity" the Canal Zone, a strip of land in Panama surrounding the Panama Canal. The perpetuity clause over time generated opposition in Panama, including riots in both 1959 and 1964. After the unrest in 1964, the United States and Panama began negotiations aimed at transferring the Canal Zone to Panama, but those discussions had stalled prior to **Jimmy Carter**'s election.

Carter sought to bring the negotiations to fruition for several reasons. He believed that turning the Canal Zone over to Panama would improve the United States' standing in Latin America. It would demonstrate his desire to give more emphasis to Third World issues. Finally, he worried that failure to turn the Canal Zone over to Panama could lead to renewed unrest and, possibly, an attempt by Panamanians to close or sabotage the canal. After intense negotiations, Carter and Panamanian president **Omar Torrijos** signed two treaties. The first would turn the Canal Zone over to Panama at the end of 1999. The second would grant the United States the right to protect the canal from external threats, leaving it up to Panama to handle any internal menace. Ratifying the treaties was another matter. Some lawmakers, including Senators **George McGovern** of South Dakota and **Sam Nunn** of Georgia, favored their passage. McGovern and Nunn were joined by former secretary of state **Henry Kissinger** and former president **Richard Nixon**, who sought to use their influence to see the Upper House ratify the agreements. However, other U.S. senators, among them **Strom Thurmond** of South Carolina, **Robert Dole** of Kansas, and Mississippi's **John Stennis**, as well as most Americans, opposed the pacts. The Carter administration thus began an intense lobbying campaign that succeeded not only in changing the minds of Americans but also of senators. In March and April 1978, the Senate passed the first and second treaties, respectively. The two agreements were among President Carter's greatest **foreign policy** successes.

See also BYRD, ROBERT CARLYLE (1917–2010); CHRISTOPHER, WARREN MINOR (1925–2011); CHURCH, FRANK FORRESTER (1924–1984); GOLDWATER, BARRY MORRIS (1909–1998); GRIFFIN, ROBERT PAUL (1923–); HELMS, JESSE ALEXANDER, JR. (1921–2008); LINOWITZ, SOL MYRON (1913–2005); LONG, RUSSELL BILLIU (1918–2003); MONDALE, WALTER FREDERICK (FRITZ) (1928–); MOORE, FRANK (1935–); PASTOR, ROBERT A. (1947–); REAGAN, RONALD WILSON (1911–2004); TALMADGE, HERMAN EUGENE (1913–2002); WEXLER, ANNE LEVY (1930–2009); WRIGHT, JIM (JAMES CLAUDE WRIGHT JR.) (1922–).

PARDON POLICIES FOR VIETNAM WAR DRAFT EVADERS. During the 1976 presidential campaign, **Jimmy Carter** had promised to offer a blanket amnesty to Americans who had evaded the draft during the Vietnam War. A day after taking office, Carter did just that, engendering an outcry from members of Congress and veterans' groups.

PASTOR, ROBERT A. (1947–). Democrat. The Latin American specialist on the National Security Council (NSC) from 1977 to 1981, Robert Pastor was born in New Jersey. He received his bachelor's degree (1969) from

Lafayette College and both his master's (1974) and Ph.D. (1977) from Harvard University. While teaching at Harvard, he joined the Linowitz Commission; headed by **Sol Linowitz**, President Lyndon B. Johnson's ambassador to the Organization of American States (OAS), the commission issued a report in 1977 calling for a review of U.S. policy toward Latin America, including normalizing relations with **Cuba** and turning the Panama Canal Zone over to Panama. That same year, Pastor became director of the NSC's Office of Latin American and Caribbean Affairs in the **Jimmy Carter** administration. As the top NSC specialist on Latin America, Pastor's work encompassed numerous policy matters, including the **Panama Canal treaties**, the possibility of normalizing relations with Cuba, **human rights**, arms control, economic and military aid, combating the drug trade, and promoting democracy.

After Carter's term in office ended, Pastor's career included teaching positions at universities in both the United States and Mexico, working as a fellow and director of the **Carter Center**'s Latin American and Caribbean Program, and serving as an adviser to Senator Al Gore during Gore's 2000 bid for the presidency. Presently, he is professor of International Relations, director of the Center for North American Studies, and codirector of the Center for Democracy and Election Management at American University.

PAVAROTTI, LUCIANO (1935–2007). The most recognizable of the "Three Tenors," and certainly the most flamboyant, Luciano Pavarotti was born in Modena, Italy. His career in **opera** began in Italy in 1961, and seven years later, he debuted at the famous Metropolitan Opera in New York City. By the mid-1970s, Pavarotti was one of opera's most renowned performers. His ability to hit a high C was one of his most remarkable singing feats, which audiences adored. By the end of the 1970s he graced the cover of *Time*. In 1990 Pavarotti performed with **José Carreras** and **Placido Domingo** to raise money for the José Carreras International Leukemia Foundation. Their performance led to many concerts worldwide as the Three Tenors. Pavarotti took great pride in his ability to please his audiences. He held a white napkin during his concerts, which became his signature prop. He appeared on **television** as both a guest and a singer, as well as starring in one movie, *Yes, Giorgio* (1982). Diagnosed with pancreatic cancer in 2006, he displayed a positive attitude until the illness finally ended his life.

PEOPLES TEMPLE. *See* JONES, JAMES WARREN "JIM" (1931–1978).

PERCY, CHARLES HARTING (1919–2011). Republican. A U.S. senator from 1967 to 1984, Charles Percy was born in Pensacola, Florida, but his family moved shortly thereafter to Chicago. Following his graduation in 1941 from the University of Chicago, he began working for the camera company Bell and Howell. The following year, he left the firm to serve in the U.S. Navy during World War II. After the war ended, he returned to Bell and Howell, becoming its president by 1949. Under his leadership, the corporation saw record profits. In the 1950s, Percy became active in the Republican Party at both the state and national levels, and he chaired the platform committee at the party's 1960 national convention. Six years later, he ran for and won a seat in the U.S. Senate.

Percy's liberal stance on social issues set him apart from many members of his own party, including President **Richard Nixon**. Conversely, he tended to support the agenda of the **Jimmy Carter** administration, which further strained his relationship with fellow Republicans. However, he did have his disagreements with Carter. Most notably, as the highest-ranking minority member of the Senate Governmental Affairs Committee, it was Percy who helped force the resignation of **Bert Lance**, the head of the Office of Management and Budget and a close personal friend of the president's. While his liberal views had alienated Republicans and his attacks on Lance had upset many Democrats, Percy was able in 1978 to win a third term in the Upper House. The continued movement of the Republican Party to the right, though, cost him the support he needed to win reelection in 1984. Afterward, he established a consulting firm in Washington, D.C., where he resided until his death from Alzheimer's disease in September 2011.

PETERSON, ESTHER EGGERTSON (1906–1997). Born in Provo, Utah, Esther Peterson received her bachelor's degree in 1927 from Brigham Young University and a master's in education from Columbia University three years later. While at Columbia, she met Oliver Peterson, whom she later married. Influenced by Oliver's political activism, she became a union organizer who focused on the welfare of female employees. In 1961, President John F. Kennedy appointed her assistant secretary of **labor**; in that post, she helped Kennedy achieve passage of the Equal Pay Act of 1963, which required **women** to receive the same pay as men for doing the same work. Under President Lyndon B. Johnson, she oversaw the White House Office of Consumer Affairs. In 1971, Peterson became vice president for consumer affairs for Giant Food Inc., a grocery store chain along the mid-Atlantic Coast.

Peterson's work gained the attention of the country's top consumer advocate, Ralph Nader, who encouraged President **Jimmy Carter** to name Peterson as special assistant for consumer affairs. Carter, who as governor of Georgia and a presidential candidate supported consumer rights, agreed. Moreover, he named Peterson as head of a new Consumer Affairs Council (CAC), thereby giving her a powerful voice in all White House initiatives affecting consumers. She influenced passage of laws requiring that food labels provide a product's nutritional value, gave consumers advice on saving money on food and energy, and convinced Carter to sign Executive Order

12264, which banned the export of goods regarded as unsafe within the United States. For her work, Carter awarded Peterson the Presidential Medal of Freedom.

Peterson continued her advocacy for consumers while out of government. She became consumer adviser to the National Association of Professional Insurance Agents and lobbied for the International Organization of Consumers Unions. In that latter role, she convinced the United Nations General Assembly to establish a list of restricted or banned goods, thereby making all countries aware of such products. In 1993, President Bill Clinton appointed her to work with the United Nations Educational, Scientific and Cultural Organization (UNESCO). In December 1997, she passed away from a stroke.

PHILIPPINES, RELATIONS WITH. *See* MARCOS, FERDINAND (EMMANUEL EDRALIN) (1917–1989).

POL POT (1928–1998). The leader of the Khmer Rouge, a communist organization in Cambodia, Pol Pot was born Saloth Sâr in Prek Sbauv, Cambodia. He fought alongside the Viet Minh, a Vietnamese revolutionary organization that sought to end French control of Indochina, and in 1967 launched a rebellion against the Cambodian government. After seizing power in 1975, he instituted a campaign of terror against those people he regarded as threats. Approximately one-quarter of the entire population was killed in the process. Despite his clear violations of **human rights**, though, President **Jimmy Carter** did not take action against Pol Pot. Pol Pot was a close ally of communist **China**, with which Carter wanted to improve relations, and punishing the Khmer Rouge could undermine that initiative.

In 1979, Vietnam invaded Cambodia as a result of a border conflict between the two countries. Pol Pot fled, spending time in exile in Thailand. After the Vietnamese withdrew a decade later, he returned to Cambodia and again took up arms against the Cambodian government. By the mid-1990s, the Khmer Rouge began to fall apart; when officials of the Khmer Rouge tried to negotiate with the government, Pol Pot had them killed. Infuriated, the Khmer Rouge arrested Pol Pot and in 1998 announced it would turn him over to an international tribunal. But before he could face trial, Pol Pot died. It is unclear if he committed suicide or was poisoned.

See also FOREIGN POLICY.

POLAND, RELATIONS WITH. *See* WALESA, LECH (1943–).

POWELL, JODY (JOSEPH LESTER POWELL JR.) (1943–2009). The press secretary for President **Jimmy Carter** from 1977 to 1981, Jody Powell was born in Cordele, Georgia. He graduated from Georgia State University in

1966 and began graduate work at Emory University. In 1969, he volunteered for Carter, who at that time was seeking the office of Georgia governor. The two became close friends. After Carter's victory in the gubernatorial election the following year, Powell devoted ever more of his time to answering reporters' questions. Impressed with Powell, who had become one of his closest confidants, Carter appointed him press secretary.

Powell was active in Carter's campaign during the **1976 election**. In light of their close relationship and his previous work, it was no surprise that now-President Carter again named Powell press secretary. There was a love-hate relationship between the media and Powell, with reporters finding him combative and quick to anger yet also humorous, frank, and witty. As one of the president's top advisers, he was also present during many of the administration's most significant policy deliberations. While his closeness to the president allowed him to be more forthright than was the case with many of Carter's other aides, Powell avoided partaking in actual decision making, contending that doing so could make it difficult for him to gather the information he needed to do his job and would deleteriously affect his credibility. Following Carter's defeat in the **1980 election**, Powell became a syndicated

Press Secretary Jody Powell (left) and Carter's chief staff aide, Hamilton Jordan. Powell and Jordan opposed the inflation-fighting proposals of Council of Economic Advisers chairman Charles Schultze. Courtesy of the Jimmy Carter Library.

columnist and gave lectures around the country. He later chaired a Washington, D.C.-based public relations firm. He passed away from a heart attack outside his Maryland home.

See also ANDERSON, JACK (JACKSON NORTHMAN) (1922–2005); JORDAN, HAMILTON (1944–2008); RAFSHOON, GERALD (1934–).

POWELL, LEWIS FRANKLIN, JR. (1907–1998). An associate justice of the **Supreme Court** from 1972 to 1987, Powell was born in Suffolk, Virginia. He attended Washington and Lee University, where he received both his bachelor's and law degrees in 1929 and 1931, respectively. In 1932, Powell earned a master's in law from Harvard University. Afterward, he worked at a prestigious law firm in Richmond, Virginia. During World War II, he served as an intelligence officer in the U.S. Army Air Force. Discharged in 1946, he returned to his job in Richmond, where he remained until his appointment to the Supreme Court. As an associate justice, it was Powell who wrote the majority opinion in the 1978 **affirmative action** case *University of California Board of Regents v. Bakke*. Pointing to both his age and health problems, he retired from the court in 1987. He passed away from pneumonia in 1998.

POWERPLANT AND INDUSTRIAL FUEL USE ACT. *See* NATIONAL ENERGY ACT.

PRECHT, HENRY (1932–). Democrat. Born in Georgia in 1932, Henry Precht was a career Foreign Service officer who, at the time of **Jimmy Carter**'s election, had spent 15 years in Washington, D.C., and at posts in Europe, the Middle East, and Africa. In the middle of 1978, he became head of the State Department's **Iran** Desk. In that role, he was a critic of the shah of Iran, **Mohammed Reza Pahlavi**, whom Precht believed stood little chance of surviving widespread opposition to his rule. He found resistance from the National Security Council (NSC) and even President Carter to giving thought to relations with a post-shah Iranian government. After the shah left Iran, Precht hoped the United States might be able to develop a relationship with moderates in the government of **Ruhollah Khomeini**. He advised against admitting the shah to the United States so that the ex-monarch could get cancer treatment, fearing it might cause a violent anti-American backlash in Iran. During the **Iran hostage crisis**, Precht took part in the negotiations to seek the hostages' release. He retired from the Foreign Service in 1987.

PREGNANCY DISCRIMINATION ACT. In 1964, Congress passed and President Lyndon B. Johnson signed into law the Civil Rights Act. Title VII of that bill prohibits employers from hiring, firing, or promoting individuals solely because of that person's race, gender, or ethnicity. The Pregnancy Discrimination Act, signed into law by President **Jimmy Carter** in 1978, amended Title VII. It proscribes an employer from refusing to hire a **woman** because she is pregnant. The law further bars harassment of pregnant employees and requires employers to treat women who cannot perform their job because of pregnancy the same way they would treat employees who suffer from a temporary disability. Finally, any employer-funded health insurance must include pregnancy-related expenses.

PRESLEY, ELVIS (1935–1977). Born in Memphis, Tennessee, Elvis Presley revolutionized American **music** in the 1950s. As a child and young adult, he had been influenced by the sounds of white country and rock as well as **African American** soul, gospel, and R&B. From these diverse styles, he developed his own version of rock and roll, which appealed both to whites and African Americans. Indeed, at a time when segregation was law in parts of the United States, Presley oftentimes played before integrated audiences. His physical gyrations during a 1956 appearance on the *Ed Sullivan Show* offended many viewers yet also drew even more attention to him. Later that year, he appeared in *Love Me Tender*, the first of nearly three dozen movies in which he starred. In 1959, he met Priscilla Ann Wagner, whom he married in 1967. They had one child, Lisa Marie, born in 1968.

By the early 1970s, Presley's life was on a downward spiral. His marriage began to break up, and in 1973 he and Priscilla divorced. Though he continued to record songs, he started to abuse drugs, became overweight, and suffered from numerous ailments, among them high blood pressure, liver damage, and glaucoma. In August 1977, he died from a drug overdose. Yet he remains influential to the present. Hundreds of impersonators portray him on and off stage, Elvis Presley Radio airs from the singer's Graceland Mansion in Memphis, and over 1 billion of his albums have sold worldwide, making him the best-selling artist ever.

PRIVACY PROTECTION ACT. In 1971, a violent confrontation took place between Palo Alto, California, police and protestors on the campus of Stanford University. In an attempt to identify some of the demonstrators, law enforcement officers searched the offices of Stanford University's student newspaper, the *Stanford Daily*. Although the *Daily* charged that the police had violated both the First and Fourth Amendments, the U.S. **Supreme Court** in the 1978 case *Zurcher v. Stanford Daily* upheld the search. In response, Congress in 1980 passed the Privacy Protection Act, which requires government officials to obtain a subpoena before having the right to search newsrooms or journalists' homes or to seize documents. Exceptions to the rule include those instances where the person in question was believed to have broken the law or if seizure of such materials would prevent injury or death to another person.

PROPOSITION 13. Proposition 13 represented the start of an antitax, anti-government rebellion that swept the nation. In California, rising property taxes caused by an increase in the value of housing, a rapid growth in the number of local and state government workers, and legislation requiring tax dollars from more affluent school districts to go to less-wealthy ones made many residents believe their taxes were being misappropriated. Leading this rebellion was Howard Jarvis, a retiree and conservative **Republican** who charged that the state's politicians cared more about spending money than in relieving Californians' tax burden, a burden he declared many living in the state could not afford. He and other antitax advocates therefore proposed the "People's Initiative to Limit Property Taxation," otherwise known as Proposition 13. It called for restricting increases in property assessments to no more than 2 percent a year and limiting local property taxes to 1 percent of a property's assessed value. It passed by an overwhelming margin in 1978. In the 1992 case *Nordlinger v. Hahn*, the U.S. **Supreme Court** declared Proposition 13 constitutional.

PROXMIRE, EDWARD WILLIAM (1915–2005). Democrat. Born in Lake Forest, Illinois, to a well-off family, William Proxmire served in the U.S. Senate from 1957 to 1989. He attended Yale University (B.A., 1938) and then Harvard University, receiving a master's in business administration in 1940. He worked for a time with J. P. Morgan but then joined the U.S. Army to serve in World War II. Discharged in 1946, he went back to Harvard to get another master's degree in public administration. Moving to Wisconsin, he worked for a time for a newspaper in Madison. In 1950, he ran for and won a seat in the state assembly. Seven years later, he successfully campaigned for the seat left vacant by the death of U.S. senator Joseph McCarthy, thereby beginning a 32-year career in the Upper House.

Though liberal in ideology, Proxmire developed a reputation as a maverick. He became famous for his Golden Fleece Awards, which he gave to examples of what he regarded as unnecessary government spending. He was one of the first members of the Upper House to call for the resignation of **Bert Lance**, President **Jimmy Carter**'s director of the Office of Management and Budget who became the focus of a scandal involving questionable banking practices. He disliked big business and fought against a White House plan in 1979 to bail out Chrysler Motor Corporation. He defended the policies of Federal Reserve chairman **Paul Volcker** despite charges from both liberals and conservatives that Volcker was pushing the nation toward a recession. He was less involved in matters of **foreign policy** but did oppose the **Strategic Arms Limitation Treaty (SALT II)** on the grounds that it failed to curb the arms race. Proxmire's maverick status allowed him to survive the swing toward conservatism that took place in 1980. Pointing to his age, he decided not to run for reelection in 1986. In retirement, he wrote a syndicated column and continued to dole out Golden Fleece Awards. He ended his column in 1998 after he learned he had Alzheimer's disease. He passed away in Maryland in 2005.

PRYOR, RICHARD (1940–2005). An **African American** actor and comedian, Richard Pryor was born in Peoria, Illinois. A high school graduate, he gained fame in the 1960s on **television** with appearances on several programs, including *The Tonight Show*. He was a writer for the **Norman Lear** television series *Sanford and Son*. His first **cinematic** role was in the 1972 hit movie *Lady Sings the Blues*. He won an Emmy and five Grammy Awards during the 1970s and 1980s. He died of a heart attack.

R

RAFSHOON, GERALD (1934–). The staff assistant in charge of communications in the **Jimmy Carter** administration from 1978 to 1979, Gerald Rafshoon was born in Brooklyn, New York. Following his graduation from the University of Texas in 1955, Rafshoon worked for an Austin radio station, served four years in the U.S. Navy, joined Twentieth Century Fox, and then, in 1966, opened an advertising company in Atlanta. He met Carter during Carter's 1966 bid for the governorship. Carter liked Rafshoon and asked him to oversee his media campaign. Though Carter did not win in 1966, he had Rafshoon assume a similar role when Carter launched his successful gubernatorial campaign in 1970. When Carter decided in 1972 to run for the U.S. presidency, Rafshoon oversaw the campaign's public relations. In each of these campaigns, Rafshoon had Carter emphasize style over substance, with a focus on the candidate's work ethic, honesty, and support for minority rights.

After Carter won the **1976 election**, Rafshoon acted in an unofficial capacity, offering advice to the administration. However, when Carter's poll numbers began to sag in 1978, Rafshoon accepted a request to oversee communications. While Press Secretary **Jody Powell** focused on the day-to-day communication issues, Rafshoon concentrated on general themes and improving Carter's public image. Rafshoon's effort proved relatively successful. He oversaw the administration's speechwriters and made sure Carter stayed on message. He helped put together what became known as the **"malaise" speech** of 1979, though the term given that oration hides the fact that it was well received at the time. When Carter ran for reelection a year later, Rafshoon again led the candidate's public relations and communications. Following Carter's defeat in the **1980 election**, Rafshoon returned to private life. He has become increasingly involved in producing films for cable and television. He has also remained politically active, seeking to generate interest in a third-party alternative in presidential elections.

REAGAN, RONALD WILSON (1911–2004). Republican. The governor of California from 1967 to 1975 and president of the United States from 1981 to 1989, Ronald Reagan was born in Illinois and graduated from Eureka College in 1932 with a degree in economics. He began his **cinematic** career in 1937 and in 1940 married actress Jane Wyman. Their marriage ended in 1948, and in 1952 he wed actress Nancy Reagan. Two years later, he became the host of the *General Electric Theater*, a weekly **television** program that ran until 1962.

Reagan began his political career as a **Democrat**, but as time passed, he began to embrace Republican values. Changing parties in 1962, he ran for and won the governorship of California in 1966. During his two terms, he became the voice for the GOP's conservative wing. Leaving office in 1975, he sought the Republican nomination for the presidency in that year and proved a formidable challenge to President **Gerald Ford**'s bid to get the party's nod. Although Ford received the nomination, Reagan had developed a widespread following among Republicans.

Over the next four years, Reagan prepared for another bid for the White House. He bolstered his conservative credentials by denouncing the **Panama Canal treaties**, calling for cutting taxes across the board to stimulate growth of the **economy**, and demanding the United States take a tougher stand against the **Union of Soviet Socialist Republics (USSR)**. When the Republican Party formally nominated him for the presidency in July 1980, Reagan had a commanding 28-point lead over President **Jimmy Carter** in public opinion polls. But Carter, who received the Democratic nomination in August, began to close the gap by charging that Reagan might lead the country into a war with Moscow. Moreover, a series of gaffes hurt the Republican nominee. Ultimately, however, the economy, the **Iran hostage crisis**, and Reagan's performance at the only debate between himself and Carter—which was held a week before the election—convinced Americans to vote for the former California governor in the **1980 election**.

Reagan served two terms in the White House. His tenure witnessed a long period of sustained economic growth, the beginning of the end of the Cold War—for which some analysts give Reagan sole credit—and an effort to curb government spending on social and welfare programs. Upon his departure from Washington, he went on the lecture circuit. Diagnosed with Alzheimer's in 1994, he withdrew from the public arena. He passed away in 2004 at age 93.

See also DERIAN, PATRICIA MURPHY (1929–); FOREIGN POLICY; GOLDWATER, BARRY MORRIS (1909–1998); KISSINGER, HENRY ALFRED (ALFRED HEINZ) (1923–); LABOR; MONDALE, WALTER FREDERICK (FRITZ) (1928–); MOYNIHAN, DANIEL PATRICK (1927–2003); MUSKIE, EDMUND SIXTUS (1914–1996); O'NEILL, TIP

(THOMAS PHILLIP O'NEILL JR.) (1912–1994); RELIGION; SCHLE-SINGER, JAMES RODNEY (1929–); SCHULTZE, CHARLES LOUIS (1924–); THATCHER, MARGARET (1925–).

REFUGEE ACT. In 1951, the United Nations adopted the Convention Relating to the Status of Refugees, which assigned refugee status to people affected by events taking place prior to that year. This was generally defined as those individuals who had become refugees because of World War II. But a 1967 protocol expanded that definition to include anyone who feared persecution if he or she returned to his or her homeland. Moreover, the 1951 convention spelled out the responsibilities of nations offering asylum to refugees as well as the rights of those granted asylum. The United States signed the 1967 protocol, but there ensued a debate as to exactly what the nation's obligations were to those seeking asylum or refugee status.

The purpose of the Refugee Act was to delineate those responsibilities. Signed into law in early 1980, the act adopted the definition of refugee established by the 1967 protocol and set up an elaborate system to provide asylum or refugee status. Persons granted the right to stay in the United States could become American citizens after residing in country for a year. About a month after the Refugee Act became law, tens of thousands of people fled **Cuba** to the United States in what became known as the **Mariel Boatlift**. Under the law, the U.S. government could accept only 19,500 Cubans annually, and it appeared that many of them were not eligible for protection. Before the boatlift came to an end, approximately 125,000 Cubans had come to the United States, where they were put into refugee camps or prison pending documentation. Ultimately, only about 2,700 of them were denied U.S. citizenship.

REGENTS OF THE UNIVERSITY OF CALIFORNIA V. BAKKE. *See* BAKKE, ALLEN PAUL (1940–); SUPREME COURT.

REHABILITATION, COMPREHENSIVE SERVICES, AND DEVELOPMENTAL DISABILITIES AMENDMENTS. In 1973, the U.S. government passed the Rehabilitation Act, the first law to protect people with disabilities. It prohibits discrimination against disabled persons working for the federal government, in programs conducted by federal agencies or receiving federal aid, or in businesses with federal contracts. Amendments to this law were adopted in 1978 and established a nationwide Independent Living Program for people with disabilities; the National Institute of Handicapped Research to improve services for the disabled; the National Council of the

Handicapped (now called the National Council on Disability) to lobby the president and Congress on matters affecting the disabled; and new programs for the handicapped, among them recreation and employment initiatives.

REHNQUIST, WILLIAM HUBBS (1924–2005). An associate justice of the **Supreme Court** from 1972 to 1986 and chief justice of the Supreme Court from 1986 to 2005, William Rehnquist was born in Milwaukee, Wisconsin, ironically on the same day and year as **Jimmy Carter**. He grew up in a family of devoted **Republicans**. He dropped out of college to fight in World War II with the Army Air Corps. Afterward, he received a bachelor's and master's degree from Stanford University, a second master's from Harvard University, and then, in 1952, a law degree from Stanford. Later that year, he served as a clerk for Supreme Court justice Robert Jackson. In that role, he wrote what became an infamous memo that rejected the call for school integration in *Brown v. Board of Education* (1954) and defended the Court's finding in *Plessy v. Ferguson* (1896), which had established that segregation was legal as long as the facilities provided to whites and blacks were equal. Rehnquist defended his conclusion on the grounds that judges should accept majority will. That philosophy would continue to guide him throughout his career.

In 1953, Rehnquist began working with a law firm in Arizona. He also became active in Republican Party politics. His defense of the power of the executive branch of government, including the right of the president to withhold information from Congress, garnered him the attention of President **Richard Nixon**. When two positions became available on the Supreme Court in 1971, Nixon nominated Rehnquist to fill one of them. During his confirmation hearing, Rehnquist's memorandum related to the *Brown* case became a matter of contention. He replied to critics that he now realized how important it was for minorities to defend their rights. The Senate subsequently confirmed him.

Rehnquist developed a reputation as one of the Court's most intelligent and most conservative justices. His decisions repeatedly demonstrated deference to states' rights. He was one of only two justices to dissent in the **abortion**-rights case *Roe v. Wade* (1973), asserting that the states should determine whether to permit abortions. In the even-more-divisive *University of California Board of Regents v. Bakke* (1978), he made clear that the Court should not determine whether race should be a factor in university admissions. In 1986, President **Ronald Reagan** appointed Rehnquist chief justice. Though diagnosed in 2004 with thyroid cancer, he continued to serve on the Court until his death in September 2005.

RELIGION. During its history, the United States has witnessed periods of intense religiosity. The First Great Awakening of the 18th century and the Second Great Awakening of the 18th–19th centuries are examples, as is the religious fundamentalism that spread across the country after World War I. By the early 1970s, religion again had become an important factor in American politics. The 1960s, marked by "free love," **women** demanding the right to contraception and **abortion**, and homosexuals insisting upon the same rights as heterosexuals generated a backlash from those Americans who believed the country had lost its sense of morality. This backlash included the New Right, which sought to establish a United States based upon Christian values. In 1976, an evangelical fundamentalist, **Jerry Falwell**, started holding "I Love America" assemblies in the hopes of moving the country in directions he favored; these rallies provided the foundation for the **Moral Majority**, a lobbying organization Falwell founded in 1979.

Religion had an impact on the **1976** and **1980 elections**. **Jimmy Carter**'s born-again Baptist upbringing resonated with religious Americans who believed he would promote an agenda favorable to their interests. His talk of bringing honesty to Washington and promoting **human rights** in U.S. **foreign policy** made sense to those upset with what they regarded as a lack of morality in the country's previous leadership. Similarly, the **Republican** candidate in 1980, **Ronald Reagan**, used the language of religion to tout the superiority of American values and to denounce an evil, godless **Union of Soviet Socialist Republics (USSR)**.

See also CIVIL RIGHTS; *GOOD TIMES*; IRAN-IRAQ WAR; JONES, JAMES WARREN "JIM" (1931–1978); TRANSCENDENTAL MEDITATION.

REPUBLICAN PARTY. By the **1976 election**, the Republican Party was reeling. The Watergate scandal, President **Gerald Ford**'s pardon of **Richard Nixon**, and a moderate-conservative split within the party between wings represented by Ford and former California governor **Ronald Reagan** had torn the GOP apart and hurt its standing in the eyes of the American people. Yet had Ford not erred in one of the debates against **Democratic Party** nominee **Jimmy Carter** and declared that there was no domination of Eastern Europe by the **Union of Soviet Socialist Republics (USSR)**, he might have won. Despite the setbacks it faced, though, the party was able to recover. The country continued to move in a more conservative direction and Carter's economic and foreign policies hurt him in the eyes of voters. In the **1980 election**, Reagan defeated Carter, and the Republicans gained control of the Senate, the first time in a generation that the GOP dominated in one of the houses on Capitol Hill.

See also ANDERSON, JOHN BAYARD (1922–); BAKER, HOWARD HENRY, JR. (1925–); BAKER, JAMES ADDISON, III (1930–); BUSH, GEORGE HERBERT WALKER (1924–); DEFENSE; DOLE, ROBERT JOSEPH (1923–); FOREIGN POLICY; GOLDWATER, BARRY MORRIS (1909–1998); GRIFFIN, ROBERT PAUL (1923–); HELMS, JESSE ALEXANDER, JR. (1921–2008); HOFFA, JAMES "JIMMY" (1913–1975); JAVITS, JACOB KOPPEL (1904–1986); KISSINGER, HENRY ALFRED (ALFRED HEINZ) (1923–); PERCY, CHARLES HARTING (1919–2011); REHNQUIST, WILLIAM HUBBS (1924–2005); ROCKEFELLER, NELSON (1908–1979); ROOSEVELT, ALICE LONGWORTH (1884–1980); SAFIRE, WILLIAM (1929–2009); SCHLAFLY, PHYLLIS (1924–); WOMEN.

REVERSE DISCRIMINATION. *See* BAKKE, ALLEN PAUL (1940–).

RHODESIA, RELATIONS WITH. *See* SMITH, IAN (1919–2007).

RIBICOFF, ABRAHAM ALEXANDER (1910–1998). Democrat. A U.S. senator from 1963 to 1981, Abraham Ribicoff was born into a poor New Britain, Connecticut, family. He began working for a zipper and buckle manufacturer after he graduated from high school. The firm sent him to its Chicago office, during which time Ribicoff also attended classes at the University of Chicago. Receiving a law degree in 1933, Ribicoff returned to Connecticut and entered politics. He was elected to the state legislature in 1938 and, a decade later, to the U.S. House of Representatives. In 1952, he sought a seat in the U.S. Senate but lost. He returned to law, only to run for and win the state governorship in 1954. Following his election in 1960 to the presidency, John F. Kennedy appointed Ribicoff secretary of **health, education**, and welfare (HEW). Ribicoff, however, disliked the job. After 16 months, he resigned, returned to Connecticut, ran again for the U.S. Senate in 1962, and won.

As a senator, Ribicoff championed President Lyndon B. Johnson's Great Society programs but became a determined opponent of the Vietnam War. He promoted Senator **George McGovern**'s bid for the Democratic Party nomination in 1972. Though he lobbied for ratification of the second **Strategic Arms Limitation Treaty (SALT II)**, signed between President **Jimmy Carter** and the **Union of Soviet Socialist Republics (USSR)**, his overall relationship with the Carter administration was not good. Ribicoff criticized the White House's energy and welfare programs, neither of which he believed would work. He was also one of the loudest voices calling for the resignation of Office of Management and Budget Director **Bert Lance**, who had been charged with questionable banking practices. Upon his election to the Senate, Ribicoff had promised that if reelected, he would serve until age 70. Keeping that pledge, he decided not to seek another term in 1980. Instead, he joined a law firm in New York City and largely dropped out of politics. He passed away in 1998 from Alzheimer's disease.

RICKOVER, HYMAN GEORGE (1900–1986). One of the most important figures in **Jimmy Carter**'s life, Hyman Rickover served as admiral in the U.S. Navy from 1953 to 1982. Born in Makow, Poland, he came to the United States as a child. In 1922 Rickover graduated from the United States Naval Academy and continued his education in electrical engineering at Columbia University, receiving his master's in 1929. He then began his service on submarines and became a proponent of submarine warfare. During World War II, he participated in the repair of two battleships damaged at Pearl Harbor. Certain of his abilities, he oftentimes found himself at odds with his superiors. Yet he was also driven and intelligent and, after the war, participated in the development of nuclear-powered submarines. Though his personality continued to cause conflict with those around him, he rose up the ranks, becoming a rear admiral in 1953 and a vice admiral in 1958.

Rickover, who later became referred to as the "father of the nuclear navy," interviewed numerous officers to command America's new generation of warships. One of the people with whom he spoke in the early 1950s was

The Carters with Admiral Hyman Rickover and his wife, Eleonore. Rickover was an influential person in the president's life. Courtesy of the Jimmy Carter Library.

Carter, who had recently graduated from the Naval Academy. Both were hardworking, sanctimonious, and detail oriented. During the interview, Rickover asked Carter if he had done his best in his studies at Annapolis. When Carter replied he had not, Rickover asked, "Why not?" The future president never forgot that question, believing that he had been challenged always to do better.

Carter had told Rickover that if he was elected president, he wanted his former commander's views on military and political matters. Following Carter's victory in the **1976 election**, Rickover obliged, writing the president on such matters as **defense** contracts, **human rights**, and the nuclear navy. On some matters, such as Rickover's complaint that defense contractors overcharged the government, Carter was sympathetic. On others, among them the admiral's support for adding a nuclear-powered aircraft carrier to the U.S. naval fleet, the president was not. Yet throughout, Carter never lost respect for Rickover and had him over for dinner on more than one occasion.

Following the incident at **Three Mile Island**, Rickover began to have doubts about nuclear power. He retired from the navy in 1982. In declining health, he passed away in July 1986.

RIGHT TO FINANCIAL PRIVACY ACT. In 1976, the **Supreme Court** ruled in the case *United States v. Miller* that a person's bank records were the property of that bank rather than the customer's. Accordingly, it was possible that the federal government could access an individual's financial records without telling that person. Determining *Miller* an infringement on one's privacy, Congress in 1978 passed the Right to Financial Privacy Act, which states that no government entity can access a person's financial records unless that individual permits such access or the government is authorized to do so via a subpoena or warrant.

ROBINSON, FRANK (1935–). Born in Texas, Robinson was a professional **baseball** player who began his career in 1956 with the Cincinnati Reds. Hitting 38 home runs, he was named Rookie of the Year. Over the next 20 years, Robinson, who played both left and right field, was a member as well of the Baltimore Orioles, Los Angeles Dodgers, California Angels, and Cleveland Indians. During that time, he won two World Series with the Orioles. He also became the first and only player to be named Most Valuable Player in both the American and National leagues. Robinson set another first when, in 1975, the Cleveland Indians gave him the title player-manager, making him the first **African American** to manage in Major League Baseball. After spending two years in Cleveland, he went on to manage the San Francisco Giants, the Baltimore Orioles, and the Montreal/Washington Expos. In 1982, while with the Giants, he received induction into the National

Baseball Hall of Fame. His managerial career ended in 2006 when the Expos decided not to renew his contract. He now works for Major League Baseball commissioner Bud Selig, who has asked Robinson to find a way to speed up the pace of baseball games.

See also SPORTS.

ROCKEFELLER, DAVID (1915–). Son of multimillionaire John D. Rockefeller, David Rockefeller was educated at Harvard University (B.A., 1936) and received his doctorate from the University of Chicago in 1940. Rockefeller was involved in the creation of the Trilateral Commission, the purpose of which was to promote cooperation among the world's leading countries. He was instrumental in helping the shah of **Iran, Mohammed Reza Pahlavi**, come to the United States for medical treatment for cancer. For many years Rockefeller headed the Chase Manhattan Bank. In 1981 he retired from his position at Chase. Afterward, he continued to manage the family's wealth and to support various charities and institutions.

See also LINOWITZ, SOL MYRON (1913–2005).

ROCKEFELLER, NELSON (1908–1979). Republican. The governor of New York State from 1958 to 1973 and vice president of the United States from 1974 to 1977, Nelson Rockefeller was the grandson of industrialist John D. Rockefeller. Born in Maine, Rockefeller attended Dartmouth College, graduating in 1930. He then devoted himself to philanthropy, giving donations to many foundations and businesses. A liberal Republican, he was unsuccessful in his three tries to become the party's presidential candidate; however, in 1974, **Gerald Ford** chose Rockefeller to serve as his vice president.

Ford reached the conclusion by 1976 that he faced a formidable challenge from conservative Republicans if he hoped to win the party's nomination for the presidency. Therefore, he successfully pressured Rockefeller to drop his name from consideration as Ford's running mate. Instead, Ford selected Senator **Robert Dole** of Kansas. Rockefeller continued his philanthropy, including support for the arts. He died of a heart attack in January 1979.

See also KISSINGER, HENRY ALFRED (ALFRED HEINZ) (1923–); SAFIRE, WILLIAM (1929–2009).

ROE V. WADE. *See* ABORTION; SUPREME COURT.

ROOSEVELT, ALICE LONGWORTH (1884–1980). The daughter of President Theodore Roosevelt, Alice Roosevelt's behavior throughout her life was fodder for the media. Her mother, and the president's first wife, died in childbirth. Theodore Roosevelt remarried but had little to do with Alice since she reminded him of his first wife. He fathered four children with his second wife. Feeling that she did not belong in her father's new family, Alice became known as the presidential wild child. She smoked, drove recklessly, and interrupted her father's meetings. Her father once said that he could run the country or control Alice, but he could not do both. Although she married and had one daughter, her marriage was not happy, and her relationship with her only child was strained. Famous for loving gossip and expressing her opinions without consideration for others, her home was always open to guests of the media, entertainment, and politics. She was dubbed "the other Washington monument." A **Republican**, she was cordial with President **Gerald Ford**; however, she believed President **Jimmy Carter** lacked the social graces necessary for her to meet him. She had a pillow made with a message on it, stating that if the guest had something bad to say about another person, that person should sit by Alice.

ROOTS. In January 1977, about 80 million viewers watched the American Broadcast Corporation's (ABC) **television** miniseries *Roots*, based upon **Alex Haley**'s best-selling book about his family's African heritage. Unsure that white people would watch a miniseries about the history of an **African American** family, ABC showed it on eight consecutive nights. Instead, each evening the audience grew, and by the time the series ended, *Roots* had become a media event in the United States. During the 1977 Emmy Awards for the best television programs, *Roots* was nominated for 36 awards and won nine.

See also LITERATURE.

ROSE, PETE (PETER EDWARD, SR.) (1941–). Nicknamed "Charlie Hustle" for his prowess on the **baseball** field, Pete Rose was born in Cincinnati. His father had been a semi-pro **football** player, and Rose was pushed into athletics at a young age. His professional baseball career began in his hometown in 1960 when the Cincinnati Reds signed him to a contract. The Reds sent Rose to their minor league team, but in 1963 he was playing in Cincinnati. He was named Rookie of the Year that same year. Rose became a major star of the Reds, helping them to be the most successful National League team in the 1970s. In the early 1980s stories began to circulate that Rose was involved with gamblers. Baseball commissioner Bart Giamatti's investigation concluded that Rose had bet on baseball games. In the 1990s Rose served five months in prison for tax evasion. These problems kept Rose from being named to the Baseball Hall of Fame. To this day Rose is considered one of baseball's greatest players, but his past has marred his reputation. Controversy continues today as to whether he should be in the Baseball Hall of Fame.

See also SPORTS.

ROSTENKOWSKI, DANIEL DAVID (1928–2010). Democrat. A Member of the House of Representatives from 1959 to 1994, Daniel Rostenkowski was born in Chicago. His father and grandfather were members of the city's Democratic Party machine, so from the start Rostenkowski was immersed in politics. After graduating from a private military school in 1946, he spent two years in the U.S. military. Rather than complete a college degree, he dove into politics, where with his father's help he was able to get elected to the Illinois state legislature. When his district's U.S. representative decided to retire in 1958, Rostenkowski was able to use his political connections to run largely unopposed.

Rostenkowski turned out to be an able negotiator, one who was willing to shake hands with members of the **Republican** opposition to get things done. His deal making earned him respect in Congress. He helped write the legislation that developed the Medicare program. In 1976, he played a key role in the appointment of **Jim Wright** as House majority leader. In return, Wright appointed Rostenkowski deputy majority whip. That same year **Jimmy Carter** was elected president. Carter and Rostenkowski did not work well together. The lawmaker believed the president did not do a good job of consulting Congress. On specific matters, Rostenkowski opposed the White House's proposals for tax breaks for businesses and believed a plan for hospital cost containment would not work.

In 1981, Rostenkowski became chair of the powerful Ways and Means Committee; thus, he had even more influence in Congress. In that role, in 1986, he helped achieve passage of the Tax Reform Act, a major revision of the nation's tax code. In time his power began to erode. In the early 1990s, a grand jury looked into reports of Rostenkowski's misconduct at the House Post Office. The investigation soon learned that Rostenkowski had illegally turned over $20,000 of postage stamps into cash. Additional accusations included misuse of personal vehicles, charging Congress for furniture and china, and obstruction of justice. In 1994, he had to resign his post as Ways and Means chair. Though he ran for reelection that year, he lost. In 1996 he pled guilty to mail fraud and served 15 months in jail. In 2000, he received a pardon from President Bill Clinton. He died of lung cancer in 2010.

S

SADAT, (MUHAMMAD) ANWAR AL- (1918–1981). The president of **Egypt** from 1969 to 1981, Anwar Sadat was born north of Cairo. His family moved to Egypt's largest city when he was a child. Though growing up in abject poverty, Sadat recalled a happy childhood. He came to share the desire of many other Egyptians to see their nation freed of British control. To achieve this goal, he attended the Royal Military Academy, graduating as an officer in 1938. Soon thereafter, he joined other officers in preparing for a revolt against the British. During World War II, he spent time in jail for conspiring with Nazi agents against the British presence in Egypt. In 1952, he joined revolutionaries led by Colonel Gamal Abdel Nasser. Unable to maintain control of their former colony, the British withdrew and Nasser became Egypt's president. Sadat at first held a variety of secondary posts in the new government, but in 1964 Nasser decided to appoint him vice president. When Nasser passed away in 1970, Sadat succeeded him.

In 1973, Egypt and **Syria** launched an attack on **Israel** during what became known as the Yom Kippur War. Though Israel was able to inflict heavy losses on the Egyptians and Syrians, the war's initial battles had gone in Egypt's favor, which bolstered morale among Arabs throughout the Middle East and Sadat's prestige in the region. The Yom Kippur War also encouraged the Middle East peace process. U.S. Secretary of State **Henry Kissinger** had engaged in intense diplomacy to end the war. He and Sadat became close, and Kissinger succeeded in getting Israel and Egypt to sign limited peace agreements in 1974 and 1975. But a more comprehensive peace remained elusive until 1978, when **Jimmy Carter** was able to get Egypt and Israel to sign the **Camp David Accords**. Sadat's willingness to make peace with Israel drew criticism from many of his Arab friends. Egypt's membership in the Arab League was suspended. In October 1981, members of the Egyptian Islamic Jihad, an organization seeking to overthrow Egypt's government and turn Egypt into a strict Islamic state, assassinated Sadat during a parade commemorating the 1973 war.

See also FOREIGN POLICY.

SAFIRE, WILLIAM (1929–2009). Formerly a speechwriter for **Richard Nixon**, Safire was best known as a *New York Times* political columnist who made frequent **television** appearances. Born in 1929, he attended Syracuse University but dropped out so he could take on a job with the *New York Herald Tribune*. From 1951 to 1954, he served in the U.S. Army, returning to journalism afterward. He grew increasingly involved in **Republican Party** politics, working for both Nixon and **Nelson Rockefeller**. After Nixon's victory in the 1968 presidential election, Safire became one of his speechwriters. In 1973, he left the White House to accept the *Times*' political columnist position. Though angered after learning that Nixon had taped their conversations, he continued to think highly of his former boss. Indeed, it appears that he believed Nixon was unfairly targeted by a liberal press for crimes that were no worse than those committed by Nixon's predecessors. Moreover, he criticized what he considered **Jimmy Carter**'s "self-righteousness." His respect for Nixon and distaste for Carter may explain why he censured Carter's director of the Office of Management and Budget, **Bert Lance**, for reportedly using his office to obtain a loan with deferred interest from a Chicago bank. His reports on Lance earned him the Pulitzer Prize in 1978. He also accused Carter of questionable financial practices during the **1976 election**, though a grand jury investigation found no malfeasance on Carter's part.

A year after winning the Pulitzer Prize, Safire began a column titled "On Language." Appearing in the *New York Times Magazine*, Safire explained the origins of various words or phrases and what they meant. He became known for pointing out words or phrases that were coming into common use as well as examples of improper use of English. Calling himself a "libertarian conservative," Safire was highly critical of President Bill Clinton and, even more so, First Lady Hillary Clinton. Following the terrorist attack on the World Trade Center in 2001, he became a leading proponent of going to war with Iraq. Safire stopped writing his political column in 2005 and "On Language" in 2009. In 2006, President George W. Bush awarded him the Presidential Medal of Freedom. He passed away in 2009 from pancreatic cancer.

SANDINISTAS. Named after Augusto César Sandino, a Nicaraguan resistance leader in the late 1920s to early 1930s, the Frente Sandinista de Liberación Nacional (Sandinista National Liberation Front, or FSLN) was formed in 1961. Socialist in orientation, its leaders waged guerrilla warfare against the governments of Luis Somoza Debayle and his successor, **Anastasio Somoza Debayle**. The Somozas' repression and corruption garnered the Sandinistas growing support. In 1979, Anastasio Somoza fled Nicaragua in the face of widespread unrest. The Sandinistas assumed power, which they would hold until 1990.

See also AARON, DAVID LAURENCE (1938–); CARTER, JAMES EARL, JR. (JIMMY) (1924–).

SATURDAY NIGHT LIVE (SNL). Premiering on **television** in 1975, shortly after the end of the Vietnam War and the Watergate scandal, *SNL* was a perfect answer to the public's disgust with the world situation and politicians. The skits were irreverent and sarcastic. No one was free from their humorous comments. Often people who had been picked on in a skit became the host of the show. Gradually, some of the original cast left *SNL* to pursue a career on the big screen.

See also CARLIN, GEORGE (1937–2008); CINEMA; DANCES; *NATIONAL LAMPOON'S ANIMAL HOUSE.*

SCHLAFLY, PHYLLIS (1924–). Republican. One of the most conservative figures in the **women**'s movement, Phyllis Schlafly was born in St. Louis. She graduated from Washington University (B.A., 1944). A member of Phi Beta Kappa, she continued her education at Harvard University from which she received her master's degree in government in 1945. In 1978 Schlafly received her law degree from Washington University Law School. She is the author or the editor of 20 books. During the 1970s she formed Stop Taking Our Privileges ERA, or STOP ERA, the purpose of which was to prevent the **Equal Rights Amendment (ERA)** from becoming part of the U.S. Constitution. Declaring that the ERA would cause more harm to women than good, her powerful grassroots movement succeeded in its goal. The *Ladies Home Journal* named Schlafly as one of the 20th century's most important women.

SCHLESINGER, JAMES RODNEY (1929–). The secretary of energy from 1977 to 1979, James Schlesinger was a native of New York. After receiving his doctorate from Harvard University in 1956, he taught at the University of Virginia before leaving in 1963 to join the RAND Corporation. In 1969, he started a long governmental career when he became assistant director of the Bureau of the Budget in the **Richard Nixon** administration. Over the next six years, he served as chairman of the Atomic Energy Commission, director of the **Central Intelligence Agency (CIA)**, and finally, beginning in 1973, secretary of **defense**. It is interesting that Nixon and his successor, **Gerald Ford**, kept Schlesinger on, for Schlesinger was a strong opponent of **détente**, and his brusque and patronizing personality wore on both presidents. Matters came to a head, however, when Ford received word that Schlesinger favored **Ronald Reagan** for the 1976 **Republican** nomination for president. In November 1975, he asked Schlesinger to resign.

Schlesinger, though, was not finished as a government official. When Reagan failed to win the Republican nomination, Schlesinger threw his support behind the **Democratic** nominee, **Jimmy Carter**. Carter, for his part, found the former defense secretary highly intelligent and respected Schlesinger's extensive experience in government. Following his victory in the **1976 election**, Carter named Schlesinger to develop a comprehensive national **energy** program. The president also asked Congress to establish a new Department of Energy. Working in secret, Schlesinger presented to Carter in the spring of 1977 a plan with over 100 proposals, including a tax on gas-guzzling cars, a wellhead tax to raise oil prices and force down consumer demand for gas, and incentives for energy conservation. In August 1977, lawmakers established the department, and Carter nominated Schlesinger to head it. By that same month, Speaker **Tip O'Neill** had pushed the energy program through the House of Representatives largely unscathed. However, the bill met intense opposition in the Senate. It did not pass until the fall of 1978, and in a severely watered-down form.

Carter meeting with his cabinet. Around the table, starting on the left, are James Schlesinger, Jay Janis, John C. White, Michael Blumenthal, Walter Mondale, Griffin Bell, uncertain (either Robert J. Brown or Richard Moe), Andrew Young, Joseph Califano, Cecil Andrus, Cyrus Vance, Jimmy Carter, Harold Brown, Juanita Kreps, Brock Adams (?), Bert Lance, and Robert Strauss. Robert Lipshutz, Douglas M. Costle, Stuart Eizenstat, and Jane L. Frank are along the wall at the right. Courtesy of the Jimmy Carter Library.

Schlesinger by this time had begun to ruffle feathers in both the executive and legislative branches. Individuals such as White House Special Assistant **Stuart Eizenstat** and Treasury Secretary **Michael Blumenthal** were upset that Schlesinger had not consulted them as he put the energy program together. Schlesinger's determined effort to push the original bill through Congress disgruntled some lawmakers. Outside government, he upset conservationists by playing down the danger posed by the 1979 **Three Mile Island** nuclear reactor accident and urging petroleum drilling in Alaska. Fed up with the criticism, he decided to resign.

Leaving Washington, Schlesinger took a job as a senior adviser with Lehman Brothers, Kuhn Loeb Inc., in New York City. He also served on numerous governmental bodies, including the Commission on National Security for the 21st Century, the Homeland Security Advisory Council, and a commission to look into the torture of inmates at the U.S.-run Abu Ghraib prison in Iraq. In the meantime, he remained steadfast in opposing any policies he believed endangered U.S. defense, including the Comprehensive Nuclear Test Ban Treaty (CTBT); though approved by the United Nations in 1996, the United States to this day has yet to ratify it. Schlesinger presently is director of the board of trustees of the MITRE Corporation and serves on the boards of several other firms.

SCHMIDT, HELMUT HEINRICH (1918–). Possibly the most vocal of President **Jimmy Carter**'s European critics was Helmut Schmidt, who served as the chancellor of **West Germany** from 1974 to 1982. Schmidt was born in Hamburg, Germany, fought in World War II, joined the Social Democratic Party (SDP) in 1946, and received his college degree in 1949. He rose up the SDP's ranks, becoming defense minister under his predecessor, Willy Brandt. When a scandal forced Brandt's resignation, Schmidt assumed the chancellorship.

Schmidt sought to normalize relations with the communist nations of Eastern Europe. In that effort, he developed a good relationship with French officials. Dealing with the United States was another matter. Schmidt believed American officials too often ignored West German concerns when it came to **foreign policy** or **defense**. The tension between the chancellor and the United States increased during Carter's tenure in office. The two clashed on numerous topics, including the **neutron bomb**, West Germany's plan to sell a nuclear power plant to Brazil, the U.S. response to the **Union of Soviet Socialist Republics' (USSR)** invasion of **Afghanistan**, and the deployment of nuclear missiles in Europe. After losing a no-confidence vote in 1982, Schmidt became coeditor of the weekly news **magazine** *Die Ziet*. In more recent years, he has argued against permitting Turkey to join the European Union and has criticized the U.S.-led war against Iraq.

Carter and West German chancellor Helmut Schmidt. Schmidt was one of Carter's strongest international critics. Courtesy of the Jimmy Carter Library.

See also GISCARD D'ESTAING, VALERY (1926–); GREAT BRITAIN, RELATIONS WITH.

SCHULTZE, CHARLES LOUIS (1924–). The chairman of the Council of Economic Advisers (CEA) from 1977 to 1981, Charles Schultze was born in Alexandria, Virginia. He had just begun his college career when the United States entered World War II. Dropping out of college, he joined the armed forces and fought in Europe. After the war, he completed his studies, earning a Ph.D. in economics from the University of Maryland. He taught for two years at the university level before getting a position as assistant director of the Bureau of the Budget (BOB) in 1962. In 1965, President Lyndon B. Johnson appointed him BOB's director. By the time of the **1976 election**, Schultze had become known as one of the **Democratic Party**'s top economic minds.

Although Schultze did not know **Jimmy Carter**, he offered to help the new president. Carter accepted, naming Schultze to head the CEA. In that post, Schultze called for giving priority to combating the nation's high unemployment rate rather than **inflation**, which set him apart from Carter and other advisers. Schultze, though, came around to accepting the president's determination to focus on inflation and backed the White House's call in the fall of 1978 to cut the budget, limit pay increases for federal employees, and deregulate industry as a means to curtail rising prices. But the revolution in **Iran** resulted in higher oil costs and made it hard for the administration to bring inflation down. Accordingly, in 1979, Carter, over Schultze's objections, endorsed Federal Reserve chairman **Paul Volcker**'s decision to fight inflation by selling Treasury bonds on the open market, even though that would mean higher interest rates and slower economic growth. It was the state of the **economy** that played a part in Carter's eventual loss in the **1980 election**.

Schultze returned to private life, working at Stanford University and as a senior fellow at the Brookings Institution. He criticized the **Ronald Reagan** administration's economic policies. In the 1990s, he appeared frequently on the NBC program *Nightly Business Report*. In 2011, he joined nine other former CEA heads to call for bringing down the federal deficit, which they stated posed a threat to the nation's well-being. He presently is senior fellow emeritus at the Brookings Institution.

See also MEANY, GEORGE (1894–1980).

SCIENCE FICTION. The decade of the 1960s had seen the "new wave" in science fiction **literature**, whereby authors were more concerned with style and prose over accuracy. The period also witnessed more **women** joining the genre, among them Joanna Russ and Ursula Le Guin. The new wave remained active in the 1970s. Meanwhile, numerous other science fiction authors who had been writing for years continued to do so in the 1970s, including Isaac Asimov, Ray Bradbury, Arthur C. Clarke, and Robert Heinlein. Michael Crichton, who had published his first novel in the 1960s, saw many of his works turned into movies. Possibly the best known of the science fiction authors whose stories appeared on the big screen is **Stephen King**. If novels sold well, the same could not be said for science fiction **magazines**, few of which succeeded.

Science fiction **cinema** of the 1950s and 1960s had focused primarily upon monsters, aliens, and the danger posed by modern technology (particularly the atomic bomb), and many of these themes continued into the 1970s. In *Colossus: The Forbin Project* (1970), based upon a 1966 novel by Dennis Feltham Jones, a U.S. defense computer and a similar device in the **Union of Soviet Socialist Republics (USSR)** take over the world by controlling the two countries' nuclear arsenals. (One might see *Colossus* as a precursor to the 1984 film *The Terminator*.) In *West World* (1973), written and directed by Crichton, robots at a theme park turn on the human visitors. Android police control humans in *THX 1138* (1971), directed by **George Lucas**. Extraterrestrials are central to the plots of *The Andromeda Strain* (1971), *Close Encounters of the Third Kind* (1977), and *Invasion of the Body Snatchers* (1978). Both *The Andromeda Strain* and *Invasion of the Body Snatchers* were based upon novels. In the former, an extraterrestrial microbe threatens human life, while in the latter, pods replace humans. The aliens are far less threatening in *Close Encounters*, directed by **Stephen Spielberg**, where the subject is contact between humans and extraterrestrials.

Close Encounters was also reflective of a trend in the 1970s toward movies with bigger budgets and superior special effects. Among the most important of these films was Lucas's *Star Wars*; using what is referred to as "motion control photography," a technique pioneered in the 1968 movie *2001: A Space Odyssey*, Lucas gave his machines more natural movement than the stop motion animation used for years in the film industry. Other movies that received note for their effects were *Superman* and *Star Trek: The Motion Picture*, both of which appeared in 1978. *Star Trek*, furthermore, revitalized that 1960s **television** series and generated both several new TV series and numerous movie sequels.

Television viewers watched a number of popular science fiction programs. The main characters in *The Six Million Dollar Man* and *The Bionic Woman* had superhuman abilities thanks to science. *Battlestar Galactica*, with a plot line similar to *Star Wars*, appeared late in the decade and prompted an ultimately unsuccessful lawsuit by Lucas, who claimed that Universal Studios, which produced the series, had committed plagiarism. In the comedy *Mork and Mindy*, an alien arrives on earth to study its inhabitants. *Buck Rogers in the 25th Century* focused on an astronaut from the 20th century who came out of suspended animation 500 years later.

SCORSESE, MARTIN (1942–). Academy Award–winning movie director of some of the best films of the 1970s, Martin Scorsese was born in Long Island, New York. He tried to become a Catholic priest but was not successful. He enrolled at New York University where he graduated with a bachelor's degree in 1964, followed by his graduate degree in 1966, both in filmmaking. In 1973 he was critically acclaimed for his movie *Mean Streets*, which was followed with the violent film *Taxi Driver*. **Robert De Niro** became one of Scorsese's most valuable and talented actors, appearing in eight of the director's movies, including *Mean Streets*, *Raging Bull*, and *Goodfellas*. Scorsese continues to direct, both for the big screen and television.

See also CINEMA.

SICK, GARY GORDON (1935–). A member of the National Security Council (NSC) from 1976 to 1981, Gary Sick was born in Beloit, Kansas. He received a bachelor's degree from the University of Kansas in 1957, joined the U.S. Navy, and received a Ph.D. from Columbia University in 1973. His work for the navy took him to a number of diplomatic posts, including within the Middle East. It was his knowledge of that region of the world that prompted President **Gerald Ford** to ask Sick to join the staff of the NSC, and Sick retained that post under **Jimmy Carter**.

Sick developed a reputation as an expert on **Iran**. That nation's leader, Shah **Mohammed Reza Pahlavi**, was a close ally of the United States. Despite Sick's warnings during 1978 that the shah's political future looked bleak, most intelligence and State Department officials, including U.S. ambassador to Iran **William Sullivan**, painted a rosier picture. Not until late that year did Sullivan caution that the shah's position was precarious, prompting Sick to criticize the ambassador for having earlier issued misleading reports.

Sick left the government following **Ronald Reagan**'s inauguration and retired from the navy in 1982. Several years later, he wrote the book *October Surprise*, in which he contended that officials from the Reagan campaign convinced Iran not to release dozens of Americans it was holding hostage so as to guarantee Reagan a victory in the **1980 election**. Presently, he is an adjunct professor at Columbia University's School of International and Public Affairs.

SILKWOOD, KAREN (1946–1974). A **labor** union member who worked at an Oklahoma plant run by the energy company Kerr-McGee, Karen Silkwood achieved national fame when she publicly accused the firm of giving more attention to meeting production demands than to caring for the **health** of its workers. Born in Texas, Silkwood went to Lamar State College and had worked for a time in a hospital before getting work with Kerr-McGee. Following tests in November 1974 that showed she had been exposed to a dangerously high level of plutonium, she decided to make her case public. She claimed to have documentation proving wrongdoing by Kerr-McGee but died under mysterious circumstances before she could deliver her evidence to a newspaper. Afterward, her estate sued Kerr-McGee and eventually settled out of court for $1.4 million. Silkwood's life was the topic of the 1983 movie *Silkwood*.

SILLS, BEVERLY (1929–2007). One of **opera**'s greatest singers during the 1970s, Belle Miriam Silverman was born in Brooklyn, New York. She began her singing career as a child and in 1947 debuted on the operatic stage. In the 1950s she was singing with the New York Opera Company and in the Metropolitan Opera. By the time she retired from performing at age 50, Sills had appeared on several **television** talk shows. She served as a guest host of *The Tonight Show* for **Johnny Carson**. Her ability to perform in many genres made her one of America's most effective leaders in the arts. She held many titles, including chair of the Lincoln Center and general director of the New York Opera. She passed away from cancer in July 2007.

See also WOMEN.

SIMPSON, "O. J." (ORENTHAL JAMES) (1947–). One of **football**'s greatest professional players, O. J. Simpson was born and raised in San Francisco. He played football at the University of Southern California (1967–68) and won the Heisman Trophy in 1968. Besides playing for the Buffalo Bills, he also became a **cinema** star, appearing in several films including *The Towering Inferno* (1974) and *The Naked Gun* (1988). Simpson was accused of killing his wife in 1994, and the trial on **television** became a media circus. Simpson was found not guilty, but to this day many people believe Simpson murdered his wife.

See also ADVERTISEMENTS; SPORTS.

SISKEL AND EBERT. This popular **television** program began in the mid-1970s on public television (PBS) as *Coming Soon to a Theater Near You*. It paired movie critics Gene Siskel (*Chicago Tribune*) and Roger Ebert (*Chicago Sun-Times*). The program presented clips from new films, with the critics debating whether the movie was worth seeing. After only two seasons, the show was renamed *Sneak Previews* and became a biweekly production. By the fourth season it was a weekly show, and in 1980 PBS sold it to a network station. The show changed its name to *At the Movies*.

See also CINEMA.

SMITH, IAN (1919–2007). The prime minister of Rhodesia from 1965 to 1979, Smith was born in Selukwe, located in the then-British colony of Southern Rhodesia. He had fought in World War II and, after the war, rose up the ranks of Southern Rhodesia's apartheid system, in which a minority of whites ruled over the majority-black population. In 1964, he became prime minister of Southern Rhodesia. Angered by the unwillingness of **Great Britain** to grant Southern Rhodesia its freedom until it permitted universal suffrage, Smith in 1965 declared his country, renamed Rhodesia, independent. London responded by imposing economic sanctions on Rhodesia, and the United Nations followed suit in 1968. Meanwhile, black nationalists in Rhodesia took up arms, hoping to overthrow the Smith government.

President **Jimmy Carter** saw ending apartheid as part of his larger effort to promote **human rights** worldwide and endorsed the policy of sanctions. Smith, however, refused to budge. The Rhodesian head of state in 1978 proposed an "internal settlement" that would give blacks some power within his government, but that would allow him to retain the prime ministership and give whites enough power in Parliament to prevent any changes to the nation's constitution. The proposal was unacceptable to blacks, and the fighting in Rhodesia continued.

By late 1979, Carter was giving far less attention to Rhodesia than he had in 1977 or even 1978. The U.S. ambassador to the United Nations, **Andrew Young**, had championed greater attention to Africa and its problems, but he had been forced to resign in July 1979 after meeting with a member of the **Palestine Liberation Organization**. Furthermore, Carter's focus was elsewhere, including the **Iran hostage crisis** and his own desire to win another term in office. But the sanctions had an impact upon the Rhodesian economy, as did the ongoing civil war. Facing internal and external pressure, Smith in 1979 accepted a British plan that allowed for black majority rule. In June of that year, he gave up the prime ministership; the following year, elections were held that gave blacks majority control over the newly renamed nation of Zimbabwe. After retiring, Smith wrote his memoir and was a critic of the black Zimbabwean government. He died in November 2007.

See also FOREIGN POLICY.

SOCIAL SECURITY DISABILITY AMENDMENTS. In 1956, the U.S. Congress amended the Social Security Act to provide disability insurance benefits to employed persons aged 50 to 65 who were insured but disabled, or to the disabled children of insured workers. Sixteen years later, lawmakers again made changes to the Social Security system, creating a program called Supplemental Security Income (SSI) for the Aged, Blind, and Disabled. SSI provided financial assistance to individuals aged 65 and over who were blind or disabled and received little or no Social Security.

By the mid-1970s, both Social Security and SSI appeared headed for insolvency because of a sizeable increase in the number of people seeking government assistance. Therefore, in June 1980 Congress passed and President **Jimmy Carter** signed the Social Security Disability Amendments to strengthen the system and provide more equity to those receiving benefits. The changes included limits on the amount of aid insured workers and their dependents could receive, incentives in both disability insurance and SSI to convince disabled workers to seek employment, and provisions to make sure there was uniformity among state disability programs.

SOLZHENITSYN, ALEKSANDR (1918–2008). Born in the Caucasus region of the **Union of Soviet Socialist Republics (USSR)**, Aleksandr Solzhenitsyn became a famous Soviet novelist and historian. He was raised by his mother, his father having died prior to his birth. Encouraged by his mother to pursue his interests in science and **literature**, Solzhenitsyn studied math, science, and history in college. During World War II, he served in the Red Army. Throughout, Solzhenitsyn had loyally followed the communist line, but in 1945, he wrote letters to friends criticizing how Soviet leader Josef Stalin had conducted the war. Shortly thereafter, Solzhenitsyn was arrested.

He served seven years in prison and three more in internal exile. A few years after regaining his freedom, he began writing *One Day in the Life of Ivan Denisovich* (1962), a novel based upon his own life experience. The story made Westerners aware of the terrors of the Soviet labor camp system.

While the Soviet government had permitted the publication of *One Day*, by the mid-1960s, Solzhenitsyn had become a target of the Soviet secret police, better known as the KGB, which seized many of his papers. Undeterred, he secretly prepared what would become his most subversive and critical work, *The Gulag Archipelago*. Published in 1973 and based upon primary research, it described in frightening detail the history of the Soviet system of labor and concentration camps. The next year, he was arrested, kicked out of the USSR, and had his Soviet citizenship taken away. He spent most of the next two decades living in the United States, where he continued his writing. His Soviet citizenship was restored in 1990, and he returned to his home country four years later. He published several more works, including a memoir of his time in the West. He died of heart failure in 2008.

SOMALIA, RELATIONS WITH. *See* HORN OF AFRICA.

SOMOZA DEBAYLE, ANASTASIO (1925–1980). The president of Nicaragua from 1967 to 1972 and from 1974 to 1979, Anastasio Somoza Debayle was the third and last member of a dynasty that had ruled Nicaragua since the 1930s. The first was Somoza's father, Anastasio Somoza García, who led the country from 1936 until his assassination in 1956. Luis Somoza Debayle, García's oldest son, took over the reins of power, where he remained until his death from a heart attack in 1967. Anastasio Somoza Debayle then became the nation's president. Though the law did not permit him to run for consecutive terms, he was effectively Nicaragua's leader from 1972 to 1974, when a *junta* ran the country. The Somozas' repressive and corrupt leadership fueled an opposition movement made up of several groups. The most radical of them was the Sandinista National Liberation Front, or **Sandinistas** for short, a leftist organization formed in 1961 that used guerrilla warfare against the government.

Despite his avowed support for **human rights**, President **Jimmy Carter** and his advisers saw little reason to convince Somoza to change his ways or give up the presidency, for the opposition seemed too weak. That began to change during 1978. One reason was the murder in January 1978 of Pedro Joaquín Chamorro, a well-known critic of the Somoza government. Then, in June, Somoza published a letter sent to him by Carter in which the U.S. president expressed his support for the Nicaraguan leader. Ever more of Somoza's opponents endorsed the Sandinistas and made the White House realize the Nicaraguan leader's days were numbered. Starting in mid-1978, the Carter administration sought to find a moderate alternative to both the Sandinistas and Somoza, but by then the moderates had fled, been killed, or joined the Sandinistas. In June 1979 the Carter administration convinced Somoza to leave Nicaragua, after which the Sandinistas assumed power. When Carter refused to permit him to enter the United States, Somoza traveled to Paraguay. A year later, a team of Sandinista commandos killed the former Nicaraguan president.

See also AARON, DAVID LAURENCE (1938–); FOREIGN POLICY.

"SON OF SAM". The "son of Sam" was the alias given to David Berkowitz, a serial killer whose exploits were made into the 1999 movie *Summer of Sam*. Born in 1953 in the Bronx, New York, David was adopted by Nathan and Pearl Berkowitz. Having been given up by his mother, growing up in a family that loved him but was rather introverted, and finding few friends, he developed a reputation as a loner and a bully. He became depressed when Pearl died of **breast cancer** in 1967. Shortly after remarrying, Nathan and his new wife moved, leaving the 18-year-old David behind. In 1971, David joined the U.S. Army and was dishonorably discharged three years later. Not long thereafter, he located his birth mother, only to find out to his dismay that he had been illegitimately conceived.

Driven by anger, paranoia, and depression, in 1975 Berkowitz began a crime spree that lasted for two years. He shot and killed six people and wounded at least eight others, leaving one permanently paralyzed and another blind in one eye. Following one of the attacks, he sent a letter to the New York City Police Department (NYPD) in which he called himself the "son of Sam," and the name stuck. In August 1977, following an extensive investigation, the NYPD arrested Berkowitz, after which he admitted to the shootings. The following year, he was sentenced to six life sentences for each of the murders and sent to the Attica Correctional Facility, where he remains. After Berkowitz tried to profit from selling his story, the state of New York passed what became known as the Son of Sam Law, which prohibits criminals from receiving financial benefit from their stories. Nearly every other state has since passed similar legislation.

SONDHEIM, STEPHEN (1930–). One of Broadway's most celebrated composers and lyricists, Stephen Sondheim was born in New York City. His parents were wealthy; however, Stephen rarely saw them. Oscar Hammerstein II taught him to write lyrics, and that knowledge made Sondheim one of the most successful songwriters on Broadway. He provided all of the lyrics for *West Side Story* and created the music and lyrics for some of the most popular plays that also became great motion pictures, among them *A Funny Thing Happened on the Way to the Forum* and *Sweeney Todd.*

SOUTH KOREA, RELATIONS WITH. The Korean War of 1950–53, fought between North and South Korea, had ended with the United States retaining tens of thousands of troops in South Korea to defend that country. In 1969, though, President **Richard Nixon** had proposed withdrawing those forces as a way to save money, and to encourage South Korea to spend more for its own defense. Yet continued tensions on the Korean peninsula convinced him and his successor, **Gerald Ford**, to stay any action.

At the time **Jimmy Carter** won the **1976 election**, there were about 41,000 U.S. soldiers stationed in South Korea. Hoping to cut costs, and disliking the repressive nature of the South Korean government of President Park Chung-hee, Carter announced shortly after his inauguration that he would remove those forces (though he would provide Seoul with military equipment necessary for its **defense**). Both South Korea and **Japan** reacted angrily, as neither had received advance notice of the decision. Further, both saw the presence of those forces as important to their security. Members of the U.S. Congress, including fellow **Democrats**, joined the chorus. So did General John K. Singlaub, the chief of staff of American forces in South Korea. Angered by Singlaub's commentary, Carter had him relieved of command and ordered him to return to the United States.

Adding to the tension in U.S.-South Korean relations was the "Koreagate" scandal. Predating Carter's election, it involved payments sent from the Korean Central Intelligence Agency to members of Congress in the hopes of influencing U.S. policy toward South Korea. The *Washington Post* broke the story in 1975, and Capitol Hill began an investigation in 1977. Several lawmakers were censured and reprimanded, and at least three others, including Richard T. Hanna (D-California), were tried on charges including bribery and conspiracy. Only Hanna, however, faced prison time.

All the while, discussion and debate over the withdrawal of U.S. troops continued. The issue became moot following a report by the *Army Times* in January 1979 that determined that North Korea's military was stronger than originally believed. Afterward, Carter announced his intention to suspend any plan on removing the soldiers, and there the matter stayed through the remainder of his term. To this day, the United States retains sizeable military forces on the Korean peninsula.

See also FOREIGN POLICY; HUMAN RIGHTS; NUNN, SAM (SAMUEL AUGUSTUS) (1938–).

SPACE PROGRAM. *Sputnik*, the world's first space satellite, launched by the **Union of Soviet Socialist Republics (USSR)** in 1957, jump-started the U.S. space program. President Dwight D. Eisenhower increased funding for science programs in universities and oversaw the creation of the National Aeronautics and Space Administration (NASA). NASA established facilities from Florida to Texas to oversee its Apollo program, which landed humans on the moon in 1969, shortly after **Richard Nixon** became president. Nixon also approved development of the space shuttle. Yet funding for NASA declined during Nixon's years in office, and both **Gerald Ford** and **Jimmy Carter** devoted relatively little attention to the U.S. space program.

However, NASA was not inactive. Work on the space shuttle continued. In 1975 *Viking 1* was sent to land on Mars. The following year *Viking 2* was launched. Like *Viking 1*, *Viking 2* landed on the red planet, and both sent back images as well as data about the Martian surface. In 1977 NASA sent a pair of spacecraft, *Voyagers 1* and *2*, on a five-year mission to study Jupiter and Saturn, with *Voyager 2* also doing flybys of Uranus and Neptune. The space probes continue to send back information. In 1978 NASA launched *Pioneer Venus* to study the atmosphere on Venus.

In June 2012, NASA reported that *Voyager 1* had reached the edge of the solar system. When it leaves the solar system, it will become the first man-made object to enter interstellar space.

See also TECHNOLOGICAL ADVANCES.

SPIELBERG, STEVEN (1946–). Filmmaker Steven Spielberg was born in Cincinnati, Ohio. His interest in **cinema** began as a very young man. Indifferent to classes unrelated to film, he did not do well in college, but his filmmaking abilities were so extraordinary that he became one of the youngest directors at Universal Pictures. His first major film was *Duel* (1971). In time Spielberg enjoyed creating movies that were unique in their special effects. Some of his best and most highly praised **science fiction** films include *Close Encounters of the Third Kind* (1977) and *E.T.* (1982). In 1994, he was awarded his only Academy Award for the 1993 film *Schindler's List.*

See also WILLIAMS, JOHN (1932–).

SPORTS. The major change in sports in the 1970s was that professional athletes became free agents, which meant they no longer were "owned" by a team. **Television** changed the world of sports, and team owners profited from the exploitation of their players. The players retaliated by becoming negotiators of their own contracts. Baseball great **Pete Rose** was earning a million dollars a year by 1979; before 1970, only a small number of sports figures made $100,000 a year.

Moreover, athletes became spokespersons for various products, appearing in **magazines**, newspapers, and on television. Television also gained its own sports channel in 1979 when **ESPN (Entertainment and Sports Programming Network)** debuted on cable television. At first it was only on for a limited time each day, but by 1980 it was broadcasting 24 hours a day. ESPN covers sporting events worldwide.

Another significant change was Title IX, part of the Educational Amendments of 1972, which guarantees **women** attending educational institutions receiving federal financial aid the same rights and opportunities as their male counterparts. In 1975 and again in 1979, the U.S. government clarified what this change meant for college athletics. As a result of Title IX, women who play sports are eligible for scholarships and have had opportunities to play in sports once denied them. The law also forced colleges and universities to reevaluate what sports they would offer to guarantee equal opportunity for men and women.

See also AARON, HANK (1934–); ABDUL-JABBAR, KAREEM (1947–); ALI, MUHAMMAD (1942–); BASEBALL; BASKETBALL; BICYCLING; BOXING; CLAY, CASSIUS MARCELLUS; COMANECI, NADIA (1962–); COSELL, HOWARD (1918–1995); ERVING, JULIUS (1950–); FIXX, JAMES (1932–1984); FOOTBALL; FULLER, MILLARD (1935–2009); GOLF; JORDAN, HAMILTON (1944–2008); KING, BILLIE JEAN (1943–); McKAY, JIM (JAMES) (1921–2008); *MONDAY NIGHT FOOTBALL*; OLYMPICS; ROBINSON, FRANK (1935–); ROSE, PETE (PETER EDWARD, SR.) (1941–); SIMPSON, "O. J." (ORENTHAL JAMES) (1947–).

STAGFLATION. Stagflation refers to a combination of **inflation** and little or no economic growth. It was one of the reasons for President **Jimmy Carter**'s defeat in the **1980 election**.

See also ECONOMY; FULL EMPLOYMENT AND BALANCED GROWTH ACT.

STEINEM, GLORIA (1934–). Perhaps one of the most well-known **women** of the 1970s, Gloria Steinem was born in Toledo, Ohio. She graduated from Smith College in 1956, worked at various times for two **magazines**, and in 1972 introduced her own magazine, called *Ms.* It became and remains one of the icons of the women's movement. While Steinem and other feminists acknowledged President **Jimmy Carter**'s effort to do more for women, she criticized him and his wife, **Rosalynn**, for not being more outspoken in defense of women's rights.

STENNIS, JOHN CORNELIUS (1901–1995). Democrat. Born in De-Kalb, Mississippi, John Stennis served as a U.S. senator from 1947 to 1989. He attended Mississippi State University (B.S., 1923) and the University of Virginia (LL.B., 1928). He then got a seat in the Mississippi House of Representatives and afterward worked in the state as a lawyer and judge. In 1947, he ran for and won a seat in the U.S. Senate. While he was not willing to defend the **civil rights** movement that had taken hold in the South starting in the 1950s, he was equally unprepared to defend those who used the race card for political gain. He became particularly well known, however, for his work on the Armed Services Committee, which he came to chair starting in 1969. Stennis supported increases in **defense** spending during the 1960s yet had apprehensions about the expanding U.S. role in Vietnam as the decade continued. Believing that congressional decision making in the 1960s had given the president too much power to make war, he was a sponsor of the 1973 War Powers Act, which restricted the executive branch's ability to send troops into harm's way.

Stennis had favored Texas senator Lloyd Bentsen's candidacy for the 1976 Democratic nomination for president, which **Jimmy Carter** eventually received. While Stennis's relationship with President Carter was not contentious, the two did not see eye to eye. Stennis opposed Carter's decision to cut funding for several water projects, including one favored by the senator; voted against the **Panama Canal treaties**, despite Carter's best effort to change his mind; and had serious qualms about the **Strategic Arms Limitation Treaty (SALT II)**, which he believed endangered America's defense. Indeed, when it came to defense, Stennis's philosophy was similar to his Armed Services Committee colleague, **Henry Jackson**, though his personality was less abrasive.

Stennis began to suffer personally and physically during the 1980s. In 1983, his wife, to whom he had been married for over a half century, passed away, and the following year he lost a leg to cancer. In 1988, he announced he would not seek reelection. After leaving the Senate, he returned to Mississippi, living for a time in Starkville. As his health continued to decline, he moved to a nursing home in Jackson, where he died at age 93.

STEVENS, JOHN PAUL (1920–). A native of Illinois, John Paul Stevens was an associate justice of the **Supreme Court** from 1975 to 2010. He received his bachelor's degree from the University of Chicago in 1941, served as a naval intelligence officer during World War II, and, upon his return to the United States, went to Northwestern University, from which he received his law degree in 1947. Afterward, Stevens worked as a clerk for U.S. Supreme Court justice Wiley Rutledge and then joined a law firm in Chicago. In 1952, he opened his own legal office, focusing on antitrust law. Eighteen years later, President **Richard Nixon** appointed Stevens to the Seventh Circuit Court of Appeals. There, he developed a reputation as a moderate, which served Stevens well when President **Gerald Ford** nominated him to the U.S. Supreme Court. The Senate approved the nomination unanimously.

Throughout his career, Stevens was someone who preferred to write his own opinions rather than join those of other justices, and he was unpredictable in what position he might take. For instance, in the 1978 case *University of California Board of Regents v. Bakke,* Stevens dissented from the majority, contending that **affirmative action** violated the 1964 Civil Rights Act. Yet 25 years later, he agreed with four other justices in upholding the University of Michigan's affirmative action program. In *Houchins v. KQEL* (1978), he rejected the majority view that officers of the law could prevent press access to prisons or prisoners; a year later, though, in *Gannett Co. v. dePasquale,* he joined the majority in stating that a court could exclude the media from a pretrial hearing if requested by the defendant. In the early part of his career Stevens defended the death penalty, but, by the end of it, he had concluded that sentencing a person to death was unconstitutional. Since leaving the Supreme Court, he has been writing his memoir and frequently comments on Court decisions.

STEWART, POTTER (1915–1985). An associate justice of the **Supreme Court** from 1958 to 1981, Potter Stewart was born in Jackson, Michigan, and raised in Ohio. He attended Yale University, where he received his undergraduate and law degrees (B.A., 1937; LL.B., 1941). He fought with the U.S. Navy during World War II. After the war, Stewart worked in a Cincinnati law firm before joining local politics. He supported **Republican** presidential candidate Dwight D. Eisenhower in the 1952 election. Two years later, Eisenhower appointed Stewart to the Sixth Circuit Court of Appeals, followed by the U.S. Supreme Court in 1956.

Stewart's rulings reflected a desire to balance the right of free speech with the good of society and to defend a person from overly intrusive government. He dissented from the majority of the justices in *Miranda v. Arizona* (1966), which required police to read criminals their legal rights. He joined the majority, though, in *Roe v. Wade* (1973), which granted a woman the right to an abortion. In *Regents of the University of California v. Bakke* (1978), Stewart agreed with four of the other justices that the University of California's quota system for minorities was unconstitutional. In 1981 Stewart resigned and was replaced by the first **woman** justice, Sandra Day O'Connor. He died in December 1985 shortly after suffering a stroke.

STRATEGIC ARMS LIMITATION TREATY (SALT II). In 1972, the United States and **Union of Soviet Socialist Republics (USSR)** signed and ratified the Strategic Arms Limitation Treaty, or SALT I, which restricted the number of antiballistic missile (ABM) systems and offensive nuclear missiles each nation could build. Although the ABM treaty had no expiration date, the restriction on offensive missiles did, in 1977. President **Jimmy Carter,** therefore, sought to achieve a SALT II agreement, one broader in scope and with even greater cuts in the number of missiles. After two years of negotiations, he and Soviet general secretary **Leonid Brezhnev** signed

SALT II. Its provisions included reducing the number of ballistic missile launchers to 2,250 by the year 1981, prohibiting any increase in the destructive power of their missiles, limiting the number of missiles with more than one warhead as well as cruise missiles to 1,320, and permitting each country to construct one new missile system. Additionally, each superpower had to allow the other to verify that it was complying with the treaty.

This was as far as SALT II got. Part of the problem was strong opposition in the Senate, which would have to ratify the treaty. Although some members of the Upper House, such as **Frank Church, Jacob Javits**, and **Abraham Ribicoff** endorsed the treaty, many, including **Bob Dole, Henry Jackson, William Proxmire, Jesse Helms, Sam Nunn, John Stennis, Howard Baker**, and **Daniel Patrick Moynihan**, registered reservations or outright rejection. But what killed SALT was the USSR's invasion of **Afghanistan** in December 1979. Afterward, Carter had the Senate put the agreement on ice.

See also AARON, DAVID LAURENCE (1938–); BROWN, HAROLD (1927–); BYRD, ROBERT CARLYLE (1917–2010); CHINA, RELATIONS WITH; CHURCH, FRANK FORRESTER (1924–1984); CUBA, RELATIONS WITH; CUTLER, LLOYD NORTON (1917–2005); DEFENSE; FOREIGN POLICY; GREAT BRITAIN, RELATIONS WITH; HORN OF AFRICA; JACKSON, HENRY MARTIN "SCOOP" (1912–1983); McGOVERN, GEORGE STANLEY (1922–2012); NIXON, RICHARD MILHOUS (1913–1994); TURNER, STANSFIELD (1923–); VANCE, CYRUS ROBERT (1917–2002); WARNKE, PAUL CULLITON (1920–2001).

STRAUSS, ROBERT SCHWARTZ (1918–). Democrat. A jack-of-all-trades, Robert Strauss served as President **Jimmy Carter**'s special trade representative from 1977 to 1979, then as Carter's Middle East negotiator from 1979 to 1980, and finally as the chair of the Carter reelection campaign in 1980. Born in Lockhart, Texas, Strauss received his bachelor's and law degrees from the University of Texas (LL.B., 1941) and then worked for the Federal Bureau of Investigation during World War II. He founded his own legal practice in 1946. Through his work as an attorney and his real estate investments, he became wealthy enough to spend time working in Democratic Party politics. He raised money for John Connally when Connally sought the governorship of Texas in 1962. Six years later Connally named Strauss to the Democratic National Committee, of which he became treasurer in 1972. That same year, he promised to raise $1 million for the Democratic Party and, to the surprise of House Speaker **Tip O'Neill**, did just that. Shortly thereafter, Strauss was elected the party's chair.

Strauss first met Carter in early 1973, at which time they talked about raising money for Democrats running for Congress. Strauss shortly thereafter asked Carter to cochair, along with the former governor of North Carolina, Terry Sanford, the Committee to Elect Democrats. Carter used that position not only to stump for those seeking office but to set the stage for his own presidential bid. Though Strauss favored other Democrats seeking the party's presidential nomination, once Carter had it, Strauss loyally raised large sums of money for the campaign. In return, Carter appointed Strauss special trade representative, giving the Texan the job of negotiating all U.S. trade agreements. Strauss's success in this role, which included a major commercial pact with **Japan**, convinced observers that he was an exceptional diplomat. Carter was impressed enough with Strauss's abilities that, following the **Camp David Accords** of 1978, he named Strauss special envoy to the Middle East. Both Secretary of State **Cyrus Vance** and National Security Adviser **Zbigniew Brzezinski** did not like Strauss's appointment, seeing it as usurping their authority. Strauss himself, though at first excited with his new responsibilities, soon came to see little chance of getting **Israel** and the Palestinians to sit down and engage in serious talks. He was thus thrilled when Carter in 1980 asked him to step down as Mideast envoy and instead head his reelection campaign. Despite Strauss's best efforts, however, the **economy**, the **Iran hostage crisis**, the split within the party between Carter and Senator **Edward Kennedy**, and Carter's poor showing in his debate with **Republican** candidate **Ronald Reagan** all took their toll and helped Reagan win the **1980 election**.

Strauss continued his role as a Washington insider. He became close friends with Reagan's vice president, **George H. W. Bush**. In 1991, Bush named Strauss ambassador to the **Union of Soviet Socialist Republics (USSR)**. Later that year, the USSR began to dissolve, to be replaced by the Russian Federation; Strauss thus became the first ambassador to the new nation. In 1992, he resigned his post and returned to law. He currently maintains legal offices in both Washington, D.C., and Dallas, Texas.

See also LINOWITZ, SOL MYRON (1913–2005); McDONALD, AL (ALONZO LOWRY) (1928–).

STUDIO 54. Located in a former **opera** house and Columbia Broadcasting System (CBS) studio in New York City, in 1976 the property was purchased by Steven Rubell, Tim Savage, Ian Schraeger, and Jack Dushey, who agreed to turn it into a **disco**. It was these men who gave it the name Studio 54 after its address at 254 W. 54th Street. Numerous celebrities, including **Michael Jackson**, Cher, Liza Minnelli, Robin Leach, and Debbie Harry, attended on opening night. Studio 54 soon became the most famous nightclub in the city. This was not just because of the artists who performed there, such as Gloria Gaynor and Donna Summer, but also because of its dance floor and hedonistic activities that took place on site, such as sex and drugs. One of the people accused of drug use at Studio 54 was President **Jimmy Carter**'s chief of staff, **Hamilton Jordan**, though he was never formally charged. In 1980, after Rubell and Schraeger were given prison sentences for tax evasion,

Studio 54 closed down. It then reopened in 1982 under new ownership. Artists such as Madonna, Wham, Boy George, and KISS were among those who performed. In 1986, Studio 54 again shut its doors. In 1998, the building was rediscovered and has since been the home of the Roundabout Theatre Company.

See also CINEMA; CIVILETTI, BENJAMIN RICHARD (1935–); DANCES.

SULLIVAN, WILLIAM HEALY (1922–). Democrat. The U.S. ambassador to **Iran** from 1977 to 1979, William Sullivan was born in Rhode Island. He received his bachelor's degree in 1942 from Brown University and then served in the U.S. Navy during World War II. After receiving his master's from Tufts University's Fletcher School of Law in 1947, he joined the Foreign Service. During the next 30 years, his stints included Thailand, India, **Japan**, Italy, and Laos. He then received an offer from President **Jimmy Carter** to take up the post as ambassador to Iran. Though he had preferred Mexico as his assignment, he accepted the offer.

At the time of Sullivan's appointment, Iran was the scene of growing unrest against that nation's leader, Shah **Mohammed Reza Pahlavi**. Despite evidence that the shah's days might be numbered, Sullivan believed Pahlavi could remain in power if he instituted political and economic reforms, and he sent his superiors in Washington rosy reports about the shah's political future. But in November 1978, he warned that Pahlavi was on the verge of losing power; it was time, wrote Sullivan, for the United States to prepare for a new Iranian government headed by the shah's leading opponent, Ayatollah **Ruhollah Khomeini**. Sullivan's sudden change of heart regarding the shah's future angered officials within the Carter administration, particularly National Security Council (NSC) adviser **Zbigniew Brzezinski** and the NSC's Iran expert, **Gary Sick**. Two months later, the shah fled, and Khomeini assumed power. Sullivan criticized President Carter for not sending an emissary to meet with Khomeini, a move the ambassador believed necessary to maintain good relations with the new Iranian leadership. Carter later wrote he should have fired Sullivan for insubordination but permitted the ambassador to remain at his post. Concluding that he could not accept the administration's Iran policy, Sullivan resigned in protest in February 1979. In the years since, he has written two books on his Foreign Service career and served as president of Columbia University's American Assembly.

See also LAINGEN, (LOWELL) BRUCE (1922–).

SUPREME COURT. Generally, the decisions rendered by the Supreme Court during **Jimmy Carter**'s term in the White House reflected its largely liberal makeup. Of the nine justices, **William Brennan, Thurgood Mar-**

shall, **Warren Burger**, **Lewis Powell**, and **Harry Blackmun** tended toward the liberal side of the sociopolitical spectrum. **William Rehnquist**, who later became chief justice, was known for his conservatism. **Potter Stewart** and **Byron White** could be regarded as moderates who generally made their decisions on a case-by-case basis, while **John Paul Stevens** became known for his ideological inconsistency.

The most important of the cases the Court decided in the second half of the 1970s focused on issues related to discrimination, equal opportunity, and First and Eighth Amendment rights. In *Ingraham v. Wright* (1977), the justices decided by a 5–4 vote that the use of corporal punishment by Florida's public schools neither violated the "cruel and unusual punishment" clause of the Constitution, nor required notification or hearings beforehand. The following year, in *Foley v. Connelie*, the Court in a 6–3 decision struck down a New York state law requiring state police to be American citizens. In *Houchins v. KQED* (1978), the justices determined 4–3 that government officials had the right to prohibit reporters from interviewing prisoners; upheld in the 5–3 decision *Zurcher v. Stanford Daily* (1978) that police had the right to search a newsroom in an attempt to identify criminals; and by a 5–4 vote in *Gannett Co. v. DePasquale* (1979) permitted closing pretrial hearings to the media. However, in *Richmond Newspapers v. Virginia* (1980), the Court largely reversed *Gannett*, with seven of the justices declaring that under the First Amendment, trials could be closed to the press only under extraordinary circumstances. The comedian **George Carlin**'s comedy routine in which he referenced the "seven dirty words" became central to the Court's 5–4 decision in *Federal Communications Commission v. Pacifica Foundation* (1978). In that case, the justices upheld the right of the Federal Communications Commission to prohibit the broadcasting of indecent material.

None of the cases to appear before the Court, however, drew more attention than ***Regents of the University of California v. Bakke***. **Allan Paul Bakke**, who was white, charged that to uphold **affirmative action** mandates, the medical school at the University of California at Davis had set aside seats solely for minorities. Bakke's lawyers contended that as a result, their client had been denied admission despite the fact that he had a higher grade point average and standardized test score than minority students who had been allowed to enroll. By a 5–4 ruling, the justices upheld affirmative action programs but declared it unconstitutional to use quotas.

See also ABORTION; CIVIL RIGHTS; GRIFFIN, ROBERT PAUL (1923–); LIPSHUTZ, ROBERT JEROME (1921–2010); MINORITY SET-ASIDES; MONDALE, WALTER FREDERICK (FRITZ) (1928–); NATIONAL ORGANIZATION FOR WOMEN (NOW); NATIVE AMERICANS; PRIVACY PROTECTION ACT; PROPOSITION 13;

RIGHT TO FINANCIAL PRIVACY ACT; *UNITED STEELWORKERS OF AMERICA V. WEBER*; WEDDINGTON, SARAH RAGLE (1945–); WOMEN; WRIGHT, JIM (JAMES CLAUDE WRIGHT JR.) (1922–).

SURFACE MINING CONTROL AND RECLAMATION ACT. Desirous to find a way to confront America's **energy crisis** through coal mining while protecting both farmland and the **environment**, lawmakers and President **Jimmy Carter** worked together to see passage of the Surface Mining Control and Reclamation Act in 1977. It forbids mining companies from using land that might be put toward residential, commercial, agricultural, or forestry use unless the land in question can be returned to its premining state. Additionally, the bill authorizes the states to oversee its enforcement.

SUSAN B. ANTHONY DOLLAR COIN. Minted starting in 1979, this coin depicted one of the leaders of the **women**'s suffrage movement, with an American eagle on the tail side. It soon aroused complaints that it was smaller than earlier dollar coins and too easily confused with quarters. Nearly 900 million were produced before the U.S. Treasury stopped minting them in 1981.

SYRIA, RELATIONS WITH. *See* ASSAD, HAFEZ AL- (1930–2000).

T

TAIWAN, RELATIONS WITH. *See* CHINA, RELATIONS WITH.

TALMADGE, HERMAN EUGENE (1913–2002). Democrat. A critic of **Jimmy Carter**, Herman Talmadge served as governor of Georgia from 1948 to 1955 and as a U.S. senator from 1957 to 1981. He was born in Georgia, received a law degree from the University of Georgia, and saw battle with the U.S. Navy during World War II. His father, who had served as Georgia's governor, died shortly after being reelected in 1946 to a fourth term. Talmadge successfully succeeded his father in a special election held two years later. After holding the governorship for seven years, he ran for and won a seat in the U.S. Senate, where he remained until 1981. As both a governor and senator, Talmadge played both sides of the coin on such matters as social welfare programs and race. He supported segregation and declared himself an admirer of **Lester Maddox**, an Atlanta businessman and segregationist who ran for Georgia governor in 1966. Furthermore, he opposed most of President Lyndon B. Johnson's Great Society programs. Yet he also backed equal pay for black and white teachers and was central to the development of the Great Society's food-stamp initiative.

Talmadge had been close to Jimmy Carter's father, who had been one of Talmadge's most avid supporters. The same was not the case for the younger Carter. After Carter won in the 1970 gubernatorial election, Talmadge believed Carter would seek his Senate seat. Accordingly, he and his allies in Georgia tried to stop Carter's effort to reorganize the state's government. Though happy to learn that Carter had his eyes instead on the White House, Talmadge gave his fellow Georgian only a lukewarm endorsement. Talmadge voted in favor of the **Panama Canal treaties** and supported the **Camp David Accords** but was for the most part critical of Carter's presidency. He rejected the administration's national **health** care proposal, believing the White House's call for hospital cost containment went too far; criticized Carter's **human rights** initiatives; and opposed the president's nomination of **Andrew Young** for the United Nations ambassadorship on the grounds that Young was too willing to back leftist governments in Africa.

In the meantime, Talmadge suffered both personal and political misfortune. Between 1975 and 1977, one of his sons drowned, and Talmadge and his wife divorced. He began to drink heavily and had to spend time in a treatment program. After completing the program in 1978, he came under investigation for misappropriation of campaign funds. The Senate subsequently found him guilty and denounced him for "reprehensible conduct." This scandal, combined with the growing power of the **Republican Party** in the South, cost Talmadge his bid for reelection in 1980. Afterward, he retired to Georgia, where he spent a quiet life. He died of cancer in 2002.

See also JACKSON, MAYNARD HOLBROOK, JR. (1938–2003).

TECHNOLOGICAL ADVANCES. If one subject was to appear in a list of the 1970s technological innovations, the **computer** and its ability to make life and business easier has to be first on the list. The first computers took up entire rooms; by the 1970s, one could purchase a device that would fit on a desk. Computer games appeared, as did the floppy disk. In 1975, **Bill Gates** founded Microsoft, which would add to the computer's incredible performance. Computers were used in the **space program**, in the space shuttle, and in the production of movies. Pocket calculators also appeared during the decade.

The 1970s saw other innovations. The Sony Walkman allowed people to listen to their **music** on an audiocassette, while video cassette recorders (VCRs) permitted one to tape **television** programs or watch movies at home. In combination with air-conditioning—not an innovation of the 1970s but one that had become very popular by then—the VCR allowed people to stay inside rather than go out to watch a film. Thanks to Mr. Coffee, one could enjoy a cup of drip brew at home. Post-it Notes were invented in 1974.

Transportation, both inside and outside earth's atmosphere, changed. The year 1976 saw the Concorde, a supersonic commercial jet, enter service, significantly cutting down travel time between New York and Europe. The next year, the space shuttle *Enterprise* conducted a successful test flight. A total of six shuttles were constructed, which would conduct 135 orbital missions between 1981 and 2011.

The global positioning system, or GPS, which today is common, was created in the 1970s by the Department of Defense for military use. The **B-1 bomber**, first envisioned in the 1960s, was developed the following decade. The U.S. military tested the **neutron bomb** and also began development of a stealth fighter capable of evading enemy radar.

See also APPLE COMPUTER; CENTRAL INTELLIGENCE AGENCY (CIA); TURNER, STANSFIELD (1923–).

TELEVISION. Television in many respects reflects the times in which the shows on it appear, and this was true for the 1970s. The Western, which had been popular during the 1950s and 1960s, gave way to programs that oftentimes had social and political overtones. The influence of the **African American civil rights** movement appeared in the miniseries *Roots*, which depicted the lives of African slaves. *Good Times* addressed the difficulties faced by lower-class blacks, while *The Jeffersons* suggested that African Americans had greater opportunity than in the past to become members of the upper crust. *All in the Family*, though focused on a lower-class white family, attacked head-on the prejudices faced by minorities in the country. The challenges faced by single **women** and mothers appeared in the comedies *One Day at a Time*, *Laverne and Shirley*, and *The Mary Tyler Moore Show*. Sex and sexuality became more open, as seen in *Three's Company*, a comedy about two women and a man living together, and the drama *Charlie's Angels*. *Three's Company* was also significant in that it reflected the burgeoning **gay rights** movement: though Jack Tripper, played by the actor John Ritter, was heterosexual, he pretended to be a homosexual. Homosexuality appeared as well in the comedy *Soap*, a parody of soap operas in which one of the main characters, Jodie Dallas, was gay. The variety show *Saturday Night Live* began airing in 1975, with many skits having political or social connotations. Other popular variety shows during the decade were *The Carol Burnett Show* and *The Sonny & Cher Comedy Hour*. The comedy *M*A*S*H* centered around doctors during the Korean War, *Barney Miller* focused on detectives working in a New York City police station, and *WKRP in Cincinnati* gave Americans a humorous depiction of the lives of employees at a radio station.

If *Barney Miller* gave Americans a laugh about the nation's crime fighters, police dramas ran the gamut from funny to serious and even outlandish. Aside from *Charlie's Angels*, Americans watched *The Rockford Files*, *Barnaby Jones*, *Columbo*, *Baretta*, *Starsky and Hutch*, *Hawaii Five-O*, *Kojak*, and *CHiPs*. *The Dukes of Hazzard*, in which a bumbling county police force plays a role, reflected not only the growing influence of southern culture in the country but the widespread use of **citizens band (CB) radio**. **Science fiction** appeared in numerous programs on TV during the decade, among them *The Incredible Hulk*, *The Six Million Dollar Man*, *The Bionic Woman*, *Wonder Woman*, and *Battlestar Galactica*. *Fantasy Island*, an hour-long weekly drama, in many respects was part of the science fiction genre. Other dramas included *The Love Boat* and *Dallas*. Game shows, among them *Let's Make a Deal*, *The Gong Show*, *The Joker's Wild*, *The Newlywed Game*, *Password*, *The Price Is Right*, *Family Feud*, *Hollywood Squares*, and *Tic Tac Dough* had large audiences.

Numerous TV actors and actresses became household names. John Ritter appeared in other series on the small screen and a number of big-screen movies prior to his untimely death in 2003. Erik Estrada achieved fame from his work on *CHiPs*; Billy Crystal, who played Jodie Dallas on *Soap*, would go on to star in numerous films and repeatedly host the Academy Awards; and Lynda Carter's career took off through her portrayal as Wonder Woman. Carter also became a sex symbol, as did **Farrah Fawcett** (*Charlie's Angels*), Suzanne Somers (*Three's Company*), Loni Anderson (*WKRP in Cincinnati*), and Catherine Bach (*Dukes of Hazzard*). Others who appeared on the small screen during the decade had already established themselves. Lorne Greene, who played Commander Adama on *Battlestar Galactica*, previously had been known to Americans as Ben Cartwright on the series *Bonanza*, which aired from 1959 to 1973. Telly Savalas, who played Theo Kojak on *Kojak*, had been in numerous movies and had received an Academy Award for best supporting actor in the 1962 film *Birdman of Alcatraz*.

Sports remained as popular as ever. ***Monday Night Football*** began airing in 1970, with **Howard Cosell** offering commentary. At the end of the decade, Americans could watch the first sports-only channel, **ESPN (Entertainment and Sports Programming Network)**. For those favoring news and politics, viewers found themselves at the start of the decade limited to the big three networks and anchors and commentators such as **Walter Cronkite** and **William F. Buckley**. By 1980, they could watch the **Cable News Network** and **C-SPAN**. Television was also a key player in the outcome of both the **1976** and **1980 elections**. Children got their own station in **Nickelodeon**. Increasingly, the sets on which American television programs were filmed were made outside the United States, as changes in the world **economy** convinced American TV manufacturers to move their plants elsewhere.

See also ACTION FOR CHILDREN'S TELEVISION; ALI, MUHAMMAD (1942–); CADDELL, PATRICK H. (1950–); CARLIN, GEORGE (1937–2008); CARSON, JOHNNY (1925–2005); CINEMA; DOMINGO, PLACIDO (JOSE PLACIDO DOMINGO EMBIL) (1941–); EASTWOOD, CLINTON, JR. (1930–); FALWELL, JERRY (1933–2007); GREENE, "MEAN JOE" (CHARLES EDWARD) (1946–); HALEY, ALEX (1921–1992); HENSON, JIM (1936–1990); INFOMERCIALS; JACKSON, MICHAEL (1958–2009); KING, BILLIE JEAN (1943–); KISSINGER, HENRY ALFRED (ALFRED HEINZ) (1923–); LEAR, NORMAN MILTON (1922–); LUCAS, GEORGE (1944–); McKAY, JIM (JAMES) (1921–2008); McMAHON, ED(WARD) (1923–2009); McMURTRY, LARRY (1936–); PAVAROTTI, LUCIANO (1935–2007); PRYOR, RICHARD (1940–2005); REAGAN, RONALD WILSON (1911–2004); SILLS, BEVERLY (1929–2007); SIMPSON, "O. J." (ORENTHAL JAMES) (1947–); *SISKEL AND EBERT*; TECHNOLOGICAL ADVANCES; TURNER, TED

(ROBERT EDWARD, III) (1938–); WALTERS, BARBARA (1929–); WILLIAMS, JOHN (1932–); WILSON, FLIP (CLEROW WILSON JR.) (1933–1998).

TEST-TUBE BABIES. July 1978 witnessed the birth of Louise Brown, the first "test tube baby." The process that led to Brown's conception was (and is) known as in vitro fertilization, or IVF. IVF is generally used where other methods to assist pregnancy, such as hormones, have failed. In IVF, eggs are removed from a **woman**'s ovaries and placed in a liquid medium, where sperm cells fertilize them. One or more fertilized eggs are then placed into the woman's uterus, with the anticipation that this will result in a successful pregnancy. While IVF does not guarantee that pregnancy will occur, advancements in the technology have seen an increasing number of test-tube births. The process also offers potential complications, particularly the possibility of multiple births.

THATCHER, MARGARET (1925–). Margaret Thatcher was the first **woman** to serve as prime minister of **Great Britain**, a post she held from 1979 to 1990. She was born in Grantham, Lincolnshire, to grocers Alfred and Beatrice Roberts. She attended Oxford University where she majored in chemistry. However, she was attracted to politics, in part because her father was a local councilor. In 1950 and 1951 she ran as the Conservative Party candidate for the parliamentary seat for Dartford, which was then held by the Labour Party. Though she lost both times, her youth and gender attracted widespread media attention, and she succeeded in cutting into Labour's majority. One of the people who supported her campaign was Denis Thatcher, a businessman whom she married in 1951. Two years later she got her law degree. In 1959, she won a seat in Parliament, became education minister during Edward Heath's prime ministership (1970–74), and then won the seat of Conservative Party leadership, the first woman ever to lead a political party in the West.

In 1979, a British electorate disgruntled with the Labour Party gave the Conservatives the majority of seats in Parliament. A day later, Thatcher became prime minister. She liked President **Jimmy Carter** as a person but regarded him as a poor politician. Even so, she sought to continue the close relationship between her country and the United States that had existed for over a century. Alongside her foreign secretary, Peter Carrington, she arranged an agreement that ended apartheid in **Rhodesia** and allowed for black majority rule; this was a goal of Carter's since he had assumed office. She supported Carter's call to boycott the 1980 Summer **Olympics** following the **Union of Soviet Socialist Republics'** invasion of **Afghanistan** (though she proved unable to prevent the British Olympic team from participating). She developed a much closer relationship with Carter's successor, **Ronald Reagan**, in part because of their shared aversion for communism.

The end of the Cold War and a talk within Europe of economic integration bred divisions within the Conservative Party. Members of the party began to desert Thatcher's leadership. In 1990, she resigned as prime minister. Following several strokes, she announced in 2002 that she would refrain from public speaking. One poll taken in 2011 found her the most competent of Britain's prime ministers over the past three decades.

See also FOREIGN POLICY.

THEATER. Broadway offered some shows in the 1970s that later became successful movies. *Chicago* was introduced in 1975 and made into a movie in 2002. Other Broadway productions were based on the **music** of groups that were active in the decade. These include *Mamma Mia!* (using songs by the group **ABBA**) and *Dreamgirls* (focusing on the success of The Supremes). Ira Levin's *Deathtrap*, which premiered in 1978, was one of Broadway's longest running plays.

See also CARRERAS, JOSÉ (JOSEP CARRERAS I COLL) (1946–); WILSON, FLIP (CLEROW WILSON JR.) (1933–1998).

THREE MILE ISLAND. A commercial nuclear power reactor originally operated by Metropolitan Edison and General Public Utilities, Three Mile Island is located in Londonderry Township, Pennsylvania, or about 10 miles south of Harrisburg, Pennsylvania's capital. In March 1979, the core in one of the plant's two reactors (TMI-2) partially melted down because of a malfunction in the cooling system. The accident released a large amount of radioactivity into the **environment**, though there is some debate whether any humans suffered ill effects. The accident received national and international media coverage, and prompted worldwide protests; that *The China Syndrome*, a movie about a nuclear reactor accident, appeared in **theaters** less than two weeks before the meltdown probably added to the uproar. It also led to changes in the construction and operation of nuclear power plants, including upgrades to make them stronger and safer, programs to improve human performance, and expansion of the Nuclear Regulatory Commission's (NRC) inspection process.

In 1985 TMI-1, which had been shut down at the time of the accident, received permission to resume operations, but TMI-2 remained closed. In 1998, AmerGen Energy Company, today a subsidiary of Exelon Corporation, acquired TMI-1; five years later, Exelon purchased the contract to maintain

TMI-2. In 2009, the NRC renewed Exelon's license to permit TMI-1 to continue operating until 2034, at which point TMI-1 will also be decommissioned.

See also CINEMA; RICKOVER, HYMAN GEORGE (1900–1986).

THURMOND, (JAMES) STROM (1902–2003). A U.S. senator from 1956 to 2003, Strom Thurmond was a member of the **Democratic Party** until 1964, when he switched to the **Republicans**. Born in Edgefield, South Carolina, Thurmond attended Clemson College, joined the South Carolina bar in 1930, worked as an attorney in Edgefield, and then saw service in World War II in both the Atlantic and Pacific theaters. A year after the war ended, he ran for and won the state governorship. He received national fame in 1948 when he campaigned as the presidential candidate for the "Dixiecrats," a faction of the Democratic Party that endorsed segregation. Failing to win the White House, he remained as South Carolina's governor until 1951, when he returned to law. Three years later, he ran as a write-in candidate for a seat in the U.S. Senate. He won, making him the first individual in American history to obtain a major U.S. governmental post via a write-in campaign. By holding on to his seat until his retirement in 2002, Thurmond became one of the longest-serving members of the Senate in its history.

A segregationist, Thurmond fought the Civil Rights Act of 1957 by conducting the longest filibuster in Senate history by a lone senator. During the 1970s, he opposed ratification of the **Panama Canal treaties** and was critical of **Jimmy Carter**'s **human rights** policy, contending that Carter too often targeted friendly, right-wing governments for human rights violations. He died a year after his retirement. Shortly thereafter, the nation learned that despite Thurmond's opposition to **African American** rights, he had fathered a daughter with a black maid.

TORRIJOS, OMAR (1929–1981). The leader of Panama from 1968 to 1981, Omar Torrijos was born in Santiago, Panama. He attended a military academy and, in 1952, joined the National Guard, Panama's equivalent of the U.S. Army. In 1968, then-Lieutenant Colonel Torrijos participated in a military coup that overthrew the government of Arnolfo Arias. Afterward, Torrijos promoted himself to brigadier general and president of his nation. Within a few years, he had crushed all opposition to his leadership and assumed full control over Panama.

The most important subject for Torrijos was the Panama Canal. In 1903, the United States and Panama had signed a treaty giving the former control "in perpetuity" over a strip of land in Panama that became known as the Canal Zone. Many Panamanians viewed the perpetuity clause as an infringement on their nation's sovereignty. Frustration turned into violence in both

1959 and 1964, when Panamanians rioted against U.S. control of the Canal Zone. After the unrest in 1964, U.S. and Panamanian officials began negotiations to turn the Canal Zone over to Panama, but those talks had yet to achieve fruition at the time **Jimmy Carter** became president of the United States. Torrijos wanted the Canal Zone given to Panama, a sentiment shared by Carter. After months of negotiations, Torrijos and Carter signed the **Panama Canal treaties**. Not only did the treaties encounter intense opposition in the United States, where many Americans contended that the waterway was U.S. property, but it did as well among Panamanians, who did not like the idea of waiting 20 years to have the canal given to them. After intense lobbying by the White House, the U.S. Senate agreed to ratify the treaties. In Panama, the evidence suggested that the Torrijos government had used fraud to get the treaties approved.

In 1978, Torrijos ostensibly named Aristides Royo as president, though actual power still rested in Torrijos's hands. After **Iran**'s leader, Shah **Mohammed Reza Pahlavi**, fled his country and found few nations willing to take him in, Torrijos, at Carter's request, permitted the shah to spend time in Panama. Torrijos died in a plane crash in 1981.

See also FOREIGN POLICY.

TOYS AND GAMES. The 1970s introduced some very unusual but popular toys. Boys loved Matchbox cars and the game Battleship, while girls enjoyed the Easy Bake Oven. Popular toys for boys and girls were the Slip 'n Slide, Legos, and Nerf balls. Games included Twister and the Rubik's Cube. Very young children could ride and enjoy the Big Wheel.

TRADE AGREEMENTS ACT (TAA). In December 1974, the U.S. Congress passed and President **Gerald Ford** signed into law the Trade Act, the purpose of which was to restrict the number of barriers to trade while offering protections to U.S. corporations. It permits the president to negotiate trade agreements with other nations; gives him the power to defend U.S. companies from imports, even in instances where there is no evidence of unfair trade practices; and allows the U.S. government to impose restrictions upon imports from nations that engage in unfair trade practices against American products. In 1979, with the U.S. **economy** registering little growth, President **Jimmy Carter** came under pressure to raise tariffs to protect domestic manufacturers from imports. Instead of doing so, he sent to Congress a bill that lawmakers passed in July 1979. Called the Trade Agreements Act, it authorized the president to implement agreements reached on barriers to trade other than tariffs at ongoing trade negotiations then taking place in Tokyo, such as a requirement that the U.S. government give preference to purchasing items from American companies. It also expanded the power of the president to sign commercial agreements with other nations aimed at reducing nontariff trade barriers.

TRANSCENDENTAL MEDITATION. A new-wave **religious** movement, transcendental meditation started in India, where Swami Brahmananda Saraswati Maharaj (1870–1953) was its first teacher. A type of mantra meditation, its defenders argued that by quietly sitting and chanting, a person improved his or her physical well-being and intelligence. After Maharaj died, one of his disciples, Maharishi Mahesh Yogi (1914–2008), took over the effort to spread the movement. Even so, transcendental meditation remained little known until the media reported in 1967 that the Maharishi had become a "spiritual adviser" to the rock group the Beatles. Afterward, transcendental meditation spread rapidly and gained many followers in the United States. However, its popularity had begun to wane as the 1970s came to an end.

TURNER, STANSFIELD (1923–). Democrat. The director of the **Central Intelligence Agency (CIA)** from 1977 to 1981, Stansfield Turner was born in Illinois. He attended college in Massachusetts for two years and then transferred to the U.S. Naval Academy, graduating in 1947. In 1972, he received promotion to the rank of vice admiral and appointment as president of the U.S. Naval War College in Rhode Island. In 1975, Turner became a full admiral and commander of the North Atlantic Treaty Organization's (NATO) southern region. However, he did not enjoy his work with NATO and gladly accepted President **Jimmy Carter**'s offer to become director of the CIA. Carter intended for Turner to oversee the entire national intelligence community, including the National Security Agency and the foreign intelligence divisions of the Federal Bureau of Investigation and the State Department.

Turner later admitted that as director of the CIA, his record was less than stellar. He encountered resistance from other intelligence agencies to give him the information he desired, and within the CIA he was seen by many as an unwanted outsider. Moreover, he believed that **technological advances** offered a better way to gather intelligence than humans. He accordingly fired 800 of the CIA's 1,200 personnel involved in covert activities, many of whom had years of experience, which only served to add to the resentment he faced within the agency. Finally, he found himself with increasingly little access to the president, though there is some debate whether that was the work of Carter himself or National Security Council (NSC) adviser **Zbigniew Brzezinski**. During the **Strategic Arms Limitation Treaty (SALT II)** negotiations, Turner raised concerns about the **Union of Soviet Socialist Republics (USSR)** encrypting information about its missiles, thereby making it more difficult to guarantee that the Kremlin complied with SALT. Neither he nor the CIA was prepared for the revolution in **Iran** or the **Iran hostage crisis**, in part because of the CIA's removal of key personnel and in part because experts outside of the intelligence community did not foresee the events that occurred in that country. There is also evidence that Turner was at fault for providing intelligence discounting the possibility of a Soviet intervention in **Afghanistan**.

After Carter's term in office, Turner left the CIA. He joined other former CIA directors in calling for the establishment of a director for national intelligence who would oversee the nation's intelligence agencies. He opposed the 2003 invasion of Iraq and charged Vice President Dick Cheney with favoring the torture of prisoners. He presently is a senior research scholar at the University of Maryland's School of Public Policy.

TURNER, TED (ROBERT EDWARD, III) (1938–). Businessman and philanthropist, Ted Turner was born in Cincinnati, Ohio, but his **television** programming dynasty began in Atlanta, Georgia. He started his college education at Brown University but was expelled in 1960 for having a **woman** in his dormitory room. Turner returned home after his expulsion from Brown, and in 1963, upon his father's suicide, he took over his father's successful advertising business. Doing well at advertising, Turner gradually entered the world of entertainment. He bought the film studio of MGM/UA and used his interest in films to introduce Turner Network Television (TNT) and Turner Classic Movies (TCM). He also founded the **Cable News Network (CNN)**, the first news station to air 24 hours a day, seven days a week. Turner gave a $1 billion gift to the United Nations in 1998 for use in its causes. He has been married three times, including a 10-year marriage (1991–2001) to actress Jane Fonda.

U

UDALL, MORRIS (MO) KING (1922–1998). Democrat. The younger brother of Stewart Udall, who had served as secretary of the interior in the John F. Kennedy and Lyndon B. Johnson administrations, Morris Udall served in the House of Representatives from 1961 to 1991. Born in St. Johns, Arizona, Morris fought in the U.S. military during World War II and received his law degree from the University of Arizona in 1949. He practiced law in Arizona afterward. However, in 1961, he sought and won the seat in the U.S. House previously held by his brother, who had accepted the Department of Interior secretaryship. In 1974, Udall announced his decision to seek the Democratic nomination for the presidency. He did fairly well in the race, but not well enough to win any primary. He therefore withdrew in June 1976.

Like Stewart, Morris had a strong interest in the **environment**, and his succession in 1977 to the chairmanship of the House Committee on Interior and Insular Affairs gave him great influence over the country's environmental policy. He drafted numerous environmental bills, including legislation designed to protect land from development. He also sponsored the Indian Child Welfare Act (1978), which gives **Native American** tribes influence over the adoption or foster care of Native American children. In 1991, Udall suffered severe injuries from a fall down a flight of stairs and resigned from Congress. He passed away from Parkinson's disease in December 1998.

ULLMAN, AL (ALBERT CONRAD) (1914–1986). Democrat. A member of the House of Representatives from 1957 to 1980, Al Ullman was born in 1914 in Montana and raised in Oregon. He received a bachelor's degree from Whitman College in 1935 and a master's from Columbia University in 1939. He served in the U.S. Navy during World War II, went into real estate development after the war, and then won a seat in the U.S. House of Representatives as one of Oregon's lawmakers. In 1975, he became chairman of the Ways and Means Committee when the incumbent chair, Wilbur Mills, had to resign as a result of a scandal involving a stripper.

257

Ullman did not get along with President **Jimmy Carter**. He did not like Carter's 1977 proposal for a $50 tax rebate but pushed it through the House anyway; he was infuriated when Carter then decided to forego the rebate. He looked less favorably upon Carter's **energy** and welfare reform programs than did House Speaker **Tip O'Neill**. In both cases, O'Neill attempted to get around Ullman by forming special ad hoc committees on both energy and welfare reform. While the House speaker was able to get a watered-down energy program passed, Ullman succeeded in killing welfare reform. In 1980, Ullman suggested a national sales tax along the lines of the value-added tax used by many European countries. His proposal, regarded by many observers as particularly harmful to lower-class Americans, got little traction and may have cost Ullman his bid for reelection in 1980. Ullman, however, blamed Carter, stating that the president's decision to concede that year's presidential election before the polls had closed on the West Coast convinced many Democrats in that part of the country not to vote. Afterward, he opened a consulting firm in the U.S. capital. He passed away in Maryland from prostate cancer.

UNION OF SOVIET SOCIALIST REPUBLICS (USSR), RELATIONS WITH. Established five years after the Bolshevik revolution of 1917 that overthrew Russia's czarist government, the Union of Soviet Socialist Republics became in the eyes of the United States the greatest threat to it and its worldwide interests. Inspired by a communist ideology anathema to the capitalist and democratic values Americans considered dear, the United States and USSR became the primary protagonists in the Cold War that emerged after World War II. Throughout much of that period, a consensus existed among American officials that Moscow was the locus of a worldwide communist conspiracy aimed at destroying the United States and its allies. To stop the spread of communism, Washington enacted a policy of containment. Using political, economic, and military measures, including monetary assistance to foreign countries, and forming and joining alliances such as the North Atlantic Treaty Organization and the Southeast Asia Treaty Organization, Washington attempted to give teeth to containment doctrine. The Cold War even entered into outer **space**. The Soviet launch in 1957 of *Sputnik*, the world's first space satellite, shook American prestige. To avoid losing the "space race," Congress in 1958 passed legislation creating the National Aeronautics and Space Administration. Eleven years later, the United States became the first (and only) country to send humans to the moon.

President **Richard Nixon** sought to improve relations with the USSR through a policy that became known as **détente**. His efforts reached their apex in 1972, when he and Soviet general secretary **Leonid Brezhnev** signed the **Strategic Arms Limitation Treaty** (SALT I). But by 1976, when **Jimmy Carter** was elected, détente had shown signs of weakening. The two superpowers had differing interpretations of what détente meant: to Moscow, détente permitted it to aid communist nations and movements, just as Washington did for noncommunists; to U.S. officials, détente prohibited the Kremlin from trying to upset the international status quo. Additionally, the United States denounced the USSR for mistreating its nationals, while the publication of **Aleksandr Solzhenitsyn**'s book *The Gulag Archipelago* gave impetus to American calls that the Kremlin respect the **human rights** of its people. To the Soviet government, such criticism amounted to undue interference in its internal policy.

As part of his **foreign policy**, Carter wanted to revive détente. With SALT I due to expire in 1977, he hoped to sign a SALT II agreement with the Soviets. Achieving that goal proved harder than anticipated. Part of it was Carter's fault. A strong believer in human rights, he publicly lambasted the Soviet leadership for the mistreatment of its people and sent a personal letter to the Soviet dissident Andrei Sakharov. He also sought to cut the nuclear arsenals of the two superpowers more deeply than Brezhnev favored, and despite warnings from the Kremlin that it would not accept such reductions. An infuriated Kremlin threatened that it would not agree to SALT II if Carter failed to back off on both criticizing it on human rights grounds and insisting upon deep cuts in its atomic weaponry. On both demands, Carter gave ground in the name of getting SALT. Finally, the president sought to normalize relations with communist **China**. Once close allies, the relationship between the Soviet Union and China had soured. To Brezhnev and his aides, Carter's effort to improve Sino-American ties was part of a broader effort to force the USSR to make concessions on matters such as SALT and made Moscow even less willing to bargain at negotiations aimed at producing a treaty acceptable to it and Washington.

Yet there was also mutual misunderstanding, particularly insofar as the meaning of détente. Especially irksome to the Carter administration was Moscow's decision to give military aid to the African nation of **Ethiopia**, which was in a border war with its neighbor, **Somalia**. By the middle of 1978, the White House began to suggest that it would link Soviet activities in the **Horn of Africa** to cooperation with Moscow on such matters as SALT.

It was not until June 1979 that Carter and Brezhnev signed SALT II. Getting it ratified by the U.S. Senate was another matter. The USSR's activities worldwide had convinced many Americans and members of Congress that the Kremlin could not be trusted. Some lawmakers contended that SALT cut the U.S. nuclear arsenal too much. Then, in December 1979, the USSR invaded **Afghanistan** in the name of defending that country's communist government from an internal rebellion. An infuriated Carter told the Senate to shelve SALT II. Believing the invasion posed a threat to the oil-rich Persian Gulf, Carter warned that he would use "any means necessary" to defend that part of the world from a Soviet attack. Furthermore, he imposed an embargo on grain shipments to Moscow, instituted a large-scale U.S. **defense** buildup, and called for an international boycott of the 1980 Summer **Olympics**, which were to be held in the USSR. It was not until the second half of the 1980s, during the **Ronald Reagan** presidency, that détente showed signs of revival.

See also AARON, DAVID LAURENCE (1938–); BRZEZINSKI, ZBIG-NIEW KAZIMIERZ (1928–); CASTRO, FIDEL (1926–); CENTRAL IN-TELLIGENCE AGENCY (CIA); CUBA, RELATIONS WITH; DONO-VAN, HEDLEY WILLIAMS (1914–1990); EGYPT, RELATIONS WITH; FOLEY, THOMAS STEPHEN (1929–); GISCARD D'ESTAING, VAL-ERY (1926–); GREAT BRITAIN, RELATIONS WITH; JACKSON, HEN-RY MARTIN "SCOOP" (1912–1983); KENNEDY, EDWARD MOORE "TED" (1932–2009); KLUTZNICK, PHILIP MORRIS (1907–1999); LIT-ERATURE; MOYNIHAN, DANIEL PATRICK (1927–2003); SCHMIDT, HELMUT HEINRICH (1918–); STRAUSS, ROBERT SCHWARTZ (1918–); THATCHER, MARGARET (1925–); TURNER, STANSFIELD (1923–); VANCE, CYRUS ROBERT (1917–2002); WALESA, LECH (1943–); WARNKE, PAUL CULLITON (1920–2001); YOUNG, ANDREW JACKSON, JR. (1932–).

UNITED FARM WORKERS. *See* CHAVEZ, CESAR ESTRADA (1927–1993).

UNITED MINE WORKERS (UMW). Founded in 1890, the United Mine Workers **labor** union had begun in the 1940s to negotiate three-year contracts with the Bituminous Coal Operators Association (BCOA), which represented firms that ran the mines. In December 1977, about 165,000 members of the UMW went on strike when they proved unable to reach a new agreement with BCOA. By February 1978 power companies began to feel the effect and asked customers in various parts of the nation to use less electricity. In some cases, schools closed or businesses shortened their work-weeks. Growing frustration within and outside Congress forced President **Jimmy Carter** in early March to invoke the Taft-Hartley Act of 1947, which allowed the federal government to force the miners to return to work, and to threaten a federal takeover of the mines. Carter took neither action, however, and later that month, the miners and BCOA reached a new contract. The 110-day strike hurt Carter, with miners angry at his invocation of Taft-Hartley, mine owners upset by his threat to seize the mines, and many other Americans frustrated that he did not attempt to end the strike earlier.

See also ENVIRONMENT.

UNITED STEELWORKERS OF AMERICA V. WEBER. In 1964, President Lyndon B. Johnson signed the **Civil Rights** Act, Title VII of which banned discrimination in the workplace against any person because of that individual's race, ethnicity, **religion**, or gender. During the next three years, the U.S. government issued orders favoring **affirmative action**, the purpose of which was to give minorities the same opportunities as afforded white men. Kaiser Aluminum and Chemical Company, in an agreement reached with the United Steelworkers of America, aimed at meeting affirmative action requirements by offering a training program that admitted whites and **African Americans** on an equal basis, even though there were more whites seeking entry into that program. Brian White, a worker at Kaiser, was one of those whites unable to get into the training program. In 1974, he sued Kaiser, claiming that the company was in violation of Title VII of the Civil Rights Act. Although lower courts decided in his favor, the U.S. **Supreme Court** in 1979 sided with United Steelworkers. According to the Court, the training program's one-for-one admission standard was a lawful means of complying with affirmative action standards.

UNIVERSITY OF CALIFORNIA BOARD OF REGENTS V. BAKKE. *See* BAKKE, ALLEN PAUL (1940–).

V

VANCE, CYRUS ROBERT (1917–2002). Democrat. President **Jimmy Carter**'s first secretary of state, a post he held from 1977 to 1980, Cyrus Vance was born in West Virginia. He attended Yale University (B.A., 1939; LL.B., 1942) and served with the U.S. Navy during World War II. He returned to law after the war and joined the Council on Foreign Relations. He served in both the John F. Kennedy and Lyndon B. Johnson administrations prior to becoming **Jimmy Carter**'s secretary of state.

Vance sought to downplay the centrality of the **Union of Soviet Socialist Republics (USSR)** in U.S. **foreign policy**, which placed him at odds with Carter's other top foreign policy adviser, **Zbigniew Brzezinski**, who headed the National Security Council (NSC). While Brzezinski also believed the USSR should not be the most important diplomatic concern of the United States, Vance judged the NSC adviser too willing to blame foreign crises upon Moscow when in fact those crises might actually be the result of internal factors unrelated to Soviet activities. Furthermore, Vance contended that Brzezinski's anti-Sovietism jeopardized important foreign policy initiatives, particularly the **Strategic Arms Limitation Treaty (SALT II)**. Carter had intended for Vance to be his preeminent adviser when it came to foreign policy, but to the secretary of state's frustration, it was Brzezinski who gradually gained the president's ear. The final straw for Vance was the president's approval in 1980 of a military mission to rescue Americans being held hostage in **Iran**. Not only did Brzezinski (as well as other Carter advisers) favor the rescue mission, but the president reached his decision without Vance's input. Tired of having his advice pushed aside, in April of that year Vance resigned in protest. **Edmund Muskie** succeeded him as secretary of state.

After leaving the White House, Vance returned to law and wrote his memoirs. He served as a negotiator in a number of United Nations peacekeeping missions. He passed away from Alzheimer's in January 2002.

See also CHINA, RELATIONS WITH; CHRISTOPHER, WARREN MI-NOR (1925–2011); DONOVAN, HEDLEY WILLIAMS (1914–1990); HORN OF AFRICA; MARCOS, FERDINAND (EMMANUEL EDRALIN) (1917–1989); STRAUSS, ROBERT SCHWARTZ (1918–); WARNKE, PAUL CULLITON (1920–2001).

VOLCKER, PAUL ADOLPH (1927–). The chairman of the Federal Reserve Board from 1977 to 1987, Volcker was born in New Jersey. He received a bachelor's degree from Princeton University in 1949 and a master's in political **economy** from Harvard University in 1951. He then began his doctoral studies but never completed his Ph.D. A year after graduating from Harvard, Volcker took a job at the Federal Reserve Bank in New York City. From 1957 to 1962, he worked for the Chase Manhattan Bank and then took a position in the Treasury Department. Impressed with Volcker's knowledge of international monetary policy, Treasury Secretary C. Douglas Dillon promoted Volcker to deputy undersecretary for monetary affairs. In 1965, Volcker returned to Chase Manhattan Bank, but his reputation and knowledge of finance moved President **Richard Nixon** in 1969 to offer him the position of undersecretary of the Treasury for monetary affairs. In that position, Volcker was key to Nixon's decision to withdraw the United States from the gold standard. He grew frustrated with the Nixon administration, particularly because of the Watergate scandal, and resigned in 1974.

Volcker got a position with Princeton University's prestigious Woodrow Wilson School of Public and International Affairs. He stayed only a year, accepting an offer to become president of the Federal Reserve Bank of New York, the most important of the nation's 12 Federal Reserve banks. In 1979, President **Jimmy Carter** reassigned Federal Reserve Board chairman **G. William Miller** to the Treasury Department and asked Volcker to take over Miller's old job. Volcker had an excellent reputation on Wall Street, but he proved a serious problem for the White House. With the nation facing double-digit **inflation**, Volcker's solution was to allow the market to determine interest rates, which slowed economic growth and increased unemployment. By the time of the **1980 election**, the United States was in the middle of a recession. While it is impossible to know whether a different Fed chairperson could have averted such an economic downturn, it is clear that the nation's economic troubles had a significant impact upon **Ronald Reagan**'s victory in 1980.

Volcker remained at his post at the Federal Reserve until 1987 when, under pressure from the Reagan White House, he resigned. He joined a New York investment banking company and made a sizable profit when Bank-America Corp. purchased the firm in 1996. He has remained active since, including participating in investigations of the Arthur Andersen accounting firm and the United Nations' Iraq Oil for Food program. He presently is an economic adviser to President Barack Obama.

See also KAHN, ALFRED EDWARD (1917–2010); PROXMIRE, EDWARD WILLIAM (1915–2005).

W

WALESA, LECH (1943–). One of the founders of the Polish **labor** union Solidarity, Lech Walesa was born in Popowo, **Poland**. His father had been in a Nazi concentration camp and died shortly after the end of World War II. Walesa went to a vocational school, spent time in the Polish military, and then began working at the shipyard in the city of Gdańsk. He had a strong interest in the rights and needs of workers and organized a strike in 1970 to protest high food prices. Over the next decade, he had trouble finding work because of his activism, was arrested multiple times, and was carefully watched by Polish secret police.

Though an independent nation, Poland was an Eastern European satellite of the **Union of Soviet Socialist Republics (USSR)**. During the 1970s, the USSR had allowed Poles greater freedoms, such as wider freedom of speech, in the hopes of curbing dissent. But in the second half of the 1970s, Poland went into a recession, prompting the government to raise food prices. Walesa, who was once again working in Gdańsk, helped lead another strike that began in August 1980; similar work stoppages followed throughout the country. Walesa became the head of the Inter-Plant Strike Committee to coordinate these strikes; the committee shortly thereafter became known as the National Coordinating Committee of the Solidarność Free Trade Union, or Solidarity for short. The **American Federation of Labor and Congress of Industrial Organizations (AFL-CIO)** sent Solidarity money to assist its efforts.

While the **Jimmy Carter** administration was not happy with the AFL-CIO's involvement in Poland's affairs, it had taken a great interest in what was happening in Poland. In part this was because Carter's national security adviser, **Zbigniew Brzezinski**, was a native of Poland. But it was also because the White House hoped to drive wedges between Moscow and its Eastern European satellites, and saw the strikes and liberalization in Poland as proof that Poles wanted to be free of Soviet domination. In 1977, Carter traveled to Poland and laid a wreath at a monument commemorating the 1944 Warsaw Ghetto uprising against Nazi Germany. A year later, Brzezinski and First Lady **Rosalynn Carter** visited Poland. That same year, Polish cardinal Karol Józef Wojtyla became Pope John Paul II and began pressing for an end to communism in his home country.

In light of the activities of the United States and the pope, Walesa's 1980 strike was viewed by the USSR as part of a broader conspiracy to destroy its control over Poland. If it failed to act, then similar uprisings might take place in the other countries it dominated in Eastern Europe. U.S. intelligence received information that the USSR was preparing to invade Poland to crush the strikes. Both the White House and its European allies warned Moscow against military action. By the end of 1980, the USSR had decided against an invasion, not because of the warnings, but because Moscow was not sure it could expect even the support of the Polish government if it attacked.

Though the collapse of communism in Eastern Europe did not take place until the end of the 1980s, the rise of Solidarity and the decision by the Kremlin not to attack Poland signified the first cracks in the Soviet bloc. In 1989, Poland became the first Eastern European nation to name a noncommunist prime minister. The following year, Walesa became Poland's first democratically elected president. He served until 1995, when he lost a bid for another term. However, he remains well known internationally and continues to speak on issues relating to European and world politics.

WALLACE, GEORGE CORLEY (1919–1998). Democrat. The three-time governor of Alabama (1963–67, 1971–79, and 1983–87), and four-time presidential candidate (1964, 1968, 1972, and 1976), George Wallace became nationally famous as a defender of segregation. He was born in Clio, Alabama, into a lower-class family. At age 15, he got a job as a page in the state legislature, which offered him his first introduction to politics. Enthralled by the experience, he ran for class president during his freshman year at the University of Alabama. He received his bachelor's degree there, followed by a law degree in 1942. Afterward, he joined the U.S. Army Air Force, where he saw service in the Pacific Theater during World War II. Returning home, he won a seat in 1947 in the state legislature and earned a reputation as a liberal who sought to promote industrial investment in Alabama. Six years later, he became a state judge; however, his ultimate goal was to become governor. In 1958, he made a bid for that office, but his opponent, John Patterson, ran on a blatantly racist platform and won. Although Wallace supported segregation, he had never been overtly racist. Yet determined to become governor, Wallace followed Patterson's lead, adopting a vehemently anti–**African American** campaign in 1962 and aligning himself with white supremacist groups, including the Ku Klux Klan.

Wallace's tactics having proved successful, he decided to continue his racist, segregationist policies. He fought integration of all public schools and the University of Alabama, contending that the states, not the federal government, had the power to determine when and how to end segregation. His stance against big government drew him applause from segments of the U.S. public and convinced him to make a bid for the Democratic nomination for president in 1964. Though he did well, he decided to withdraw after **Barry Goldwater**, who held a similar position to Wallace's, won the **Republican Party**'s nomination. When he was unable to seek a consecutive term as governor, Wallace's wife of 23 years, Lurleen, ran for the post and won, but she died while in office. In 1971, Wallace returned to the governor's mansion after conducting another racist campaign.

In 1972, Wallace again sought the presidency, but an assassin's bullet nearly killed him and forced him to withdraw. Left paralyzed below the waist, Wallace made yet another bid for the White House in 1976. He posed a significant challenge to the other southern candidate, former Georgia governor **Jimmy Carter**. Though he himself had once sought the governorship using a racist platform, as governor, Carter had demonstrated himself a moderate on racial issues; in that respect, he symbolized a more open-minded South when it came to race relations. In a key primary in Florida, Carter defeated Wallace, who not long thereafter withdrew. Still, Wallace remained powerful and popular in Alabama. A change to the state constitution allowed him to run for a consecutive term, and he successfully won reelection in 1974. He had to leave the governor's mansion in 1979 but returned following another victory in 1982. By the end of that fourth term, his health had deteriorated, and he chose to retire rather than run for a fifth term.

Wallace left a subpar legacy in Alabama. He raised salaries for teachers and state employees and increased funding for state roads. However, he inflicted severe harm on race relations in the state and tended to ignore the needs of the state's universities, Auburn and the University of Alabama. He overlooked the corruption of his brother, Gerald, who made a fortune by overcharging the state for construction projects it awarded him. Wallace died in 1998 from septic shock and cardiac arrest.

See also WOODCOCK, LEONARD FREEL (1911–2001).

WALTERS, BARBARA (1929–). Journalist, writer, and one of **television**'s most recognizable **women**, Barbara Walters was born in Brookline, Massachusetts. Her father was a booking agent and producer in theater. In 1951 she received her B.A. from Sarah Lawrence College. Her career in television began at the Columbia Broadcasting System (CBS), where she was a writer for the news programs. That was followed by her move to the popular *Today Show*, and, in 1974, she became the first female cohost of *The Today Show*. Her career took her to the American Broadcasting Company (ABC) from 1976 to 1978, and then to back CBS. She was known for her work on ABC's

20/20 beginning in 1979. During the **1976 election**, she was the moderator in the first and third debates between **Jimmy Carter** and **Gerald Ford**. Today she is one of the cohosts of the program *The View*.

WARNKE, PAUL CULLITON (1920–2001). Democrat. The director of the Arms Control and Disarmament Agency (ACDA) from 1977 to 1978, Paul Warnke was born in Massachusetts. He graduated from Yale University in 1921, served in the U.S. Coast Guard during World War II, received a law degree from Columbia University after the war, and then began a career in law. In 1966, he agreed to join the Lyndon B. Johnson administration as general counsel for the Department of Defense, where he remained until 1969. During the 1972 presidential campaign, he advised two Democratic nominees, **Edmund Muskie** and then **George McGovern**, on foreign and national security policy. Three years later, Warnke published an article in which he cited the arms race as the main cause of political instability in the world and urged both the United States and **Union of Soviet Socialist Republics (USSR)** to halt their weapons buildups.

Warnke's position on arms control drew him the attention of **Jimmy Carter**, who nominated Warnke to head both the ACDA and the U.S. delegation to the **Strategic Arms Limitation Treaty (SALT II)** negotiations. Carter's selection drew the ire of hawks inside and outside the Senate, who contended that Warnke's desire to limit the superpowers' nuclear stockpiles jeopardized America's atomic deterrent. Although Warnke received Senate confirmation, he found himself at odds with both National Security Council (NSC) adviser **Zbigniew Brzezinski** and Secretary of Defense **Harold Brown**, who were less prepared than Warnke or Secretary of State **Cyrus Vance** to make concessions at the SALT talks. The criticism he received from both within and outside the Carter administration convinced Warnke that he could not have the influence over the SALT negotiations that he had hoped. Therefore, in November 1978, he resigned his post and returned to law. He died in October 2001 as a result of a pulmonary embolism.

See also GRIFFIN, ROBERT PAUL (1923–).

WATSON, JACK HEARN, JR. (1938–). Jack Watson served as special assistant to President **Jimmy Carter** from 1977 to 1979 and then as Carter's chief of staff from 1980 to 1981. Born in El Paso, Texas, Watson received his undergraduate degree from Vanderbilt University in 1960, spent two years in the U.S. Marine Corps, and then obtained a law degree from Harvard University (LL.B., 1966). Afterward, he joined an Atlanta law firm run by **Charles Kirbo**, who was himself a close friend of then-state senator Carter. Shortly thereafter, Watson met Carter and immediately took a liking to him. He served as a volunteer for Carter's successful 1970 campaign for the Georgia governorship. In return, Carter named Watson to the state's Board of Human Resources alongside **Robert Lipshutz**.

Watson also played an active role in Carter's bid for the White House in 1976. He had hoped to become Carter's chief of staff, but the new president believed such a post gave the person who held it too much power over who had access to the Oval Office. Instead, Carter gave Watson the dual appointments of cabinet secretary and special assistant for intergovernmental affairs. Both were new positions aimed at coordinating administration policy. As cabinet secretary, Watson's job was to make sure Carter's foreign and domestic initiatives were enacted. As special assistant, Watson was to see to it that officials from the federal level on down worked out any differences among themselves as they implemented White House programs. In both cases, he found his authority challenged, if not undercut, by other administration officials, including **Zbigniew Brzezinski**, **Stuart Eizenstat**, and **Hamilton Jordan**. In 1979, Carter finally decided he needed a chief of staff, but he gave the nod to Jordan; he asked Watson to oversee presidential appointments. When Jordan took over Carter's reelection campaign, the president replaced him with Watson. The White House staff agreed that Watson proved a far more capable chief of staff than Jordan.

After Carter lost the **1980 election**, Watson supervised the transition to the **Ronald Reagan** government. He then returned to Georgia to practice law. He also acted as a consultant to the governments of Brazil and Zambia, and as the chief legal strategist for Monsanto Company. He presently lives in Atlanta.

WEBBER, ANDREW LLOYD (1948–). Composer, **musician**, and one of Broadway's most popular and successful people, Andrew Lloyd Webber was born in London, England. In 1981 he entered Oxford University to study history. He remained at Oxford for only one term. Meeting lyricist Tim Rice made Webber and Rice one of the most successful duos in the world of musicals. The team won worldwide acclaim for their musical plays, including *Jesus Christ Superstar*, *Evita*, *Cats*, and *The Phantom of the Opera*. Some of the duo's collaborations ended with films made from their plays.

WEDDINGTON, SARAH RAGLE (1945–). President **Jimmy Carter**'s special assistant for **women**'s affairs from 1978 to 1979 and assistant to the president from 1979 to 1981, Sarah Weddington was born in Abilene, Texas. She attended McMurray College and then received her jurisprudence degree from the University of Texas in 1967. Unable to find a legal firm willing to hire a woman, she worked for a variety of women's causes. Most famously, it was she who argued before the U.S. **Supreme Court** in the case of *Roe v.*

Wade that states did not have the power to prohibit **abortions**. Though only 26 years old, and never having argued a case in court, she won. Her victory made her famous within and outside her home state and prompted her allies to ask her to run for public office. In 1973, she did so, winning a seat in the Texas legislature. There, she continued her fight for women's rights.

In 1977, Weddington headed to Washington, D.C., first to work as general counsel in the U.S. Department of **Agriculture** and then, in 1978, as President Carter's special assistant for women's affairs. She spent much of her time seeking ratification of the **Equal Rights Amendment (ERA)**. But she also worked to give women more opportunities in the armed forces, supervised a federal interdepartmental task force aimed at giving more attention to matters relating to women and women's rights, and provided women's groups with briefings on administration policy. In 1979, she was promoted to assistant to the president. This gave her additional responsibilities, among them arranging briefings for foreign officials and overseeing the White House's Speaker's Bureau. She was also actively engaged in Carter's bid for reelection. In the years following Carter's defeat, Weddington taught at Wheaton College in Massachusetts, the University of New Mexico, and the University of Texas. She maintains a law office in Austin, Texas.

WEST GERMANY, RELATIONS WITH. *See* FOREIGN POLICY; SCHMIDT, HELMUT HEINRICH (1918–).

WEXLER, ANNE LEVY (1930–2009). The deputy undersecretary of commerce from 1977 to 1978 and head of the Office of Public Liaison from 1978 to 1981, Anne Levy was born in New York City. She married Richard Wexler in 1951, the same year she graduated from Skidmore College. Wexler was both a housewife and a champion of liberal politicians and causes. She served on the campaign staffs of Minnesota senator Eugene McCarthy and South Dakota senator **George McGovern**, who sought the **Democratic** nomination for president in 1968 and 1972, respectively. In 1973, she joined the nonprofit advocacy group Common Cause and developed a reputation as one of the most influential **women** in U.S. politics. A year later, she divorced her husband and married Joseph Duffey, an influential minister in Washington, D.C.

In 1976, Wexler left Common Cause to join **Jimmy Carter**'s presidential campaign. Following his victory, Carter named Wexler as deputy undersecretary of commerce. However, she became best known for her work as head of the Office of Public Liaison (OPL), a job she assumed following **Midge Costanza**'s resignation. In that post, she devoted much of her attention to those initiatives that Carter considered most important, and then developed outreach programs aimed not at lobbying organizations or party leaders but at the grassroots. Yet she also took care to include lawmakers in her efforts, such as asking them for the names of individuals who could join her outreach programs. Her efforts were key to the passage of the **Panama Canal treaties** and **deregulation** of the trucking and airline industries. Additionally, she organized social events at the White House, among them state dinners. Throughout, however, she believed that Carter did not fully appreciate her work for the administration.

Wexler left the White House in 1981 and formed a lobbying firm called the Wexler Group (now named Wexler and Walker Public Policy Associates). By the end of the following decade, she was regarded as one of the most influential lobbyists in the U.S. capital. She died in 2009 from cancer.

WHITE, BYRON RAYMOND (1917–2002). Democrat. A brilliant student who graduated at the top of his Yale University Law School class (LL.B., 1946), Byron White served as an associate justice of the **Supreme Court** from 1962 to 1983. Born in Fort Collins, Colorado, White attended the University of Colorado, where he excelled in both the classroom and in several **sports**. Upon graduation in 1938, he had offers of both a Rhodes scholarship and a contract to play professional **football**; he did the latter for a season before heading to Oxford University in 1939 to continue his studies. The outbreak of World War II later that year, however, forced him to return to the United States. He went to Yale Law School, played two more seasons of professional football, and then joined the U.S. Navy following **Japan**'s attack on Pearl Harbor.

After the war, White completed his law degree and became a clerk for U.S. Supreme Court justice Fred Vinson. In that post, he developed a close relationship with Senator John F. Kennedy, whom he had first met at Oxford. In 1962, now-President Kennedy nominated White to replace Justice Charles Whittaker, who had resigned. Upon his approval by the Senate, White became at age 44 one of the youngest people ever to serve on the Court. As a justice, White favored the rights of citizens over criminals, opposed **abortion**, believed in protecting the rights of the disadvantaged, and mistrusted the power of the press. He oftentimes found himself in the minority. He dissented from most of the justices in *Miranda v. Arizona* (1966), which required police to read criminals their legal rights. Believing abortion was a political as opposed to a legal matter, he joined the minority in opposing *Roe v. Wade* (1973), which granted **women** the right to end a pregnancy. He was among the four justices who opposed the Court's decision in *Regents of the University of California v. Bakke* (1978), which declared unconstitutional admission quotas for minority students. That same year, he wrote the Court's opinion in *Zurcher v. Stanford Daily*, which determined that the First Amendment did not protect the media from search warrants. A private person, which was also a reason for his distrust of the media, White gave up his Court offices upon his retirement in 1993. He returned to Colorado, where he died from pneumonia.

WHITE, DANIEL JAMES "DAN" (1946–1985). *See* MILK, HARVEY (1930–1978).

WILLIAMS, JOHN (1932–). A composer and conductor, John Williams was born in New York City. His father was a drummer for a **jazz** band, and Williams followed his father's footsteps into **music**. The family moved to California in 1948, and not long thereafter, Williams entered the University of California at Los Angeles. He also took private instruction from the famous Italian film composer Mario Castelnuovo-Tedesco. Drafted into the U.S. Air Force in 1952, he arranged and conducted musical scores. In 1955, he left the military and moved to New York City, where he took classes at the prestigious Julliard School. Following graduation, he returned to Los Angeles, where he joined the film industry. He started off as a piano player for studios in Hollywood but then got the opportunity to write his own scores. His compositions left a positive impression, and his credits soon included such **television** shows as *Lost in Space* (1965–68) and *The Time Tunnel* (1966–67) and the movies *Valley of the Dolls* (1967) and *The Reivers* (1969). His adapted score for *Fiddler on the Roof* (1971) won him his first Academy Award.

Williams's work drew him the attention of a young director, **Steven Spielberg**, who asked him to write the score for what would be Spielberg's second film, *Jaws* (1975). Not only did the soundtrack win Williams another Academy Award, but it began a long collaboration between the two; *The Color Purple* (1985) is the only Spielberg-directed movie for which Williams did not write the music. It was Spielberg, moreover, who introduced Williams to director **George Lucas**, for whom Williams composed the music for all six *Star Wars* films. Williams's other compositions include the soundtracks for *Superman* (1978), *JFK* (1991), *The Patriot* (2000), and *Harry Potter and the Sorcerer's Stone* (2001). His scores have earned him 6 Oscars, 3 Emmys, 4 Golden Globes, and 21 Grammy Awards.

See also CINEMA.

WILSON, FLIP (CLEROW WILSON JR.) (1933–1998). Born Clerow Wilson in Jersey City, New Jersey, Flip Wilson spent his childhood in foster homes and reform school. He decided to quit high school and, by lying about his age, was able to join the U.S. Air Force at age 16. His comedic and outgoing personality led his fellow servicemen to declare that he was consistently "flipped out," giving Wilson his new moniker. After leaving the armed forces in 1954, Wilson worked at a San Francisco hotel both as a bellhop and in the hotel's nightclub, where he portrayed a drunk. He decided to leave the West Coast and head to New York, where he became a regular at Harlem's famous Apollo Theater and appeared on numerous **television** talk shows. In 1970, the National Broadcasting Corporation (NBC) gave him his own variety program, called *The Flip Wilson Show*. Many **African American** entertainers, including the Jackson Five, appeared on it. After the show was canceled in 1974, Wilson continued to appear on comedy and variety programs. In the 1980s, he hosted the short-lived game show *People Are Funny* and was the star of the final episode of *Charlie and Company*, a sitcom that lasted only one season. He passed away in California from liver cancer.

WOMEN. The 1970s witnessed women continuing their efforts to achieve equality. They became more prominent politically. **Betty Ford** and **Rosalynn Carter** were among the most activist First Ladies in the nation's history and spoke loudly in support of women's rights. President **Jimmy Carter** appointed **Bella Abzug** as cochair of the National Advisory Committee on Women (NACW)—though he later fired her from that position—**Patricia Derian** as assistant secretary for **human rights**, and **Shirley Hufstedler** as the first secretary of **education**. Women became increasingly involved in the **Democratic** and **Republican** parties. They made up 40 percent of the delegates at the 1972 Democratic National Convention, nearly 30 percent higher than in 1968. The same proved to be the case for the Republican Party, with the number of women at its national convention nearly doubling between 1968 and 1972 to 30 percent. In 1972, Shirley Chisholm, an **African American** member of the House of Representatives, ran for the presidency on the Democratic Party ticket but failed to win many delegates. Though few women were elected to Congress during the decade, the year 1973 saw Pat Schroeder become one of the youngest women elected to the U.S. House of Representatives; five years later, Nancy Kassebaum of Kansas become the first woman elected to a full term in the U.S. Senate.

The women's rights movement used its growing influence to sway both legislation and court decisions. Title IX of the Higher Education Act (1972) mandated equal opportunity for women in educational programs that received financial assistance from the federal government. In 1976, the U.S. military service academies began to admit women. The **Pregnancy Discrimination Act** of 1978 declared it illegal for employers to discriminate against women who were pregnant. Other women sought greater control over their bodies by revising rape laws and seeking the right to an **abortion**. On both scores, they saw triumphs, with rape laws changed so women would not feel intimidated about reporting assaults against them, and the **Supreme Court** deciding in the 1973 case *Roe v. Wade* that women had the right to an abortion.

Defenders of women's rights sought to break down barriers to their equal treatment through means other than education and politics. In 1973 tennis star **Billie Jean King** accepted a challenge from Bobby Riggs, a men's tennis champion who wanted to prove men's superiority; Americans who watched the match on **television** saw King defeat Riggs. **Gloria Steinem**, a leading advocate of the **Equal Rights Amendment (ERA)**, founded the feminist **magazine** *Ms*. Television programs such as *The Dukes of Hazzard*, *Charlie's Angels*, *The Mary Tyler Moore Show*, *Laverne and Shirley*, *Wonder Woman*, and *The Bionic Woman* depicted women who were capable of competing in a male-dominated world. The same was true for movies. Jane Fonda played a determined TV news reporter in *The China Syndrome*, while Sigourney Weaver battled an alien entity in the **science fiction** blockbuster *Alien*.

Other women became well respected in media and business circles. **Ann Landers** and **Dear Abby** offered nationally syndicated advice columns, while **Erma Bombeck** offered a humorous look at the life of a housewife. Bombeck also used her fame to call for passage of the Equal Rights Amendment. Mary Kay Ash, the founder of Mary Kay cosmetics, saw her business take off in the 1970s.

Yet for proponents of women's equality, much remained unachieved. Women complained that in the business world, a "glass ceiling" prevented their advancement. They could point as well to the Equal Pay Act of 1963, which stated that women should receive the same wage as a man for doing the same job. Effort to enforce that act did not get very far: whereas women made 59 cents for every dollar a man earned in 1963, the gap had closed by only 19 cents by 2010. Proponents of the ERA failed to see it added to the U.S. Constitution; indeed, some of the leading opponents of the ERA were women, among them **Phyllis Schlafly**. The abilities of female characters on television and **cinema** were offset by what feminists saw as a particularly disturbing message: while a woman could successfully compete against men, she was simultaneously an object to be ogled by those same men.

It was in part because they saw a world dominated by men as not affording them truly equal treatment that women increasingly focused on their differences from men and their needs. Shelters for battered women and rape crisis centers sprang up around the country. Psychologists began to consider physical, social, and intellectual differences in male and female development. Lesbians, who previously had identified themselves with the **gay rights movement**, began to associate instead with feminism, believing that the rights of lesbians were part and parcel of the larger women's rights movement.

See also ADVERTISEMENTS; ALASKA PIPELINE; ALBRIGHT, MADELEINE KORBEL (1937–); ART; BAYH, BIRCH EVANS, JR. (1928–); BURGER, WARREN EARL (1907–1995); CARTER, ELEANOR

ROSALYNN SMITH (1927–); CARTER, LILLIAN GORDY (1898–1983); CIVIL RIGHTS; COSTANZA, MIDGE (MARGARET) (1932–2010); DISCO; ELECTION, 1976; FADS AND FASHIONS; FAWCETT, FARRAH (1947–2009); HARRIS, PATRICIA ROBERTS (1924–1985); JORDAN, BARBARA (1936–1996); KREPS, JUANITA MORRIS (1921–2010); LENNON, JOHN (1940–1980); LITERATURE; MARSHALL, THURGOOD (1908–1993); MASTERS, WILLIAM HOWELL (1915–2001), AND JOHNSON, VIRGINIA ESHELMAN (1925–); PETERSON, ESTHER EGGERTSON (1906–1997); SUSAN B. ANTHONY DOLLAR COIN; TEST-TUBE BABIES; THATCHER, MARGARET (1925–); WEDDINGTON, SARAH RAGLE (1945–); WHITE, BYRON RAYMOND (1917–2002).

WONDER WOMAN. Based upon a comic book character who first appeared in 1941, *Wonder Woman* was a **television** movie starring Cathy Lee Crosby. Renamed *The New Adventures of Wonder Woman*, it became a weekly television show starring Lynda Carter that appeared on the American Broadcasting Company (ABC) from 1975 to 1977 and the Columbia Broadcasting System (CBS) from 1977 to 1979. *Wonder Woman* exemplified the conflict that had begun in the 1960s between traditionalism and feminism. On the one hand, Wonder Woman was a sexual object who was beautiful and dressed in little more than a swimsuit. Even as her alter ego, Diana Prince, she was essentially a secretary. On the other, she was intelligent, powerful, and highly capable of succeeding in a world dominated by men (and threatened by both humans and the periodic alien).

See also WOMEN.

WOODCOCK, LEONARD FREEL (1911–2001). Democrat. Leonard Woodcock was the first U.S. ambassador to communist **China**, serving from 1979 to 1981. He was born in Providence, Rhode Island. The company for which Woodcock's father, Ernest, worked transferred him and the family to Germany in 1914, where Ernest was interned during World War I. The family came back to the United States in 1926 and took up residence in Michigan, where Ernest became involved in trade union activities. Woodcock himself spent two years in college, but the Depression forced him to quit so he could get a job. He followed in his father's footsteps, working for the **American Federation of Labor** and then the United Auto Workers (UAW), and eventually become the UAW's president in 1970.

In the **1976 election**, the UAW endorsed **Jimmy Carter**, both because it did not want to see **George Wallace** get the nomination and because Woodcock knew Carter through their mutual membership in the Trilateral Commission. In 1977, Woodcock decided not to seek another term as UAW president. Desirous to repay Woodcock for supporting him in 1976, and believing he had the requisite personality traits, Carter asked Woodcock to head the U.S. Liaison Office in the People's Republic of China (PRC). As such, Woodcock played a central role in the negotiations that led to normalization of Sino-American ties. With that goal achieved, Carter nominated Woodcock as the first U.S. ambassador to Beijing, which the Senate approved by an overwhelming margin.

Following the **1980 election** of **Ronald Reagan**, Woodcock resigned his post and took a job teaching political science at the University of Michigan. He also remained active in U.S.-Chinese relations, including an effort to see an extension of the PRC's most-favored-nation status, which the United States had granted Beijing in 1980. He passed away at his Michigan home in 2001.

See also FOREIGN POLICY.

WRIGHT, JIM (JAMES CLAUDE WRIGHT JR.) (1922–). Democrat. Jim Wright was a member of the House of Representatives from 1955 to 1989, during which time he was majority leader (1977–97) and speaker (1987–89). A native of Texas, Wright was a brilliant student who skipped a number of grades and who, though admitted to the University of Texas, never finished his degree. Instead, a day after **Japan**'s attack on Pearl Harbor, he signed up for the U.S. Army Air Corps. During World War II, he received the Distinguished Flying Cross and returned to his home state following the end of hostilities.

Even as a college student, Wright had demonstrated an interest in politics and supported a liberal agenda. In 1946, he successfully ran for a seat in the Texas state legislature, where he served a single term. Failing to win reelection in 1948, he turned his attention to the mayoral race of his hometown of Weatherford, which he won in 1950. Four years later, voters in his district elected him to the U.S. House of Representatives. There, he demonstrated himself to be a moderate: he joined only a small number of southern lawmakers who rejected the Southern Manifesto that rebuked the 1954 U.S. **Supreme Court** decision integrating schools, and endorsed both President Dwight D. Eisenhower's national highway initiative as well as most of President Lyndon B. Johnson's Great Society programs. Desirous to rise up the political ranks, Wright sought, but did not win, a bid for the U.S. Senate. Though dejected, he turned his attention to gaining more power in the House, eventually becoming in 1969 one of the Democrats' deputy whips. When House Majority Leader **Tip O'Neill** assumed the post of speaker in 1976, Wright saw another chance at promotion. Thanks in part to O'Neill's backing, Wright got the party's endorsement.

In 1976 Wright saw fellow Democrat **Jimmy Carter** elected as president. Though he backed the **Panama Canal treaties** and Carter's decision not to develop the **B-1 bomber**, and worked with O'Neill to meet the president's call for legislation aimed at reducing the nation's dependence on foreign **energy** sources, the relationship between Wright and the president was difficult. Politically, the majority leader opposed Carter's decision to kill a number of water projects that the president considered a waste of money, and he believed Carter's enormous list of initiatives unnecessarily overburdened Capitol Hill. Personally, he found the president self-centered and sanctimonious. Indeed, in the **1980 election**, Wright was one of a number of Democratic Party leaders who refused to champion Carter for the party's nomination, announcing instead that he would support whomever the party chose.

In 1987, Wright became Speaker of the House upon O'Neill's retirement. Though he took a far left position on some matters, such as opposing development of the MX missile, he tended to be conservative in his orientation. His political career suffered a fatal blow when the House Ethics Committee in 1989 ruled that he had used the publication of a book to earn royalties and speaking fees larger than permitted by law. In June of that year, Wright resigned from Congress. Afterward, he worked as a consultant to the American Income Life Insurance Company, served as an adjunct professor of political science at Texas Christian University, and was inducted in 2004 into the Texas Trail Hall of Fame. He currently resides in Fort Worth.

See also ROSTENKOWSKI, DANIEL DAVID (1928–2010).

YOUNG, ANDREW JACKSON, JR. (1932–). Democrat. The ambassador to the United Nations from 1977 to 1979, Andrew Young was born into a middle-class **African American** family in New Orleans. He gained fame as a member of the **civil rights** movement. Unlike many blacks, who were members of the Southern Baptist Church, Young's family were Congregationalists, which gave him an opportunity to spend a greater amount of time with northern whites living in the South than would be the case for many southern African Americans. He continued his association with the church, deciding after getting his bachelor's degree from Howard University (B.S., 1951) to become a minister; accordingly, he attended Hartford Theological Seminary in Connecticut and was ordained in 1955.

A year before his ordination, Young married his first wife, Jean Childs. The Youngs lived for a time in New York City, but the burgeoning civil rights movement convinced them to move to Atlanta in 1961. Like Martin Luther King Jr., Young had been inspired by Mohandas Gandhi's use of civil disobedience. Young, therefore, associated himself with King's efforts to end segregation via peaceful means and soon became one of King's closest aides. In 1968, he was with King when King was murdered in Memphis, Tennessee. To Young, King's loss was a serious blow to the efforts of civil rights advocates to break down the barriers established by whites in the South.

Shortly thereafter, Young decided to turn his focus to politics. In 1970 he tried, but failed, to win a seat in the U.S. House of Representatives, but succeeded in his second effort in 1972. During the next four years, he demonstrated himself to be a champion of **affirmative action** and social programs within the United States, and also of **human rights** in Africa. Indeed, it was Young's promotion of human rights that brought him to the attention of **Jimmy Carter**. Young became the first nationally known black leader to endorse Carter's bid for the presidency, and he introduced Carter to important leaders within both the African American community and liberal interest groups. Furthermore, he actively campaigned for Carter once the Georgia governor clinched the Democratic nomination. In return for his loyalty, Carter nominated Young as ambassador to the United Nations.

It did not take long following Senate approval of his nomination for Young to become a lightning rod for controversy. On the one hand, his appointment was highly praised by defenders of human rights and by nations in Africa. Additionally, Young helped to impose sanctions on **Rhodesia**'s apartheid government and to develop a closer U.S. relationship with Nigeria. On the other hand, he made statements that appeared to endorse the presence of **Cuban** soldiers in Angola and to downplay the terrible conditions faced by dissidents in the **Union of Soviet Socialist Republics (USSR)**. Moreover, he criticized the incarceration of "political prisoners" in the United States. Then, in July 1979 he violated a State Department policy prohibiting official meetings with the **Palestine Liberation Organization (PLO)** when he secretly met a PLO representative. The outcry prompted Carter to fire Young in August of that year.

Young subsequently returned to Atlanta. Since then, he has been involved in numerous political, civil rights, and religious organizations. From 1981 to 1989 he served as mayor of Atlanta, during which time he helped win that city's bid for the 1996 **Olympics**. In 1990, he tried, but failed, to win the Georgia governorship. In 1995, a year after Jean passed away from cancer, Young married his second wife, Carolyn McClain. The following year, he and Carlton Masters cofounded Good Works International, which seeks to promote business investments abroad. Currently he is the chair of that organization. He was president of the National Council of Churches from 2000 to 2001. Finally, he remains an outspoken advocate of efforts to combat both racism and poverty.

See also FOREIGN POLICY; ISRAEL, RELATIONS WITH; JACKSON, JESSE LOUIS (1941–); JACKSON, MAYNARD HOLBROOK, JR. (1938–2003); TALMADGE, HERMAN EUGENE (1913–2002).

YOUNG, COLEMAN ALEXANDER (1918–1997). Democrat. The mayor of Detroit from 1974 to 1994, Coleman Young was born in Alabama in 1918. He and his family moved to Detroit when he was still a child. Young hoped to attend college but, failing to receive a scholarship, began to work for the Ford Motor Company. During World War II, he served with the Tuskegee Airmen, the famous all–**African American** Army Air Force fighter squadron. For a time after the war, Young worked for the Congress of Industrial Organizations (CIO) and then held several jobs before deciding to enter politics. In 1964, he won a seat in the Michigan state senate. Nine years later, he successfully ran for mayor of Detroit, becoming that city's first African American mayor and one of the first black mayors in the nation. Young also was one of the first African American political leaders in the nation to endorse Georgia governor **Jimmy Carter**'s bid for the presidency and helped secure Carter's victory in the May 1976 Michigan primary. He served as mayor until 1994 when, facing several scandals and deteriorating health, he chose not to run for another term. Young died in 1997 from respiratory failure.

See also JACKSON, MAYNARD HOLBROOK, JR. (1938–2003).

Bibliography

INTRODUCTION

The 1970s was long regarded as the "lost decade," but scholars have recently begun giving more attention to the significance of those years. The best examination of the 1970s and their influence upon the United States is Bruce J. Schulman's *The Seventies: The Great Shift in American Culture, Society, and Politics*. For studies that look at the decade from an international perspective, consult Niall Ferguson, et al., *The Shock of the Global: The 1970s in Perspective*, and Thomas Borstelmann, *The 1970s: A New Global History from Civil Rights to Economic Inequality*.

For the growing influence of conservatism in America, which had an impact upon both the 1976 and 1980 presidential elections, see Bruce Schulman and Julian Zelizer, eds., *Rightward Bound: Making American Conservative in the 1970s*, and Laura Kalman, *Right Star Rising: A New Politics, 1974–1980*.

Jimmy Carter has written over two dozen books on topics ranging from his boyhood to religion to foreign policy. Three particularly important ones for anyone wanting to learn about him and his presidency are his 1976 campaign biography, *Why Not the Best?*; his presidential memoir, *Keeping Faith: Memoirs of a President*; and *White House Diary*, which contains excerpts from his diary while he served in the Oval Office.

For more on Rosalynn Carter, the place to start is her autobiography, *First Lady from Plains*; her coverage of life in the White House is in many ways more revealing than her husband's. Readers should also consult Scott Kaufman's *Rosalynn Carter: Equal Partner in the White House*, which includes both archival research and interviews with Carter administration officials, including both President and Mrs. Carter.

No one has yet written a top-notch biography of Carter, but there are several monographs to which readers may wish to refer. Though over 30 years old, Betty Glad's *Jimmy Carter: In Search of the Great White House* is solid but ends with his 1976 campaign. *Jimmy Carter: A Comprehensive Biography from Plains to Post-Presidency*, written by Carter friend Peter Bourne, is not surprisingly sympathetic toward the country's 39th president. Kenneth E. Morris's *Jimmy Carter: American Moralist* is more critical. Morris charges that Carter's focus on morality blinded, and continues to blind, him to key issues affecting the United States and its people.

Just as the biographers are split over Carter, so are those scholars who have written on his presidency. Some view his tenure in office as one marked by poor managerial skills, a lack of vision, and ultimately a mediocre record of accomplishment. Others contend that Carter deserves far more credit for what he did, or even tried to do, for the country, and that he oftentimes was the victim of forces beyond his control. For a critical analysis, see Burton I. Kaufman and Scott Kaufman, *The Presidency of James Earl Carter, Jr.*, 2nd ed. A more positive portrayal can be found in Jonathan Dumbrell's *The Carter Presidency: A Re-evaluation*, 2nd ed.

The literature on Carter's foreign policy is extensive and growing rapidly. Zbigniew Brzezinski's *Power and Principle: Memoirs of the National Security Adviser, 1977–1981*, and Cyrus Vance's *Hard Choices: Critical Years in America's Foreign Policy* are detailed and present to the reader a good sense of the sometimes intense arguments that divided the president's top two foreign policy aides.

Just as there was a split between Brzezinski and Vance, so there is one among scholars who have written surveys of Carter's foreign policy. The earliest study, Gaddis Smith's *Morality, Reason, and Power: American Diplomacy in the Carter Years*, is critical. While giving Carter credit where due, he contends that the administration's record was lacking and places much of the blame at the president's feet. More recent works share Smith's conclusions, among them Scott Kaufman's *Plans Unraveled: The Foreign Policy of the Carter Administration* and Betty Glad's *An Outsider in the White House: Jimmy Carter, His Advisors, and the Making of American Foreign Policy*. Robert Strong disagrees with Smith, Kaufman, and Glad. In

Working in the World: Jimmy Carter and the Making of American Foreign Policy, Strong concludes that Carter was a better president who accomplished more than his detractors are willing to admit.

Despite the fact that Carter gave a great deal of emphasis to promoting human rights in U.S. foreign policy, few book-length works have been produced on this subject. Mary Stuckey, in *Jimmy Carter, Human Rights, and the National Agenda*, credits the 39th president for making human rights a key component of American diplomacy, not only in the 1970s but beyond. Readers should also consult A. Glenn Mower's *Human Rights and American Foreign Policy: The Carter and Reagan Experiences*.

On relations with specific countries, the revised edition of Raymond L. Garthoff's massive and detailed *Détente and Confrontation: American-Soviet Relations from Nixon to Reagan* is excellent in its coverage of the relationship between the United States and the Union of Soviet Socialist Republics. That Soviet-style communism might take hold in Nicaragua became a matter of concern for U.S. officials during the Carter years. For more on this subject, see Robert Kagan, *A Twilight Struggle: American Power and Nicaragua, 1977–1990*, and Morris H. Morley, *Washington, Somoza, and the Sandinistas: State and Regime in U.S. Policy toward Nicaragua, 1969–1981*. The Panama Canal treaties and their impact upon domestic U.S. politics are well addressed in Adam Clymer's *Drawing the Line at the Big Ditch: The Panama Canal Treaties and the Rise of the Right*.

No one has yet written a definitive account of the Camp David Accords. However, William Quandt's *Camp David: Peacemaking and Politics* is certainly the place to begin. Quandt served on the National Security Council during Carter's tenure and was responsible for addressing Arab-Israeli relations. Useful as well are Burton I. Kaufman's *The Arab Middle East and the United States: Inter-Arab Rivalry and Superpower Diplomacy*, and George Lenczowski's *American Presidents and the Middle East*.

Possibly no subject affecting the Carter administration's diplomacy has received more attention than U.S. relations with Iran and the Iran hostage crisis. Excellent studies of these topics are *Taken Hostage: The Iran Hostage Crisis and America's First Encounter with Radical Islam*, by David Farber; David Harris's *The Crisis: The President, the Prophet, and the Shah—1979 and the Coming of Militant Islam*; and Mark Bowden's *Guests of the Ayatollah: The First Battle in America's War with Militant Islam*. Farber offers a brief well-written overview. The books by Harris and Bowden are more detailed and include interviews with participants. Important, too, is *American Hostages in Iran: The Conduct of a Crisis*. Written by over a half dozen Carter administration officials, among them Deputy Secretary of State Warren Christopher and National Security Council member Gary Sick, it details the difficult and lengthy negotiations to free the hostages.

There is far less published on Carter's domestic initiatives than on his diplomacy. Carl Biven, in *Jimmy Carter's Economy: Policy in an Age of Limits*, defends the president for trying to come to grips with the country's economic troubles at a time when resources were limited. Welfare reform is addressed in *The President as Policymaker: Jimmy Carter and Welfare Reform*, by Laurence E. Lynn and D. F. Whitman. Kevin Mattson, in *"What the Heck Are You Up To, Mr. President?": Jimmy Carter, America's "Malaise," and the Speech That Should Have Changed the Country* on the one hand criticizes Carter's handling of the energy crisis and, on the other, implies that had Americans listened to him, the country would have headed down a path that could have prevented the current difficulties in which it finds itself. A study of Carter's lifelong commitment to improving education is Deanna L. Michael's *Jimmy Carter as Educational Policymaker: Equal Opportunity and Efficiency*.

While most analyses of Carter's postpresidency are positive in their assessments, a few are not. Douglas Brinkley's *The Unfinished Presidency: Jimmy Carter's Journey beyond the White House* falls into the former category. Brinkley sees Carter using his post–White House years to continue his presidential agenda, particularly insofar as concerns promoting human rights and world peace. The title of Steven F. Hayward's *The Real Jimmy Carter: How Our Worst Ex-President Undermines American Foreign Policy, Coddles Dictators and Created the Party of Clinton and Kerry* reflects his take on the 39th president's post–White House initiatives.

In 1990, Hofstra University hosted a conference on the Carter administration that included academics and members of the administration. The presentations and commentaries from that conference have been published in a fascinating two-volume work edited by Herbert D. Rosenbaum and Alexej Ugrinsky. *The Presidency and Domestic Policies of Jimmy Carter* and *Jimmy Carter: Foreign Policy and Post-Presidential Years* cover just about every aspect of Carter's term in office and his activities since.

There are several websites where one can find more about the Carter administration, but a good place to begin is www.whitehouse.gov/about/presidents/jimmycarter, which offers a brief overview of the Carter presidency. A chronology of Carter's life that focuses primarily upon his tenure in office can be found at http://www.pbs.org/wgbh/americanexperience/features/timeline/carter.

Anyone wishing to do primary research on the Carter administration will want to begin at the Jimmy Carter Library in Atlanta, Georgia, which contains the president's papers as well as those of many of the officials who worked in his administration. The website for the library is http://www.jimmycarterlibrary.org. Secretary of State Cyrus Vance's papers are located at Yale University. A guide to his papers can be found via Yale's manuscript and archives site, located at http://www.library.yale.edu/mssa.

George Washington University is the home of the National Security Archive (NSA), which uses the Freedom of Information Act to declassify documents. Some of these materials are available only in hard copy, while others have been published on microfilm. For more information, go to http://www.gwu.edu/~nsarchiv. The Woodrow Wilson International Center for Scholars publishes the *Cold War International History Project* (*CWIHP*), where one can find translated Cold War–era documents from the Union of Soviet Socialist Republics, communist China, Cuba, and numerous other nations. The *CWIHP* can be found at http://www.wilsoncenter.org/program/cold-war-international-history-project. As of mid-2012, the Department of State was in the process of declassifying its papers from the Carter administration. Those papers are held at the National Archives and Records Administration in College Park, Maryland; its website is http://www.nara.gov. Once available, a sizeable number of those State Department papers will be published in *Foreign Relations of the United States* (*FRUS*), a multivolume product of the State Department's Office of the Historian. *FRUS* is available both in hard copy and online. Currently, some of the volumes from the Gerald Ford administration are available. Go to http://history.state.gov/historicaldocuments to access the volumes.

BIBLIOGRAPHIES, DICTIONARIES, AND ENCYCLOPEDIAS

Commire, Anne, ed. *Historic World Leaders*, 5 vols. Detroit: Gale, 1994.

Concise Dictionary of American Biography, 5th ed. New York: Scribner, 1997.

Daniel, Clifton, ed. *Chronicle of the 20th Century*. Liberty, Mo.: JL International, 1997.

Findling, John E. *Dictionary of American Diplomatic History*, 2nd ed., rev. and expanded. Westport, Conn.: Greenwood, 1989.

Finkelman, Paul, and Peter Wallenstein, eds. *The Encyclopedia of American Political History*. Washington, D.C.: CQ Press, 2001.

Grossman, Mark. *Encyclopedia of the United States Cabinet*, 2nd ed., 2 vols. Armenia, N.Y.: Grey House Publishing, 2010.

Kaufman, Burton I. *The Carter Years*. New York: Facts on File, 2006.

Kohn, George Childs, ed. *Dictionary of Historic Documents*. New York: Facts on File, 2003.

Nolan, Cathal J. *Notable U.S. Ambassadors since 1775: A Biographical Dictionary*. Westport, Conn.: Greenwood, 1997.

Olson, James Stuart. *Dictionary of United States Economic History*. Westport, Conn.: Greenwood, 1992.

Rodger, Liam, ed. *Chambers Biographical Dictionary*, 9th ed. London: Chambers Harrap, 2011.

Ware, Susan, ed. *Notable American Women: A Biographical Dictionary Completing the Twentieth Century*. Cambridge, Mass.: Harvard University Press, 2004.

Who's Who in 20th Century America. New Providence, N.J.: Marquis Who's Who, 2000.

Wieczynski, Joseph L., ed. *The Modern Encyclopedia of Russian and Soviet History*. Gulf Breeze, Fla.: Academic International, 1980.

GENERAL SURVEYS

Brinkley, Alan, and David Dyer, eds. *The Reader's Companion to the American Presidency*. Boston: Houghton Mifflin, 2000.

Friedman, Robert, ed. *The Life Millennium: The 100 Most Important Events and People of the Past 1,000 Years*. New York: Life Books, 1998.

Geisst, Charles R. *Wall Street: A History*. New York: Oxford University Press, 1997.

Genovese, Michael A. *Encyclopedia of the American Presidency*, rev. ed. New York: Facts on File, 2010.

Henretta, James A., David Brody, and Lynn Dumenil. *America: A Concise History*, vol. 2, *Since 1865*, 4th ed. Boston: Bedford/St. Martin's, 2009.

Hughes, Jonathan, and Louis B. Cain. *American Economic History*, 8th ed. Boston: Pearson Addison-Wesley, 2011.

Levy, Leonard W., and Louis Fisher, eds. *Encyclopedia of the American Presidency*, 4 vols. New York: Macmillan, 1998.

O'Brien, Steven. *American Political Leaders: From Colonial Times to the Present*. Santa Barbara, Calif.: ABC-CLIO, 1991.

Paletta, Lu Ann, and Fred Worth. *The World Almanac of Presidential Facts*. New York: World Almanac, 1988.

Patterson, James T. *America in the Twentieth Century: A History*, 5th ed. Fort Worth, Tex.: Harcourt College Publishers, 2000.

Peters, Gerhard, John T. Woolley, and Michael Nelson, eds. *The Presidency A to Z*, 4th ed. Washington, D.C.: CQ Press, 2008.

Post, Robert C., ed. *Every Four Years*, rev. ed. Washington, D.C.: Smithsonian Books, 1984.

Shields-West, Eileen. *The World Almanac of Presidential Campaigns*. New York: World Almanac, 1992.

Tindall, George Brown, and David E. Shi. *America: A Narrative History*, 7th ed. New York: Norton, 2007.

Whitney, David C. *The American Presidents*, 11th ed. Pleasantville, N.Y.: Reader's Digest Association, 2009.

Wilson, Robert A., ed. *Character above All: Ten Presidents from FDR to George Bush*. New York: Simon and Schuster, 1995.

Yergin, Daniel. *The Prize: The Epic Quest for Oil, Money, and Power*. New York: Free Press, 2008.

THE 1970S

Bailey, Beth, and David Farber, eds. *America in the Seventies*. Lawrence: University Press of Kansas, 2004.

Berkowitz, Edward D. *Something Happened: A Political and Cultural Overview of the Seventies*. New York: Columbia University Press, 2006.

Carroll, Peter N. *It Seemed Like Nothing Happened: The Tragedy and Promise of the 1970s*. New York: Holt, Rinehart, and Winston, 1982.

Frum, David. *How We Got Here: The 1970s, the Decade That Brought You Modern Life (for Better or Worse)*. New York: Basic Books, 2000.

Hurup, Elsebeth, ed. *The Lost Decade: America in the Seventies*. Oakville, Conn.: Aarhus University Press, 1996.

Jenkins, Philip. *Decade of Nightmares: The End of the Sixties and the Making of Eighties America*. New York: Oxford University Press, 2006.

Sandbrook, Dominic. *Mad as Hell: The Crisis of the 1970s and the Rise of the Populist Right*. New York: Knopf, 2011.

JIMMY CARTER

Abernathy, M. Glenn, Dilys Hill, and Phil Williams, eds. *The Carter Years: The President and Policymaking*. New York: St. Martin's, 1984.

Campbell, Colin. *Managing the Presidency: Carter, Reagan, and the Search for Executive Order*. Pittsburgh: University of Pittsburgh Press, 1986.

Fink, Gary. *The Carter Presidency: Policy Choices in the Post-New Deal Era*. Lawrence: University Press of Kansas, 1998.

———. *Prelude to the Presidency: The Political Character and Legislative Leadership Style of Governor Jimmy Carter*. Westport, Conn.: Greenwood, 1980.

Godbold, E. Stanly. *Jimmy and Rosalynn Carter: The Georgia Years, 1924–1974*. New York: Oxford University Press, 2010.

Hargrove, Erwin C. *Jimmy Carter as President: Leadership and the Politics of the Public Good*. Baton Rouge: Louisiana State University Press, 1988.

Hult, Karen M., and Charles E. Walcott. *Empowering the White House: Governance under Nixon, Ford, and Carter*. Lawrence: University Press of Kansas, 2004.

Jones, Charles O. *The Trusteeship Presidency: Jimmy Carter and the United States Congress*. Baton Rouge: Louisiana State University Press, 1988.

Kucharsky, David. *The Man from Plains: The Mind and Spirit of Jimmy Carter*. New York: Harper and Row, 1976.

Mazlish, Brice, and Edwin Diamond. *Jimmy Carter: A Character Portrait*. New York: Simon and Schuster, 1979.

Miller, William Lee. *Yankee from Georgia: The Emergence of Jimmy Carter*. New York: Times Books, 1978.

Mollenhoff, Clark. *The President Who Failed: Carter Out of Control*. New York: Macmillan, 1980.

Nielsen, Niels C. *The Religion of President Carter*. Nashville: Thomas Nelson, 1977.

Norton, Howard, and Bob Slosser. *The Miracle of Jimmy Carter*. Plainfield, N.J.: Logos International, 1976.

Pippert, Wesley G. *The Spiritual Journal of Jimmy Carter: In His Own Words*. New York: Macmillan, 1978.

Rozell, Mark J. *The Press and the Carter Presidency*. Boulder, Co.: Westview, 1989.

Shoup, Laurence H. *The Carter Presidency and Beyond: Power and Politics in the 1980s*. Palo Alto, Calif.: Ramparts, 1980.

Thompson, Kenneth W., ed. *The Carter Presidency: Fourteen Intimate Perspectives of Jimmy Carter*. Lanham, Md.: University Press of America, 1990.

Wooten, James. *Dasher: The Roots and Rising of Jimmy Carter*. New York: Summit Books, 1978.

Zelizer, Julian E. *Jimmy Carter*. New York: Henry Holt, 2010.

AFRICAN AMERICANS

Anderson, Terry H. *The Pursuit of Fairness: A History of Affirmative Action*. New York: Oxford University Press, 2004.

Ball, Howard. *The Bakke Case: Race, Education, and Affirmative Action*. Lawrence: University Press of Kansas, 2000.

Bell, Griffin B., with Ronald J. Ostrow. *Taking Care of the Law*. New York: William Morrow, 1982.

DeRoche, Andrew J. *Andrew Young: Civil Rights Ambassador*. Wilmington, Del.: Scholarly Resources, 2003.

Dreyfuss, Joel, and Charles Lawrence III. *The Bakke Case: The Politics of Inequality*. New York: Harcourt Brace Jovanovich, 1979.

Gates, Henry Louis, Jr., and Cornel West. *The African-American Century: How Black Americans Have Shaped Our Country*. New York: Free Press, 2000.

Lawson, Steven F. *In Pursuit of Power: Southern Blacks and Electoral Politics, 1965–1982*. New York: Columbia University Press, 1985.

O'Neill, Timothy J. *Bakke and the Politics of Equality: Friends and Foes in the Classroom of Litigation*. Middletown, Conn.: Wesleyan University Press, 1985.

Sindler, Allan P. *Bakke, DeFunis, and Minority Admissions: The Quest for Equal Opportunity*. New York: Longman, 1978.

WOMEN AND WOMEN'S RIGHTS

Abzug, Bella, and Mim Kelber. *Gender Gap: Bella Abzug's Guide to Political Power for American Women*. Boston: Houghton Mifflin, 1984.

Berry, Mary Frances. *Why ERA Failed: Politics, Women's Rights, and the Amending Process of the Constitution*. Bloomington: Indiana University Press, 1986.

Borrelli, MaryAnne. *The Politics of the President's Wife*. College Station: Texas A&M University Press, 2011.

Davis, Flora. *Moving the Mountain: The Women's Movement in America since 1960*. New York: Simon and Schuster, 1991.

Hartmann, Susan M. *From Margin to Mainstream: American Women and Politics since 1960*. Philadelphia: Temple University Press, 1989.

Hoyt, Mary. *East Wing: Politics, the Press, and a First Lady; A Memoir*. Philadelphia: Xlibris, 2001.

Levine, Suzanne. *Bella Abzug: How One Tough Broad from the Bronx Fought Jim Crow and Joe McCarthy, Pissed Off Jimmy Carter, Battled for the Rights of Women and Workers, Rallied against War and for the Planet, and Shook Up Politics along the Way: An Oral History*. New York: Farrar, Straus, and Giroux, 2007.

Martin, Janet M. *The Presidency and Women: Promise, Performance, and Illusion*. College Station: Texas A&M University Press, 2003.

Masbridge, Jane J. *Why We Lost the ERA*. Chicago: University of Chicago Press, 1986.

Mathews, Donald G., and Jane Sherron de Hart. *Sex, Gender, and the Politics of ERA: A State and the Nation*. New York: Oxford University Press, 1990.

Troy, Gil. *Mr. & Mrs. President: From the Trumans to the Clintons*, 2nd ed. Lawrence: University Press of Kansas, 2000.

Wandersee, Winifred D. *On the Move: American Women in the 1970s*. Boston: Twayne, 1988.

Women, a Documentary of Progress during the Administration of Jimmy Carter, 1977 to 1981. Washington, D.C.: Executive Office of the President, 1981.

SUPREME COURT

Barnhart, Bill, and Gene Schlickman. *John Paul Stevens: An Independent Life*. DeKalb: Northern Illinois University Press, 2010.

Bland, Randall. *Private Pressure on Public Law: The Legal Career of Justice Thurgood Marshall, 1934–1991*, rev. ed. Lanham, Md.: University Press of America, 1993.

Eisler, Kim Isaac. *A Justice for All: William J. Brennan, Jr., and the Decisions That Transformed America*. New York: Simon and Schuster, 1993.

Greenhouse, Linda. *Becoming Justice Blackmun: Harry Blackmun's Supreme Court Journey*. New York: Times Books, 2005.

Hutchinson, Dennis J. *The Man Who Once Was Whizzer White: A Portrait of Justice Byron R. White*. New York: Free Press, 1998.

Jeffries, John C., Jr. *Justice Lewis F. Powell, Jr.* New York: Scribner, 1994.

Maltz, Earl M. *The Chief Justiceship of Warren Burger, 1969–1986*. Columbia: University of South Carolina Press, 2000.

Rosenkranz, E. Joshua, and Bernard Schwartz, eds. *Reason and Passion: Justice Brennan's Enduring Influence*. New York: Norton, 1997.

Schwartz, Bernard. *The Ascent of Pragmatism: The Burger Court in Action*. Reading, Mass.: Addison-Wesley, 1990.

———. *A History of the Supreme Court*. New York: Oxford University Press, 1993.

Sickels, Robert Judd. *John Paul Stevens and the Constitution: The Search for Balance*. University Park: Pennsylvania State University Press, 1998.

Starks, Glenn L., and F. Erik Brooks. *Thurgood Marshall: A Biography*. Santa Barbara, Calif.: Greenwood, 2012.

Stern, Seth, and Stephen Wermiel. *Justice Brennan: Liberal Champion*. Boston: Houghton Mifflin Harcourt, 2010.

Stevens, John Paul. *Five Chiefs: A Supreme Court Memoir*. New York: Little, Brown, 2011.

Williams, Juan. *Thurgood Marshall: American Revolutionary*. New York: Times Books, 1998.

Yarbrough, Tinsley E. *Harry A. Blackmun: The Outsider Justice*. New York: Oxford University Press, 2008.

FOREIGN RELATIONS

Andrianopoulos, Gerry Argyris. *Kissinger and Brzezinski: The NSC and the Struggle for Control of U.S. National Security Policy*. New York: St. Martin's, 1991.
Christopher, Warren. *Chances of a Lifetime: A Memoir*. New York: Scribner, 2001.
Maga, Timothy P. *The World of Jimmy Carter: U.S. Foreign Policy, 1977–1981*. West Haven, Conn.: University of New Haven Press, 1994.
McLellan, David S. *Cyrus Vance*. Totowa, N.J.: Rowan and Allanheld, 1985.
Moens, Alexander. *Foreign Policy under Carter: Testing Multiple Advocacy Decision Making*. Boulder, Co.: Westview, 1990.
Rosati, Jerel. *The Carter Administration's Quest for Global Community: Beliefs and Their Impact on Behavior*. Columbia: University of South Carolina Press, 1987.
Skidmore, David. *Reversing Course: Carter's Foreign Policy, Domestic Politics, and the Failure of Reform*. Nashville: Vanderbilt University Press, 1996.
Thornton, Richard C. *The Carter Years: Toward a New Global Order*. New York: Paragon House, 1991.

CAMP DAVID ACCORDS

Brands, H. W. *Into the Labyrinth: The United States and the Middle East, 1945–1993*. New York: McGraw-Hill, 1994.
Charney, Leon H. *Special Counsel*. New York: Philosophical Library, 1984.
Christison, Kathleen. *Perceptions of Palestine: Their Influence on U.S. Middle East Policy*. Berkeley: University of California Press, 1999.
Dayan, Moshe. *Breakthrough: A Personal Account of the Egypt-Israel Peace Negotiations*. New York: Knopf, 1981.
Fraser, T. G. *The USA and the Middle East since World War II*. New York: St. Martin's, 1989.
Merkley, Paul Charles. *American Presidents, Religion, and Israel*. Westport, Conn.: Praeger, 2004.
Spiegel, Steven L. *The Other Arab-Israeli Conflict: Making America's Middle East Policy, from Truman to Reagan*. Chicago: University of Chicago Press, 1985.

Stivers, William. *America's Confrontation with Revolutionary Change in the Middle East, 1948–83*. New York: St. Martin's, 1986.

CENTRAL INTELLIGENCE AGENCY AND THE ARMED FORCES

Auten, Brian J. *Carter's Conversion: The Hardening of American Defense Policy*. Columbia: University of Missouri Press, 2008.

Gates, Robert M. *From the Shadows: The Ultimate Insider's Story of Five Presidents and How They Won the Cold War*. New York: Simon and Schuster, 1996.

Gray, Colin. *The MX ICBM and National Security*. New York: Praeger, 1981.

Herspring, Dale S. *The Pentagon and the Presidency: Civil-Military Relations from FDR to George W. Bush*. Lawrence: University Press of Kansas, 2005.

Kotz, Nick. *Wild Blue Yonder: Money, Politics, and the B-1 Bomber*. New York: Pantheon, 1988.

Scoville, Herbert, Jr. *MX: Prescription for Disaster*. Cambridge, Mass.: MIT Press, 1981.

Turner, Stansfield. *Burn before Reading: Presidents, CIA Directors, and Secret Intelligence*. New York: Hyperion, 2005.

———. *The CIA in Transition*. Boston: Houghton Mifflin, 1985.

Wasserman, Sherri. *The Neutron Bomb Controversy: A Study in Alliance Politics*. New York: Praeger, 1983.

HUMAN RIGHTS

Muravchik, Joshua. *The Uncertain Crusade: Jimmy Carter and the Dilemmas of Human Rights*. New York: Hamilton Press, 1986.

Schoultz, Lars. *Human Rights and U.S. Policy toward Latin America*. Princeton, N.J.: Princeton University Press, 1981.

Vogelgesang, Sandy. *American Dream, Global Nightmare: The Dilemma of U.S. Human Rights Policy*. New York: Norton, 1980.

IRAN AND THE HOSTAGE CRISIS

Arjomand, Said Amir. *The Turban for the Crown: The Islamic Revolution in Iran*. New York: Oxford University Press, 1988.

Beckwith, Charlie, and Donald Knox. *Delta Force*. New York: Harcourt Brace Jovanovich, 1983.

Bill, James A. *The Eagle and the Lion: The Tragedy of American-Iranian Relations*. New Haven, Conn.: Yale University Press, 1988.

Houghton, David Patrick. *US Foreign Policy and the Iran Hostage Crisis*. New York: Cambridge University Press, 2001.

Huyser, Robert E. *Mission to Iran*. New York: Harper and Row, 1986.

Jordan, Hamilton. *Crisis: The Last Year of the Carter Presidency*. New York: Berkley Publishing, 1982.

Kyle, James H., with John Robert Eidson. *The Guts to Try: The Untold Story of the Iran Hostage Rescue Mission by the On-Scene Desert Commander*. New York: Ballantine, 1995.

Rubin, Barry. *Paved with Good Intentions: The American Experience in Iran*. New York: Oxford University Press, 1980.

Ryan, Paul B. *The Iranian Rescue Mission and Why It Failed*. Annapolis, Md.: Naval Institute Press, 1986.

Salinger, Pierre. *America Held Hostage: The Secret Negotiations*. Garden City, N.Y.: Doubleday, 1981.

Seliktar, Ofira. *Failing the Crystal Ball Test: The Carter Administration and the Fundamentalist Revolution in Iran*. Westport, Conn.: Praeger, 2000.

Sick, Gary. *All Fall Down: America's Tragic Encounter with Iran*. New York: Random House, 1985.

Sullivan, William H. *Mission to Iran*. New York: Norton, 1981.

NICARAGUA AND THE PANAMA CANAL TREATIES

Furlong, William L., and Margaret E. Scranton. *The Dynamics of Foreign Policymaking: The President, the Congress, and the Panama Canal Treaties*. Boulder, Co.: Westview, 1984.

Hogan, J. Michael. *The Panama Canal in American Politics*. Carbondale: Southern Illinois University Press, 1986.

Jorden, William J. *Panama Odyssey*. Austin: University of Texas Press, 1984.

LaFeber, Walter. *Inevitable Revolutions: The United States in Central America*. New York: Norton, 1984.

———. *The Panama Canal: The Crisis in Historical Perspective*, updated ed. New York: Oxford University Press, 1990.

Lake, Anthony. *Somoza Falling: A Case Study of Washington at Work*. Amherst: University of Massachusetts Press, 1989.

Leo Grande, William M. *Our Own Backyard: The United States in Central America*. Chapel Hill: University of North Carolina Press, 1998.

Pastor, Robert. *Condemned to Repetition: The United States and Nicaragua*. Princeton, N.J.: Princeton University Press, 1987.

———. *Whirlpool: U.S. Foreign Policy toward Latin America and the Caribbean*. Princeton, N.J.: Princeton University Press, 1992.

Pezzullo, Lawrence, and Ralph Pezzullo. *At the Fall of Somoza*. Pittsburgh: University of Pittsburgh Press, 1993.

UNION OF SOVIET SOCIALIST REPUBLICS AND SALT II

Cynkin, Thomas M. *Soviet and American Signalling in the Polish Crisis*. New York: St. Martin's, 1988.

Freeman, Robert O. *The Soviet Union and the Carter Administration*. Pittsburgh: University of Pittsburgh Center for Russian and European Studies, 1987.

LaFeber, Walter. *America, Russia, and the Cold War, 1945–2002*, 9th ed. Boston: McGraw-Hill, 2004.

MacEachin, Douglas J. *U.S. Intelligence and the Confrontation in Poland, 1980–1981*. University Park: Pennsylvania State University Press, 2002.

Newsom, David. *The Soviet Brigade in Cuba: A Study of Political Diplomacy*. Bloomington: Indiana University Press, 1987.

Powaski, Ronald E. *The United States and the Soviet Union, 1917–1991*. New York: Oxford University Press, 1998.

Sanders, Jerry W. *Peddlers of Crisis: The Committee on the Present Danger and the Politics of Containment*. Boston: South End Press, 1983.

Sarantakes, Nicholas Evan. *Dropping the Torch: Jimmy Carter, the Olympic Boycott, and the Cold War*. New York: Cambridge University Press, 2011.

Talbott, Strobe. *Endgame: The Inside Story of SALT II*. New York: Harper and Row, 1979.

INTERNET RESOURCES

history.state.gov/historicaldocuments
www.askjimmycarter.com
www.gwu.edu/~nsarchiv
www.habitat.org
www.jimmycarterlibrary.gov
www.library.yale.edu/mssa
www.nara.gov
www.nps.gov/jica
www.pbs.org/wgbh/americanexperience/features/timeline/carter

www.whitehouse.gov/about/presidents/jimmycarter
www.wilsoncenter.org/program/cold-war-international-history-project

About the Authors

Diane Kaufman received her master's degree from Kansas State University. While teaching in Kansas, she received both a state and national award for her work in economics, as well as recognition as one of the Outstanding Leaders in Elementary and Secondary Education in 1976. She has served on the board of Scholastic Books and was a reference librarian at Manhattan (Kansas) Public Library. At the Newman Library of Virginia Tech, she was head of conservation. She has also headed the Western College Memorial Archives at Miami University of Ohio. She was coauthor of *The Historical Dictionary of the Eisenhower Era* for Scarecrow Press.

Scott Kaufman received his bachelor's degree from Kansas State University, and his master's and Ph.D. from Ohio University. He is professor of history at Francis Marion University (FMU) and an FMU Board of Trustees research scholar. He is the author of six books, including *Rosalynn Carter: Equal Partner in the White House* (2007) and *Plans Unraveled: The Foreign Policy of the Carter Administration* (2008), and coauthored with his father, Burton I. Kaufman, the revised edition of *The Presidency of James Earl Carter, Jr.* (2006). His most recent publication is *Project Plowshare: The Peaceful Use of Nuclear Explosives in Cold War America* (2013). He presently is editing *The Companion to Gerald R. Ford and Jimmy Carter*.